THE
LIVERPOOL SCOTTISH
1900—1919

THE
LIVERPOOL SCOTTISH
1900—1919

BY

A. M. McGILCHRIST

LIVERPOOL
HENRY YOUNG & SONS, LTD.
1930

CONTENTS

TO

ABSENT FRIENDS

PREFACE

THIS history of the Liverpool Scottish, from the Battalion's earliest days in 1900 to the return of the cadre from Antwerp in 1919, has been compiled with a double purpose. It is meant to be, in the first place, a record to help ex-members to keep fresh the memory of the days when they themselves were making the Battalion's history and, secondly, an encouragement and an example to the new members whose duty it is to carry on and to uphold the high reputation inherited from those who have gone before.

Accuracy is, of course, the first essential in the writing of history and every effort has been made to secure it. There is no incident recorded in the pages that follow which has not been confirmed by an officer or man—or both—who was present at the time. But in spite of these precautions minor errors may have crept in, especially, perhaps, in such cases as the nominal roll of the 1st Battalion, where the old list from which it was taken has evidently been hurriedly written and is not always easily decipherable. If any such errors are noticed I shall be grateful if the reader will write to me at 5, Fraser Street, Liverpool, and give chapter and verse for his complaint, criticism or correction. Steps will then be taken to ensure that mistakes are rectified in any future edition.

Those who read the account of the First Action at Bellewaarde, on 16 June, 1915, in the Official History of the War, Volume IV, will find few references to the Liverpool Scottish. The explanation is simple and the fault lies very largely with the Battalion itself. The Official History is compiled from the war-diaries of divisions, brigades and battalions. Only in the case of ambiguity or contradictory narratives is application made to battalion commanders for special accounts of their units' part in any action. Much, therefore, depends on the fulness of detail with which battalions describe an operation in their war-diaries. The Liverpool Scottish war-diary sums up the Action at Bellewaarde in a bald statement of less than one hundred words, and gives no details of the Battalion's share in the fight beyond a reference to the fine work of the bombers and stretcher-bearers. After an engagement in which seventy-five per cent. of the Battalion were casualties it is not surprising that a comprehensive account could not be written at the time, but the result has been to deny to the Liverpool Scottish in the Official History of the War the just recognition of the prominent part they played in that costly minor engagement. Thanks to a personal introduction which Lieut.-General Sir Hugh S. Jeudwine was kind enough to give me I took the matter up with Brigadier-General J. E. Edmonds, the Official War Historian, and I am glad to say that he arranged to insert in the next volume a corrigendum modifying the narrative in Volume IV and bringing out more fully the share of the Liverpool Scottish in the action. I should like to express publicly to General Edmonds my indebtedness to him for the courteous way in which he received my criticism and for the action he has taken.

I have tried in these pages not only to record the dry facts but to paint a picture of the country we fought in, battle zone and back areas, of the hardships imposed by the enemy and the weather and of the fatalistic life we led, and I have particularly sought to bring out the patience, courage, cheerfulness and unfailing humour of the man in the ranks. This is his book.

In addition to the war-diary and other official sources I have received the greatest assistance from the diaries, correspondence and personal narratives of many individuals, too numerous to mention here by name, and I take this opportunity of thanking them all for making possible whatever success this history may achieve.

A. M. McGILCHRIST,
Major, The Liverpool Scottish.

LIVERPOOL,
  8 *August,* 1930.

ILLUSTRATIONS

MAPS

xi

THE BATTALION PRE-WAR

THE BATTALION PRE-WAR

On 27 January, 1900, a letter, signed " G. Forbes Milne,"
appeared in the daily press suggesting that in view of
1900   the great wave of patriotic feeling roused by the Boer
War the time might be opportune for the raising of a
volunteer corps of young Scotsmen in Liverpool on similar lines
to the London Scottish.

The idea was enthusiastically taken up, meetings were
arranged, a large number of men anxious to be enrolled gave
in their names, a very influential general committee was formed
which included such prominent Scotsmen as Lord Balfour of
Burleigh—then Secretary for Scotland—and the Earl of Wemyss
and March, and a petition, signed by Mr. David McIver, M.P.,
was forwarded to the War Office requesting permission to raise
the proposed battalion. The War Office was not slow to respond
and authority was granted on 80 April, 1900, the Battalion to
be called the 8th (Scottish) Volunteer Battalion, The King's
Liverpool Regt.

In the meantime a local working committee of leading
business men in Liverpool had been formed, with two honorary
secretaries, to do the necessary spadework but, although the
machinery was ready, there were unaccountable delays and it
was not until 24 October that the first Commanding-Officer,
Captain and Hon. Major C. Forbes Bell, V.D., was appointed.
It would be impossible to suggest a more suitable commanding-
officer for a new battalion. Colonel Forbes Bell had already a
very long and varied experience of the Volunteers. He was
gazetted to the 1st Cheshire Rifle Volunteers as far back as 1872
and served with them and with the 2nd V.B. The King's
Liverpool Regt. until 1891, when he retired. In 1895 he was
persuaded to rejoin the 2nd V.B. as Quartermaster and he
remained with them in that capacity until 1898 when he was
compelled to resign owing to ill-health. He thus had a thorough
knowledge not only of the training side but also of the administrative side, which was particularly valuable to a new formation.

On 21 November the first Adjutant, Captain J. C. Robertson,
West India Regiment, arrived, and the Commanding-Officer
and he at once made preparations to enrol the first recruits.

3

Colonel Forbes Bell had already rented a small room at 12, Alexandra Buildings, Ormond Street, as Headquarters, and it was from there that the first Battalion Orders were issued on 3 December, 1900, stating that recruits would be enrolled the following day beginning at 12-30 p.m., and also giving details as to lectures to the Officers and drills. These orders are now framed and hang on the wall of the Commanding-Officer's room at Fraser Street.

A large number of recruits presented themselves the following day and, by dint of hard work on the part of the doctors conducting the medical examination, 80 were examined in the hour allotted for recruiting and of these 60 were accepted. The Liverpool Scottish determined at the outset to insist on a very high standard of physical fitness and they have never relaxed their standard at any time in an attempt to bring the Battalion up to strength.

It is interesting to note that at this time, in addition to the annual subscription of 10/-, each man on joining the Battalion had to pay an entrance-fee of £2. Later the entrance-fee was reduced to 10/-, but each man paid a clothing subscription of 20/-.

Recruiting proceeded steadily until, at the end of February, 1901, the numbers were 305. Up to this
1901 time the members of the Battalion had been carrying out their drills in the shed of the 4th V.B., K.L.R., Shaw Street, which had been very kindly placed at their disposal, and also in the North Haymarket, but it became evident that recruiting was suffering owing to the Liverpool Scottish having no drill-shed of their own, and Colonel Forbes Bell therefore secured new Headquarters at 22, Highgate Street, where there was accommodation for parade work. A new difficulty now arose. The Scottish no longer had access to the rifles of the 4th V.B., and the Government would not issue rifles to them until a suitable armoury was provided. To get over the difficulty two hundred old trade guns were hired which, although they were useless for range work, were serviceable enough for arms-drill training.

Another bar to recruiting was the lack of uniforms but on 16 April, 1901, Highland dress was officially sanctioned for the Battalion and permission to wear a tartan was given. There could be no question as to which tartan the Battalion should wear, and the Forbes tartan, which was chosen out of compli-ment to the first Commanding-Officer, will always remind us of what the Battalion owes to him. By a happy coincidence the Forbes tartan will also remind us of Mr. Forbes Milne whose letter to the papers had been the spark which set alight the enthusiasm of the Scotsmen of Liverpool. Mr. Forbes Milne did more than write to the papers. He was himself one of the first recruits enrolled and, as he was a piper, he took in hand the training of a pipe band and became the first Pipe-Major.

The Battalion was now in a position to go ahead. Colour-Serjeants C. Lindsay and J. Biggs and Serjeant J. Meecham had joined as Instructors on the Permanent Staff, uniforms were issued as fast as they could be got and rifles were received from the Government. It was felt, however, that it would be bad policy to allow the Battalion, in the first year of its existence, to go to camp with more experienced troops. A standing camp for the Scottish alone was, therefore, formed at Altcar on 27 June and lasted for three weeks. Those who could obtain leave from their employers spent ten days under canvas while others travelled to and from Liverpool daily and attended drills in the evenings and early mornings.

The Battalion had its first Annual Inspection on 27 July, 1901, at the Old Exhibition Grounds, Edge Lane, when Colonel E. H. FitzHerbert, commanding the 8th and 40th Regimental Districts, expressed himself as greatly pleased with all he saw and congratulated Colonel Forbes Bell on the rapid progress made. Over 400 were on parade on that occasion.

On 17 February, 1902, the Right Honourable Donald Alexander Lord Strathcona and Mount Royal was *1902* appointed to the Hon. Colonelcy of the Battalion. Lord Strathcona probably did more than any other man for the commercial development of Canada, and Strathcona's Horse which he raised there at his own expense made a great name for themselves in the South African War. The Liverpool Scottish were greatly honoured when he accepted the Hon. Colonelcy, and his appointment was enthusiastically received by the Battalion.

In response to a call for volunteers a service section, consisting of 1 officer, 1 serjeant, 1 corporal, 1 drummer and 18 privates, embarked at Southampton on 25 March, 1902, for South Africa, where they were attached to the 1st Battalion, Gordon Highlanders. They arrived too late to take part in any major engagements but did valuable work on detachment in various blockhouses. The officer in charge, Lieut. J. Watson, was a son of the Revd. John Watson, D.D., Chaplain to the

B

Battalion, better known perhaps outside Liverpool under his *nom-de-plume*, "Ian Maclaren."

Another officer, Lieut. J. A. Bingham, had already volunteered for active service early in 1901. He was seconded to the Imperial Yeomanry with whom he took part in many severe actions, ultimately receiving wounds at Klip River as a result of which he died in February, 1902. He was the first battle casualty of the Liverpool Scottish and his name will always be honourably remembered.

On 26 July, 1902, Colonel Forbes Bell was compelled, owing to ill-health, to resign his commission, a sad misfortune for the Battalion, but in Major A. L. Macfie, who succeeded him, it found another keen and experienced Commanding-Officer who had been an active member of the Volunteers for more than twenty years.

By this time the Liverpool Scottish were fit to take their place in camp with other troops and accordingly they proceeded to their first camp proper at Aldershot, where, as in the two succeeding years at Stobs, they were attached to the 2nd Lothian Brigade from whose Commander, Brigadier-General William Gordon, they received the highest praise.

21 November, 1902, is a date to be recorded as it was on that day that there took place at St. George's Hall the first Annual Prize-Distribution and Ball, which have since been such features in the social life of the Battalion.

By the end of the training year in 1903 the strength of the Battalion was just short of 700 all ranks and it *1903* remained constant at slightly above or below this figure for some years. It became obvious that a Headquarters more worthy of the Battalion was an absolute necessity, and an appeal was made for donations to meet the cost of erecting a suitable building. When £4,000 had been raised by public subscription the actual work of construction was put in hand, and the present Headquarters in Fraser Street was completed *1904* in October, 1904, and formally declared open by Colonel Courtenay, A.A.G., North-Western District. The funds raised were, however, not sufficient to meet the entire cost, and to pay off the deficit a strong committee took in hand the organization of a Bazaar. This was held in St. George's Hall in November, 1904, and lasted three days, the daily opening ceremony being performed in turn by Lord Crewe, Lord Strathcona and General Sir Henry Mackinnon. A sum of about £8,000 was realized, which entirely freed the building from debt.

In this year, too, the Regimental Hut at Altcar was erected.

On 18 September, 1905, H.M. King Edward VII held a review
in Edinburgh of the entire Scottish Volunteer Force,
1905   when over 38,000 troops of all arms paraded. The
Liverpool Scottish were honoured by being included in
the review. They were billeted in the Academy and were
attached to the 2nd Lothian Brigade. As the Battalion passed
the saluting point His Majesty graciously remarked on the fine
physique of the men. Twenty officers and 480 other ranks
attended. It was on this occasion that the Adjutant dropped
his eyeglass. It was picked up and pocketed by one of the
drummers and is now a treasured possession of the Serjeants'
Mess, where it is exhibited—in a highly improper and unusual
setting—on very special occasions.

On 22 October, 1906, Captain J. C. Robertson completed
his tour of duty and the Adjutancy of the Battalion
1906   was taken over by Major C. J. Simpson, 1st
Battalion, Gordon Highlanders.

On 31 March, 1908, the Battalion underwent a very material
change as on that date the Volunteer Force ceased
1908   to exist and the Territorial Force was formed. The
difference between the two forces was considerable.
Under the old régime a recruit was simply enrolled a member of
the Battalion. As a Territorial he had to swear an oath of
allegiance and bind himself to serve for four years. In addition,
the Territorial Force could, on a state of national emergency
being declared, be mobilized for home defence, while this was
not so in the case of the Volunteers. The new system necessitated the disbanding of the old Battalion and the re-enlistment
of all those prepared to serve under the new conditions. The
response was very satisfactory, but many felt that they could
not undertake the obligations demanded of them and for a time
the strength of the Battalion dropped to about 600. Within
a year, however, it had risen to 29 officers and 991 other ranks.
As a Territorial unit the Battalion now became the 10th
(Scottish) Battn. The King's (Liverpool) Regt. and formed part
of the South Lancashire Brigade.

In this year at Peel Camp, Isle of Man, "C" Company
(Captain J. R. Davidson), won the Brigade Cup for the most
efficient company in the Brigade.

On 5 July, 1909, a Royal Review was held at Knowsley by
H.M. King Edward VII.   Before the Review the
1909 King's and Regimental Colours were received by
Lieutenants E. G. Thin and D. A. Campbell from the
hands of His Majesty.   The Colours were the gift of Lord
Strathcona to the Battalion and were consecrated by the Lord
Bishop of Liverpool, assisted by the Revd. Alexander Connel,
M.A., B.D., Chaplain to the Battalion.

On 21 October, 1909, Captain the Hon. A. H. Maitland,
Queen's Own Cameron Highlanders, took over the duties of
Adjutant from Major Simpson.   Captain Maitland was a most
popular Adjutant and under his efficient guidance the Battalion
made very rapid progress.   It was with deep regret and a sense
of personal loss that the Battalion received the news of his
gallant death in action with his Regiment on 14 September,
1914, at the Battle of the Aisne.

On 3 October, 1911, Colonel Macfie was appointed to
command the South Lancashire Brigade, and Major
1911 Willlam Nicholl took over command of the Battalion.
Once more the Scottish were fortunate in having as
their Commanding-Officer one with long experience of volunteer-
ing, whose heart and soul were in the work of increasing the
efficiency of the Battalion.

Annual training in 1912 took an unusual form.   Instead of
attending Camp with the remainder of the Brigade, the
1912 Scottish proceeded alone to Gailes, in Ayrshire, and
after a week's camp there devoted the second half of
their training to a route-march through a large part of the
Southern Highlands.   Starting from Balloch, at the south end
of Loch Lomond, they marched north along the side of the loch
through Luss and Ardlui to Crianlarich and thence via Luib,
Lochearnhead, Callander and Dunblane to Stirling, where they
entrained for Liverpool.   The march was a huge success and
was greatly enjoyed by all ranks in spite of rather disappointing
weather.

Captain Maitland rejoined his Regiment on 22 October,
1913, and Captain C. P. James, Argyle and
1913 Sutherland Highlanders, took over the duties of
Adjutant.

The Battalion suffered a severe loss in January, 1914, in the
death of its Hon. Colonel, Lord Strathcona.   He
1914 had always taken a keen interest in the Battalion,
had visited it on several occasions and, in addition

to his gift of the Colours, had given the Scottish many proofs of his generosity. To find a worthy successor was a matter of very serious thought, but later in the year the Battalion learnt with pride and satisfaction that the Marquis of Tullibardine— now the Duke of Atholl—had consented to become its Hon. Colonel, his appointment being dated 13 June. The Marquis of Tullibardine was heir to one of the oldest titles in Scotland, he had seen service in South Africa with his own Regiment, the Scottish Horse, which he commanded, and no more suitable or popular appointment could have been made. He lost no time in arranging to make the acquaintance of the Battalion and on 15 July a review was held in Sefton Park when the Liverpool Scottish, wearing white spats for the first time in their history, were led past the saluting base by their new Hon. Colonel. Since that day, both during the Great War and afterwards, the Battalion has on numerous occasions had cause to congratulate itself on having an Hon. Colonel who always has the interests of the Liverpool Scottish at heart and for whom no trouble is too great to take if it is for the benefit of the Battalion.

The Scottish were due to proceed to Hornby for annual training on 2 August, 1914. When the day arrived France, Russia and Germany were already mobilizing and it appeared probable that Great Britain, too, would be involved. However, the Battalion duly paraded at Headquarters and moved off to Camp, which was reached late in the afternoon. At 2 a.m. the following morning orders were received that the Battalion should return at once to Liverpool. On arrival at Fraser Street, Colonel Nicholl addressed the men and they were then dismissed to their homes with orders to be prepared to report at Headquarters at a moment's notice.

The Ultimatum to Germany from the British Government expired at midnight on 8 August. The following day saw the mobilization of the Territorial Force.

THE FIRST BATTALION

MOBILIZATION AND TRAINING

1914

The first three days of mobilization were occupied in issuing equipment, drawing stores from Ordnance, medical inspection, attestation of recruits to bring the Battalion up to strength, and all the hundred and one activities of the transition from a peace to a war footing. Captain Harrison, the Transport Officer, was engaged meantime in collecting horses for his section. He succeeded in getting together a magnificent lot of animals, too magnificent as it turned out, for they attracted the attention of a Regular Battalion, billeted in St. George's Hall and feverishly making ready for service overseas, and to Captain Harrison's unutterable disgust most of his beautiful steeds were commandeered and he had to start afresh.

So far the men had been sleeping in their own homes but at 10 p.m. on 7 August an urgent call was sent out to all ranks to parade at Headquarters immediately. In all, about six hundred reported at Fraser Street that night and were billeted in the Shakespeare Theatre. The following day the men received their embodiment grant of £5 each and their 10/- kit-allowance, and ball ammunition was issued. The Companies were now disposed—" A " to " F " in the Stadium, " G " and " H " in the Shakespeare Theatre. The managers of the Stadium did all in their power to give the Battalion a good time. Their private offices were placed at the Commanding-Officer's disposal for an officers' mess, while boxing exhibitions and concerts were organized in the ring each night for the benefit of the men.

In addition to its normal training—route-marches, parades in Sefton Park, etc.—the Battalion furnished working parties at the Docks, principally unloading and warehousing shipments of frozen meat, until on 18 August it entrained for Edinburgh where, with the remainder of the South Lancashire Brigade, it formed part of the Forth Defences, the Liverpool Scottish and the 5th South Lancashires being encamped in the King's Park close to Holyrood Palace, and the other half of the Brigade being stationed at Dunfermline.

It was a disappointment to the Liverpool Scottish that they were not quartered in the historic Castle, which was occupied by a khaki battalion. The Civil Authorities approached the Scottish

Command and suggested that as a kilted battalion was available
it should become the garrison of the Castle, but the necessary
permission was not forthcoming.

Training was now begun in earnest. A severe programme
of work was laid down calculated to weed out the weaklings,
if any, and the Battalion proceeded to get fit. The day started
at 6-45 a.m. with an hour's physical drill which frequently took
the form of company races to the top of Arthur's Seat. After
breakfast, company and battalion training continued till
4-80 p.m., and lectures after tea were not unknown. Discipline
was tightened up, only 20% of the trained men and 25% of the
uniformed recruits being allowed leave out of camp after parade.
The recruits still awaiting uniform fared better. They were all
allowed out after duty, to the envy of their less fortunate
comrades, and they were able also to slip over the wall, at the
morning break, to a shop near by where they consumed vast
quantities of soup washed down by a schooner of ale each. The
Battalion throve on the hard work, every man was keen and a
genuine trier, the inter-company rivalry was prodigious, and
the rapidity with which partially trained civilians were turned
into a very fair imitation of whole-time soldiers was really
astonishing.

The burning question in everyone's mind was, "What
will the Government do with the Territorials?" Colonel
Nicholl had already in Liverpool offered the Battalion
to the War Office for garrison duty abroad to relieve
a regular unit, and there were various rumours that
the Scottish might be sent to India, Egypt or Malta.
Eventually, on 27 August, definite news came from the War
Office that, provided 80% volunteered for foreign service wherever
they might be required, the Battalion would be allowed to go as
a unit. If less than that percentage volunteered they might be
attached to another Battalion. Naturally many men with
relations dependent on them did not feel, at that early stage,
that they were called upon to go and many of the younger men
could not get the necessary permission from their parents but
the general response was magnificent. All the officers and more
than 800 other ranks volunteered at once and the continued
existence of the Liverpool Scottish as a separate entity was
assured. Authority was now given to enlist a further 300 recruits,
and Major Blair and Captain Anderson went to Liverpool to
make the requisite arrangements. There was no difficulty in
finding the men. In three days the full three hundred had been
attested and medically examined and, had it been possible to

take them, double the number would have joined. These recruits duly arrived in Edinburgh and were posted to their companies. The old members who had not been able to volunteer for service overseas were formed into two new companies, " I " and " K," and afterwards did their training separately from the Battalion.

On 17 August Lieut.-General Sir James Grierson, K.C.B., to whom had been entrusted the command of the II Army Corps of the British Expeditionary Force, died suddenly in a train at Amiens. His body was brought back to Glasgow for burial and representatives of every Scottish battalion attended the funeral ceremony. The Liverpool Scottish were honoured in being ordered to send a party, and the twelve men—specially chosen for their height and physique—who paraded under the command of Lieutenant W. J. H. Renison, worthily represented the Battalion.

All who served with the Liverpool Scottish in Edinburgh will look back to those days with pleasure and a wistful longing that the clock could be put back and that they might again camp in the King's Park and re-live the old life. But of all the memories of that time the one which will stand apart in the minds of many is that of the Church Parades in St. Giles' Cathedral. The noble setting, the almost overpowering weight of tone in the singing of the soldiers' hymns by the huge congregation led by the splendid brass band of the Battalion, and the ever-present thought at the back of everyone's mind of the future and what it might hold, combined to make these services both moving and memorable.

After about two months, orders were received for a move to Tunbridge Wells, which was carried out on 10 October, the Battalion on arrival being billeted in schools and empty houses. The same programme of work was adhered to as far as possible but the training facilities were nothing like so good as in Edinburgh and everyone was delighted when, on 27 October, a warning order was received to be ready to embark for service abroad on the 30th. The next few days were hectic. All leather equipment was called in and full web equipment issued, kit inspections seemed to occur at every hour of the day and night, and Battalion Headquarters at " The Dell " hummed like a bee-hive. One strange item of procedure was the withdrawal of every rifle in the Battalion and the issue to each man of a new rifle which he would have no possible chance of trying before going overseas.

At the last minute orders came that those men who had not

fired their musketry course were not to proceed with the Battalion, which meant that many of the last 300 recruits had to be left behind, to their bitter disappointment. Neither in Edinburgh nor at Tunbridge Wells had there been adequate range accommodation, and it had been found quite impossible to put all the men through their course. As it turned out, this loss of part of the Battalion proved a blessing in disguise because all these men subsequently came out to France with the first draft at a time when fresh and fit men were very badly needed, and they materially stiffened the Battalion.

One other member, too, was refused permission to go over-seas. Lieut.-Colonel Nicholl, to his keen regret, could not find a doctor—and he tried many—who would pass him fit for active service and he was compelled to hand over the command to Major Blair. It was indeed a cruel blow that after commanding the Liverpool Scottish for so many years and training them for active service he was not allowed to lead them in the field, and his disappointment was shared by every man in the Battalion.

At last the expected final orders arrived and on the morning of 1 November the Battalion entrained for Southampton, which was reached during the afternoon, and embarked on the *s.s. Maidan.* The Military Landing Officer, after compli-menting the Commanding-Officer on the expeditious way in which the men had gone on board, remarked that he had been responsible for the shipping overseas of a large part of the British Expeditionary Force but had not seen any battalion the equal in physique of the Liverpool Scottish. Also on board the *Maidan* were the Queen's Westminsters, one of the leading London Territorial Units, and very cheery and friendly shipmates they proved to be. The crossing, in company with other trans-ports and escorting destroyers, was uneventful and Havre was reached at 7 a.m. on the 2nd, but for some reason the steamer put to sea again and cruised about the Bay until 10 p.m. when she tied up alongside the wharf for the night. The ship was so overcrowded that no one relished the thought of another night on board, but that, after all, was a minor discomfort, and at 8 a.m. on the 3rd the Battalion landed on French soil.

The Liverpool Scottish were not the first Territorial Infantry Battalion to reach France; that distinction is held by the London Scottish; but they were specially selected, along with twenty-two other Territorial Battalions, on account of their record and their progress since mobilization, to assist the sorely-tried Regular Army to hold the line during the first winter campaign while the new armies were being raised and trained. It speaks volumes for the pre-war efficiency of the officers and the keenness of the men that the junior Territorial Battalion of Liverpool should be the only one selected to go overseas in 1914.

The officers now had to undertake that unpalatable daily duty, the censoring of the men's letters. It was an embarrassing duty, that reading another man's most intimate messages to his nearest and dearest, but it was very necessary, though not often, perhaps, from the point of view of preventing the leakage of important military information. The average Tommy—and for that matter the average officer—was only on very rare occasions possessed of information which would have been of any real use to the enemy. Rather was the censorship useful in suppressing the type of letter written by the more imaginative man entirely for effect and with no thought of the anxiety it might bring to his relatives. For instance, one bright spirit wrote from Havre on the day the Battalion landed, " Dear Mother, you " will see by the address that we are in the thick of it. And it " is Hell !" Censoring had its ironic side, too, as witness the case of the young subaltern who was compelled each day to read the most impassioned screeds from a private in his platoon to a lady for whom he himself entertained more than a passing fancy.

After a night spent under canvas on the heights above the town, the Battalion entrained on the 4th for St. Omer and the men learnt the meaning of the words on the cattle-trucks, " Hommes 40, Chevaux 8." The journey, some two hundred miles, took twenty-seven hours but, as the train stopped for a considerable time at nearly every station and there was much that was novel and interesting to see, no one was too bored. At Abbeville the Medical Officer, Lieutenant N. G. Chavasse, and one or two others astonished the natives by having a cold bath in the tank below the pump used to supply water to the loco-motives. St. Omer was reached at 9-45 p.m. on the 5th and after a long wait in pouring rain the Battalion moved off to Blendecques, three miles away, and went into billets. Here the men had their first experience of the sort of dwelling that was to be theirs for many a long day, the typical French barn, and here, too, many of them first made the acquaintance of those unwelcome little visitors which later formed part of the stock-in-trade of every music-hall comedian.

With the exception of two days' trench digging the training at Blendecques consisted entirely of practice attacks across miles of country through every phase, from column-of-route to the final assault, and as the weather was consistently atrocious the fitness and stamina of the Battalion were severely tested, particularly as there were no facilities for drying wet clothes. It says much for the general condition of the Battalion that only about twenty men broke down and had to be left behind when orders to move were received.

Training was broken by a sad but proud duty. Field-Marshal Lord Roberts, who had been paying a visit to the Indian Troops at the Front, returned to Sir John French's headquarters at St. Omer suffering from a chill and died there of pneumonia on 14 November. On the 17th his body was to be taken to the Hotel de Ville for a short service and thence to the railway station to be removed to England for burial. The Liverpool Scottish had the honour of being detailed to line the Place Gambetta, in which the Hotel de Ville is, and also the street leading into it. One officer, Lieutenant F. H. Turner, and twenty picked men were also detailed to take part in the procession, and a splendid looking lot they were, none of them under six feet in height. The previous day intensive practice, under the able instruction of Colour-Serjeant S. Jennings, in the reversing of arms and resting on arms reversed was carried out, a new drill to many of the Battalion, but the men acquitted themselves well at the ceremony.

One of those whose health broke down under the severe conditions was Major Blair and he was compelled to give up the command and return to England. Whilst sympathising with him in this cruel stroke of bad luck the Battalion knew that in his successor, Major J. R. Davidson, they had an ideal commanding-officer. A first-class soldier in every sense of the word, he was peculiarly fitted by his civil profession of engineering to command a Battalion destined to spend many months in wet trenches, where indeed his expert knowledge of water levels and drainage did prove of the utmost value.

While at Blendecques the Scottish were in reserve for the First Battle of Ypres but were not called on, though lorries were ready to rush them up the line if required in a hurry. Continuous gun fire could be heard and even, when the wind was favourable, the rattle of musketry, and there was much speculation as to what was going on, reliable and recent news being rare in those days.

Before leaving Blendecques, the Quartermaster, Lieutenant A. C. Jack, deposited at the Infantry Barracks, St. Omer, the pipes and drums of the Pipe Band and the Officers' swords which they had taken out with them. It is an interesting fact that he recovered them intact a year later. The swords were then sent home and the pipes and drums taken up the line for the use of the Battalion.

At length, on 19 November, a General Staff-Officer from Sir John French's Headquarters, having inspected the Scottish in the attack and expressed himself as immensely pleased with the improvement shown, gave orders that they should be prepared to move nearer the line—the following day to Hazebrouck and the day after to Bailleul. A great part of that night was occupied in issuing new boots, tunics, etc., which had been indented for some time previously but had, as usual, arrived at the last moment. No one got much sleep.

The 20th was, for a change, fine but it had frozen hard all night and the roads were solid ice. The march was rather a nightmare, particularly to the rear company, whose job it was to keep the transport on the road if possible and put it back on the road when it got ditched. Many men had bad falls—no joke with a rifle and full pack—but Hazebrouck was at last reached at 4 p.m. and troubles seemed over. Unfortunately there proved to be no billeting accommodation in the town, which was already full of troops out on rest, and the Battalion had to set off by companies into the surrounding country to try and find shelter in farm buildings. It was not until midnight that all were housed.

The march next day to Bailleul was considerably easier and there the Battalion found first-class billets and quite a busy town in which to amuse itself.

Little training was attempted in Bailleul, parades under company arrangements being the usual routine except for two Battalion route-marches up towards the trenches. During one of these one of our 6-inch guns in a camouflaged position near the road without warning fired a round over the column, a rather startling experience as few had realised that they were so close to the war as to be in front of some of our artillery.

On 28 November orders came through that the Battalion would join a Regular Brigade on the 25th, and here a word must be said about organization.

The Regular Army, early in 1914, had adopted the double-company system but the Territorial Force continued to be organized under the old eight-company system. It was obvious that on joining a regular formation the Scottish would have to conform to their method and the Battalion was reorganized

accordingly, " A " and " B " becoming one company, " C " and
" D " another and so on. The difficulty arose of deciding by
what style the double-companies should be known. To call them
" A," " B," " C " and " D " might easily have led to confusion
and they were therefore known for some time as numbers 1, 2,
3 and 4 companies. This system, however, had disadvantages
and subsequently they were called " V," " X," " Y " and " Z,"
which they have remained ever since and by which names they
will be alluded to throughout this history.

On the morning of the 25th the Battalion formed up in mass
in a field near Bailleul and was addressed by General Sir
H. Smith Dorrien, G.O.C., II Corps, who was accompanied
by the Prince of Wales. The General, in his speech, welcomed
the Liverpool Scottish into his Corps and complimented them
on their appearance. He described what their duties would be
and gave it as his personal opinion that if the British and French
Armies pinned the enemy down in the West during the winter
the Russians would smash through to Berlin from the East
during the spring and the war would be over in the summer.
At that time most of the Battalion were surprised to learn that
the Staff expected the war to last so long !

After the General's address the Battalion moved off to
Westoutre, where it joined the 9th Brigade (Brigadier-General
W. Douglas Smith), 3rd Division (Major-General A. Haldane),
and was billeted, " Z " Company in the Church, the remainder
in barns and cottages.

The 9th Brigade was composed of the following units :—
1st Northumberland Fusiliers, 1st Lincolns, 1st Royal Scots
Fusiliers, 4th Royal Fusiliers. They had taken part with distinction in every engagement of the war from Mons onwards and
held a record in the Army second to none. Quite naturally they
were somewhat dubious at the prospect of having attached to
them a wholly untried territorial battalion which might prove
a liability and not an asset. How the Scottish overcame the
initial doubts of the Brigade and gained the confidence and
friendship of all its battalions will be told in due course.

The first sight the Battalion had of a company of Regulars on
the march was something of a shock. Many of the men had
beards, their clothing was stained and muddy, and quite a
number were wearing cap-comforters instead of the regulation
flat cap. Anything more unlike the traditional smart Tommy it
would be impossible to imagine. But there was one thing about
them that did particularly attract the eye. Every man's rifle

was absolutely spotless, not a bad illustration for civilian soldiers of the distinction between the superficial and the essential.

The Battalion received orders to move to the trenches at Kemmel on the evening of 27 November, and on the 26th, at a meeting of officers, the Brigade-Major, Captain Wavell, explained the principles of trench-warfare as it was in those early days and also issued instructions regarding the routine to be carried out in the line. Some of these, in the light of later experience, were rather humorous. For instance, " In the front line there will be no smoking whatever, and no matches will be struck," and " Day and night every other man will be on sentry duty."

The Liverpool Scottish were ordered to find 150 rifles for the front line, 100 as supports, and two platoons as local reserves, and there was a long argument amongst the company-commanders as to who should take the front line. Captain Anderson claimed that as his old company, " B," held the Battalion Efficiency Shield and with it the privilege of leading the Battalion on the march it should also lead into the trenches, but Captain Twentyman insisted that as senior Company-Commander it was his right to be the first into action, and his argument won the day. " Y " Company, less one platoon, therefore, had the honour of being the first into the firing-line, while one platoon of " V " and the remaining platoon of " Y " were detailed as supports, and two platoons of " Z " Company to local reserve.

C

THE FIRST WINTER

Adequately to realize the difficulties and hardships of
life in the trenches that first winter it is necessary
1914 to understand something of the general situation
at the time.

The first Battle of Ypres was just over and the enemy's
advance on the Channel Ports had definitely been brought to a
standstill. The weather and the state of the ground made further
movement by either side impossible, and so there began that
siege-warfare which was totally unforeseen and therefore found
us with no organization ready to deal with it. The enemy, of
course, was in similar case but, though stopped, he had been
able practically everywhere to seize and hold what high ground
there was and thus he not only, from the field of view which
he had, precluded any movement on our part near the line
during the day but had the advantage of a much drier situation
for his trenches. The siting of the British trenches was quite
haphazard, the line on which a counter-attack had been held
up and the men had dug themselves in frequently becoming
the fire-trench with no regard to field of fire or even to the
direction of the enemy. Many of the Kemmel trenches were
open to enfilade fire, either from rifles or artillery, while from
some parts of them the enemy's trenches could not be seen at all.
There was, naturally, no trench-system as it was understood in,
say, 1916. The front line of trenches was the only line and it
was by no means continuous. Support-trenches did not exist nor
were there, at any rate when the Liverpool Scottish first went
into the line, any strong-points or defended localities in rear to
serve as rallying points or to hold up an attack which might
break through the fire-trenches. The only defence scheme,
therefore, was, "If the front line is captured it must be retaken
immediately," the rôle of supports and reserves being entirely an
offensive and not a defensive one.

Communication-trenches, too, were non-existent at Kemmel
except for one of perhaps fifty yards long on the extreme right
of the Brigade front. Reliefs had, therefore, to be carried out
over the open by night, a difficult business if the night was very
dark and a dangerous one if it was clear and the enemy got wind

of what was going on. There were two methods of carrying out relief. Either the men were lined up along the back of the trench and took over simply by jumping in and hoisting the other people out or the incoming troops filed in at one end of the trench and gradually pushed the outgoing troops out at the other end. The latter method, though safer and less noisy, gave the men no chance of learning from their opposite numbers where the danger spots were nor any other details that might be of use to them during their tour in the line.

The trenches themselves were far from being the comfortable homes that they became later in the war. There were no dug-outs, no duckboards, no pumps, and all material required for revetting had to be improvized from planks and lumber taken from ruined houses. Even sandbags were rare and were mostly the special perquisite of the R.E. The state of these trenches after heavy rain or during a thaw is indescribable. Men had frequently to be dug out of the mud by their friends, being quite incapable of movement unassisted, and many a man discovered after walking a considerable way towards billets after a relief that he had left a shoe and spat behind in the trench, sucked off by the mud—the loss unnoticed until circulation began to return to the feet. Shoes and spats are clearly not a suitable dress for trench-warfare and they were soon withdrawn and boots and puttees issued.

Sanitation, to all intents and purposes, was a dead letter, and the condition of the ground behind the trenches and indeed of the trenches themselves must be left to the imagination.

Figures will describe more vividly than words the terrible conditions which the Battalion had to face during its first few weeks in the line. Twenty-six officers and 829 other ranks strong on 27 November, and as fit as training could make it, it was reduced by the end of the first week in January to a total strength of 370. During that period actual battle losses totalled 32. Trench-foot was responsible for most of the casualties and those men who had it badly were never fit for active service again.

A contributory cause of the great amount of sickness in the Battalion was, no doubt, the lack of hot food in the trenches. At night hot tea was sent up in dixies from headquarters but as it had to be carried a mile and a half, frequently over shockingly bad ground, much was spilt on the way and there was not much heat left in the rest when it did arrive. Hot stews were impossible as the Transport did not at first include field-cookers in which meals might have been brought up reasonably near the line under cover of darkness.

Another drawback was the impossibility of getting the men properly dried and clean when back in billets after duty in the trenches, and the constant living in wet clothes was responsible for much illness. The officers fared better as they were able to get a complete change, thanks to their valises, while their soaked things were drying. One concession was made which had an amusing sequel. It was, of course, impossible to shave in the trenches—there was no water to spare for that—and orders were issued that the men were not to be compelled to shave when the Battalion was out of the line. The natural result was that practically every man started to grow a beard and at the end of a few weeks the appearance of the Battalion was so ghastly that a special inspection of beards was held, and only those men who showed signs of being able to grow a respectable one were allowed to continue unshaven. The others had to remove the fungus at once.

The Scottish suffered from another inconvenience. They went to the front armed with the old long Lee Enfield Rifle. The Regular Army were, of course, armed with the new S.M.L.E., but there were not sufficient supplies to arm any except the Regulars with it. This was a perfect nuisance, as the bolt of the long rifle was not designed to withstand the heavier charge of cordite in the new Mark VII ammunition and, therefore, special stocks of Mark VI, in addition to the 150 rounds carried by each man, had to be taken into the trenches. The old rifle, too, was not so easily protected from the mud as the new, its protruding barrel being particularly prone to fill itself with dirt and, though a good target weapon, it was not so well adapted for rapid fire, a much more desirable attribute in close-range warfare.

Early in 1915 these rifles were replaced by the new weapon but for some time men from hospital, or who had been detached for special duties, rejoined the Battalion still in possession of the old rifle. Drafts, too, arrived armed with it and it was not until immediately before the Battle of the Somme in 1916 that the Battalion was uniformly armed with the S.M.L.E.

But to return to the Battalion :

It was an eerie experience, that march up to the trenches for the first time. No chances were taken, smoking and talking being stopped fully three miles from the line. In Kemmel the companies were met by guides and set off independently to their positions. "Y" Company reached the front line without incident except that it got its baptism of fire, but no casualties, from the stray bullets which always seemed more numerous and closer to one at Kemmel than anywhere else. Curiously enough the first unit to be relieved by the Scottish was another territorial battalion, the Glasgow Highlanders (H.L.I.), who had just completed their first 48 hours in the line.

The trenches themselves were decidedly peculiar. The right section was quite a reasonable trench. It had no traverses but the parapet was sound enough, and one could move freely up and down. The left section was not a trench at all. It consisted of a series of unconnected pits which held three or four men each and were so shallow that in many of them no one could sit upright without exposing his head. The first obvious duty was to deepen these pits and get them joined up, and the men set to work with their entrenching-tools to such good purpose that by the end of the tour it was possible to go from one end of the position to the other without leaving the trench.

A patrol of two men, Lance-Serjeant W. V. Dumbreck and Private G. A. Spencer, went out the first night and worked their way over close to the enemy's line. They were fired on but returned safely to our trenches with useful information as to the nature of the ground in no-man's-land and the state of the enemy's wire.

The distance from the enemy varied. On the left it was about 200 yards but on the extreme right, where he had run out a sap, it was only 85 yards. From this point the trench ran sharply back and was manned by the Royal Fusiliers.

This sap was responsible for the Battalion's first casualty.

The first day passed quietly except for incessant sniping, a great deal of which appeared to be directed at the parapet of the trench at the corner nearest to the enemy. The parapet was repaired at night but it was not strong, and Captain Twentyman realised that if it did not hold the whole trench would be enfiladed from the German position on higher ground to the right. The sniper who was doing the damage appeared to be lying out in front of the sap-head, and as soon as it was light on the 29th Captain Twentyman went down through the trench of the Royal Fusiliers to an R.E. Dump to get a jam-tin bomb with which to dislodge him. Unfortunately, in his eagerness to save time, he came back over the open instead of up the trench, thinking, no doubt, that a thin hedge in front of the position would screen him from view. He was seen and shot down just outside the Royal Fusiliers' trench and was dead when they got him in. His death was a sad blow to his Company and to the Battalion. A most efficient and popular officer, he had thrown himself with zest into the task of training his men for war and they all respected and loved him. He was always cheery, always reliable and always considerate of those whom he commanded. He was buried the same night in the wood fringing the grounds of Kemmel Château.

The remainder of the tour was quiet enough, the only other casualty being Private W. Parry, slightly wounded. The third day was consistently wet and the Battalion had a taste of what Flanders mud can be when churned up by men's feet into a thick sticky paste, but these trenches were, comparatively, very dry and the real experience of mud at its worst was to come later.

The chief hardship was thirst. One waterbottle per man, even with the nightly addition of a small quantity of tea—" Y " Company had good reason to be grateful to that first carrying party of volunteers from " V " Company—is not enough to last three days, and by the end of the second night no one had any water left. The third day, the 30th, was very trying and seemed interminable, but at last the relieving battalion appeared and the Company set off down the road to Kemmel where it managed to " cadge " hot tea from some friendly tommies to strengthen it for the march back to Westoutre.

During their first tour in the line the Scottish definitely accounted for three enemy snipers and two or three more were believed to have been hit, and they were warmly complimented on their steadiness and keenness by the regular battalion on their right, the 4th Royal Fusiliers.

Kemmel Village itself, though scarcely more than a mile from the trenches, had suffered surprisingly little damage, and a number of the inhabitants were still going about their daily affairs apparently oblivious of the fact that there was " a war on." Their houses made excellent billets for the battalion or companies in reserve to the brigade in the trenches, and the men were able to vary the monotony of the army bill-of-fare by patronizing the numerous *estaminets*. One of these gained a deserved reputation for its omelettes which, for some obscure reason, were always served in the shape of a short-bodied and rather corpulent fish. It was somewhat puzzling that, although the men never had the slightest difficulty in buying omelettes, the officers could not buy eggs for love or money. The president of one of the company-officers' messes finally decided that it was time to take a firm line and sent out two of the batmen into the surrounding country with orders that they were not to come back without eggs. The batmen—as usual—won the trick. They returned late at night with ninety-one eggs, and as the Battalion was moving next day most of them had to be handed over to the men of the company.

Kemmel Church was practically intact—a Private of the Honourable Artillery Company played its organ delightfully—and its clock, which faced the German line, was put to a most ingenious use. It was noticed that although the clock was not going, the hands did not always remain in the same position. A watch was kept on the Church and at length the gentleman who was responsible for the strange behaviour of the clock was caught red-handed and suitably dealt with. He was using the hands to signal to the enemy and was no doubt responsible for the noticeably greater liveliness on relief nights.

On 3 December, while still at Westoutre, the Battalion lined the road and was inspected, quite informally, by H.M. the King, who was paying one of his frequent visits to the Front. With him was the Prince of Wales, who must have noticed a considerable change in the general appearance of the men since he saw them at Bailleul only a few days before.

It is not possible within the scope of this history to detail every tour of duty in the trenches carried out by the Battalion. Each company in turn took its place in the front line and all alike suffered from the exposure and the mud, for, with the exception of Headquarter and Transport personnel, every member of the Battalion at this time went into the trenches, even Company Quartermaster-Serjeants and Company Pipers. A Private of " X " Company put the situation in a nutshell. One night, in a particularly bad trench, Serjeant Ferguson found this man standing looking over the parapet with mud and water up to his knees and asked him : " Well, Barker, are you the sentry here ? " " No," said Barker, " I'm a bulrush ! "

The behaviour of the Battalion in the line had done much to allay the doubts of the Brigade as to its reliability, and on 8 December an incident occurred which was to have a material effect on its relations with at least one other Battalion. A company of the Lincolns, which had been two days in the front line, was ordered to attack an advanced trench of the enemy and the Scottish were detailed to find supports and reserves in case of a counter-attack. Accordingly " Y " Company took up a position across a field, close behind the firing-line, while " Z " Company and half " X " Company were posted farther back. The trenches from which the Lincolns had to attack were as bad as any in the sector, and after 48 hours in them many of the men were quite incapable of dragging themselves out on the signal being given. Of those who did manage to get out some reached the German trench in spite of heavy rifle and machine-gun fire, but they were too few to hold what they had won and were forced to retire to their starting point after suffering heavy casualties. Captain D. McLeod, now O.C. " Y " Company, seeing the pitiful condition of the men, suggested that his Company should take over the trenches for the remaining 24 hours of the tour, and Lieut.-Colonel Smith, of the Lincolns, gladly accepted the offer. Of the trenches it is sufficient to say that some men spent the whole of the next day in running water waist deep. On relief the following night, " Y " Company was met at the Laiterie on the Kemmel-Vierstraat Road by the company of the Lincolns which it had relieved, and not a man was allowed to go past until he had had a tot of rum and hot tea, changed his socks and warmed himself at a brazier. From that day the Lincolns always called the Liverpool Scottish the " Lincolnshire " Scottish, and the Battalions were the closest of friends.

On 14 December, the 8th Brigade carried out an attack with two battalions, Gordon Highlanders and Royal Scots, on the enemy's position in the Petit Bois. They jumped off from the trenches held by the Liverpool Scottish and Northumberland Fusiliers, whose men were withdrawn to Kemmel except for covering parties. The Scottish left in the line one platoon each of " X " and " Z " Companies, under Lieuts. F. H. Turner and A. A. Gemmell, and the machine-gun section under Lieut. B. McKinnell.

Owing to a misunderstanding, part of " X " Company's platoon left the trenches with the remainder of the company, and Lieut. Turner, thinking it hardly worth while to keep such a small covering party as the few men who were left, asked the Royal Scots for permission to join them in the attack but this request was refused. The machine-gun section had orders to cover the left flank of the attack and found good targets. The attack was at first successful and many prisoners were taken but at the end of the day only one of the captured trenches was still in British hands. While taking over this trench, J3, from the 1st Middlesex on 21 December, a clear moonlight night, " Y " Company was seen in the open by the enemy and lost 4 killed and 6 wounded before getting into the trench.

The Scottish had the good luck to be out of the line on Christmas Day. There had been frost the night before and, for a change, the ground was hard and dry. The Battalion paraded at 12.30 p.m. in a field close to billets to receive the presents sent out by the officers' wives and relations, and afterwards was addressed by Lieut.-Colonel Davidson. Then there were selections by the Pipe Band, Christmas hymns by the Battalion, and finally the Quartermaster made a dramatic entry at full gallop on a G.S. Wagon which contained Princess Mary's gifts—a pipe and tobacco in a gilt box for every man. Lord Derby materially contributed to the success of the day by sending out plum-puddings for the men, a cigar each for the N.C.O.'s and a full Christmas dinner for the officers.

The Christmas mails were colossal. More than 250 sacks were received, nearly all of which contained eatables of various descriptions. For some days the men showed a strange disinclination to draw their ordinary rations and when the Battalion again moved up to the line, on 31 December, they were still loaded fore and aft with the unconsumed portions of their Christmas fare.

The Liverpool Scottish throughout the war owed a very real debt to those at home who did so much to lighten the hardships of the campaign by their gifts of clothing and food. The Ladies' Committtee, under the able direction of Mrs. C. Forbes Bell, Mrs. Wm. Nicholl and Mrs. J. R. Davidson, worked indefatigably at the knitting and collecting of socks, cap-comforters, cardigans, etc. Large stocks of these were accumulated at Fraser Street and sent to the Front as required.

That the men fed a good deal better than the average battalion on service was also largely due to the generosity of friends at home. To mention only one name, Mr. John Rankin for a considerable time gave £60 per month to provide extra rations for the men and when a request was sent home for Primus stoves he combed England from one end to the other to get the number required. Lieut. Chavasse, too, regularly received from friends in Liverpool drugs and medicines which it was difficult or impossible to obtain through the ordinary channels from the Army Medical Authorities. On one occasion a particular drug which he required, and which could not be obtained in England, was ordered by cable from the United States and reached him in a fortnight.

No want, however staggering or however trivial, ever went unsatisfied. What the Commanding-Officer asked for he received, in full measure and at once.

The Battalion was fortunate, too, in those of its own members who were responsible for its feeding, and to the Quartermaster, Lieut. A. C. Jack, and all his staff, the greatest credit must be given for the inventive and organizing ability which they showed in varying the bill of fare and in evolving systems for the quick distribution of rations when the Battalion was in the trenches. The Liverpool Scottish were the first battalion in France to own a sausage-making machine—"found" in Ypres early in 1915—and they claim also to have been the first to joint and dress meat ready for the stewpot, and to be the originators of the system of trench-rationing whereby the rations were divided proportionately at the transport-lines and packed in sandbags, so many men's rations to a bag. This method, which became general throughout the Army, had great advantages. On arrival at the forward dump the rations could be correctly distributed in the dark without fuss, and so quickly that the carrying parties from the trenches were not kept hanging about in what was frequently a dangerous area. One unique distinction on the "Q" side the Liverpool Scottish hold. R. A. Scott Macfie was certainly the only Quartermaster-Serjeant in the British Army to compile and publish a practical and comprehensive Army Cookery Book. It was entitled *Things that Every Cook Should Know* and contained, in addition to nearly 70 recipes, a wealth of information on such matters as cleanliness, economy and cookhouse routine.

January was a trying month and the weather was atrocious but much was done to ameliorate the wintry con-
1915 ditions. Braziers, on which the men could make tea, became general in the front line and goatskin coats were issued which were a real godsend. When the Battalion was out of the line, concerts and boxing matches were organized in the school at Locre and football matches were played against the other Battalions in the Brigade in which the Scottish team was generally successful. All these activities helped considerably to keep the men in good heart and spirits.

Owing to its reduced strength it was necessary to send practically the whole Battalion into the line to hold the front allotted to it by Brigade. Inter-company reliefs were carried out to avoid leaving the same men too long in the worst places but the strain on all was severe and it was with very genuine feelings of thankfulness that the first draft of four officers (2nd Lieuts. G. K. Cowan, L. G. Wall, W. Turner and C. Dunlop) and 302 other ranks was welcomed on 30 January. The draft was distributed amongst the companies, the men being allotted as far as possible to the companies of which they had been members at Tunbridge Wells, and they very quickly settled down to the routine of trench-warfare.

On 15 February, the 9th Brigade received sudden orders to move to Ypres and take the place of the 85th Brigade in the 28th Division. The Scottish were ordered to follow the Brigade but these orders were cancelled and instead the Battalion remained in the Kemmel sector and was attached to the 85th Brigade when it arrived from Ypres. It was a great disappointment to the Scottish to be detached from the 9th Brigade but the disappointment was not altogether one-sided as the following special order by Brig.-General W. Douglas Smith will show :—

" The G.O.C. 9th Infantry Brigade hears with great regret
" that the 10th (Scottish) Battn. The King's Liverpool
" Regt. is leaving his command. He would like it placed
" on record that the Battalion since it joined this Brigade
" has throughout a most trying time in the trenches
" carried out its duties in a most efficient manner, and he
" has nothing but praise to bestow for the hard work it has
" done and the cheerful spirit in which that work has been
" conducted. He wishes Lieut.-Colonel Davidson and all
" ranks success and he feels sure that the Battalion will
" always maintain its present reputation for good discipline
" and fine soldierly qualities."

The Battalion did one tour in the trenches with the 85th Brigade and was then relieved by the 1/4th South Lancs., another Lancashire Territorial Battalion, whom it was to know very well later on in the 55th Division.

While resting at Westoutre the Battalion learnt, on 28 February, that its old friends the 6th King's (Liverpool Rifles) had arrived at Bailleul. Many men had relations and all had friends in the Sixth, and leave was given to a large number of the Battalion to go to Bailleul and see them. The same day the Scottish heard with great delight that they were to rejoin the 9th Brigade in Ypres, and on 2 March they moved north to Ouderdom. At mid-day, whilst they were fallen out for "dinners" in a field at the roadside, the Liverpool Rifles, also bound for Ypres, marched past them and were given a great ovation.

As the 9th Brigade was now part of the 28th Division, the Scottish on rejoining it ceased to belong to the 3rd Division and Lieut.-Colonel Davidson received the following letter from Major-General A. Haldane :—

"I would have liked to see the Liverpool Scottish and "bid them this morning a farewell which I hope would have "proved only to be temporary, before they left to rejoin "the 9th Brigade. Unfortunately I could not manage it "as I was obliged to inspect two battalions and drafts at "Locre at the same time as you were starting from "Westoutre.

"I wish to thank you for all the excellent service which "you have performed during the three months you have "been with the 3rd Division. To part with so fine a "Battalion as yours is a grievous loss for any General but, "as I hope to have the 9th Brigade back in the Division "after they have done what is required of them where they "now are, I shall look forward to having the Liverpool "Scottish with me again. They have invariably done their "duty in thoroughly soldierlike fashion and to my entire "satisfaction, and I feel confident that wherever they go "they will maintain under your command the good reputa-"tion which they have so quickly earned in the field.

"With all good wishes and best of luck to you all."

The Battalion was billeted in farms in the Busseboom area, close to Ouderdom, where it remained until 10 March, the time being devoted to company training and route-marching. Many entertainments also were organized there, amongst them a competition for a prize presented by the Commanding-Officer for the best company mouth-organ band. This was won by a band of 12 performers from No. 10 Platoon, complete with drum-major, big drummer with a goatskin in place of a leopard-skin, and ten instrumentalists, each with a Tickler's jam tin for a hat. The music they made was hardly first-class but their general turnout was most inspiring.

Headquarters Officers and Company-Commanders went on the 9th to see the new trenches and on the 10th the Battalion marched off to Ypres and its first experience of the Salient of unblesséd memory.

THE SALIENT—SPRING, 1915

1915   The historic town of Ypres, as the Battalion found it on 10 March, 1915, was very different from the battered and pathetic ruin which it became later in the war. It had already been shelled, of course, but the damage was largely confined to the vicinity of the Grande Place and to the houses near the two easterly exits from the town, the Menin and Lille Gates. The Cathedral and Cloth Hall had suffered and the latter had been completely gutted by fire, but there was still stained glass in some of the windows of the Cathedral, and it was a fairly simple matter to climb up ruined stairs into the tower of the Cloth Hall. Most of the civilian population had gone, but enough were left to give the place quite a busy air. These were mostly of the shopkeeper class who were prepared to take a certain amount of risk in order the separate the fabulously well-paid British soldier from some of his wealth. There were several restaurants, teashops and *estaminets* open, where good food and drink could be had—how and where the owners got their supplies was something of a mystery. A good trade was done in the shops where picture-postcards, lace and knick-knacks of all sorts could be bought, while the tobacconists must have made small fortunes. There was even a first-class photographer's shop which was well patronized.

Such was Ypres when the Liverpool Scottish marched into it on their way to the trenches at Hill 60, east of Zillebeke. " X " and " Y " Companies were detailed for the front line and supports, Battalion-Headquarters being in a cellar just behind Zillebeke, while " V " and " Z " Companies were in reserve in the Infantry Barracks, Ypres.

After Kemmel the new trenches were a nine days' wonder. They were deep and dry, there were shelters where the men could sleep when off duty and there was a communication-trench by which supports could reinforce the firing-line. It was no hardship to occupy trenches such as these, but there were disadvantages. This was a much livelier part of the line and there was a great deal more shelling of the trenches themselves than there had been at Kemmel, where most of the enemy's shells had been directed at Kemmel village and certain selected points behind the British line. Although no heavy shells were used against the trenches at Hill 60 there were plenty of "whizz-bangs," from which the Battalion suffered many casualties both in the front line and supports. Mining operations, too, were being carried on by both sides, and on 12 March the Scottish were involved in that most unpleasant of all wartime experiences, the explosion of an enemy mine.

The afternoon had been unusually quiet, no shelling and no sniping, always an ominous sign of trouble to come, when suddenly the ground rocked and there was a violent rumbling explosion immediately to the left of the Scottish position, and a vast quantity of earth, bricks and debris of all sorts was hurled high into the air. The mine had been placed under a trench occupied by a platoon of the Royal Scots Fusiliers, nearly all of whom were buried. Unfortunately the ruins of a house were immediately over the mine and the falling bricks from it caused thirteen casualties, some of them serious, in No. 9 Platoon of the Liverpool Scottish, which was on the extreme left of the Battalion sector. The vibration from the explosion was so great that 2nd Lieut. W. E. Lloyd, who was standing fully one hundred yards away beside one of the mine-shafts in our trenches, was shaken off his feet, fell down the shaft and broke the arm of an unfortunate member of the Monmouthshire Mining Battalion who happened to be on the point of climbing out.

The destruction of the Royal Scots Fusilier platoon left a dangerous gap in the line, and it was very largely due to the energy and ability of Captain B. McKinnell, the Liverpool Scottish machine-gun officer, that the situation was quickly got in hand. He at once ran to the scene of the explosion and posted a machine-gun to cover the gap. He took command of the remnant of the Royal Scots Fusiliers and himself helped, under heavy fire, to dig out those men who could be got at. Later he superintended the digging of a new trench behind the crater. Meantime part of No. 11 Platoon, under Serjeant Dickinson, had been rushed up from the supports to strengthen the left flank in case of an attack by the enemy, but this did not come, though the explosion of the mine had been accompanied by very heavy shelling. If it had been the enemy's intention to attack it is probable that the violence of the explosion upset his plans, for it was plainly seen that his own trenches were damaged by it.

Major Dick, commanding the Royal Scots Fusiliers, forwarded a report to Brigade expressing his high appreciation of the steadiness and resource of all ranks of the Scottish, and particularly mentioning the pluck and coolness of Captain McKinnell and Privates C. Smith of the machine-gun section and J. C. Darroch of " Y " Company. These two men had done great work in digging out and attending to buried men.

In the early morning of 15 March Lance-Corporal B. L. Rawlins, the very capable N.C.O. in charge of the Battalion Engineering Section, was out in front of the trenches on the right of the sector putting out barbed-wire. At this point the enemy's trenches were only about 80 yards away and he was seen and mortally wounded by a sniper. Captain Ronald Dickinson, O.C. " X " Company, in front of whose trench Rawlins was lying, wished to go out himself to bring him in but was forcibly held back by his men, who would not allow him to take the risk. Four men, Lance-Corporal A. G. Davidson, Privates W. W. Howarth and J. L. Wallace of " X " Company and Private S. G. Gibson of the Engineering section, at once went out and under heavy fire brought Rawlins in. Private Howarth was selected for special recognition and received the Distinguished Conduct Medal for his gallant action. He was the first member of the Battalion to be so decorated.

In the Hill 60 sector the right flank of the Battalion rested on the Ypres-Comines Railway which here ran through a deep cutting where there were a number of old and disused French dugouts. Lieut.-Colonel Davidson decided to enlarge and adapt some of them to make a new Battalion-Headquarters, about four hundred yards behind the front line. This work was put in hand and so quickly finished that on the night of 15 March Headquarters were able to occupy their new residence, which consisted of a series of dugouts to accommodate the Officers, Signallers and Headquarter units, and included a kitchen and a mess. It was the first work of its kind to be constructed and excited much interest. The great advantage of the " Davidson Dugout " was that the Commanding-Officer could come up to the trenches in daylight, by the railway-cutting, a thing he had never been able to do in any other sector, and his advice on the work to be done, siting of loopholes, etc., was of great assistance to the officers in the line.

The Battalion remained in the Hill 60 sector twelve days, inter-company reliefs taking place every two or three days and companies on relief going back to Ypres. The total casualties during this period were fourteen killed and forty-two wounded.

The Liverpool Scottish were relieved on the night of 21 March by their friends the Liverpool Rifles, who were going into the trenches for the first time as a unit.

The next sector to be occupied by the 9th Brigade was the Bluff and lay south of Hill 60, between it and the Ypres-Comines Canal. It included two well-known features, Slaughter Hill, which was the easterly end of the ridge formed by the spoil bank of the Canal, and the International Trench, which was occupied both by the British and the enemy. Each held an end of it with a sort of no-man's-land between them about twenty yards in length, and each had a strong sandbag barricade in the trench. This sector was better suited to a four than to a five battalion brigade, and the Liverpool Scottish were therefore split up and attached by companies to the other units, " V " Company to the Northumberland Fusiliers, " X " to the Lincolns, and " Z " Company and half " Y " to the Royal Scots Fusiliers, the remainder of " Y " being put into reserve dugouts on the Canal bank. The Royal Fusiliers were very strong in numbers at this time and did not require extra men.

Slaughter Hill was very heavily shelled on 1 April and " X " Company and one team from the machine-gun section, who were holding it, suffered severely. They were again shelled that night while being relieved and altogether lost eight killed besides a number wounded.

Otherwise this tour was without particular incident except the first daylight patrol attempted by the Battalion. It was carried out by Corporal S. Smith and Private Pyke of " Y " Company, who obtained useful information regarding the enemy's positions and were warmly complimented by Major Dick, of the Royal Scots Fusiliers.

The 9th Brigade was relieved on the night of 3/4 April by the 85th Brigade, and all ranks were pleased to learn that they were to rejoin the 3rd Division which was occupying the St. Eloi sector. " X " and " Z " Companies went straight into the trenches there the same night, the other half of the Battalion being in huts behind Dickebusch. The Liverpool Scottish remained in this sector until 26 May, always holding the same trenches and carrying out inter-company reliefs every four days.

In order that the two companies out of the line might be within easier distance of the trenches, if required in an emergency, dugouts were constructed in a wood, christened Scottish Wood, on a ridge behind Voormezeele—where the Battalion Headquarters was—and here that part of the Battalion nominally on rest came after relief, only the Quartermaster's

Stores and Transport-section remaining at Dickebusch. Scottish Wood was immediately in front of our 18-pounder positions, and the terrific din when these guns were firing—with an occasional "premature" for luck—added to the daily ration of shrapnel from the enemy, made the wood anything but a haven of rest. The companies in the wood supplied working parties every night, practically every man going out, usually under the supervision of the Royal Engineers, and before long the men came to look forward to their tours of trench duty as being safer and much less exhausting than their four days' "rest" in Scottish Wood.

A tremendous amount of work was done to the firing-trenches and in making communication-trenches during this time. Q2, the front trench, was immensely improved; Q3, the support-trench, which was little more than a succession of dugouts to begin with, was converted into a fire-trench and wired; one communication-trench was made joining up these two trenches and another back from Q3 to Voormezeele, a distance of more than half a mile. In addition to the work done on its own sector, the Battalion supplied carrying and digging parties to other parts of the Brigade front and, as there were epidemics of measles and Flanders 'flue, specialists and all batmen had occasionally to be pressed into service to provide the numbers required by Brigade.

The Scottish, perhaps, got more than their fair share of navvying on account of a reputation they had very quickly acquired with the R.E. of being particularly good diggers. No doubt the amateur soldier in the early days of the war looked on working-parties as a means of getting much-needed exercise, whereas to his Regular brother they were fatigues pure and simple and not down in the book of words. The fact remains that the Officer Commanding the Royal Engineers—who afterwards became A.A.G. on Sir Douglas Haig's Staff—made no secret of his preference for the Liverpool Scottish as workers.

One germ victim was Lieut.-Colonel Davidson, who contracted paratyphoid and was sent down the line on 7 April and subsequently to England. Major E. G. Thin took over command of the Battalion and Major A. S. Anderson became Second-in-Command.

St. Eloi was on the whole a quiet sector, the enemy's activities being mainly confined to sniping at night, with fixed rifles, on to exposed parts of the road up to the trenches, which made reliefs rather unpleasant, and to shelling, principally of

D

Q2, with whizzbangs and 5.9's. The trench was too strong for whizzbangs to have much effect on it, and as the enemy, methodical as ever, always turned on his 5.9's at about 4-30 in the afternoon, it soon became a matter of routine just before that hour to move the men to the right along the trench, away from the portion of it which was invariably shelled, and to send them back again when the half-hour's hate was over. The Battalion did, however, suffer several casualties before the danger-spots were known and avoided.

On 14 April the Liverpool Scottish were again involved in an enemy mine explosion. Relatively to each other the St. Eloi trenches were, as it were, in echelon, and the left end of Q2 was masked by a small advanced trench, Q1, about eighty yards in front. This trench was in the sector occupied by the Northumberland Fusiliers, and it was under the left portion of it that the enemy had dug his mine. At 11 p.m. he suddenly opened rapid fire on our trenches, accompanied by very heavy shelling with whizzbangs, and a few minutes later, with a roar, Q1 went up into the air. The half-stunned survivors of its garrison ran back into Q2. Captain G. B. L. Rae, O.C. " Y " Company, at once sent these men and fifteen of " Y " Company, under Captain McKinnell, up to Q1 to re-occupy it. All stretcher-bearers and first-aid men available were also sent up, and later fifteen men of " V " Company, under Second-Lieutenant J. P. White. All these did magnificent work. It was found that the left end of Q1 was totally wrecked and that thirty-five men had been buried. Many of them were dug out and they and the other wounded were carried into the shelter of a ruined house where they were dressed by Lance-Corporal C. Elliott of " Y " Company, and Privates D. Carr and A. Jones of " V " Company. These men had to do their work under a steady bombardment of bombs and rifle-grenades. All three were afterwards mentioned in despatches and the two privates received the Military Medal—when that decoration was introduced, in 1916—for their gallant conduct. Captain McKinnell meanwhile set about repairing the trench and reorganizing the garrison, and so well was the work done that when Northumberland Fusilier reinforcements came up and the Liverpool Scottish withdrew at dawn to their own trenches Q1 was again in a fit state for defence.

There is little doubt that on this occasion the enemy intended to rush Q1 under cover of his bombardment and the confusion caused by the explosion of the mine, but Private D. McDonald, of the Scottish Signal Section, realising as soon as the shelling started that something serious was afoot, sent the S.O.S. to

Battalion-Headquarters without waiting for orders. It was lucky that he did so, as immediately afterwards the wires both to Headquarters and Q3 were cut by shells. Another Signaller, Private D. H. Thomson, in Q3, finding his wire gone, at great personal risk got out of the trench and continued to send the S.O.S. back to Battalion-Headquarters by lamp until our guns opened. Our counter-barrage was splendid and made it impossible for the enemy to leave his trenches, and it is beyond question that the prompt action of these two signallers and the quick response of our guns saved the Battalion a counter-attack on Q1, which the enemy could have captured without opposition.

The following Special Order was published in Battalion Orders of 17 April :—

" I. Lieut.-Colonel A. S. Ainslie, Commanding 1st " Battalion 5th Northumberland Fusiliers, has expressed his " high appreciation of the prompt action taken by the " Officer Commanding the trench Q2 (Captain G. B. L. Rae) " on the occasion of the mine exploding in Q1, and of the " excellent work done by Captain McKinnell and his " N.C.O.'s and men, and later Second-Lieutenant J. P. " White and his party, who at once went forward to assist " the men of that battalion.

" II. The Commanding-Officer wishes to put on record " the good work done by the men in the trenches during the " night of the 14th inst. when the mine exploded, as referred " to above. The thirty men, stretcher-bearers, first-aid men " and signallers who were called on responded magnificently, " and their services will always be remembered in the history " of the battalion."

For his work on this occasion and previously at Hill 60 Captain McKinnell received the Military Cross; he was the first officer of the Battalion to win this decoration.

Thus for the third time since they had joined the 9th Brigade the Liverpool Scottish had had the opportunity of rendering valuable and valued assistance to another battalion of the Brigade at a critical juncture and had risen to the occasion. Small wonder that all the Brigade now treated them as equals and trusted them as they trusted their Regular comrades.

On 22 April the enemy launched his first gas-attack against the French in the north of the Ypres Salient. The Liverpool Scottish were too far away to suffer any real inconvenience from the gas, but the north-east wind brought down sufficient of it

to set men's eyes watering. As it was a day or two before the
news came through that the enemy was using poison-gas there
was much speculation as to what the irritant in the air could
be and many theories were propounded by the knowing ones.
The authorities were very quick to provide means of protection
against the gas and many and varied types of mask were issued.
The first of all was simply a portion of a body belt soaked in
some chemical solution, placed over the mouth and nose and
held in position by tapes tied behind the head. Then came a very
similar one, a pad of cotton waste in a length of gauze-like
material which also had to be tied behind the head. The first
helmet was a bag made of flannel shirting. This was slipped
over the head and the end tucked into the tunic. It had a talc
eyepiece let into it which, of course, soon became clouded by
the man's breath. Afterwards a mouthpiece was added with a
valve which allowed the man to exhale but not to inhale through
it. It was not until 1916 that the small-box-respirator was
evolved and issued to the troops.

It was at the time of the first gas-attack that the enemy
shelled Ypres from Houthulst Forest with his 17-inch howitzers.
To the Liverpool Scottish, although they were three miles from
Ypres, each of these shells in its flight sounded like an express-
train in a tunnel, and on detonation the shock of the explosion
could be distinctly felt on the ears. All civilians were evacuated
from Ypres on account of this shelling.

The success of the first gas-attack and the fighting subsequent
to it caused such a critical situation in the Salient that it was
believed the whole of it would have to be given up and the
British line withdrawn to the west of Ypres. Preparations were
so far made for this eventuality that a new line was dug and the
fire-trenches, including those held by the Liverpool Scottish, were
cleared of all stores and reserve ammunition in readiness for the
move to the new positions. The Battalion was under orders to
move at a moment's notice to a specified place in the new line,
but the British troops in the Salient just managed to hold on
and the withdrawal was avoided. How many lives might have
been saved later on if the Ypres Salient had ceased to exist
in 1915!

On 26 May the Battalion was relieved by the Queen Victoria
Rifles, 13th Brigade, and moved back to the huts at Dickebusch.
Two days later the 9th Brigade again took over trenches in the
Salient, this time to the east of Potijze, but the Lincolns and
Liverpool Scottish remained in reserve in a camp near

HOOGE, 16 JUNE, 1915.

Vlamertinghe and supplied working-parties at night, digging support-trenches and strong-points behind the line.   These working-parties had to pass through Ypres and it was interesting to notice the change in the condition of the town since the beginning of April.   The 17-inch shells had done enormous damage and as the enemy was still shelling the town regularly, though with guns of smaller calibre, it was a matter of some difficulty to get through the streets, blocked with fallen masonry and also made dangerous by fires which were of nightly occurrence.

The Battalion again went into the line on 2 June, to trenches along the east edge of Armagh Wood, east of Zillebeke. This tour was without incident worth particular mention, but the disposition of the Liverpool Scottish in the line is interesting. With the exception of a garrison of one N.C.O. and nineteen men in a redoubt in Sanctuary Wood and thirty-eight rifles in a supporting-trench the whole trench-strength of the Battalion, 470 rifles and four machine-guns, was in the front-line trenches.

On relief from this sector on 6 June the Battalion moved back to Vlamertinghe and on the 10th orders were received that the 3rd Division was to go farther back for ten days' rest, and it was reported that a considerable number of the men would be granted leave. This happy prospect faded away when all leave was unexpectedly cancelled and the Battalion moved to a bivouac camp near Busseboom and commenced special training. As bomb-throwing practice and getting through and over barbed-wire were the points which received particular attention, it was not difficult to deduce that something other than trench-warfare might be expected in the near future, and it was no surprise, therefore, to learn that the 9th Brigade was to attack Hooge on the morning of 16 June and that the Liverpool Scottish would participate in the attack. The Battalion had proved itself a worthy member of the Brigade in trench-warfare. It was now to have the opportunity of demonstrating that it could pull its weight in the open too.

HOOGE—16 JUNE, 1915

The Battle of Hooge or, as it is now officially and more correctly named, the First Action at Bellewaarde, was *1915* a holding action to pin down enemy reserves and so assist the operations which were being carried out on the same day at Givenchy by the British and at Vimy by the French. It had as its object the capture of the enemy's system of trenches lying between the Menin Road and the Ypres-Roulers Railway. Here the German line formed a salient and their front-line trenches south from Railway Wood were on a ridge from which they had a clear view of all the country behind the British lines right down to Ypres itself. The attack, if successful, would deny to the enemy this advantage of position and would straighten out the uncomfortable re-entrant in our own line.

According to the operation orders the attack was to be in three stages. First, the Royal Fusiliers, Royal Scots Fusiliers and Northumberland Fusiliers were to assault the enemy's front line of trenches. When this line was taken the Lincolns (on the right) and the Liverpool Scottish were to go through and capture the second line from a house 100 yards south of Y 17 to Y 11, the dividing line between the battalions being a hedge 150 yards south of Railway Wood, running east from Cambridge Road, and thence the track leading to Bellewaarde Farm. Flanks during this second phase were to be secured, on the right, by the 7th Brigade, which was ordered to work up under Y 20 and the trench from that point to the second T in Eclusette and, on the left, by the Northumberland Fusiliers who were to work to Y 7 and Y 8 by bombing parties. The Royal Fusiliers and Royal Scots Fusiliers were to reorganize and support the second phase if necessary. After the capture and consolidation of the second line the three battalions which had taken the first objective were to go through again and capture the third objective, which was from the south-west corner of Bellewaarde Lake, through Y 18, Y 12 and Y 8, to Y 7.

The 7th Brigade was ordered to support the 9th Brigade closely, to occupy trenches vacated by the 9th Brigade, to dig communication-trenches linking up our trench-system with the enemy's and, after the capture of the third objective, to consolidate the line gained.

No. 3 Motor Machine-Gun Company was also to support the attack from the Menin Road.

It will be seen from the above orders that the battalions engaged were to do a double leap-frog. First the Lincolns and Liverpool Scottish were to pass through the other battalions to assault the second objective, and then the Royal Fusiliers, Royal Scots Fusiliers and Northumberland Fusiliers were to go through again and attack the third objective.

The disposition of the Liverpool Scottish for the attack was as follows :—

" X," " Y " and " V " Companies, from right to left, attacking each with two platoons in the first wave and two in close support, and " Z " Company supporting the whole.

Every battalion drew from Brigade 400 bombs, including 150 of the Mills pattern—then a new invention—125 wire-cutters, and 10 small flags, for the bombers to indicate their positions. It was arranged that one platoon in each battalion should carry spades to help in the work of consolidation. In the Liverpool Scottish these were distributed—7 to each of the front companies and 30 to " Z," the supporting company. The supply of bombs was hopelessly inadequate, but no more were available. The total brigade reserve amounted only to 1,200.

Each man carried 200 rounds S.A.A., an extra day's ration in addition to the emergency ration, and had two sandbags tucked through his belt. Haversacks were worn on the back, all packs being marked and stored.

A section of the 1st Cheshire Field Company, R.E., was attached to the Battalion to assist in consolidation.

The Battalion marched off from Busseboom at 4 p.m. on the 15th. The prospect of really having a go at the enemy after sitting still in the trenches for months appealed to everyone and the men were in tremendous form, singing and joking most of the way up. After a very slow march with many halts the assembly position in Cambridge Road was reached about midnight. The enemy had undoubtedly got wind of the impending attack. Indeed he could hardly have failed to notice the unusual concentration of troops in and near our trenches and also the fact that a number of new trenches had been dug behind Cambridge Road. These were to accommodate units of the 7th Brigade during the first stages of the attack. At any rate, Cambridge Road was shelled steadily with 5.9 and 8-inch shells from soon after midnight and many casualties were incurred.

Our artillery bombardment opened at 2-50 a.m. and continued until 4-15 a.m. with three pauses, at 3-10, 3-40 and 4 o'clock, to mislead the enemy as to the actual hour of the attack. After many months' experience of being shelled in trenches and knowing that our own supply of shells was so inadequate that the reply of our guns, if any, would amount to only a very small fraction of the weight of metal which the enemy was sending over it was a " sicht for sair e'en " to see the Germans for once getting the worst of the bargain. Our bombardment was very accurate and heavy enough to satisfy the most critical.

At 4-15 the three battalions detailed for the first phase got out of their trenches for the assault. Very soon there appeared at various points on the enemy's parapet screens stuck in to indicate to our gunners what portions of the position had been captured. These screens which were of canvas nailed to two poles were about six feet long by three deep and were coloured red and yellow. Each company carried six of them. They proved singularly ineffective. In the morning haze and the smoke and dust from the shelling they were not easy to see, and as, after zero hour, our artillery were not working to a time programme it happened again and again during the action that they continued to shell trenches which had been captured and not a few of the Battalion's casualties were caused by our own guns. The enemy's counter-bombardment was so heavy that the telephone lines laid by the gunner signallers who, with the Forward Observation Officers, were close up behind the attacking troops, were constantly being blown away and communication by runner was too slow and unreliable to be of much assistance. The artillery were therefore working very much in the dark—this being long before the days of creeping barrages and contact aeroplanes—and it was quite unavoidable that we should run into our own shelling.

The Lincolns and Liverpool Scottish, according to plan, as soon as they saw that the enemy's front line had been taken left their assembly position in Cambridge Road and moved forward over our front line to just short of the parapet of the enemy's front trench, where they lay down to reorganize and await the signal to go on to the second objective. In carrying out this operation " V " Company, which had to advance through Railway Wood, found that on its front the attack had been held up by machine-gun fire and that the enemy was still holding his front line. After a pause, during which they were reinforced by part of " Z " Company, the men dashed forward and carried the position, bayoneting those of the enemy who still offered resistance and taking about forty prisoners. Other parts of the front line also were still holding out and three men, Corporals W. E. Blackburne and S. Smith and Lance-Corporal A. Moir, "Y" Company, seeing a machine-gun in action bombed their way along the trench to it, capturing the gun and killing a number of the enemy. Corporal Smith for his share in this feat and for his gallant conduct throughout the day received the D.C.M.

After a wait of about 15 minutes while our artillery bombarded the second objective, the line moved on and without great difficulty, except for heavy cross machine-gun fire from the vicinity of the railway cutting at Y 6, captured the line from the pond beside Bellewaarde Farm to Y 11. This proved to be in most places a very shallow trench only two or three feet deep and was not occupied by the enemy. It would have been quite impossible to hold against a counter-attack unless there had been time to deepen and improve it considerably which, of course, there was not. Undoubtedly the best thing to do was to go straight on to the final objective, and Lieut.-Colonel E. G. Thin gave orders to this effect. He himself was wounded immediately afterwards. Most of the Battalion, with a few men of the Royal Scots Fusiliers and Northumberland Fusiliers, moved forward again, some men going over the open and some by the communication-trenches. Unfortunately a certain number of the Liverpool Scottish on reaching the second line, which they knew to be their final objective, did not go on with the rest but began to dig in where they were. These men suffered very severely from the enemy's shelling and hardly a man who remained in the second line escaped injury. In spite of lack of numbers the third line was taken and the work of consolidation started. Some men, carried away by excitement and over-keenness, went even farther and were seen pushing on towards Dead Man's Bottom but of these none got back.

For a time all went well and, as the third-line trench was a very deep and well-made one, it appeared likely that the Battalion would be able to hold what it had won, but they were a very small band who had got thus far and reinforcements were urgently needed. Messages were sent back asking for more men, and three small parties of the Liverpool Scottish managed to make their way up to the most advanced trench, followed later by a platoon of the Northumberland Fusiliers. But the enemy's shelling was very heavy, the communication-trenches were entirely destroyed in some places and were choked with dead and wounded so that movement of troops from the rear was a matter of very great difficulty. The leap-frogging and the moving up of the supporting Brigade into trenches vacated by the 9th Brigade caused serious congestion, and units became badly mixed up with one another. Some of the Royal Irish Rifles, of the 7th Brigade—true Irishmen and unable to see a fight without joining in—actually took part in the attack and had to be collected and sent back to their correct position. In spite of this chaos, it might have been possible to hold all the third line had the section of it on the right of the Liverpool Scottish been captured but, so far as can be ascertained, the attack there had never been able to get beyond the second line and thus the Battalion's right flank was in the air.

A stubborn fight went on all morning in the network of trenches between Y 8 and Y 11. The enemy had a covered access to this part of his system from the railway-cutting, Y 5 to Y 6, and he launched counter-attack after counter-attack, sometimes over the open but mostly by bombing parties. These were all repulsed and the left flank temporarily secured. The duty of looking after this flank, as has been told, devolved upon the Northumberland Fusiliers but some of the Liverpool Scottish also took part in its defence. Two men in particular did magnificent work, Corporal Bartlett and Private W. Short, both of " V " Company. They were detailed by Captain Sandilands, of the Northumberland Fusiliers, to join one of his bombing squads which were engaged in clearing the enemy out of those parts of the trenches on the left which he was still holding. After much heavy fighting Corporal Bartlett was killed but Private Short continued to take part in alternate attack and counter-attack until well on into the afternoon. He afterwards received the D.C.M. and the French Croix de Guerre for his invaluable work.

Those of the Liverpool Scottish who had reached the final objective remained in possession for some hours. They were not seriously attacked but they broke up an attempt at a counter-attack from the northerly side of Dead Man's Bottom. They were continually under the fire of machine-guns from the railway cutting between Y 5 and Y 6, which were able to enfilade parts of the trench they were holding, and a number of men were hit. About noon, bodies of the enemy were seen emerging from the south end of Dead Man's Bottom and moving across towards the trenches about Y 18. To counter this threat to the right flank of the position Captain W. J. H. Renison organized a defensive flank in the communication-trench immediately north of Bellewaarde Farm. About the same time an enveloping movement by the enemy developed on the left flank and it was also noticed that the British troops on the right were retiring from the second German line.   Threatened on both flanks, the troops in the third objective were now in an impossible position and a general retirement was ordered to the second line. where a stand was made for a short time.   The enemy, however, had already re-occupied his second line of trenches south of Bellewaarde Farm and his bombing parties could be seen and heard working their way northwards.   The Scottish by this time had used up every bomb they had and were forced to continue the withdrawal to the German first-line trenches.

One incident during the retirement must be recorded. Captain Dickinson, O.C. " X " Company, was lying severely wounded in the second line, just beside the small pond in front of Bellewaarde Farm, and his wounds were of such a nature that it was impossible to get him away.   With him were twelve or fifteen of the Battalion, nearly all wounded.   When the Germans were observed bombing up the trench these men, although they had no bombs left, determined not to leave Captain Dickinson but to fight it out where they were.   It was only when directly ordered by him to retire that they did so and by that time the enemy were practically on top of them.   All were hit and only one or two succeeded in getting back to the first line of trenches.

During the afternoon a fresh attack on the German second line was launched by units of the 7th Brigade but only a few men were able to reach the enemy's trenches, where they were soon overpowered, and it was then decided to consolidate the first line.

The German shelling which had been severe throughout the day reached its height between 7 and 8-30 p.m.   During that time it is estimated that 100 shells per minute fell on the Brigade front.   The enemy made desperate efforts to recapture his front line but all his attacks were repulsed, the Liverpool Scottish doing their full share in beating them off, and when, about 11-30 p.m., the 8th Brigade relieved the 7th and 9th Brigades the whole of the German front-line system of trenches was handed over intact.   Not a little of the credit for the successful holding of the German front-line must be given to Company-Serjeant-Major W. G. Flint who, when all the officers in his vicinity had become casualties, organized the defence of the line with great skill.

The British attack had not yielded all the results hoped for but it had none the less been of decided value, although the casualties were out of all proportion to the visible gains and were certainly far in excess of those of the enemy. The two main objects of the attack—the pinning down of the enemy's reserves and the capture of the ridge occupied by him—had been attained and the action must therefore be written down a successful one. A legitimate question is, however, was not the success too dearly won? So far as the Liverpool Scottish are concerned that question is difficult to answer. Judged by material results there is no doubt that their losses were not justified, but those who fell won for the Battalion, by their gallant conduct in the attack and their still more gallant deaths, a glorious name and established a tradition which those who came after were proud to remember and uphold. The Liverpool Scottish had fully held their own in a Brigade justly famous for its fighting qualities. They—with a few of the Royal Scots Fusiliers and Northumberland Fusiliers—were the only troops who reached the final objective and they did not withdraw from their advanced and isolated position until forced to do so by circumstances beyond their control. Of 23 officers and 519 other ranks who went into action only 2 officers—Lieutenant L. G. Wall and 2nd-Lieutenant T. G. Roddick, the latter suffering from concussion—and 140 men came through untouched and, as most of the casualties occurred in or near the second German line, the proportion of killed and missing was abnormally high.

In detail the casualties were :—4 Officers and 75 other ranks killed; 11 Officers and 201 other ranks wounded; 6 Officers and 103 other ranks missing. Of the missing all the officers and— with a very few exceptions—all the men were subsequently reported killed. The Liverpool Scottish had practically ceased to exist but they had definitely proved themselves as a fighting unit and set the seal to their previous record in the Brigade.

One section merits special mention for its behaviour during and after the action—the Battalion stretcher-bearers. They had done splendid work during the attack itself, they remained in the line after the Battalion was relieved, and on the night of the 16th and the succeeding night they continued to carry out their duties until they were satisfied that every wounded man had been brought in. An inspiring example was set them by the Medical Officer, Lieutenant N. G. Chavasse, to whose untiring efforts in personally searching the ground between our line and the enemy's many of the wounded owed their lives. Lieutenant Chavasse received the Military Cross, and one of the stretcher-bearers, Private F. F. Bell, the D.C.M. in recognition of their gallantry.

After the return of the Battalion to camp at Busseboom,

Brigade Headquarters asked for a list of those recommended for decoration or mention and this was sent. This list is believed to have been destroyed by a fire which broke out in Brigade Headquarters. At any rate it never reached Division, and by the time its loss was discovered and a fresh list called for and sent in all the decorations allotted for the action had been apportioned to the various units. Thus no member of the Liverpool Scottish was decorated on the recommendation of his own unit. The three men who received the D.C.M. all did so on the recommendation of the Commanding-Officers of other units. Ten men were, however, awarded the Military Medal in 1916 in recognition of their conspicuous gallantry at Hooge—Serjeants J. Briggs, W. Sloss and P. J. Thomson, Lance-Corporals A. F. Foden and J. M. Tomkinson, and Privates B. G. Barnshaw, J. C. Darroch, W. Fitton, J. R. Pollock and D. Williams.

Major-General Haldane published the following special order on 17 June :—

" The Major-General commanding cannot adequately
" express his admiration for the gallant manner in which
" the attack was carried out yesterday. The dash and
" determination of all ranks was beyond praise, and that
" some actually reached the objective in the first rush and
" remained there under most trying circumstances is a proof
" of their superiority over the German Infantry. That the
" captured ground could not all be held is disappointing,
" more especially as the losses incurred were heavy. But
" these casualties have not been in vain. The 3rd Division
" carried out a fine piece of work and fought splendidly,
" and their Commander is deeply proud of them."

The following entirely gratuitous commentary on the Liverpool Scottish in the attack by an impartial observer is perhaps worth recording.

The present writer's father, soon after the action, happened to get into conversation with a Gordon Highlander in the train from Euston to the North. The Gordon, who was obviously just home on leave from the front, had no idea that his fellow-traveller was in any way connected with the Liverpool Scottish or even with Liverpool. On being asked from what part of the line he had come, he replied : " I've come from Wipers, Sir. My division has just been over the top at Hooge. We were in reserve close behind and I saw the finest sight I'll ever see. I saw the Liverpool Scottish make their attack and they went over just as if they were on parade."

Several excellent photographs are extant which were actually taken during the action. Private Fyfe, " Z " Company, who was wounded very shortly after the engagement began, thought that he might usefully employ his time until the stretcher-bearers came for him and, taking from one of his pouches his vest-pocket camera he obtained some very good snapshots of the ground between the British and German trenches and of supports coming up. It is hardly necessary to say that there was an order strictly prohibiting the carrying of cameras and that serious trouble was in store for the man found in possession of one. Perhaps the fact that Fyfe is by profession a press-photographer may be some excuse for his having overlooked this embarrassing order.

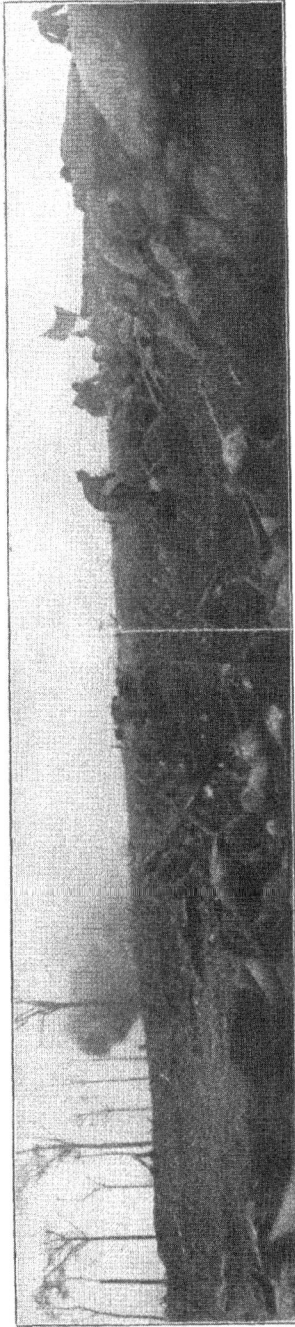

16 JUNE, 1915.

These Photographs of no-man's-land were taken by Private F. A. Fyfe, "Z" Company, who was lying wounded. The German front-line trench is on the right, with an artillery flag planted on the parapet. On the left are the British barbed-wire entanglements, in which a gap has been made to allow the attackers to pass through them. The 1st Battn. Lincolnshire Regiment and 1st Battn. Liverpool Scottish have gone on to assault the German second line. The figure on the extreme right is an artillery officer following up the attack; his signaller is about to cross the German front line. A 5·9-inch shell has just burst in Railway Wood.

LAST DAYS WITH THE 3rd DIVISION

The depleted Battalion returned to its bivouacs near Busseboom and in that area it remained for four weeks, *1915* the time being devoted to company-training and route-marching.

The regular battalions of the Brigade soon received drafts to bring them up to effective strength again but none came for the Scottish. As a matter of fact there were at the time no men available. The Second Battalion, with the other second lines of the West Lancashire Division, formed part of the force earmarked for home defence in case the enemy effected a landing on the English Coast and consequently had to be kept intact, while the Third Battalion, the draft-finding unit, had been formed only a few weeks before and none of its men were yet sufficiently trained to be fit for active service. Officers, however, were available and six reported on 2 July and were posted to companies.

On 10 July the Battalion was inspected by the Major-General with whom was Lord Derby. Lord Derby addressed the Battalion and, after complimentary references to their work in the field, announced that he had obtained permission to arrange, on his return to England, for a large draft to be sent out so that the Scottish could go over the top again. The memory of 16 June was too fresh in the men's minds for this announcement to be received with marked enthusiasm! Major-General Haldane struck a more responsive note in his speech with the welcome news that leave to England would definitely start in a few days and that every man would get six days. He also spoke in the warmest terms of the part the Liverpool Scottish had played at Hooge.

On 14 July the 9th Brigade again went into the line, slightly to the south of those St. Eloi trenches where it had spent so long a time during the Spring. The Liverpool Scottish took over three front trenches, O3, O4 and O5, and a strong-point in rear, S 8, and were soon once more engaged in the never-ending duties of trench-warfare—repairing parapets, digging shelters and putting out barbed-wire. On 20 July leave started, forty men going that day and smaller parties on each succeeding day.

This so reduced the trench strength of the Battalion that on the 22nd the Northumberland Fusiliers took over O5 and two days later S 8.

On 21 July six more officers arrived from England, amongst them one whom the Battalion was particularly glad to see, Lieut.-Colonel J. R. Davidson. He at once resumed command and Lieutenant Wall became his Adjutant.

From 23 to 26 July a platoon of the 12th Manchester Regiment was attached to the Liverpool Scottish for instruction in trench-warfare. These men were part of Kitchener's Army which was just beginning to arrive in France at that time. There was a great deal of stupid jealousy in the earlier stages of the war between the Territorials and " K's " Army. Those Territorials who had borne the brunt of the first winter and looked upon themselves as being almost in the veteran class resented the superior air which some members of " K's " Army affected, and particularly the fact that they described themselves as Regular soldiers. " K's " Army, on the other hand, were horrified at the indignity of being taught their job by mere Territorials and were not very willing pupils. One of them made the mistake, in an *estaminet* one night, of dropping a disparaging remark to a Lincoln about the Liverpool Scottish. The place and the confidant were ill-chosen. The Lincoln warned him to be careful of what he said about the " Lincolnshire " Scottish and, emphasizing his point with a bottle, temporarily reduced the strength of the 12th Manchesters by one.

The Battalion was relieved by the 12th Manchesters on the night of 28/29 July and moved back to Gordon Farm, half a mile from the line. After two nights' digging behind the front trenches a further move was made, with the remainder of the 9th Brigade, to a camp on the Ouderdom-Vlamertinghe Road and on the following night the Scottish found themselves once more in the Salient, half being in what were known as the Potijze Defences and half in the Kaaie Salient, a redoubt northeast of Ypres and about a mile behind the front line. Here they relieved their old shipmates, the Queen's Westminsters.

The enemy was still intermittently shelling Ypres with his 17-inch howitzers. As the Kaaie Salient was in the direct line of flight of these shells it was a somewhat noisy place. The terrific force of the explosion of the shells was such that, although they were bursting in Ypres, fragments occasionally landed in Kaaie Salient upwards of half a mile away. On the whole, however, Kaaie Salient received little direct attention from the enemy's guns and was a sufficiently peaceful place for the men when off duty to be allowed to disport themselves in an artificial open-air swimming-bath which was only a short distance away. This bath—a very good one, complete with diving boards—was a great boon in the hot August weather, and what a scuttering and splashing there was as the men hurried to the side for their things if a shell came anywhere near ! Why one should have felt safer clothed, even if the clothing consisted of nothing more than a shirt, than *in puris naturalibus* was one of the war's minor mysteries ! But one did.

The Battalion was relieved on 13 August and went back to camp at Ouderdom where, on the 17th, the newly-formed Divisional Band gave a performance. The Band and the Divisional Concert Party—of which several of the Liverpool Scottish were members—were both excellent and contributed very materially to the enjoyment of all ranks when units were out of the line.

On the return of the Brigade to the trenches on 19 August the Liverpool Scottish found themselves in reserve dugouts in a wood near the White Château, Kruisstraat. Here they began a special task which was to occupy them for more than a month. In connection with the attack at Loos, timed to take place towards the end of September, the 3rd Division was ordered to carry out on the same day a subsidiary operation at Sanctuary Wood—between Hill 60 and the Menin Road—with the object, as previously at Hooge, of pinning down enemy reserves. For this operation it was essential to have two communication-trenches from Zillebeke to the front line, an up-trench for the attacking troops and stores, and a down-trench for the wounded. One communication-trench, Zillebeke Street, was already in existence but it was in shocking disrepair and very wet. Working parties from several battalions had done their best with it but there was no continuity about the work and little or no improvement was noticeable. The Major-General came to Lieut.-Colonel Davidson in despair and asked him for his advice as to what should be done. The Colonel replied, " If " you will leave the job entirely to the Liverpool Scottish I will " guarantee that both trenches will be finished and fit for use " when you want them." General Haldane agreed and work was started at once with the result that when the attack took place the new trench,—Dormy House Lane—from Zillebeke to Maple Copse, was completed and both it and Zillebeke Street were bone dry, a very notable achievement, particularly as the

E

weather during September was exceptionally wet and on some nights it was quite impossible for the men to do any work at all.

In order to be on the spot for this special work the Battalion left Kruisstraat on 3 September and moved to dugouts in the bank of Zillebeke Lake, a large reservoir. Here on 11 September there arrived a draft of 105 men, the first since Hooge, and very welcome they were. They were an unlucky draft for nine of them were wounded by a shell three days later while engaged in repairing the dugouts.

In addition to this draft the Battalion had received towards the end of August a rather surprising reinforcement—five officers of the 16th King's Liverpool Regiment who were to be attached to the Liverpool Scottish for the duration of the War. Lieut.-Colonel Davidson took very strong exception to this attachment —without, of course, casting the slightest reflection on the officers themselves. He pointed out the unwisdom of sending khaki officers to a kilted battalion and also that the Liverpool Scottish had in their own ranks any number of men whom he would be only too glad to recommend for commissions in the Battalion. Brigade and Division were sympathetic but the higher authorities would do nothing and merely replied that it would not be possible in future to guarantee that Territorial units would receive Territorial officer reinforcements—which was hardly the point. However, the Liverpool Scottish never again had junior officers posted to them whom either they had not themselves chosen or who were not members of Highland Battalions.

On 27 August Lieutenant Wall was wounded by a shell splinter, and Lieutenant B. Arkle became acting-Adjutant. This appointment was confirmed and was held by him continuously, and with conspicuous success, until April, 1918—something of a record.

On 23 September part of the Battalion took over the guards on the Canal Bridges, eight in all, from the Royal Scots Fusiliers, and the following day the remainder moved back to billets in the Kruisstraat Château barns.

On the morning of 25 September the attack about Sanctuary Wood was launched by the 8th Brigade but the old trouble of uncut wire was a terrible handicap and little progress could be made. Except for the machine-gun section, under Lieutenant G. S. Duckworth, which occupied a position in the south-east corner of Sanctuary Wood, the Liverpool Scottish were kept in

Divisional Reserve during the day, but in the evening they were
sent up to the Wood to relieve a company of the Lincolns and
on arrival were set to work repairing damaged communication-
trenches. Captain N. G. Chavasse and a party of men spent the
whole night bringing in wounded of the Gordon Highlanders,
who had lost heavily in the attack.

The following evening, about 10 p.m., a terrific fusillade
began about the neighbourhood of Hooge and for some hours all
the troops in the vicinity stood to arms expecting a counter-
attack. The firing, however, gradually died down and it was
afterwards learnt that it had started from nothing more serious
than the bombing of a working party. It was extraordinary
how frequently a quite minor incident was the cause of a sudden
outburst of rifle and shell-fire which might spread for a considerable distance to both flanks of the original outbreak,
especially if there had been "a certain liveliness" in that
particular part of the line and both sides were a trifle nervy.
For a sudden flare-up of this kind the troops had their own
name, expressive but perhaps hardly suitable for publication.

For a long time before the attack the Staff had been trying
to devise some means of improving communication with the
attacking troops and some genius suggested carrier-pigeons.
Major-General Haldane was very much struck with the possi-
bilities of this suggestion and orders were sent to all battalions
in the Division to send any pigeon-fanciers in their ranks to
Divisional Headquarters where a loft was quickly erected and
stocked. When the pigeons had become accustomed to their
surroundings they were sent up in pairs in baskets to the front
line where they were put in the care of the regimental signallers
who had orders that the birds should be released with test
messages attached to them. The first pair which were sent up
(not to the Liverpool Scottish) did not return to the loft,
although the signallers were emphatic that they had been
released, and the incident was eventually written down an
unsolved problem, though there was a strong suspicion that if
the birds had actually been released it was only for a short
flight from the basket to the stewpot. This, as a matter of fact,
was the correct solution but the evidence was too circumstantial
to convict.

By the time the actual day of the attack arrived the pigeons
had been regularly employed in taking messages back from the
line and great hopes were entertained that the difficulties of
communication from front to rear were solved. A number of

birds were sent up to the attacking battalions and handed over to the company signallers. As soon as the attack was well under way the Major-General went to the loft to await the first news but no pigeons arrived. The morning dragged on but still there were no pigeons. At last, about 3 p.m., a tired-looking bird entered the loft and an orderly was despatched to get the message and bring it to the General. He did so. The General opened it, read it, crushed it in his hand, dashed it to the ground and strode away with a face like thunder. One of his staff, wondering what calamity had occurred that could bring such a cloud to the Great Man's brow, carefully smoothed out the crumpled message and read—" I'm sick of carrying this bloody bird !"

On 29 September the enemy made a counter-attack in Sanctuary Wood and succeeded in occupying part of the trenches held by the 8th Brigade. An urgent message was sent back for bombs and at 1-30 a.m. the following morning the Liverpool Scottish—now billeted in the Ramparts at Ypres—were ordered to provide three parties, each of twenty men, to carry them to Maple Copse. As most of the Battalion was already engaged on other duties there were not sufficient men available and so those of the transport who had come up to Ypres with the rations were pressed into service, to their intense surprise, and the numbers were made up. The transport men returned to Ypres after delivering their loads but the others remained in Maple Copse all day detonating bombs and carrying them to the front line. Some were wounded and some actually took a hand in the scrap themselves. Eventually the enemy was cleared out and the party from the Liverpool Scottish returned to Ypres.

The dugouts in the Ramparts in which the Battalion was housed were long tunnels, lined with brick, hollowed out of the old fortifications of the town and were proof against everything except the very heaviest shells. Successive occupants had done what they could to make these dugouts comfortable, with furniture of all sorts " scrounged " from the ruined houses round about. As a result, all the men had mattresses to sleep on and there were tables and chairs and even a piano. If only the dugouts had not been literally swarming with lice they would have been ideal billets.

During its stay in the Ramparts the Battalion was busy every night with working-parties of one sort and another, mostly up the Menin Road past the dreaded Hell Fire Corner which was the spot most consistently shelled by the enemy and where

one waited under what cover there was for a salvo to come over
and then crossed at the double before the next one arrived.

To illustrate the normal wastage, from wounds and sickness,
of a battalion in the Salient a few figures may be interesting.
The Liverpool Scottish after Hooge had a trench strength of two
officers and 140 men plus those who had not been sent up to
the attack, say 190 in all. They had received 18 officer reinforcements and a draft of 105 men, and a number of slightly wounded
men had rejoined from hospital, yet their fighting strength on
80 September was only 11 officers and 195 other ranks. During
these three and a half months the Battalion had spent one
month several miles behind the line, had been in no attack
and only for about a fortnight had occupied front-line trenches.

The Liverpool Scottish remained in the Ramparts until
12 October when they moved up to the B trenches in Sanctuary
Wood and relieved the Royal Scots Fusiliers. The next day
the enemy made a bombing attack on the 1st Middlesex
Regiment, who were holding the trenches immediately on the
right, and ten of the Scottish bombers were sent to give help if
required. They soon became involved in the fight and three of
them were wounded but the remainder were able to report, on
their return to the Battalion, that the enemy had been forced
back to his own trenches.

While in Sanctuary Wood one Company found its strength
mysteriously increased by one man for whom no one could
account. After this man had taken part in the bombing attack
referred to above and had been evacuated to hospital wounded,
it was discovered that he really belonged to the 2nd Battalion
and had no right to be in Flanders at all. It turned out that
he had been able to slip on board a returning leave-train from
London and, on arrival in France, had managed to find his
way to the 1st Battalion and quietly insinuate himself into the
ranks of one of the companies. On discharge from hospital he
was sent back to the 2nd Battalion at Maidstone under arrest
with the threat of a court-martial—for desertion—to come. The
Brigade-Commander, however, considered that the man had
already had his punishment and he was released.

Another member of the 2nd Battalion who carried out a
similar escapade in 1916 was not so fortunate. He was sent
back to England under arrest, court-martialled and sentenced
to 42 days' imprisonment.

While everyone admired the spirit shown by these men it
was obvious that discipline could not be maintained if they,

without leave, left their own battalion and made their way to the front.

The Battalion was relieved on 19 October and moved back to Ouderdom. After four days there news was received that at last the 3rd Division was to have a real rest, the first it had had since Mons, and the 9th Brigade marched via Reninghelst and Boescheppe to Godewaersvelde, nine miles behind the line. Here the men found themselves in first-class billets and unspoiled country, a pleasant change after the mud and desolation of the Salient. The mornings were devoted to training under company arrangements and the afternoons to sport of various descriptions. The Battalion Soccer Team was very successful, beating the Northumberland Fusiliers, Royal Scots Fusiliers and Royal Fusiliers on successive days. Not to be outdone, some Rugger enthusiasts got a side together and after three weeks' training took on the 23rd Brigade R.F.A. and beat them to the tune of 17 points to nil.

On 4 November the Brigade moved to a new area at Winnezeele and here a similar scheme of training was carried out and classes for the junior N.C.O.'s were held under the direction of the Regimental Serjeant-Major, S. Jennings, with excellent results. The training of the young N.C.O. on service must always be a problem. It was easy enough for him to pick up a knowledge of what was required of him in the trenches but terribly difficult for him to learn how to train his section when out on rest. Later on the N.C.O.'s schools established by all divisions at their Reinforcement Camps did much to put this right.

The Commanding-Officer, Lieut.-Colonel J. R. Davidson, went on short leave to London on the 4th and during his absence his brother, Captain A. G. Davidson, assumed command. Did Brigadier-General Douglas-Smith then perhaps recall an incident of nearly a year before when, at Westoutre, he said to the Colonel, " Davidson, I can't understand your battalion; the " men are such a curious mixture. Most of them are obviously " gentlemen, but you seem to have a number of absolute toughs " as well. Now look at this ruffian "—indicating a lance-corporal in a goat-skin walking towards them, mud to the eyes and with a three weeks' growth—" I shouldn't care to meet him alone " on a dark night. Do you know who he is?" " Yes, Sir" said the Colonel, " He's my brother !" *Tempora mutantur nos et mutamur in illis.*

On 6 November a Divisional Ceremonial Parade was held at

Steenvoorde for the bestowal of decorations awarded by the French Government, and Private W. Short received the Croix de Guerre which he had won at Hooge.

On the 21st the Scottish again found themselves *en route* for the line and, after a night spent at Reninghelst, took over the T trenches at St. Eloi. The 1st North Staffordshires, whom they relieved, had strange stories to tell of the peacefulness and mateyness of the troops, Saxons, occupying the trenches opposite. These stories were taken with a grain of salt but proved to be no less than the truth. There had been a great deal of mining activity round about St. Eloi and the opposing lines on the Battalion's front were separated by craters, each side having posts on their respective lips with the craters between. The sentry of one of the posts was surprised, on the morning after relief, to see a German head appear above the opposite lip and to hear a voice ask in very good English for a tin of bully-beef. This was thrown across to him but fell short and rolled down into the crater. Without a moment's hesitation the German clambered out of his trench and retrieved the bully. Of course, he should not have been allowed to do it but it seemed unsporting to put a bullet through a man who evidently had not the slightest suspicion that he was taking any risk.

These Saxons said they were tired of the war and did not intend to make themselves unpleasant. They meant it, too, for the Scottish transport at night brought the ration-limbers up to within a quarter of a mile of the front trenches without any interference from them, though the noise of the wagons could be heard a mile away. The Saxons even went so far as to warn the men to be careful of sniping from the flanks as they had Prussians on each side of them. This was perfectly true and the only casualties the Battalion sustained were from oblique fire. These friendly enemies were very anxious to fraternize in no-mans'-land at night but this was going a little too far and the suggestion was quietly ignored.

One incident occurred which was perfectly ludicrous. The Commanding-Officer wished to find out if one particular crater post of the enemy's was part of his front line or merely a sap joined to it by a communication-trench. In the latter case he thought it would be an easy matter some night to surprise and capture the garrison. He accordingly detailed the scout officer, Lieutenant L. B. Mill, to go out with his corporal and reconnoitre the position. The night chosen for the patrol was rather too clear for comfort and, thanks to a sharp frost, the ground had a thin hard crust on it and crackled loudly as the two crawled round the crater. When they got near the German line they were startled to hear a voice say " Very good indeed, but if " you keep to your left a little you will find the going easier !" All the men in the post were standing up and watching the patrol's progress with the greatest interest. What could one do with enemies like that? Mill and his corporal did the only possible thing. They burst out laughing and walked back to their own trenches.

The T trenches were in a deplorable state, waterlogged and deep in mud, and there seemed a prospect that the second winter would be a repetition of the first so far as casualties from exposure were concerned. The authorities were, however, fully alive to the danger and had already provided supplies of those " gum boots, thigh," which were such a boon in wet trenches and helped so much to ward off the scourge of trench-foot. Unfortunately for the Scottish, it was not particularly easy for a man in a kilt to put them on, as they had to be pulled on under the kilt and there were no trouser buttons to hold them up. Other methods of keeping the men's feet in condition were also considered, all battalion-commanders having to submit their ideas, and the system finally evolved, whereby platoon-commanders were held personally responsible that their men's feet were rubbed daily with whale-oil and that each man got a dry pair of socks in exchange for his wet pair, proved so successful that not a single case of trench-foot occurred in the Battalion throughout the whole winter.

During this tour in the line a draft of 77 men arrived. The Battalion was relieved on 29 November by the London Rifle Brigade and moved back to huts at D Camp near Reninghelst, returning to the T trenches on 6 December.

Conditions were even worse than before, the trenches being entirely flooded and almost uninhabitable. On the 9th there came into this paradise, of all unexpected people, three petty-officers from the Fleet, who spent twenty-four hours with the Battalion. They were from a large party of naval officers and ratings which was split up into small groups and sent to all parts of the line to spend a few days with the infantry in order to give the Navy an idea of the conditions which the Army had to face. All the men on their return had to lecture to their ships' companies on their experiences and to pass on in their own words the impressions they had received of life in the Junior Service. The scheme undoubtedly did much to promote good feeling between the two Services and to give each a better idea of the work of the other, "Jack" learning of the Army from personal experience and "Tommy" of the Navy from the yarns of his guests. The three men attached to the Scottish were splendid fellows and the best of company. For their especial benefit Brigade arranged quite a nice little bombardment on the trenches opposite with everything from 18-pounders to 8-inch hows. They did not ask for an encore, but on the whole they appeared to enjoy their visit though when they left all three were unanimous in saying that they did not care if they never set foot ashore again until the war was over.

Sir John Jellicoe afterwards addressed a general letter to the Army expressing his appreciation of the treatment given to his officers and men and saying that they were all enthusiastic and amazed at the cheerfulness of the "P.B.I." under such impossible conditions.

On the 18th the Battalion completed what proved to be its last tour of duty in the front line with the 3rd Division and on relief went back to Reninghelst. The remainder of the month was spent here and at Dickebusch, the men working at night on the reclaiming of old trenches near St. Eloi and on digging and carrying-parties of various kinds.

On Christmas Day the Battalion, though not in trenches, was in Brigade reserve and the usual festivities were postponed until New Year's Day which was spent at Reninghelst, the 9th Brigade being in rest-billets. The day was observed as a complete holiday except for a parade to distribute the gifts for the men sent out by the wives and relations of the officers.

On New Year's Day orders were received that the Liverpool Scottish were to be transferred to the 166th Brigade, *1916* 55th Division, which was to be composed of the units of the old West Lancashire Division.

The Battalion received the news with mixed feelings. The men knew that it would probably mean a few weeks' rest while the new Division was being assembled and organized, but it was hard to part from all the good friends they had in the 9th Brigade and face the task of learning the ways of new Generals and of finding their level amongst battalions which, though all raised in Liverpool or Lancashire, were practically strangers to them. They felt, in fact, all the emotions and fears of a boy going to a new school.

The next few days were spent in leave-taking. On 4 January

Brigadier-General Douglas Smith inspected the Battalion and in his farewell speech said, " Officers, Non-Commissioned Officers " and Men of the Liverpool Scottish, I am here to-day to say " Good-bye to you. I am sorry to say you are leaving the 9th " Brigade, in which you have now been for over a year, and " to say I am sorry to lose you does not sufficiently express " my feelings.

" You have always been foremost in all that the Brigade has " done—in fighting, in football and in concerts. In anything " like that you have always come up to the scratch, and I " know I shall miss you very much in the future.

" There is a lot of hard work before us and when I look " round for the Liverpool Scottish and find them gone, I shall " miss them very much. I wish you all the very greatest luck, " and when you come across the Germans again I hope you will " give them what you did on 16 June. You were always to the " fore and never behind on that day. Few people have not " heard of the Liverpool Scottish.

" Mind you keep up the reputation the Battalion has earned " for itself.

" You have always been well behaved which is a great thing " in a country like this, where there are so many temptations."

Two days later the Battalion was inspected by Major-General Haldane who wished all ranks good-bye and good luck and thanked them for all they had done for the 3rd Division. He also wrote the following letter to Lieut.-Colonel Davidson :—

" As your battalion—the 10th Battn. Liverpool " Scottish—is about to leave my command I wish to place " on record my high appreciation of the services of the " battalion during the thirteen months that it has formed " part of the 3rd Division in the field. The battalion has had its " full share of fighting and trench duty and is a unit upon " which I place the greatest reliance under all circum- " stances. On 16 June, 1915, when engaged with the rest " of the Division in the attack on Bellewaarde, it was " conspicuously gallant in its behaviour. Its losses were " exceptionally heavy and nearly the whole of its officers, " as you know, were either killed or wounded. This " battalion since that action has suffered from the lack of " reinforcements to replace casualties, and from other " experience I should not have been surprised if the *moral* " and state of health of the unit had been affected thereby.

"On the contrary the spirit of the Liverpool Scottish has
"remained excellent, and whereas last year at this season it
"was losing many men merely from sickness, thus far its
"wastage from this cause has been extremely small.

"The pioneer work of the battalion when so employed
"has been particularly good, and all ranks have always
"been keen and ready to undertake any work assigned to
"them.

"It is with very great regret that I find myself forced
"to lose so fine, gallant and well-commanded a unit, a loss
"which the whole 3rd Division as well as myself feel. I
"feel certain, however, that the Division of which you and
"your men will form part will find you a thoroughly trust-
"worthy, well-trained and disciplined battalion, and will
"soon appreciate you as I do.

"With my most sincere good wishes to each and all of
"you."

The move to the new area began on 8 January. The pipers
of the Royal Scots Fusiliers played the Liverpool Scottish out of
Camp, and then to Bailleul they had the Divisional Band at
their head. At Bailleul they entrained for Pont-Rémy, eight
miles from Abbeville, under sealed orders and on arrival there
marched via Airaines to Heucourt, which they reached at
1 p.m. on 9 January.

EARLY DAYS WITH THE 55th DIVISION

With very few exceptions all the units of the old West Lancashire Division had been sent overseas piecemeal *1916* during 1915 and attached—like the Liverpool Scottish— to other Divisions. The North Lancashire Brigade— 4th and 5th King's Own Royal Lancasters and 4th and 5th Loyal North Lancashires—for instance, was for some time attached to the 51st (Highland) Territorial Division in the line, while the West Lancashire Divisional Artillery sailed from England with the 2nd Canadian Division in September and served with it for three months. The troops, therefore, that were gathering in and near Hallencourt from all parts of the line were not new to the war-game, and the 55th Division was given a flying start in being composed of units which had already seen service and knew the ropes.

The new Division was constituted differently from the old so far as the brigading of its infantry battalions was concerned and it may be well to set down the new arrangement as follows :—

164th Infantry Brigade :
    1/4th Battalion King's Own Royal Lancaster Regiment.
    1/8th (Irish) Battalion The King's (Liverpool) Regt.
    2/5th Battalion Lancashire Fusiliers.
    1/4th Battalion Loyal North Lancashire Regiment.

165th Infantry Brigade :
    1/5th Battalion The King's (Liverpool) Regiment.
    1/6th   do.   do.
    1/7th   do.   do.
    1/9th   do.   do.

166th Infantry Brigade :
    1/5th Battalion King's Own Royal Lancaster Regiment.
    1/10th (Scottish) Battalion The King's (Liverpool) Regt.
    1/5th Battalion South Lancashire Regiment.
    1/5th Battalion Loyal North Lancashire Regiment.

The 2/5th Lancashire Fusiliers, who had no previous connection with the West Lancashire Division, were brought in to take the place of the 1/4th Battalion South Lancashire Regiment which had become the Divisional Pioneer Battalion.

The commander appointed to the Division was Major-General H. S. Jeudwine, C.B., a Gunner Officer with a most distinguished record in peace and war. As Canon Coop in his *Story of the 55th Division* says, " To him it was given to mould " the pliable material ready to hand. The subsequent history " of the Division is evidence sufficient of the extent to which " he succeeded. No General ever was more devoted to his " Division; no Division ever was more devoted to its " General."

No one who served in the 55th Division is likely to forget the tall figure in tin hat and trench-coat which would appear in the front line in all weathers at any hour of the day or night, frequently unattended, nor the quiet cross-examination which invariably and as if by magic brought out—if things were not quite as they should have been—the self-damning answer before the culprit even realised that he was being examined. No one will forget, either, that for those who confessed their faults " Judy " always had just the right word of advice and encouragement which made difficulties disappear and restored self-confidence. But woe betide the man who tried to bluff things out. In a moment he was laid bare to the very soul and if he were wise he did not try the experiment twice.

The Liverpool Scottish, then, arrived at Heucourt and found themselves posted to the 166th Infantry Brigade, whose commander, Brigadier-General L. Green-Wilkinson, called on the Colonel the same afternoon to welcome him and his Battalion.

Divisional and Brigade Headquarters so far consisted purely and simply of those Staff-Officers who had been posted to appointments on them. There were no rank and file to do the office work and to carry out the multifarious duties connected with the controlling, feeding and clothing of nearly 20,000 men. Thanks to the fact that the majority of the Liverpool Scottish were of the clerk rather than the artisan class, quite a number of the Battalion collected " cushy " jobs on Division or Brigade to the envy of their less fortunate brothers.

Serious training was started at once and the Battalion, reinforced by a draft of 83 men, settled down to intensive work, particularly in musketry. Each company was responsible for the construction of its own 30-yards range and, close to billets, suitable ground was also found for a large-scale battalion range where firing up to 500 yards was carried out and inter-company competitions were held. The targets and frames for this range were made by the Battalion Pioneers. Bombing, too, received a great deal of attention and practice-trenches were dug where the men were exercised in the drill of trench-clearing.

Of course the sporting side was not forgotten and there was the usual succession of football matches—against other units and in the Battalion itself—including the inevitable "Officers versus Serjeants," in which the officers were narrowly beaten. They had their revenge on 27 January when a seven-mile cross-country race was run in which all the Battalion took part, and the Doctor and Adjutant finished first and second. A rumour got about that the Quartermaster had been prevailed upon to give the men an exceptionally heavy dinner that day, with suet puddings predominating, and that by arrangement the race took place immediately afterwards, but as the Doctor was an Olympic runner it is hardly likely that a lighter meal would have affected the result and the story is possibly apocryphal.

On 29 January the whole Battalion, 22 officers and 893 other ranks strong, marched to Hallencourt, six miles away, where the Division was inspected by the Earl of Cavan, commanding the XIV Corps, of which the 55th Division formed part.

On 4 February a move was begun to a new area and the Scottish marched via Longpré and Pernois to Prouville, where they arrived on the 6th. Here miniature ranges and bombing trenches were at once begun and preparations made for further training, but, on the 9th, Divisional Headquarters issued its first operation order which entailed another march with a return to the trenches at the end of it. The Battalion set out the following day via Doullens to Amplier and the day after to Berle-au-Bois.

The trenches allotted to the 166th Brigade were in the Rivière district, some six miles south of Arras, and were occupied by the 88th French (Territorial) Division. Perhaps it should be explained that the French territorial was not, like the British one, a volunteer. He was generally a middle-aged gentleman who, having completed his military service some years before, was called back to the colours and did his bit in a quiet sector of the line or on lines of communication. The 88th Division had been in the Rivière area seven months, during which time it had suffered seven casualties !

The country around Rivière was a rolling country of low hills and wide valleys, practically undamaged and still under cultivation, a pleasing contrast to that around Ypres. It was no uncommon sight to see a man ploughing his fields in full view of the enemy a couple of miles away, and much nearer the trenches than that most of the houses were still occupied by their lawful tenants. Rivière itself—complete with Maire, a most important personage—was made up of three villages—Grosville, Bellacourt and Bretencourt. The first two had suffered scarcely at all from shelling and most of the civilian population was still in occupation. Bretencourt, on higher ground and partly visible from the German trenches less than a mile distant, had received a certain amount of attention and all its inhabitants had gone except four or five individuals. One of these was a very old lady who, although her house had been hit more than once, refused to leave it. In her opinion the only way to treat the *sâle boche* was to ignore him and this she successfully did throughout the whole war. All honour to you, Madame Veuve Dauthieu-Houllier, and thanks for your many little kindnesses to " les Écossais."

The configuration of the ground and the long communication-trenches made it possible for relief to be carried out by daylight, and in the early morning of 12 February the Battalion moved up from Berle-au-Bois to Bellacourt and halted for breakfast. Either the enemy had noticed an unusual amount of movement on the roads in the back-areas or, more probably, he had learnt that the French were to be relieved, for he sent a number of " crumps " over into the village, killing two men and wounding six others and one officer—not a very happy introduction to a new sector.

The relief was otherwise carried out without incident and the French *poilu* proved a most cheery and friendly opposite number. The troops from whom the Liverpool Scottish took over were cavalry and an extraordinarily fine body of men.

The trenches were something of a novelty. Thanks to the chalky soil it was possible to dig deep and not only were the trenches themselves well-made and very safe, but there were numerous deep dugouts immediately behind the front line, many of which contained wire bunks, a luxury undreamt of and impracticable in Flanders. Add to this that there was little risk from snipers—the enemy being from 500 to 1,000 yards away—and it will be seen that the Battalion was justified in thinking that it had at last found a good war.

So indeed it proved, for during the five months spent in this sector casualties, both in and out of the trenches, were very light and practically speaking the men had only two things to trouble them—the weather and the rats.

Never were there such rats as lived in the Rivière trenches, thousands of them, enormous brutes with an utter disregard for man. The walls of the trenches and dugouts were honey-combed with their runs and at night they swarmed over everything. The men had the greatest difficulty in keeping their food protected. It was useless to hang a loaf of bread by a string from the roof of a dugout. The rats grinned con-temptuously, waited till one's back was turned, slid down the string, and the bread vanished. The only way to preserve perishable food was to cut it into small pieces and pack it in a mess-tin. Rat-hunting became a regular trench sport and though many men developed great quickness and efficiency with stick or bayonet there was no noticeable reduction in the number of rats. One wretched officer, who had a horror of rats, was very popular with his brother subalterns because, not daring to go to sleep at night in the trenches, he always volunteered to take everyone else's tour of duty and would return, worn and haggard, to company-headquarters dugout after morning stand-to and try to snatch what sleep he could curled up on the table. Even then he would lie awake wondering if the rats would fall on him from the roof. They were erudite rats too. One of them was discovered disappearing backwards into a hole with an unopened copy of the *Weekly Times* in its mouth.

The weather, too, was a great trial. Soon after the Scottish took over the trenches a spell of hard frost set in and there was a heavy fall of snow. When the thaw came the trenches began to fall in as they had not been revetted thoroughly, and the Battalion had many weeks of hard work before they got the upper hand of the mud and made things shipshape again. Chalk may be satisfactory stuff to dig in but when wet and churned up by men's feet it became a particularly beastly sort of glue which was so adhesive that it was almost a physical impossibility to walk along some of the worst trenches.

Otherwise the Battalion had little of which to complain and settled down to the old monotonous round, so many days in the trenches—Blamont, Osiers, Ravine, Willows or Grange—so many days in support at Grosville or Bellacourt, and then back to rest at Laherlière, Gouy, or—most frequently—Saulty. An ordered existence with few thrills but any amount of hard work. Apart from the front trench and communication-trenches, the French had not worried much about other defences and before long the G.O.C. decided that a derelict trench behind the front line on the right half of the sector should be made into a fire-trench and become the main line of resistance. Then the

Soutiens, a support-line in a sunken road, was converted into a series of luxurious dugouts, fitted with bunks, where all headquarter details and the garrison for the main line of resistance could live in comfort, and where a large part of the cooking for the men in the trenches was done. Add to this the normal routine of improving and repairing the front line and communication-trenches, digging shell-shelter trenches behind the front line, constructing snipers'-posts and company observation-posts, Lewis-gun positions, etc., and it will be realized that the men's hands were not allowed to get soft.

Soon after the Battalion took over the Rivière sector several changes in kit and organization took place. Early in March a new type of gas-mask was issued—the P.H. helmet—which was a great improvement on the old and gave much better protection. Even when the small-box-respirator was issued later in the same year, each man retained his P.H. helmet as a stand-by in case of damage to his respirator. About the same time the first steel helmets arrived. There was a great deal of prejudice against them to begin with on account of their weight and the men did their best to mislay them, and only by a direct order could they be induced to put them on, even in the front line. It was not until a corporal, looking over the top one day, was knocked flat on his back in the trench by a sniper's bullet, and found on picking himself up that his tin hat had saved his life, that the men realized that a little discomfort is preferable to sudden death, however painless. After that little incident they even slept in their steel helmets. While on the subject of headgear it may be said that the glengarry had by this time entirely disappeared from the Battalion and the balmoral had taken its place. It was rumoured that the reason the glengarry was given up was that, if not the bonnets themselves, certainly the dyes for the dicing, were made in Germany. Probably, however, the authorities thought the khaki balmoral more serviceable, but it is a fact that in 1915 glengarries were issued at the front which, instead of having the dicing part and parcel of the bonnet, were dark-blue all over and simply encircled by a strip of coloured ribbon. Terrible-looking things they were and no one was sorry when the issue was discontinued.

In March the machine-gun section, under Lieutenants G. Duckworth and A. H. Noble, with its transport, was detached from the Battalion and joined the newly-formed 166th Brigade Machine-Gun Company. The men retained their Scottish uniform but no longer lived or messed with the

F

Battalion. Later, of course, out of the Brigade Companies grew the Machine-Gun Corps.

About the same time another new formation came into being, the 166th Brigade Trench-Mortar Battery, armed with the admirable 2-inch Stokes-Gun. Several men volunteered for service with the trench-mortars and with them went Lieutenant J. W. Marston.

It has been said that the enemy showed no great activity in this sector but he did occasionally remind the Battalion of his presence by shelling the trenches or villages. On one such occasion, 29 February, he shelled a new machine-gun emplacement with a 5.9-inch gun. The first shell wrecked the emplacement, killing two men and wounding another. In endeavouring to remove the wounded man to a place of safety, Captain Cunningham, who had been wounded at Hooge and had not long rejoined the Battalion, was again severely wounded. He received the Military Cross, and two men, Privates C. Taylor and J. Furlong, who afterwards assisted, under heavy shell-fire, in getting the wounded man away, received the Military Medal, as did Private J. S. Parkinson who, though himself entangled in the wreckage caused by the first shell, removed the debris from on top of the wounded man before freeing himself.

But if the enemy was, on the whole, inoffensive, it was soon found that the Divisional Commander had no intention of letting sleeping dogs lie. The platoon-commander's catechism he issued, which began " Am I as offensive as I might be?" showed very clearly his mental attitude and what he expected of his Division.

Accordingly, reconnoitring or fighting patrols were out practically every night scouring no-man's-land up to the enemy's wire, but the occasions on which Germans were seen in front of their own trenches were few and far between. A section of snipers, too, was specially trained. These men did very good work and soon obtained ascendancy over the enemy's snipers. Their best day's bag was on 4 May when they accounted for three of the enemy.

The Divisional Artillery also was active and concentrated shoots were carried out by the heavies on selected parts of the German line. Sometimes these shoots were impressive, sometimes not. On one occasion company-commanders were ordered to observe and report on the damage and effect of a shoot on a strong-point called the Blockhouse. The much advertised "strafe" was rather a tame affair when it came off, only about half-a-dozen six-inch shells coming over. Brigade, however, was eager for news, and Captain A. G. Davidson caused much excitement by reporting that he had seen the German garrison leaving. When he supplemented this statement by explaining that he had seen a man—presumably the caretaker—on a bicycle with his dog going down the road behind the enemy's trenches, the pleasantry was not too well received.

During May two matters of interest occurred. First, Colonel Davidson proceeded on short leave to London and received from His Majesty the Cross of St. Michael and St. George. He was the only officer of the Liverpool Scottish to be awarded this decoration. Secondly, on Whit-Sunday, a stout-hearted Church of England padre held a Communion Service in the front line. About two dozen men attended. The Altar was made of stacked biscuit-tins covered with a blanket taken from a dugout door. The Service was perforce simple but was strangely impressive amid such unusual surroundings.

About the middle of June whispers were heard of an impending attack on the grand scale by the British and French Armies, and things livened up considerably in all parts of the line to keep the enemy guessing as to where the blow would fall. The 55th Division arranged to carry out a number of simultaneous daylight raids by various units on selected points in the German system of trenches, and the Commanding-Officer chose for the Liverpool Scottish a sap opposite the right sector as the Battalion's objective. The raid was to be preceded by a discharge of gas mixed with smoke, so that the enemy should not notice the gas until it was upon him. Gas cylinders were brought up and dug into the front line, and the raiding party— called the Special Fatigue Party—went back from the trenches to Bellacourt for special training. The heavy artillery bombarded the sap three days running and our patrols reported that the enemy's wire was destroyed. The gaps in his wire were swept by machine-gun fire from the trenches at night to prevent the enemy repairing the damage. The stage was set but the curtain could not rise for the show until the wind blew from the right quarter. On the 28th it was favourable. The raiding party got into position in the front line and the smoke and gas were released. Just as the men were about to go over, by some strange freak of nature the wind changed and gas and smoke went rolling harmlessly along in no-man's-land between the lines. To have allowed the raid to proceed would have meant a useless waste of life and it was at once cancelled so far as the Scottish were concerned.

The following night a patrol of sixteen men, under Lieutenants Buck and Hodgson, went out and bombed the sap south of the one selected for the raid, doing much damage. This operation was repeated on 1 July, again with good results.

1 July saw the opening of the Battle of the Somme, and in connection with it a smoke and high-explosive barrage was put down along the whole front of the 55th Division to deceive the enemy as to the limits of the attack. There was a similar operation on the 14th but in neither case was there any infantry action.

On 2 July a Lewis-gun patrol found a party of Germans working inside their own wire and fired off a drum into the middle of them, causing many casualties.

The Battalion was relieved on 11 July by the 1/8th Sherwood Foresters and went back to Simencourt.

During the time they had occupied the Rivière sector the Liverpool Scottish had received six drafts totalling nearly 700 men, and in July were more than 1,000 strong. Thanks to such a long stay in the same area, much had been possible in interior organization which could not have been accomplished had the Battalion been constantly moving from one part of the line to another. The indefatigable Doctor had, of course, established a bath-house at the earliest possible opportunity. This was in the yard of a brewery at Bellacourt, and parties of men in succession were given leave to come down from the trenches to bathe. The Doctor also started a laundry for socks, which was run by the stretcher-bearers and light-duty men. A dirty pair of socks was collected each morning from every man in the line, washed, and returned to him the following morning in exchange for another dirty pair. The laundry was later extended to deal with the men's towels and finally their kilts. In the case of the kilts the owners themselves were responsible for drying and ironing them, as there was not a sufficient staff at the laundry to undertake this work. Another excellent institution started by the Doctor, who himself put up the initial working capital, was a dry canteen. Corporal W. Forbes, who had charge of it, made a tour of the trenches every morning and booked the men's orders. He then returned to Bellacourt, got the goods ready, and delivered them in the afternoon. This was a splendid arrangement as the men were able to get a number of tasty

additions to their rations, such as cocoa, condensed milk and
chocolate, and it also made them independent of the army
tobacco ration so that they did not suffer in times of scarcity.

When the Battalion left Rivière the canteen went with it
but the laundry could not be taken and this intensely annoyed
the good Doctor.

But if much had been accomplished on the administrative
side, training had not been forgotten and it is not too much to
say that at no time during the war was the Battalion more
efficient in every branch than at the time it left Rivière.
Especially is this true of the specialist sections. The work of
the snipers has already been mentioned. That of the scouts and
bombers also merits a special word. There was no doubt whatever as to which side had the initiative and the command of
no-man's-land, so much so indeed that on the night before the
Battalion was relieved the Commanding-Officer sent out a
number of fighting Lewis-gun patrols, supported by bombers,
which went right up to the enemy's wire, swept his parapets
with fire and bombed his trenches without the slightest response.
The patrols even manhandled across no-man's-land a limber
carrying extra ammunition.

The Liverpool Scottish took over trenches on the night
12/13 July in the Agny sector, two miles north of Rivière,
which was held by the 164th Brigade. Five days later they
were relieved by the 8th West Riding Regiment and returned to
Simencourt, moving on to Sombrin the next day. A further
move was made on 20 July to Bouquemaison and on the 21st
to Bernaville.

All this time the Somme maelstrom was sucking in division
after division and throwing them out again, shattered and spent,
to be transferred to quieter sectors for rest and re-organization.
It was only to be expected that the turn of the 55th Division
would come, and it was no surprise to the Liverpool Scottish
when they received orders that on 24 July the transport would
begin to move by road to Ville-sur Ancre and that the
Battalion would follow by train.

On 25 July the Scottish marched from Bernaville to Candas
where they entrained for Méricourt. On arrival there, at
6-30 p.m., they marched to billets at Ville-sur-Ancre.

THE SOMME

The Liverpool Scottish remained only two days at Ville-sur-Ancre and then marched on 27 July to a locality known *1916* as the Sand Pit Area—just ouside Méaulte, about two miles south-east of Albert—where they took over from their old friends the Northumberland Fusiliers, of the 9th Brigade. The Battalion was housed in bivouacs—draughty, but reasonably weather-proof—whose walls were empty S.A.A. boxes, of which there were thousands lying about, and whose roofs were ground-sheets. Shortly after the Scottish reached this area and had fallen out, they saw a khaki battalion of the King's Regiment with a number of Liverpool Scottish in its ranks. These men proved to be a large draft which had been sent out from Oswestry and attached to this battalion. A similar fate, unfortunately, befell several drafts of the Liverpool Scottish during the Somme battle when many battalions found their own draft-finding units depleted and received reinforcements from whichever unit happened to have men to spare at the time. Lieut.-Colonel J. R. Davidson at once gave the men permission to run across and cheer their friends as they went past in fours and also sent some of the Pipers to help them along the road.

Close to the Sand Pit Area were the Liverpool Pals, who had taken part in the opening attack of the Somme battle and in whose ranks the Scottish soon discovered numerous friends.

While in this area training in extended order was carried out and—an unusual luxury—there were daily bathing parades, the River Ancre being within easy reach.

On 30 July the Scottish moved up to Mansel Copse, three miles nearer the line and half-a-mile south of Mametz, where they stood-to all day under orders to move at a moment's notice in case they were required to assist in an attack on Guillemont which was being made by another division. They were not called upon, but they were subjected to persistent bombing from German aeroplanes, most of it—fortunately—badly aimed. The following morning they occupied the old British front-line trenches at Machine Gun Copse to the north of Maricourt and south of Montauban. Here they relieved the 18th King's—one of the Pals Battalions.

THE SOMME, AUGUST—SEPTEMBER, 1916.

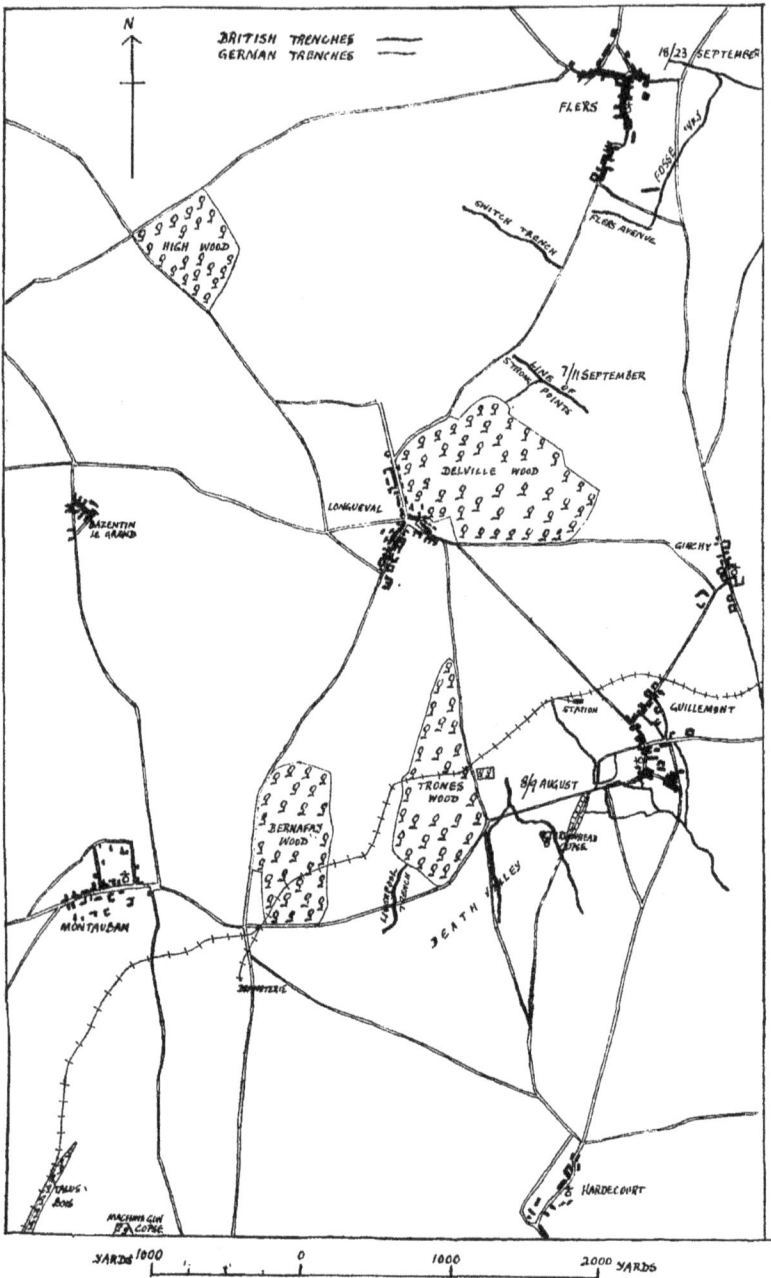

N

BRITISH TRENCHES ———
GERMAN TRENCHES - - -

18/23 SEPTEMBER

FLERS

HIGH WOOD

SWITCH TRENCH

FLERS AVENUE

COSSE WAY

LINE OF STRONG POINTS

7/11 SEPTEMBER

DELVILLE WOOD

LONGUEVAL

BAZENTIN LE GRAND

GINCHY

STATION

GUILLEMONT

TRONES WOOD

8/9 AUGUST

BERNAFAY WOOD

HOMESTEAD LINE

DEATH VALLEY

MONTAUBAN

MAMETZILE

HARDECOURT

FAVIOLE BOIS

MACHINE GUN COPSE

YARDS 1000   0   1000   2000 YARDS

For the next six days the Battalion had little rest. Large parties were out both day and night digging communication-trenches and cable-trenches in such health resorts as Bernafay and Trônes Woods, and many casualties were suffered from the enemy's shell-fire in them and also in the old trenches themselves, in front of which was a battery of heavy artillery which the Germans seemed very anxious to counter.

The utter devastation of such places as Trônes Wood, where the resistance had been most stubborn and bitter, and the grim relics of the previous month's fighting—bodies of men and animals, shattered wagons, scraps of equipment, broken and shell-twisted rifles—which scattered the ground in indescribable confusion, left on the minds of those who saw them scars which the passage of time will not easily remove.

At 11 p.m. on 6 August unexpected orders to move were received and the Battalion went back to bivouacs at Mansel Copse. The next day operation orders arrived from Division for an attack to be made against Guillemont at 4-20 a.m. on the 8th by the 164th and 165th Brigades, the 166th Brigade to be kept in reserve.

From 9 a.m. till 9 p.m. on the 7th the Heavy and Divisional Artillery bombarded Guillemont and the surrounding trenches, and from midnight until zero-hour on the 8th the bombardment was resumed with increased intensity. When the troops left their trenches for the attack, the 165th Brigade on the right gained its objective—the Guillemont/Hardicourt Road—and consolidated. On its left the 1/4th King's Own Royal Lancasters ran into a hidden belt of wire only 200 yards in front of their own trenches and could not get through, try as they might. They were compelled to fall back to their starting point. On their left again the Liverpool Irish with magnificent dash carried the German front line and pushed on as far as Guillemont railway station, but they had not mopped up as they went forward and when their supports—the 1/4th Loyal North Lancashires—reached the enemy front-line they found it fully manned again and were unable to occupy it. The remaining battalion of the 164th Brigade—the 2/5th Lancashire Fusiliers—was then sent up into the fight and the 1/5th Loyal North Lancashires were detached from the 166th Brigade to replace it as reserve battalion to the 164th Brigade. This transfer, as will be shown, led to much confusion later on.

The situation, then, on the afternoon of the 8th was that on the right the attack had succeeded, in the left centre it had

failed and on the extreme left the Liverpool Irish had broken
through the enemy's front line but were completely cut off. They
were, however, believed to be holding out.

At 5-45 p.m. the battalion-commanders of the 166th Brigade
—except the officer commanding the 1/5th Loyal North
Lancashires—were summoned to Brigade Headquarters and
verbal orders were issued that the Brigade would continue the
attack on the 164th Brigade front. At first an attack that night
was contemplated but later orders were received from Corps
that it would take place at 4-20 a.m the following morning after
several hours' bombardment. The Liverpool Scottish—with the
1/5th Loyal North Lancashires on their left—were ordered to
attack on a front of about 400 yards with the Trônes
Wood/Guillemont road as their left boundary. Their task was
to capture the German front-line and then to push on through
Guillemont and consolidate on the eastern edge of the village.
The 1/5th South Lancashires—commanded by Lieut.-Colonel
C. P. James, Argyle and Sutherland Highlanders, who had been
the Adjutant of the Liverpool Scottish at the outbreak of
war and had been wounded in the charge at Hooge—were
originally ordered to support both attacking battalions and to
occupy and consolidate the enemy's front line. Their orders
were afterwards changed and they were detailed to support the
Liverpool Scottish only. The 1/5th King's Own Royal
Lancasters were held in reserve.

The Liverpool Scottish were already under orders to move at
an instant's notice; their arms were piled and equipment stacked
at the roadside and the men were standing-by in their bivouacs.
When word was received from Brigade at 8 p.m. the Battalion
moved off at once but about an hour later a second message
—timed 9 p.m.— came from Brigade ordering the Commanding-
Officer to halt his men in any convenient place and await further
instructions. There followed a dreary wait of nearly two hours
until Brigade sent another message—timed 10-45 p.m.—with
instructions to carry on as previously arranged and the interesting news that operation orders would follow shortly. The
Scottish marched on as far as Death Valley behind Trônes
Wood. They had expected to meet at Advanced Brigade Headquarters—the Briqueterie, not far from Bernafay Wood—the
guides detailed to lead them to their positions in the front
trenches. No guides were to be found and there was a long
delay while word was sent from Brigade asking for fresh guides
to be brought down from the line. In the interval the Battalion
suffered several casualties from enemy shelling, and the men

were kept constantly on the move marching and counter-marching up and down the road to avoid the dangerous areas as the enemy switched his fire from one locality to another. Death Valley, which ran up between two small hills to just behind the front line was the only means of approach to the trenches and none knew this better than the Germans. It was, therefore, a particularly unhealthy spot and not one in which a commander would care to halt his men if he could possibly avoid it. It was already crowded with men of other units going either to or from the trenches, and by the time the Liverpool Scottish, having collected guides who appeared to know nothing whatever of the country—no unusual experience—had forced their way through and, discarding the over-busy communication-trenches, found their way across the open to their jumping-off positions, it was 3-45 a.m. The Commanding-Officer, who had at last received his operation orders, hastily called his company-commanders together and gave them his final orders. They in turn were able to give only a rough idea of the plan of attack to their platoon-commanders and serjeants when at 4-15 a.m. the barrage opened and it was time to get out of the trenches and lie down in front of them to wait the signal to attack.

Prompt at 4-20 the line moved forward, " X " Company on the right, " V " on the left with " Z " and " Y " respectively in close support. The enemy had already put down two counter-barrages, one on the support-trenches and one in no-man's-land. The attackers soon ran into the latter barrage and also met terrific machine-gun fire and were held up. Lieut.-Colonel Davidson rallied the men and led a second charge himself in which he was wounded. This attack fared no better than the first. A third and fourth time the Battalion rallied and went on but with little better result. At two places a few men succeeded in entering the enemy's trenches but they were overwhelmed by numbers. At all other points those attackers who reached the German line found uncut wire and eventually were forced to return to their own trenches or to take shelter in shell-holes in no-man's-land. So ended an attack which was doomed before it began.

For a successful assault against a strongly-organized entrenched position there are four essentials—a preliminary bombardment to destroy defences and barbed-wire entanglements and to kill or demoralize the defenders; familiarity with or at least a rough knowledge of the ground on the part of the attackers; a clearly defined scheme understood by all ranks; and—not the least important—reasonably fresh troops. Not one of these essentials was in evidence on 8/9 August.

Corps had definitely told Division that there would be a preliminary bombardment of several hours' duration. What became of it? The first shells were fired at 4-15 a.m. by the Divisional Field Artillery when the barrage opened. The enemy had had an entirely undisturbed night in which to repair the damage done to his trenches and wire the previous day, and good use he had made of his time.

So far as knowledge of the ground was concerned, only the company commanders and a few of the subalterns had been given an opportunity of going up to the front line during the previous week and seeing what was before them. None of the N.C.O.'s or men had any idea at all of what the country looked like. That might not have been so serious if there had been time to send out reconnoitring patrols before the attack. They would probably have found the nest of machine-guns established by the enemy in a sunken road in front of his trenches which was responsible for a large number of the Battalion's casualties. As the Battalion reached its position only half-an-hour before zero, patrols were out of the question. Many of the men said after the attack that it was not until the barrage opened that they knew which side of their jumping-off trench was their front and which was their rear.

Want of time was also responsible for the lack of a clear knowledge, on the part of officers and men alike, of what exactly was required of the Battalion. Brigade in their report on the action said quite rightly that it had been utterly impossible to issue detailed orders until the very last minute. Division were in the same difficulty, as they did not receive orders to attack until the afternoon of the 8th. The operation-orders which did eventually reach the Battalion were all that could be desired—as orders—but they arrived too late to be of any real use. Lieut.-Colonel Davidson, as a matter of fact, had time only to read them hurriedly through and, beyond a general outline of the scheme of attack, which had already been explained to him at Brigade Headquarters, he was unable to pass on to the company-commanders any of the carefully worded details of objectives to be taken, strong-points to be established, and all the intricacies of organization which the orders contained. The few hours between the receipt of the orders and the hour of the attack were fully occupied in getting the Battalion into its assembly position. The Colonel's difficulties were not lessened when he discovered that the Battalion

headquarters allotted to him was already taken up by the
1/5th and 1/7th King's. He was compelled to search for and
establish a new headquarters, with a consequent loss of more
valuable time.

And what of the condition of the men? They had been on
the move from 8 p.m. until 3-45 a.m., heavily shelled for a great
part of the time and with no chance whatever of getting any
rest. They had had to force their way along roads and
communication-trenches full of men from the various units who
had taken part in the attack earlier in the day, and when they
finally reached the front line they were tired out. That they
were able to attack at all when the signal was given was
creditable, that they should rally and go on again and again
when nearly all their officers were down was magnificent and
showed the stuff the Battalion was made of.

Mention has been made of the confusion caused by the withdrawal from the 166th Brigade of the 1/5th Loyal North
Lancashires. This battalion received various orders on the 8th
from its own Brigadier and from the 164th Brigade to which it
was attached, but it was not until nearly 3 a.m. on the 9th that
the Commanding-Officer—who, it will be remembered, was not
summoned to the Brigade conference the previous afternoon—
knew that his battalion was due to attack little more than an
hour later. As a consequence, except for one company which
happened to be conveniently placed, the Loyal North Lancashires did not reach their assembly trenches until 5 a.m., with
the result that the Liverpool Scottish went over with their left
flank in the air. The Loyals themselves attacked at 5-20,
without even a barrage to help them, and inevitably could make
no headway at all.

Why was the 166th Brigade sent into this disastrous attack
at such short notice? Not by the wish of Brigade or Division.
There is reason to believe that during that halt on the road,
from 9-0 to 10-45 p.m. on the 8th, an attempt was made by
Divisional headquarters to persuade the higher command to
postpone the action until it could be thoroughly organized, but
that the appeal was rejected. It is inevitable, when operations
on the scale of the Battle of the Somme are in progress, that
formations—battalions, brigades, or even divisions—should be
sent on forlorn hopes, either to help the common cause or
because a sufficiently accurate knowledge of the state of affairs
in the line has not had time to reach the higher command.
There were two reasons why the attack should take place, one

that Army had promised to do something to assist an operation by the French farther south, and the other that it was a point of honour to attempt to break through and join up with those of the Liverpool Irish who were believed to be holding out in Guillemont itself—both sound enough no doubt, but poor consolation to men who have been ordered to attempt the impossible. Most of the survivors of the Liverpool Irish, as a matter of fact, had already been captured on the afternoon of the 8th, but this news did not reach Division in time to stop the attack the following morning.

The Battalion went into action 20 officers and about 600 other ranks strong. This was not the total fighting strength but, on instruction from Brigade, a percentage of officers, specialists and N.C.O.'s, was left at the transport-lines, to form the nucleus of a new battalion in case complete disaster overtook the unit in the attack. This practice became general throughout the army, not only during offensive operations, but in some cases even in ordinary trench-warfare. The battle of Guillemont did not wipe out the Liverpool Scottish, but the casualties were very heavy. Of the officers, 5 were killed, 5 missing, and 7 wounded. Of the rank and file, 69 were killed, 27 missing, and 167 wounded. The story of the missing was that of Hooge repeated; all the officers and nearly all the men were afterwards reported killed.

The fact that a large number of the wounded were lying out in no-man's-land, either in the open or in shell-holes, made the task of dressing their wounds a very difficult and dangerous one, and many men distinguished themselves throughout the day by crawling from man to man with water and bandages under heavy fire. None carried out this work with greater disregard for personal danger than the Medical Officer, Captain N. G. Chavasse. He was deservedly awarded the Victoria Cross for exceptional bravery and devotion to duty. The official citation of the specific acts for which he received it needs no embellishment.

" During the attack on Guillemont, on August 9th, this
" officer continued to tend the wounded in the open all day
" under a heavy fire, frequently exposing himself to view
" of the enemy. He organized parties to get the wounded
" away most successfully. That night he spent four hours
" searching the ground in front of the enemy's lines for
" wounded lying out. On the following day he proceeded
" with one stretcher-bearer to the advanced trenches and

"carried an urgent case for 500 yards under a very heavy
"shell fire. During this performance he was wounded in
"the side by a shell splinter. The same night he took up
"a party of 20 volunteers, and succeeded in recovering
"three more of the wounded from a shell-hole 25 yards
"from the German trench, buried the bodies of two officers,
"and collected a number of identity-discs, although fired
"on by bombs and machine-guns. Altogether this officer
"was the means of saving the lives of 20 seriously wounded
"men under the most trying circumstances, besides the
"ordinary cases which passed through his hands. At one
"time, when all the officers were shot down, he helped to
"rally the firing-line."

Five men were decorated with the Distinguished Conduct
Medal :—

Corporal F. M. Aldritt—who carried four wounded men to
a shell-hole twenty-five yards from the German trench, and
remained with them all day; at night he sent an unwounded
man back to the British lines to collect a carrying party, but
he failed to get through. Corporal Aldritt meantime crept about
in front of the enemy's wire and, though bombed and fired on,
collected a number of water-bottles from dead men. He spent
the whole of the next day in the shell-hole and at night crawled
back to our lines and brought one of the wounded with him.
Though by this time nearly exhausted, he guided a party of
volunteers across no-man's-land and saw the remaining three
casualties carried to safety.

Corporal A. Baybut—the Doctor's orderly and shadow—who
dressed wounded in the open all morning on the 9th, and during
the evening superintended their removal and searched the
ground for others. He was one of those who volunteered to go
with Corporal Aldritt.

Lance-Corporal W. E. Pennington—who dressed wounded in
the open during the attack, and at night patrolled no-man's-land
to find those still lying out. He spent all the next day dressing
wounded in the front line, and at 5-30 p.m. went out and
carried in a badly wounded man over the open under heavy fire.

Private T. C. Duckworth—who made six journeys into
no-man's-land in broad daylight, and each time brought in a
wounded man under exceptionally heavy shell and rifle fire.

Private W. B. McCann—who, with another man, Private
H. Fildes, cut his way through the German wire and entered

the trench, where he collected bombs and held on until the other man was wounded; he then retired with him but when crossing no-man's-land found a British machine-gun, of which the crew had all been killed except one, who was mortally wounded. He remained by the gun all day and saw it brought back to our lines at night.

The Military Cross was awarded to 2nd Lieut. G. D. Morton, the Acting Adjutant, who took command when Lieut.-Colonel Davidson was hit, and showed admirable coolness and ability in the difficult task of organizing the companies and making the line secure against a counter-attack; and to 2nd Lieut. Robert McNae, who, when the other officers were shot down, rallied the firing line and led them to the third and fourth assaults. He afterwards carried in his Company-Serjeant-Major, who was badly wounded; later he re-organized the garrison of the front line, and throughout inspired everyone by his fine example.

Military Medals were won by Lance-Corporals W. C. Parker, H. Shillitoe, H. N. Lewis and A. H. George, and Privates H. Fildes, J. Cushnie, E. Herd and S. Mullock, all of whom showed great qualities of leadership or were conspicuously fearless in their attention to the wounded under fire.

This was a quite unusually large allotment of decorations to a battalion which had taken part in an unsuccessful attack. When things had gone well rewards were, as a rule, distributed on a fairly lavish scale, but they were very hard to come by after a failure.

.   .   .   .   .

The Battalion spent an uncomfortable day in the trenches from which it had assaulted and which were already crowded with the men of the 1/5th South Lancashires, who had dropped into them when they saw that the attack they were supporting had no chance of success. During the night the Scottish were relieved by the 1/5th King's Own Royal Lancasters and moved back into support in Liverpool and Lancaster trenches, where they remained until 8-30 p.m. on the 10th, when they were again relieved—by the 1st Battalion North Staffordshire Regiment— and marched to bivouacs at Great Bear, two miles south of Mansel Copse. Here they spent two days, during which refitting and reorganization were carried out, and on the night of the 12th again went up into the line and relieved the 1/6th King's Liverpools in the reserve trenches at Talus Bois. The 165th Brigade had made an attack south of Guillemont earlier in the day, in conjunction with the French, and had captured their objectives, but owing to the failure of the attack on their right they were withdrawn to their original positions. A number of the Liverpool Scottish were attached to the 1/9th King's Liverpools in the attack, for stretcher-bearer duties. When the 9th were ordered to withdraw to their original line many wounded men were perforce left lying out between the trenches. One of the Liverpool Scottish, Private John Bell Buckingham, carried out his duties with extraordinary bravery and with absolute disregard for his own safety. He went from man to man in the open and under continuous heavy fire, dressing their wounds and doing what he could for their comfort, until he was killed. He was recommended, posthumously, for the Victoria Cross. The honour was denied him but it is a privilege to pay a tribute in these pages to his gallantry and devotion to duty.

During the afternoon and evening of the 13th, the Scottish moved forward and took over the front-line trenches from the 1/9th King's Liverpools. These trenches were very shallow and had been badly knocked about, and the Scottish received orders that they must dig themselves in to a depth of five feet before daybreak—no light task. All worked with a will—subalterns and warrant-officers taking their turn with pick and spade—and when daylight came the work was complete and the trench habitable. The following night they were relieved by the 2nd Suffolks and returned to Great Bear. The enemy was in a spiteful mood and pursued them with shells for the greater part of the way. Unfortunately he caught them as they were passing through Carnoy Village and twenty men were killed or wounded.

After a night in bivouacs the Battalion marched to billets at Méaulte and here for four days training was carried on. The weather was stifling and the heat brought out swarms of flies which were very troublesome. To get a little peace the men spent most of their free time in the River Ancre.

On 16 August, Major-General Jeudwine inspected the Battalion and afterwards spoke to the men in the warmest terms on their behaviour at Guillemont. His speech was taken down by a shorthand expert in the ranks and has been preserved :—

" I am glad to see you looking so strong and well after " all you have had to do this last fortnight. You were " asked to do a considerable thing; you were asked to " attack, at very short notice and in daylight, across open " ground from bad trenches, an enemy who had been posted " strongly for a month. You did not stick at it; you went

" over at it; it was not your fault that everything did not
" go as hoped for. The attack was made as a necessity of
" the situation that existed at that time. It was necessary,
" in the opinion of the Higher Command, because certain
" advantages would accrue whether you were successful in
" getting in or not. That you were not successful in getting
" in was not your fault. What you did went very far
" towards gaining those advantages on account of which
" the order was given by the Higher Command. The
" determination and the spirit in which you took it on have
" not been wasted, either by yourselves or on the enemy
" against whom the attack was made. The enemy who see
" men coming on against them as you did will be afraid of
" meeting those men if they have to do it again.

" I had the privilege of knowing you when you were in
" the 3rd Division, and I saw you in the attack on 16 June,
" 1915. I know what the Battalion has done, what it can
" do, and what it will do; I know what sort of men it is
" made up of. I remember the dash with which you went
" and the stubbornness with which you stuck there, and
" whenever you are asked to do anything of the sort again
" you will do it with all your old dash.

" The determination and effort, not only once but
" twice, to get over shows that the Battalion is as great a
" battalion to overcome difficulties as it was before, and as
" it always will be.

" You are going, I hope, to get a bit of rest now. I may
" say you do not look as if you want it; all the same I do
" not suppose you will be sorry to get a week, a fortnight,
" or three weeks, whatever they are pleased to give us.

" We hope you will soon have a big draft coming out,
" and you will have to tell them, as I know you will, of
" the tradition of the Battalion and of what it did last year
" and now. Make them proud, as they well may be, of the
" Liverpool Scottish; I am sure they will be; and if you
" can do that it will prove you are going to have even a
" better battalion than now, if possible."

On the 19th, the Scottish entrained at Railhead—Edge Hill—
for Martainville. From here they marched to Valines and went
into billets—one company being housed at St. Marc, half a mile
away. Valines—a charming village—west of Abbeville and only
some ten miles from the coast, was far from the battle area, and
the inhabitants had never before seen a kilted battalion. Their

obvious amusement and their embarrassing remarks were a little
trying at first but quite soon the men were very much at home
in the village. Training, as usual, was begun at once and a
bombing-trench and thirty-yards-range were constructed, but as
far as possible the men were given a well-deserved holiday and
parties were granted special leave of 72 hours to visit Eu and
Ault, small seaside towns in the neighbourhood. It was hoped
that the Division might have several weeks' rest but on
27 August unexpected orders were received for a return to the
line. On the 28th the Transport, and the next day the
Battalion, set off to Moyenville where they were billeted for the
night. On the 30th they marched on to Pont Rémy and
entrained for Méricourt. Here they bivouacked in a cornfield,
the "bivvies" consisting of corn-stooks with ground-sheets
stretched over them. During the march from Valines it had
rained almost incessantly and the men had been soaked through
for forty-eight hours. They got little opportunity to dry their
sodden clothes, for the following day they moved again to
bivouacs in front of Méaulte near Bellevue Farm. Here orders
were received that the Scottish would relieve the 1st North
Staffordshires in reserve trenches north of Montauban on
1 September. These orders were cancelled and renewed alter-
nately until the relief finally took place on the 5th, the Battalion
taking over from the North Staffordshires and the 4th Royal
Fusiliers, both of its old Division. On the previous day a draft
of 1 officer and 109 other ranks had arrived and these, with
8 officers who had reported towards the end of August and 100
other ranks who had been temporarily attached to the 1/5th and
1/9th King's Liverpools, brought the strength of the Battalion
to a respectable figure.

On 7 September, the Battalion received orders to dig and
occupy a new front line in advance of the existing front line
at the north end of Delville Wood. A fresh attack was in
preparation on this sector and the object of constructing this
new trench was to lessen the distance to the enemy's line, to
give the attackers a jumping-off trench in alignment with their
objective and to avoid the shelling to which troops in Delville
Wood were constantly subjected.

The new line, which was sited by Royal Engineer officers
working under direct orders from Division, was in no-man's-land
about 400 yards in advance of the front trenches along the north-
east edge of Delville Wood. Six strong-points were marked out with
white tape and the first task of the Battalion was to complete
these. Every available man was sent up to dig and the

G

responsibility of superintending the work and of garrisoning the
strong-points when finished was given to Captain J. A. Roddick.
The whole surface of the ground in front of Delville Wood had
been churned up by shells and the digging was anything but
easy. Before daylight came, however, all the strong-points were
ready and a garrison of one platoon allotted to each of them.
The remainder of the Battalion withdrew to the reserve trenches
for the day. The following night the whole Battalion again set
to work and dug a trench joining up the strong-points to each
other. This, too, was completed in one night and the Scottish
then occupied the new line. As it was important that the
Germans should not learn that an advanced trench had been
dug the men were forbidden to look over the top or even to use
periscopes during the day. The shell-torn ground made it
impossible for the enemy to distinguish the newly-dug earth from
the surrounding shell-holes and, thanks to this fact and to the
discreet invisibility of the men in the trench, the new position
escaped observation. Consequently all the hostile shelling,
except for a few " shorts," went over the men's heads and into
Delville Wood. The Battalion, therefore, had an easy time
except for the discomfort of thirst. Casualties were always so
heavy in Delville Wood that carrying parties through it at night
were reduced to a minimum and only a very limited supply of
water could be sent up, little enough for drinking and none whatever for shaving or washing.

The Scottish spent two lazy days in the new position but
got plenty of exercise during the nights, which were devoted
to improving the fire-trenches and communication-trenches and
in salvageing material and burying dead in Delville Wood.

The Battalion was relieved in the early hours of the 11th by
the 23rd Middlesex and marched to a new billeting-area at
Ribemont, five miles south-west of Albert. The steady eastward
flow of the Somme Battle had freed Ribemont from all but long-
range shelling, and some of the civilians, who had been compelled
to evacuate it on account of the bombardment in the early days
of the battle, were already beginning to return.

The Divisional Commander in a letter to Brigadier-General
Green-Wilkinson, dated 12 September, after congratulating him
and all ranks of his Brigade on their work, went on to say :—
" The work done in pushing our line forward east of Delville
" Wood will be of the greatest help to the troops who have
" relieved us and will have an important influence on future
" operations. The value of it has been appreciated by the

" Lieut.-General Commanding the Corps.   This work is an
" instance of the immense fighting value of the spade.   Much
" fine work has also been done with the Rifle, Bayonet and
" Bombs, but unless digging had been continued, as it has been,
" regardless of fatigue and losses, the objects aimed at could
" not have been achieved."

At Ribemont twelve officers from the 4th Battalion The
Queen's Own Cameron Highlanders were attached to the
Liverpool Scottish for the duration of the War.   The Scottish
were already affiliated to the Camerons but this was the first
time that they had received reinforcements either of officers or
men from them and it marked the beginning of a real connection
with that famous regiment which has become very much closer
since the war.

After four days' training the Battalion moved to bivouacs
near Albert and was under orders to move at a moment's notice.
The following morning, 17 September, it received instructions to
proceed, in fighting order, to Pommier Redoubt—part of the old
German front system—and, after a night there, went on first
to Switch Trench and, in the evening, to Fosse Way and Flers
Avenue where it relieved the 1/6th King's Liverpools.   Here
for two days and nights work was energetically carried on,
digging and deepening a new communication-trench, and—in
conjunction with the 1/5th King's Own Royal Lancasters—
making a new front line north-east of Flers Village in readiness
for an attack timed to take place on the 25th.   The Division
was to take part in this attack and the 166th Brigade was
detailed to reserve.   The Scottish returned to Pommier Redoubt
on the night of the 23rd after handing over their trenches to the
1/6th King's.   Here three drafts, totalling 110 other ranks, joined
the Battalion.   Two Officers and 100 men of the Scottish were
attached to the 1/3rd West Lancashire Field Ambulance to
assist in carrying stretchers after the attack on the 25th.

The attack was successful and all objectives were captured
both by the 165th Brigade on the 25th and by the 164th Brigade
on the 27th, when the initial success was exploited and the gains
extended and consolidated.   Once more the Divisional Commander congratulated the 166th Brigade on its digging which
had, he said, largely contributed to the great success of the attack
by the 165th Brigade.

On 28 September the Division was relieved by the 41st
Division and took up a new billeting area at Ribemont.   The
Scottish remained there only two days and then entrained at

Méricourt for Longpré and marched thence to bivouacs at Pont
Rémy. Battalion Headquarters was established in the Château,
a magnificent place of immense size, in which was a superb
collection of portraits—one of a King of France, presented by
him to a contemporary owner of the Château—and of armour
and weapons of all sorts labelled with the names of those who
once had borne them and dating back, many of them, three or
four hundred years.

At Pont Rémy the Battalion learnt with real thankfulness
that the Division had completed its task on the Somme and
would move to a new sector immediately. The full results of
the Somme Battle were not to be realized until the retreat of
the Germans in March, 1917, showed how severely they had been
punished and how very near they had been to a crushing defeat.
To the average individual in the ranks the Somme was merely
a nightmare of endless hard work, miserable quarters and
incessant shelling with a certain amount of fighting thrown in.
It was a weary Battalion that climbed into the train at
Abbeville on 2 October and set out on the journey northwards
to Proven.

THE SALIENT AGAIN

The Battalion detrained at Proven early in the morning of 3 October and marched to K Camp at Poperinghe. *1916* Poperinghe, the " West End " of the Salient, was already familiar ground and during the next twelve months was to become more familiar still. Too far from the line to receive any except occasional shelling by long-range high-velocity guns, it drove a thriving trade in supplying the varied wants of the troops resting in the many camps in the neighbourhood after their tours of trench duty. All ranks and all tastes were catered for, and whether it was a six-course dinner or a haircut and shampoo, or only the latest A.S.C. gossip that was the pressing need of the moment, a visit to " Pop " satisfied the want. Skindles', Kiki's, the Club, Talbot House, the Red Roses—as the Divisional Concert Party now advertised themselves—all were magnets that drew officers and men released for a time from the boredom of trench routine and anxious to taste in advance some of the pleasures that they hoped to enjoy in Blighty when their turn for leave at last came round.

The Scottish were not left long in idleness to take stock of their surroundings. After one night in K Camp, they went on by train to Ypres and took over the dugouts in the Canal Bank from the 1st Border Regiment. The following night they moved on again and relieved the 2nd South Wales Borderers in the front-line trenches in the Wieltje sector.

This was the beginning of another long spell of monotonous trench warfare. Eight days in the front line and close support, eight days at B or C Camp near Brandhoek in reserve and eight days in the Canal Bank dugouts in support was the usual routine with minor changes in dispositions from time to time to suit particular conditions or to conform with alterations in the Defence Scheme for the sector. As usual in the Salient there was the everlasting struggle to gain the upper hand of the elements, and constant work on the trenches was necessary to keep them habitable. Fortunately the enemy was too fully occupied with the battle in the South to give much attention to harassing fire on the trenches and—for the Salient—there was uncannily little shelling. But if his guns were quiet and the men in the support positions could pass their days in unaccustomed peace, the front-line troops soon found that he had devised a new form of frightfulness for their especial benefit—the *Minenwerfer*. These mortars, which threw a heavy shell with great accuracy up to about 1,000 yards, were more destructive of trenches—and of life—than even the 5.9-inch howitzer, but they had one redeeming feature. The shell travelled slowly and could readily be seen in the air, so special observers were posted in the trenches whose duty it was to watch for these missiles and to shout " Minnie right " or " Minnie left " according to their judgement of where they would fall. The garrison then ran for their lives to the opposite flank and waited for the ear-splitting detonation and the resultant avalanche of mud and—if the " minnie " had landed fairly in the trench—of woodwork and sandbags, then returned to inspect the damage and get ready for the next alarm. This system reduced casualties, but there were times when most of the men were asleep in their shelters or when the observer miscalculated or, worst of all, at night when it was impossible to clear the danger-spot in time and then the damage was serious. The " minnie," lobbed out of an unrifled mortar, turned over and over in its flight and was as likely to land on its side as on its nose. It lay on the ground where it had fallen until its time-fuze operated. Its lateral effect, therefore, was tremendous and its radius of damage far greater than that of the ordinary high-explosive shell which penetrated below the surface before detonating with a consequent localizing of the effect. " Minnies " took a heavy toll of the Scottish, and the garrisons of the front line at those points which were most frequently " strafed " had to be thinned out considerably to lessen the risk.

Ypres was not greatly changed except that it was rather more dilapidated and even more depressing than it had been a year before. The enemy did not overlook the fact that troops and transport had to use its streets at night in going to and from the line, and his gunners knew exactly on which of its roads and exits their shells would do most harm. The tracks on the outskirts, too, were regularly shelled and that locality known as the Dead-end, north of Ypres, where the Yser Canal came to an abrupt stop and which all transport for the Wieltje sector had to pass, was a favourite spot for salvos, but the whole town was unhealthy and it was easy to resist the temptation to loiter in it.

The Battalion soon settled down to the usual round of trench existence. When in the forward positions two companies occupied the front-line trenches before Wieltje, with one in

close support and the fourth at St. Jean with Battalion Headquarters; trench-maintenance and repair, wiring, patrolling and
" minnie-dodging " kept the troops fully occupied.   Nor was
the life any less strenuous in the support positions whether the
Battalion was in the Canal Bank dugouts—close to the Dead-
end—or, as once happened, in Elverdinghe Château and what
was known as the L Defence-line—a succession of numbered
strong-points extending northwards from Ypres close to the
Canal Bank.   Here, too, there was the constant care of the
defences to be considered and, at night, working parties were
out, mostly near the front line—carrying, digging, draining,
cable-burying, wiring—and always liable to be involved in an
unexpected burst of shelling or machine-gun fire when cover was
scarce, as was an unfortunate party one night when twelve men
were killed and twelve wounded in a sudden bombardment.

A hard life, only made bearable by the knowledge that it was
common to all and by the extraordinary spirit of unselfishness
and comradeship that was developed in almost every individual.

There were bright spots, too, as for instance the concert
and whist-drive held in Elverdinghe Château when the Battalion
occupied that sector.   Elverdinghe Village had been entirely
flattened by shell-fire but the Château, miraculously, was almost
undamaged—rumour had it that the owner was a German—and
its rooms, long since stripped of every stick of furniture and
with sandbags built up to fill the empty window-frames, comfortably accommodated Battalion Headquarters and two companies.   The Canal Bank dugouts, too—long tunnels burrowed
into the eastern side—were good billets and safe, though lousy
and rat-infested.

The days spent near Brandhoek in one of the rest-camps were
largely given up to recreation.   The mornings were devoted to
cleaning up and mild training but for the rest of the day the
men were free to do as they liked—within the limits of the
camp.   In the afternoons there was football for the active and
sleep for the weary, and in the evenings concerts, boxing or a
visit to " Pop." for those who could get a pass.

At Brandhoek the Battalion had the rare experience of seeing
one of the British captive observation-balloons break from its
moorings and go drifting over the German lines at a great
height, pursued by shells from every anti-aircraft battery within
range but untouched, until at last it disappeared in the far
distance.

Shortly after the Battalion returned to the Salient two parties of reinforcements of an unusual character reported for duty. First, five pipers arrived and brought the pipe-band up to satisfactory strength and, a few days later, three officers of the Argyle and Sutherland Highlanders were attached to the Battalion for the duration of the war.

There was considerable excitement early in October when orders were received that five officers and 150 other ranks were to be selected to be attached to VIII Corps Headquarters for guard duties. The lucky nominees moved amongst their envious friends with a conscious air and ostentatiously added the last artistic touch to the cleaning of their clothing and equipment. When the order was almost immediately rescinded they could hardly expect sympathy. In any case they got none.

In November another party was asked for with a very different task in view and, as its orders were not cancelled, it surely deserves a chapter to itself.

"KAISER BILL" SALIENT.

TRENCH TRAMWAYS —+—+—
DUGOUTS, ETC.   ▮ ▬

THE RAID ON "KAISER BILL,"
29 NOVEMBER, 1916

1916

To devote an entire chapter in a short history such as this to what was, after all, a very minor operation, may appear out of proportion, but this highly successful raid has a general historic value in that it was, in the meticulous working out of its preliminary details and in its triumphant execution, a typical example of those whirlwind night attacks on a small portion of the enemy's front which did so much to undermine the *moral* of his troops. Most battalions of the British Army at one time or another were called upon to carry out raids on a larger or smaller scale and these raids were looked upon as part of the normal duty of the infantry. Not so with the German Army. The infrequent raids which the enemy made upon our trenches were seldom carried out by the units in the line but were entrusted to selected troops specially trained for the purpose.

On 10 November orders were received from Brigade that, on a date to be notified later, the Liverpool Scottish would carry out a raid at dusk on a small salient—known as " Kaiser Bill "— in the enemy's line about half a mile south of Wieltje, that a party of three officers and about 60 men would be required and that all those taking part in the raid should begin at once, by patrolling at night, to familiarize themselves with the ground over which they would have to operate.

This order was at once passed on to all company-commanders and to the scout- and bombing-officers with a request for volunteers. The scout section volunteered in a body, and altogether about one hundred names were sent in from which the required numbers and reserves were selected, preference being given to men with special knowledge of and aptitude for bombing. Permission was at once asked of the 1/5th King's Own, who were holding the trenches opposite " Kaiser Bill," for the raiding party to patrol on their front. They agreed and also put at the disposal of the Liverpool Scottish all the information in their possession as to the nature of the ground, state of the enemy's wire, position of his machine-guns, etc. By the time the Scottish were relieved on 18 November all members of the "Special Fatigue Party," as it was called, had a good idea of what no-man's-land was like in front of "Kaiser Bill."

On relief from the trenches the Battalion entrained at Ypres for Brandhoek and then marched to C Camp near by, which it reached about midnight. The following day intensive training for the raid was begun.

The objects of the raid were :—

(a) to kill or capture enemy ;

(b) to secure identification of the regiment holding "Kaiser Bill" ;

(c) to destroy dugouts and machine-gun and trench-mortar emplacements.

"Kaiser Bill" was believed to be strongly held, especially at night when a good deal of machine-gun fire came from it. The smoke of several fires, probably cooking, had also been noticed during the day and indicated a considerable garrison.

With the help of aeroplane photographs a full-sized replica of the Kaiser Bill salient was marked out on suitable ground, and the best way of assaulting the position was then worked out in detail. When this was finally settled the raiding party was split up into small groups each with its own task and the men were practised again and again, both by day and by night, in their particular duties until the whole operation went like clockwork and every man carried out his allotted share in it almost automatically. Two parties of Royal Engineers, of one N.C.O. and three sappers each, were attached to the raiding party to carry out the expert work of destroying dugouts and machine-gun emplacements with gun-cotton charges. They rehearsed their parts in the show with the rest of the party and so the men got to know and rely upon each other.

One most unfortunate accident occurred during practice with live bombs. A faulty bomb exploded prematurely, killing one man and wounding eleven others and two officers. This temporarily disorganized the work but, as a number of reserves had been trained in case of any such eventuality, things were soon working smoothly again.

It was decided that the raiding party should be divided into a right and left party which would enter the enemy's trenches on the south and north side respectively of the nose of the salient. These right and left parties were again sub-divided into smaller parties as follows :—

RIGHT RAIDING PARTY—

No. 1.	Scouts.	1 N.C.O. and 2 men.
No. 2.	Torpedo and wire-cutting party.	1 N.C.O. and 4 men.
No. 3.	Right bombing party.	1 officer, 2 N.C.O.'s, 2 throwers, 2 bayonet men, 2 carriers, 1 spare man.
No. 4.	Right blocking party.	1 N.C.O. and 2 men.
No. 5.	Left bombing party.	2 N.C.O.'s, 2 throwers, 2 bayonet men, 2 carriers.
No. 6.	Tape-laying party.	2 men.

LEFT RAIDING PARTY—

No. 7.	Scouts.	1 officer, 1 N.C.O., 1 man.
No. 8.	Torpedo and wire-cutting party.	1 N.C.O. and 4 men.
No. 9.	Left bombing party.	1 N.C.O., 2 throwers, 2 bayonet men, 2 carriers, 1 spare man.
No. 10.	Right forward bombing party.	1 officer, 1 N.C.O., 2 throwers, 2 bayonet men, 2 carriers, 1 spare man.
No. 11.	Left forward bombing party.	1 N.C.O., 2 throwers, 2 bayonet men, 2 carriers, 1 spare man, 1 N.C.O. R.E. and 3 sappers.
No. 12.	Left forward blocking party.	1 N.C.O., 1 thrower, 1 bayonet man, 1 carrier, 1 spare man.
No. 13.	Ditch-blocking party.	2 men.
No. 14.	Right forward clearing party.	1 N.C.O., 1 thrower, 1 bayonet man, 1 carrier, 1 spare man, 1 N.C.O. R.E. and 3 sappers.
No. 15.	Tape-laying party.	2 men.

Total strength : 1 officer and 30 other ranks in the right and 2 officers and 45 other ranks in the left raiding party, plus 2 N.C.O.'s R.E. and 6 sappers in the left party.

The Bangalore torpedoes mentioned were long thin metal tubes filled with explosive and were used to destroy wire defences. They were pushed under the wire and then exploded by detonators attached to a time-fuse sufficiently long to allow the men who lit it time to get back to a safe distance before the bang came. They were remarkably effective.

The particular duties of the small parties detailed above were :—

RIGHT RAIDING PARTY :—

No. 1.   Scouts to move forward fifty yards ahead of the main party and ascertain if the enemy's wire were cut by the artillery barrage. If sufficiently cut, to finish the work by hand and to call or signal to the main party to move up. If the wire were not sufficiently cut, to assist the torpedo party to place torpedoes in position and then rejoin the main party. After the explosion of the torpedoes to return to the gap and assist in enlarging it. Afterwards to remain and defend the gap until every other party had withdrawn.

No. 2.   To follow the scouts closely and, if required, to place the torpedoes in position, light the fuse and rejoin the main party. After the explosion to proceed to the gap and remain there to receive prisoners, until ordered to withdraw.

No. 3.   To turn south on entering the enemy's front line (at G.1) and to follow it to a point (A) where a trench leads to the tramway. To drop a bombing squad of three men at A to hold the front-line trench, the remainder to follow the side trench for about twenty yards and remain there until the signal for recall was given. This party had orders to search all dugouts and emplacements found and to destroy them by means of Stokes-mortar bombs. One N.C.O. was detailed to lay a tape from the point of entry to the farthest point reached, to guide the party back to the point of entry.

No. 4.   To follow No. 3 until they arrived at point B, then to proceed up the side-trench to their left until No. 13 party was met. To return to point B and remain there until the signal for withdrawal.

No. 5.   On entering the enemy's trench to turn north and search the front-line trench until they met the Left Raiding Party. Then to return to near G.1 and hold the trench until the signal for withdrawal.

No. 6.   To lay tape from the gap in our wire to the point

of entry (G.1) of the Right Raiding Party. To remain there and assist to escort prisoners until ordered to withdraw.

LEFT RAIDING PARTY :—

No. 7 and No. 8. Exactly as detailed for Nos. 1 and 2.

No. 9. To turn north on entering the trench at G.2 and to follow along the enemy's front line to C, about twenty yards beyond its junction with the support-line. There to blow in the trench with Stokes-mortar bombs and to hold it until the signal for withdrawal. As in No. 3, one N.C.O. was detailed to lay tape from the point of entry to the farthest point reached.

No. 10. To follow the trench running down the centre of '' Kaiser Bill '' as far as the support-line—point D. To follow the support-line to their right to where it joins the front line at A. If No. 3 were met, either to remain and assist No. 3 or to return and assist No. 14 according to circumstances. If No. 3 were not met, to establish and hold a block at the junction of the support and front trenches at A. The spare man was detailed to lay the guide-tape as before described.

No. 11, To follow No. 10 as far as the support-line—point D. To turn to their left and follow the support-line to its junction with the front line near point C, searching all dugouts on the way and doing as much damage as possible by the use of explosives, with the assistance of the N.C.O. R.E. and sappers. To connect with No. 9 in the front line but on withdrawal to return by exactly the same route as they had followed after entering. An N.C.O. was detailed to lay a guide tape.

No. 12 . To follow No. 11 to point D but to continue through the support-line about twenty yards to point E. There to form a block and hold it until the signal for withdrawal.

No. 13. To follow No. 12 as far as point F. There to turn to their right down the small side trench and continue until they met No. 4. Then to return to F and hold the trench-junction until the signal for withdrawal.

No. 14. To follow No. 13 but to continue down the trench to the support-line at point D. To turn to their right and move along the support-line until they met No. 10. To search any dugouts found and to blow them up, with the assistance of the R.E. details, also any emplacements or trench-mortars if too heavy to move and generally to do as much damage as possible.

No. 15.   To lay tape as for No. 6.

All parties were ordered to return through the gaps by which they had entered but in the reverse order. As each party passed the gap its leader had to report to the officer or N.C.O. in charge of the gap that his party was all clear. The officer or N.C.O. in charge of the two gaps had instructions to remain there with the scouts and torpedo-carriers until ordered to withdraw by the officers commanding the right and left raiding parties.

The arms and equipment to be carried by each man were laid down to the minutest detail, even a rope to tie the hands of refractory prisoners being issued to those who were to act as escort. All the men carried rifle and bayonet, except the throwers who had knobkerries instead. In order that there should be no risk of the raiding parties attacking each other in the dark the right party wore a piece of white tape round the right upper-arm and the left party round the left upper-arm. All men had a piece of tape tied round each shoulder strap.

The time of the raid was fixed for 4-50 p.m. on 28 November but that day turned out to be very misty and the operation was postponed for twenty-four hours.

On the night of 27/28 November a patrol of one officer and six men went out to cut gaps in our wire to enable the raiding party to get quickly into no-man's-land and form up for the assault. It was intended to cut six gaps in all, but the borrow-pit in front of the parapet was waist-deep in water, almost continuous and in most places too wide to bridge. Only two gaps, therefore, were cut—at the driest spots—one for the right and one for the left party. They were made specially wide and served their purpose well. Guide-boards were fixed in the front line opposite the gaps and in the gaps themselves.

The raiding party moved off from the Canal Bank, Ypres, at 2-30 p.m. on the 29th and marched to St. Jean. Here the right party turned off to the right and made their way to their place in the front line via Potijze and the Haymarket communication-trench, reaching their position at 3-45 p.m. The left party carried on through St. Jean and by means of the Garden Street and New John Street communication-trenches arrived at their position at 3-40 p.m. The firing-trenches immediately in front of " Kaiser Bill " had been vacated by their garrison about an hour earlier. This was done to avoid casualties in case the enemy artillery brought fire to bear on our trenches in retaliation for our bombardment of "Kaiser Bill." The raiding parties were ordered to remain on the right and left of the vacated portion of our trench until 4-30 p.m., and then to move into it and get into position in front of our wire.

The artillery bombardment opened at 3-55 p.m., the Divisional Artillery—18-pounders and 4·5-inch howitzers—firing three rounds per gun per minute on the Q, R, S, T, U, V, W, X, Y line (see map), and gradually creeping forward, until at 4-20 p.m. they reached the line Q, P, A, E, Y. This operation was designed to drive as many of the enemy as possible forward into the "Kaiser Bill" Salient. At the same time as the Divisional Artillery opened fire, six medium trench-mortars, placed to a flank in our front trenches, three on the right and three on the left, began to cut gaps in the enemy's wire at G.1 and G.2. Ten Vickers-guns, also, swept the enemy's front parapet for 500 yards on each side of the salient to prevent the enemy mounting machine-guns which could take the raiding party in enfilade. At 4-20 p.m. the Heavy Artillery—6-inch, 8-inch and 9.2-inch howitzers—commenced the bombardment of "Kaiser Bill" itself and fifteen minutes later eight 2-inch Stokes-mortars joined in, their targets being the front line trenches of "Kaiser Bill" and also a sap-head three hundred yards farther north from which trouble might be expected. Two of these Stokes-mortars were buried by a shell but the others made good the loss by increasing their rate of fire.

At 4-40 p.m. the Heavy Artillery lifted back to the support-trench—A to C—while part of the Divisional Artillery switched on to the front line from O to Q and Y to Z. At zero-hour—4-50 p.m.—the heavies and trench-mortars ceased fire entirely and the Divisional Artillery, which had dropped their rate of fire to one round per gun per minute while the heavies were shooting, increased their rate again to three rounds, and continued to bombard the front line on the flanks and the support-trench until, at 5 p.m., they lifted from the support-trench to the line P, S, T, W, X, Y. At 5-20 p.m. all artillery and Vickers-gun fire ceased as a signal to the raiding party to withdraw, and one and a half minutes later the barrage was resumed on the same targets until 5.40 p.m., when it began to creep forward until it reached the German front line at 5-50 p.m., and then gradually died away.

So much for the plan. Now for the execution.

In accordance with orders the right and left parties, twenty minutes before zero-hour, moved into the trenches immediately opposite " Kaiser Bill." At once the wisdom of keeping them to a flank until the last possible moment became apparent. The left party found fifty yards of their position completely blown in and their Bangalore torpedoes—which had been sent up in advance—buried. Both parties had orders to leave the trench five minutes before zero and form up in front of our wire. The right party got out up to time, but the left party were a few minutes late owing to the state of the trench which made it difficult to find the point of egress and also owing to their having four men wounded by a shell. Both parties, however, were able to move forward to the assault at zero.

The scouts of the right party could find no gaps in the enemy's wire and the torpedo party was called up. One torpedo was exploded and through the gap which was made the raiders were able to enter the German trench. They found it very little damaged, all the heavy artillery shooting on the south side of " Kaiser Bill " having been short. In spite of this the right party met with little opposition. Two dugouts were found near point B. On a bomb being thrown into one of them two Germans rushed out and gave themselves up. Another was killed in the second dugout. Otherwise the right party's stay was uneventful.

The left party found the gap at G.2 all that they could wish and they were able to enter the enemy's line straight away and proceed according to programme. The trenches in the centre and on the north of the salient had been very badly knocked about by the bombardment and consequently it was a matter of some difficulty for them to find their bearings. The right forward parties, Nos. 10 and 14, reached the support-line without opposition. On turning to the right there they found a large concrete dugout consisting of three compartments and some bombs were thrown from it. It was bombed and three prisoners taken. The dugout was then destroyed by the Royal Engineers. The left forward parties, Nos. 11 and 12, encountered considerable opposition at the junction of the support and communication-trenches, and bombs and bayonets were freely used. Many of the enemy were killed and eight gave themselves up, including two officers. No. 11 party proceeded along the support-line to the left, doing considerable damage and having a certain amount of fighting during which further prisoners were taken. Bombs were thrown at this party from a shell-hole but on a Stokes-mortar bomb being thrown into it the bombing ceased. The left bombing party, No. 9, followed the front-line trench according to plan and established a bombing-block at point C but, as the official report puts it, met with no enemy, to their great regret.

The enemy, as soon as he had definitely located the limits of the raiding party's activities, began to shell no-man's-land and his own front line pretty severely but in spite of this the break in our barrage, giving the signal for withdrawal, was easily recognized and a bugle sounded in our trenches was clearly heard. Both parties returned as ordered without special incident, the guide-tapes in no-man's-land proving particularly useful.

Our casualties were one man killed, one missing, and sixteen wounded—including the four men hit in our own front line. Of the injured, twelve had only slight wounds.

It is impossible to compute the enemy's casualties with accuracy. It is definitely known that fourteen were killed and eight wounded by rifle-fire, bombs and with the bayonet but a number of others were accounted for at the junction of the communication-trench with the support-line. Thirteen prisoners in all were taken but of these five were killed or wounded by one of their own shells before leaving " Kaiser Bill," and some of their escort were also wounded by the same shell. The remaining eight, one of whom was slightly wounded, were safely brought back to our lines, one serjeant leading his particular prisoner by a rope tied round the man's neck.

On the material side, too, the enemy's losses were heavy. Apart from the damage done to his trenches by the bombardment, seven dugouts and one machine-gun emplacement were totally destroyed by the Royal Engineers. More demolitions would have been carried out had there been sufficient time but the thirty minutes allowed proved hardly enough to complete the whole programme.

At comparatively little cost, therefore, a minimum of thirty-five casualties had been inflicted on the enemy, and the " Kaiser Bill " Salient had been temporarily rendered uninhabitable. A highly satisfactory result, which brought immediate congratulations from the Army, Corps and Divisional Commanders and, later, rewards in the shape of a Military Cross to Lieut. R. V. Clark, O.C. Raid, and Military Medals to Corporal W. E. Wyse, Lance-Corporal D. Cowie, and Private A. Arkle.

H

The raiding party took their prisoners to Brigade Head-quarters where raiders and raided all received hot drinks and a meal, after which they set out for the prison at Ypres where the A.P.M. was waiting with an escort. On the way a curious and significant incident took place. Lieut. Clark suddenly remembered that he had not given the order to unload and that his men still had a round in the chamber of their rifles. He halted the party and formed into line. As soon as he gave the command "Port Arms," all the prisoners fell on their knees and begged for mercy—which completely mystified the raiding party. It was afterwards learnt that all these men had been told by their officers that the British made a practice of treating prisoners well to start with in order to gain their confidence, but that after interrogating them they took them to a place of execution near Ypres and shot them out of hand and that it was obviously better to die fighting. Possibly their relief at finding this story untrue had something to do with the very copious information these men afterwards gave regarding the enemy's dispositions, siting of machine-guns, system of relief, rest-billets, and all the hundred and one minor details which helped the Intelligence Branch to supplement and confirm their marvellously accurate knowledge of all that went on behind the German lines.

One of the volunteers for the raid, Private Rattray, was found to be under age and on that account was told by the Commanding-Officer that he could not be allowed to take part in it. He was bitterly disappointed and, boylike, burst into tears. During the raid, however, he miraculously turned up in the German trenches and had the satisfaction of bringing back a fine large prisoner who, when Rattray fell headlong into a shell-hole in no-man's-land, politely helped him to his feet and handed him his rifle.

STILL IN THE SALIENT

The Battalion returned to the line in the Wieltje sector on 2 December and for the next few months the usual *1916* routine of trench-warfare was carried on, which is to say that for the most part the men were navvies, carpenters, plumbers or porters, rather than soldiers. Thanks to the excellent organization of the many departments run by the tireless Doctor for their benefit, there was very little sickness due to exposure to cold and wet. The Doctor had a genius for picking out those men who were near a breakdown, either in nerve or general health, but not yet so run down as to be hospital cases. Rather than send them into the trenches, where their collapse sooner or later was inevitable, he kept them at his aid post as *light-duty men*, where in comparative comfort they had a chance to rest and recover. They paid their way handsomely. Did a man from the line come in for his daily foot-rubbing by the stretcher-bearers he found when he put his boots on again that they had been dried and cleaned for him in the meantime. Did he come in from a night's digging, wearied to exhaustion, he found one of the Doctor's invalids in charge of a cocoa urn and got a hot drink that put new life into him and sent him to sleep the instant that he threw his equipment off and himself on to the ground, or on to his wire bunk if he were fortunate enough to have one. These and kindred amenities, such as sock and towel laundries and a regular battalion canteen service, could only be arranged satisfactorily if a unit spent some time in one particular sector. There was another advantage in occupying the same trenches again and again; the men knew that they themselves would reap the benefit of all the work they did on wire, trenches and dugouts and, human nature being what it is, this was an incentive to make a good job of any task they were given to do.

The Scottish were again lucky enough to find themselves out of the line at Christmas, which was spent at C. Camp, Brandhoek, where they had gone on the 18th after relief. There was a perfect spate of inspections during this rest. On 21 December, the Commander-in-Chief, Field-Marshal Sir Douglas Haig, inspected the Battalion. As it was a pouring wet day the men were not paraded but simply fell in beside their huts as Sir Douglas went round the Camp. He complimented the Commanding Officer on a fine battalion and told him to thank all ranks for the good work they had done since coming to France. Two days later, General Sir Herbert Plumer, commanding the Second Army, visited the Battalion. He, too, congratulated them on their good work generally, and particularly on the raid of 29 November, and he specifically ordered the Colonel and officers that they must teach all new drafts what a fine battalion they were joining.

Christmas Day was a general holiday, the only parade being a short one held during the morning to distribute the presents for the men from the officers' relatives. In the evening the companies had their Christmas Dinner and there was no shortage of plum-pudding or beer. Headquarter details had their dinner on Christmas Eve so that they might be free the next night to wait on the companies. The runners and cyclists, who had the reputation—not undeserved—of being the best " scroungers " in the Battalion, sat down to roast goose and vegetables, plum-pudding, peaches and custard, fruit, cakes, beer and port. It is possible, of course, that the presence of the goose was the result of an honest business transaction, but . . .

The Battalion returned to the line at Wieltje on 28 December after one night in the Canal Bank

1917 dugouts. This was an unfortunate tour. On 7 January a sudden burst of shelling caught a wiring party and one man was killed and five wounded. These men were members of a special party of two N.C.O.'s and twenty-four men whose sole duty was wiring. They had been chosen for their skill and stout-heartedness and did excellent work. Then on 10 January all men were withdrawn from the front line during the afternoon and housed in the Wieltje Dugout to avoid the enemy's barrage while the 1/5th Loyal North Lancashires raided his trenches. This dugout, which was a huge underground excavation containing dozens of rooms and passages, could accommodate a whole battalion. In spite of a heavy retaliatory bombardment, the Scottish in the support-trenches had no casualties—those in Wieltje Dugout were, of course, absolutely safe—but when things were quiet again and the front-line trenches were re-occupied they were found to have been knocked about so badly that, although every available man in the Battalion was put on to repair-work, it was not until 2 a.m. the following morning that the mess was cleared up. Finally, during relief by the 1st Hertfordshires on the night of

12/13 January the enemy opened a very heavy *Minenwerfer* barrage. This was so severe that the S.O.S. was sent up and our guns made an excellent response. If an attack or a raid had been contemplated they effectively scotched it. The " minnies," however, cost the Scottish one man killed and one officer and ten men wounded.

Nerves were further frayed during this tour by a message that the Corps Commander would inspect the Battalion in the trenches. One's own Divisional or Brigade Commanders who regularly visited the line and knew it intimately were welcome any time they cared to call, but a Corps Commander, with the inevitable group of attendant " brass-hats " who might look over the top at the wrong places or otherwise attract the attention of the German sentries, was another matter. The visitors finish their stroll round and return to the back areas but the men in the line must remain there while the news filters back from the German sentries to the gunners that there seems to be an unusual amount of traffic in the British trenches this morning and a few shells are sent over in case there may be something behind it all. In the present case, however, these gloomy forebodings were groundless. Lieut.-General Sir Hunter Weston expressed his great appreciation not only of the work being done but of the obvious goodwill with which it was being accomplished. His staff behaved with great circumspection and there were no distressing after-effects.

On arrival at B Camp in the early hours of the 13th, the Battalion learnt that the Brigade was to go farther back for a short rest. The following day the Scottish marched to the Cheese Market, Poperinghe, and from there went on by the narrow-gauge railway to Bollezeele, a village some seven miles north of St. Omer. The billets were good ones and all seemed well satisfied except Battalion Headquarters. It was bitterly cold and the Orderly Room staff, as soon as they had taken possession of their office, suggested to the landlady that the room would be cosier if she lit the fire in the stove. The outlook became distinctly chilly when the cantankerous old body refused because, she said, the heat would spoil her beautiful furniture. Luckily her dog bit the Assistant-Adjutant, and Headquarters moved at once to another and a better billet.

The training carried out at Bollezeele was considerably more ambitious than was customary during these short periods of rest in the back areas. The whole Brigade—the Machine-gun Company co-operating—practised together the assembly and deployment prior to an attack and also the trench to trench attack, and the work, besides being more interesting for the men than the usual company or platoon drill and musketry, gave the officers an opportunity of handling their commands tactically and taught many useful lessons.

Physical training was not neglected and on 20 January the whole Battalion took part in a cross-country run of 4,000 yards, after which a team was picked to compete in the Brigade run a week later.   In spite of—or perhaps because of—this preliminary canter the Scottish could not prevent the South Lancashires from winning the Cup presented by the Brigadier.

The lighter side of things was not forgotten; old and new talent sparkled on the concert platform, whist-drives were well patronized, and boxing drew the usual crowd of enthusiastic fans.

It is interesting to note that at this time the paper strength of the Battalion was 47 officers and 1,207 other ranks.   This, of course, was not the fighting strength or anything like it, for these numbers included all those employed in various capacities with Brigade and Divisional Headquarters and even outside the Division altogether.   It was a legitimate grievance of every company-commander that he not only had on his books a man who was, say, a barber at an Army Headquarters but that he was personally responsible to the Paymaster for any overpayment made to the man, although he did not pay him himself and, indeed, never saw him from one year's end to the other.

After an energetic three-weeks the Scottish returned to Poperinghe on 3 February and the same night relieved the 2/5th Lancashire Fusiliers at Mouton Farm near Elverdinghe, where they remained for six days and supplied parties for work of all descriptions in and behind the trenches.

Two days later, to the great satisfaction of everyone, Lieut.-Colonel J. R. Davidson, C.M.G., rejoined the Battalion and took over the command.   Lieut.-Colonel F. W. M. Drew, a regular officer of the South Lancashire Regiment, who had been posted to the Battalion as Second-in-Command at Bellacourt in June, 1916, had commanded it since the Battle of Guillemont and commanded it well in spite of the handicap—with a unit of such an intensely independent and clannish spirit as the Liverpool Scottish—of being both a stranger and a Sassenach. After handing over to Colonel Davidson he was given command of the 1/9th King's Liverpools.

When the Battalion went back to E. Camp on 9 February a very curious order was received from Brigade to the effect that a party from the Scottish was required to report to the 14th Royal Welch Fusiliers at the Canal Bank dugouts and to take the place of one of that Battalion's companies which had been withdrawn from the line to practice for a raid. For a company of one battalion to be attached to another unit even in its own brigade was unusual; for it to be attached to another division, except in the confusion of battle, was unprecedented. Captain L. G. Wall with his company, " V," and fifty men of " X " Company—174 other ranks in all—undertook this special duty and during its six days' absence the party lost six men killed and five wounded.

Early in March the Battalion took over a new sector—Potijze—immediately to the south of Wieltje and—except for one spell of six days in the old trenches—continued to hold it, with the usual periodical rests near Brandhoek, until the end of May. The routine was the same as in the Wieltje sector but instead of occupying the Canal Bank Dugouts when in support the Battalion was billeted in Ypres itself, most frequently in the Convent des Carmes but occasionally in the cellars of the École— a fine building only completed in 1914 and reduced to a mere heap of bricks—or in the Prison where the Orderly Room, appropriately enough, was one of the cells. The Prison had lost most of its roof but its strongly-built stone walls resisted the German shells stoutly and it shared with the Cloth Hall, the Cathedral and the Infantry Barracks the distinction of remaining a recognizable building to the end of the war.

On 17 March the inventive enemy introduced to the Battalion a new type of rifle-grenade, heavier and more accurate than his old pattern, and these gave much trouble and caused several casualties. Two days later he sprang another surprise. At 4-10 a.m. very heavy shelling broke out on the left of the Battalion front. This became so serious that the front-line companies asked for retaliation. At the same time they reported that the trenches on the right of the Scottish were also being heavily bombarded. In about half an hour the shelling died away and it was learnt that the battalion on the right had been raided and that thirteen of its men were missing. In this well-planned and well-executed raid the enemy—some twenty-four strong—had evidently formed up close in front of the British barbed-wire, slipped through a gap the instant his barrage stopped, entered the trench, collected the occupants of three shelters and got away again before the alarm could be given. He cannot have spent more than three minutes in the British line, indeed the sentries to the right and left of the short portion of trench that had been raided did not know the enemy had been in until they came across the body of a German in one of the fire-bays. This man was armed with an automatic revolver with a small bayonet attached, making a kind of trench dagger—a very handy weapon. This was quite a new type of raid and prompt steps were taken to deal with any repetition of it. Company-commanders in the front line were ordered to adapt their dispositions so that enfilade fire could be brought to bear along the immediate front of any portion of the trench which might be bombarded and, in the event of the enemy getting in, to form a defensive flank and pin him there while the supporting companies made an immediate counter-attack over the open from their trenches behind. Special gaps were cut in the wire defending the support-trenches to allow the counter-attack troops to get through. Fortunately these new arrangements never had to be put to the test.

About this time the Royal Flying Corps reported an unusual amount of activity behind the enemy's lines—movement of troops, an increase in rolling-stock on the railways, etc. These reports were confirmed by other observers and by the Intelligence Service, and there appeared to be all the symptoms of an early enemy offensive on the Ypres front. Preparations were at once made to meet the threatened attack and the Battalion received orders to concentrate on strengthening its defences. For the remainder of the tour every available man was out at night adding to and repairing the barbed-wire entanglements, and when relief took place on 27 March only the Lewis-gun teams and headquarter-details went back to D. Camp. Captain J. A. Roddick with 220 men was left behind in Ypres for further work, 2nd Lieut. Turnbull was sent with 50 men to Brielen, two miles north-west, to carry out special wiring on the defences there and a party of 110 other ranks, under Lieutenant R. V. Clark, went off by train to Proven, ten miles away, to level the ground for a new aerodrome. On the return of the Battalion to the Potijze trenches on 7 April work was concentrated on Piccadilly—the main communication-trench on the right of the sector—in which the bombing-blocks were unsatisfactory. Under the supervision of 2nd Lieut. A. Gledsdale, portions of the trench were straightened and new bombing-blocks made, with overhead wire cages to protect the defenders from hostile bombs and rifle-grenades. By the end of the tour the alterations were completed and the defences vastly improved. The expected attack, however, did not take place.

On 26 April the Battalion regretfully said good-bye to Brigadier-General Green-Wilkinson, who returned to England on reaching the limit of age for Brigadiers on active service. The relations of the Liverpool Scottish with him—and with his first Brigade-Major, Captain Hamilton, who had left to command a battalion two months before—had always been of the most cordial nature and the officers on his departure lost a friend who had always tried to help them and whose criticisms, however severe, never carried a sting in their tails. Brigadier-General F. G. Lewis, a Territorial, took over the Brigade.

8 May was an important day in the 55th Division's history, for it was then that for the first time the Divisional Badge—the red rose of Lancaster—was issued to the troops. Each unit in the Division had for more than a year worn a distinguishing mark on the back of the tunic just below the collar—that of the Scottish was two black strips of cloth like a stumpy figure eleven and was generally referred to by the men as their " Legs eleven," the name used for that numeral in the game of " House "—but the new badge, worn on the arms below the shoulder-titles, bound the whole Division together under one symbol. It was to become a very famous badge later in the War.

With the approach of summer the artillery on both sides became more active, and the back areas began to receive attention. On 1 June the Scottish—less two companies left behind for work in Ypres—were resting at B Camp. In the middle of the night their peace was disturbed by several rounds from a high-velocity gun. No one was hit but when the dose was repeated the following night one shell wrecked the officers' cookhouse and killed one and wounded three of the batmen who were sleeping there. Brigade gave permission for the Battalion to find another camp and a move was made early on the 3rd to a small copse near A Camp, Vlamertinghe—later christened Query Camp. There were no tents or huts and the men had to make such shelters as they could with their groundsheets but this was no hardship in the fine summer weather. There was a largish pond at the edge of the copse in which most of the men bathed at least once daily and if the water did soon take on the appearance and consistency of pea-soup it would have been an ultra-squeamish " Jock " who would have foregone his dip on that account.

On 5 June the two companies which had been on special duty in Ypres were relieved and marched to Machine Gun Farm and L 8 Post, but continued from there to send parties up nightly for work in the front line.   On the 11th the whole Battalion took over trenches in the Railway Wood sector, and during the move the Maltese cart and a Lewis-gun limber were damaged by shell-fire on the dreaded Menin Road.   Railway Wood, immediately to the south of the Potijze sector, had not been visited by the Battalion since the attack on Bellewaarde two years before and it had not grown more attractive in the interval. It had been the scene of much mining activity and it was with the express purpose of taking part in the explosion, and consolidation of a mine under the enemy's front trench that the Scottish were sent to this portion of the Divisional front.

The position of the mine was almost directly opposite Bellewaarde Farm and slightly in advance of and between two existing craters—Momber on the north and Hornby on the south. Zero-hour was fixed for 11 p.m. on the 12th, and the task allotted to the Scottish was to seize the near lip of the crater as soon as the mine was blown, to establish a bombing post and connect it up with the front-line trenches and to put out wire entanglements in front of the new position.   Parties from the Royal Engineers and from the Divisional Pioneer Battalion, the 1/4th South Lancashires, were attached to the Battalion to assist in consolidation.

The organization of the scheme was, of course, worked out beforehand in detail, and Captain L. G. Wall was put in charge of the operation.   " V " and " Z " Companies, which were holding the left and right portions of the front line were ordered to withdraw all their men except Lewis-gun teams of 1 N.C.O. and 2 men each from the posts in the vicinity of the mine half-an-hour before zero.   Fifteen minutes later the Lewis-gun teams, too, were to be withdrawn.   " X " Company, in support, was ordered to find the crater-jumping party of an officer, 2 N.C.O.'s and 4 bombers, the wiring parties, parties to carry up the necessary materials and a garrison for the new post when it had been consolidated.   " Y " Company was in reserve.

Everything went like clockwork.   As soon as the mine was blown the crater-jumping party, under Lieut. A. Gledsdale, rushed forward and seized the near lip of the crater.   It was immediately followed by the two wiring parties each of 1 N.C.O. and 6 men, who at once began to run out entanglements to join up with the existing wire of Momber and Hornby craters.   These wiring parties were each covered by three of the

Battalion snipers lying out in front of them. Meantime a party of Royal Engineers of 1 N.C.O. and 6 sappers was busy with the work of consolidation and, to the bombing post which they were constructing, three other parties, two from the Battalion Engineering Section and one from the 1/4th South Lancashires, were digging saps out from the old front line. All this work was covered by the fire of a section from the Brigade Machine-gun Company, the Trench Mortar Battery and the Divisional Artillery, and they played their part so well that although the enemy tried to interfere with the work by sniping and bombing the Scottish had only one man wounded.

The enemy was evidently apprehensive that more mines might be in readiness under his trench-lines for on each of the two following days he blew five *camouflets*—small mines intended simply to break down hostile galleries and not followed by offensive action. These did no harm, though one of them did just break the surface of the ground.

The Battalion was relieved on 14 June by the 2nd Northamptonshire Regiment and, after five days in camp near Vlamertinghe, went by train to Zeggers-Cappel and the next day by motor-bus to Zudausques, a pretty village five miles west of St. Omer. All were safely into billets by 3 p.m. on the 20th.

SPECIAL TRAINING

The Battalion learnt that the stay at Zudausques was to be no ordinary rest but a period of preparation for the *1917* biggest task it had yet attempted. An offensive by the Fifth Army on a very large scale was in the making on the Ypres front and the 55th Division was to be called upon at no very distant date to take part in the opening attack. There was to be no risk of a repetition of Guillemont. The ground allotted to the Division for the assault was the sector it knew so well in front of Wieltje and Potijze, and there was ample time in which to teach every man the main outline of the attack as a whole and his own particular place in it. To simplify the training and to add realism to it the first work undertaken was to map out with the aid of aeroplane photographs a facsimile not only of the enemy's front-line system of trenches with all its saps, strong-points, known machine-gun emplacements, etc., but of his defences farther back—trenches, fortified buildings and gun-positions. The stretch of country on which this full-scale plan was laid out was chosen as far as possible for its resemblance to the actual ground over which the attack would take place, and on it the Royal Engineers marked out with tapes the positions and outlines of the German defences. Then came the digging of the trenches themselves and while the companies are engaged on this laborious task we shall have time to say something of another matter that helped to make this period of the Battalion's history remarkable.

C.Q.M.S. Scott Macfie suggested that as the Scottish would probably spend some time at Zudausques it might be worth while to open a Beer-Garden which should be the centre of all the usual recreational activities of the Battalion. His suggestion was immediately adopted, and to make the necessary arrangements a general committee was formed with three sub-committees, each of one officer and one N.C.O. with one representative from each company, to look after entertainments, games and the canteen. Scott Macfie went off to St. Omer to arrange for the printing of posters and to buy a piano. St. Omer did possess a music shop but it was hardly a Rushworth and Dreaper's. There were no pianos in stock, but two were expected in the course of a week or so and might be bought for an exorbitant price. Luckily Quarters was able, by the exercise of considerable tact and persistence, to track down and secure a second-hand instrument in quite good condition from a lady music-teacher in the town. The capital necessary for the purchase of the piano and all the stores, wet and dry, for the canteen amounted to 2,000 fcs., and the Commanding-Officer and Doctor advanced to the existing canteen funds sufficient to bring them up to this figure.

Soon posters appeared at salient points in the village and the men read—

THE HORRORS OF WAR
very latest addition.

***

BEER-GARDEN
in M. Mesmacques' Pasture.

***

ATTRACTIONS.
BEER and other liquids.
MUSIC and other noises.
FAGS and other fuel.
DRAMAS and Eisteddfodau.
GAMES and other sports.
SWEETS and other silencers.
DANCING and other antics.
TINNED FOOD and other fodder.
BOXING and other combats.
EVEN SOAP.
LIBRARY, READING AND WRITING ROOMS,
RESTAURANT, GYMNASIUM AND MUSIC HALL
ALL IN ONE.
Bring your own Pots.

***

By the Blankth Scottish Battalion, the Blankth Blankety
Regiment.
ZUDAUSQUES, June, 1917.

***

The site chosen for the Beer-Garden was in a little wood. A huge marquee—the library, etc., advertised above—was erected on a grassy slope, and before it, in the middle of a clearing, was a concert-platform-boxing-ring with the piano beside it. For a dressing-room the artistes had to be content with a wigwam arrangement of draperies attached to the back of the piano.

The Beer-Garden was opened on 27 June. It was a success from the start and became the hub of the Battalion's social life.

The sub-committees worked hard to make things go and in the evenings, when digging was over for the day, the men lay on the grass, drank their ale and listened to the soloists or joined in the chorus of old favourites like " Brither Scots " and " Tipperary." When the Battalion moved unexpectedly on 30 June to a new billeting area at Esquerdes, four miles south, the Beer-Garden was re-opened there and continued to do a thriving trade, with great profit to the funds of the canteen.

Special mention must be made of one entertainment held in the Beer-Garden, for it was without doubt the most successful the Battalion ever had. The following poster advertised it :—

EISTEDDFOD,
to be held in the Beer-Garden on
Sunday, July 15, 1917.

Distinguished Patronage.   Eminent Adjudicators.

CONTESTS.

1. Male Voice Choirs.
Choirs from each company— twelve voices in each choir. Competitors to choose their own glee. Marks deducted for " Sweet and Low " and " The Soldier's Farewell."

2. Imitations of
            Charlie Chaplin.
Competitors are given permission to let their hair grow.

3. Whistling Solos.
Indents for bird-seed should be submitted at once to the Q.M.

4. Recitations.
As there is plenty of beer available the services of " Gunga Din " are not required.

5. Original Verses.
In " Limerick " or any other form. May—or may not— be read aloud. To be sent anonymously to the Secretary, Entertainment Committee, at the Orderly Room, on or before July 13. Prize-winners must acknowledge their bantlings in public or lose their prizes.

6. Pianoforte Solos.
Operatic excerpts. Competitors should reconnoitre the piano before the attack for silent keys.

7. Female Impersona-
            tions.
Don't raid the clothes-lines. Costumes will be provided. Eve, even with foliage, is not eligible—that is, Adam's wife : the " Tatler's " Eve would be welcome.

8. Mouth-Organ Contest.
Three Scottish Melodies.

9. Comic Interludes.
Anything at all that is really funny.

THIRD BATTLE OF YPRES, 31 JULY, 1917.

Warblers, Barn-Stormers, Troubadours, Whistlers, Mounte-
banks, Spring Poets, Contortionists, Wine-Bibbers, Publicans
and Sinners. Now is your chance.

———

To conform with Brigade arrangements the Eisteddfod took
place on Saturday, 14 July, and not as stated on the poster.
There was no lack of entries for the various events and there
was much excellent fooling. The villagers turned up in force
to see the fun and those ladies amongst them who had given
the free run of their wardrobes to the female impersonators
must have been considerably astonished at the originality displayed by some of the competitors in their ideas of the way to
put on the more intimate garments. The Limerick competition
was particularly popular as it gave the poets a chance to be both
scandalous and insubordinate without laying themselves open
to uncomfortable consequences. Perhaps it is as well that the
only Limerick which has survived is that written by Scott
Macfie himself as a model for those with a lesser knowledge of
scansion and rhyme.

> Our Chief is a Colonel called Davidson,
> Who asked " Here's a franc—if I gave it, son,
> " Would you squander the treasure
> " On women and pleasure
> " Or would you be wiser and save it, son?"

On 2 July the digging of the Brigade trenches was completed
and two days later training for the attack itself was begun in
earnest.

The plan of attack, so far as the 55th Division is concerned,
was as follows :—

At zero-hour two battalions of the 165th Brigade on the
right and two of the 166th Brigade on the left were to assault
the German front system of trenches and, when it was carried,
push on to the "Blue" Line, roughly a line drawn south-
east through the easterly edge of Chedder Villa and Bossaert
Farm, and there dig in. At zero, plus one hour fifteen minutes,
the remaining four battalions of these brigades were to go through
and capture the enemy's second-line system up to and including
the "Black" Line, immediately east of Canvas Trench, Wine
House and Capricorn Support. At zero, plus three hours thirty-
three minutes—or earlier if practicable—the left battalion of the
166th Brigade was to advance its left to seize Capital Trench.

This operation was to be carried out in conjunction with the 39th Division who were attacking on the north of the 55th. At zero, plus six hours twenty minutes, the 164th Brigade was to advance through the 165th and 166th and capture the enemy's rear defences as far as the " Green " Line, 1,500 yards farther on.

It will be seen that the attack was to be carried out in three main and one subsidiary bounds and that time was allowed for the cleaning up and consolidation of each position captured before the Division was committed to a further advance. Each successive advance was to be covered by the creeping barrage of the Divisional Artillery, and for the attack on the first objective the Brigade Machine-gun Companies and Trench-Mortar Batteries were also to give covering fire. If the operation was entirely successful it would mean that the enemy's defences would be penetrated to a depth of two miles.

In the 166th Brigade the task of delivering the first assault was entrusted to the 1/5th King's Own Royal Lancasters on the right and the 1/5th Loyal North Lancashires on the left. The advance to the " Black " Line was to be carried on by the 1/5th South Lancashires and the Liverpool Scottish.   The Scottish, therefore, had two objectives, first the " Black " Line and later Capital Trench, and they also had the difficult task of keeping touch on their left with the troops of another division.

On 4 July the Brigadier held a conference of officers, and afterwards the Battalion—in co-operation with the Brigade Machine-Gun Company and Trench-Mortar Battery—practised the attack over the prepared trenches. Each platoon was taken slowly over the ground representing its position in the attack and all points were explained to the men by their platoon-commanders. Training on these lines continued for two days and the fact that platoon-commanders were allowed to work out their own problems with their men and to see that each man thoroughly understood the details of the scheme from A to Z contributed in no small measure to the success of the operation when the time came to put theory into practice.

On 7 July a full-dress rehearsal was carried out by the whole Brigade with the co-operation of contact aeroplanes and tanks— of which two were attached to each battalion in the second phase. The barrage was represented by drums and Vérey lights Two further rehearsals were held, for the second of which, to approximate as nearly as possible to actual conditions, the Brigade paraded at night and attacked at dawn. Truly if any

hitch were to occur in the battle itself it would not be for lack
of forethought or training beforehand.

On 15 July a Brigade Church Parade was held at Quelmes,
near Zudausques, and this was followed by sports open to all
units of the Brigade. These provided the keenest competition
and after a ding-dong struggle the 1/5th South Lancashires beat
the Liverpool Scottish for the championship by the narrow
margin of three points.

On 20 July the Battalion said good-bye to Esquerdes and,
after marching to St. Omer, took train to Poperinghe. After a
few hours' rest there they went on in the evening and took over
the familiar trenches in front of Wieltje. The preliminary bombardment for the coming attack had begun the same day and the
enemy was replying with retaliatory fire on all roads and tracks
in the vicinity of Ypres. One heavy shell which fell right into
the middle of a platoon as it was crossing the Canal killed eight
men and wounded eight others and the platoon-commander,
Lieut. Greaves.

Further bad luck overtook the Battalion in the trenches
themselves. On the night of 21/22 July the enemy opened a
sudden and sustained bombardment with mustard-gas shells.
In spite of all precautions two officers and sixty-seven men had
to be evacuated to hospital. It was impossible to avoid
casualties in a heavy concentration of this gas. The box-
respirator protected the throat and eyes but the dense fumes
which hung about the trenches and shell-holes attacked the
skin—especially the softer parts of it—and caused painful sores.
In these circumstances the kilt is not an ideal garment. The
gas-shelling was repeated on the two following nights and
although it was not so heavy as before a number of men were
affected. On the morning of the 24th a severe barrage of high-
explosive shells fell on Bilge Trench and Garden Street and
besides doing much material damage, especially to the latter
trench, caused some casualties. Finally, when the Scottish had
been relieved by the 1/5th Loyal North Lancashires and one
company of the 1/5th King's Own on the night of the 24th, they
were again caught in a hail of mustard-gas shells near the Canal
Bank and suffered further loss. Altogether in these four days
the fighting strength was reduced by four officers and one
hundred and forty-one other ranks.

It had been originally intended that the attack should take
place on 28 July but as the French, who were co-operating by an
attack farther north, had not then completed their preparations

I

it was postponed until the 31st. On the 27th news was received that the enemy was reported to have withdrawn from his trenches on the left of the Divisional area, and the Battalion, which was busy at Derby Camp refitting, detonating bombs and getting all battle-stores ready for the show, was ordered to hold itself prepared to move at twenty minutes' notice. The next day, however, the enemy was found still to be holding his usual line and the Battalion was able to complete its final arrangements at leisure.

In accordance with general practice a nucleus of officers, non-commissioned officers and specialists was kept out of the attack. Of the four battalions in the 166th Brigade two were ordered to leave their commanding-officers behind; similarly in the companies fifty per cent. of the company-commanders and a diminishing percentage of junior officers, non-commissioned officers and men was left out. Lieut.-Colonel J. R. Davidson was one of the commanding-officers chosen to remain behind and he handed over the Battalion to Major J. L. A. Macdonald, H.L.I., his second-in-command.

THE THIRD BATTLE OF YPRES—
31 JULY, 1917

On 29 July all fighting stores were issued and at 8 p.m. the Battalion—25 officers and 475 other ranks—marched *1917* off by the tracks north of the Ypres-Poperinghe road to its assembly positions : " V " Company to cellars in Dixmude Street, " X " to the Kaaie Defences, " Y " and " Z " to Liverpool Trench and Congreve Walk, and Battalion Headquarters to a dugout in the latter trench. All companies were reported to have reached their positions by 12-50 a.m. and to have escaped casualties. The march had been a very exhausting one for the men, who were carrying two full days' rations in addition to all the paraphernalia incidental to a soldier's requirements in battle. But they were able to get a thorough rest both that night and the following day when movement of all sorts was restricted to the absolute minimum in order to lessen as far as possible the risk of detection by the enemy of the great concentration of troops.

At 5 p.m. on the 30th Battalion Headquarters went forward to Wieltje Dugout and at 8-30 p.m. the companies—after the issue of rations for an extra day, 1 August—moved up to the jumping-off trenches, " Y " and " Z " to Durham Trench, " V " and " X " to Bilge Trench, all being safely in before midnight. " X " Company found that immediately behind its portion of Bilge Trench there was a battery of heavy guns in action. They had practically nothing in the shape of camouflage to conceal their position, and the German gunners were making things hot for them and also for the infantry in the trenches near them. Captain Philpots, " X " Company's commander, realized that to occupy the section of trench allotted to him meant sacrificing a number of his men before the battle started, so with Captain Wall's permission he jammed them into that part of the trench occupied by " V " Company, not a popular move from the already over-crowded " V " Company's point of view but when the time came to go forward " X " Company was still intact. The actual hour of the attack had been kept secret, but at midnight word was received from Brigade that zero-hour was to be 3-50 a.m. and runners were at once sent out to the companies with the information. Owing to the night being an unusually dark one and to the congestion in the trenches it was fully two hours before all the companies were notified, but there was ample time left to make all final arrangements.

The Company-commanders, with the full approval of the Commanding-Officer, had arranged to take their men forward before zero-hour and to lie down in the open close behind the 1/5th Loyal North Lancashires. There were two good reasons for this manœuvre, first, that by this means the counter-barrage which the enemy was certain to lay down on our trenches as soon as the attack began would be avoided and secondly, that when the time came to go forward the Battalion would be square to its objective and would not have to waste time in the darkness and under shell-fire in checking its position and direction. The plan worked admirably. The companies left their trenches at 8 a.m. and took up their positions immediately behind Armitage Trench from which the Loyal North Lancashires were to attack. At zero-hour all companies followed the Loyals closely over no-man's-land and passed through their ranks while their mopping-up parties were dealing with such of the enemy as were still resisting in the front system of the German trenches. The Loyals made no mistake in their share of the morning's work and their quick success gave the Scottish a flying start.

About fifty yards beyond the German support-line—Call Reserve—a halt was made for reorganization and to allow platoon-commanders to check their direction by compass-bearing. Casualties so far had been negligible in numbers but " Z " Company had had the bad luck to lose its Company-Commander and No. 13 Platoon-Commander with both his serjeants, who were all hit by the same shell before they reached the enemy's front line.

After checking its position the Battalion moved forward in artillery formation under the protective barrage to the " Blue " Line and from this point it will be more convenient to follow the fortunes of each individual company.

" Y " Company, the left front company, reached the " Blue " Line with a loss of only three men and there extended into two lines and waited for the barrage to lift. On going forward no contact could be made with the 39th Division on the left, and to cover this flank No. 12 Platoon was brought up from support to extend the line northwards as was No. 6 Platoon of " X " Company shortly afterwards. A certain amount of fighting took place before the Steenbeek was reached. A machine-gun was captured at Vanheule Farm and several prisoners were taken from concrete dugouts. Only in one of these did the enemy show fight and the whole garrison of twenty to thirty were killed. The Germans were seen to be retiring from trenches on the left— out of the Battalion's area—and many of them were accounted for by the rifle and Lewis-gun fire of Nos. 6 and 12 Platoons. As the 39th Division troops had not yet got up it was necessary for the safety of the left flank to secure Canteen Redoubt, although it was not on the Company's front. This was done fairly easily by No. 10 Platoon and only two of the garrison escaped to St. Julien. Touch was at last established with the 11th Sussex on the left by a liaison-patrol sent out by No. 12 Platoon, and the Company without further trouble reached the Steenbeek which it was feared might be a formidable obstacle. Six light bridges had been carried up in case the stream should prove too wide or deep to jump or ford, but these were not required nor were any wire-entanglements encountered, the barrage had eliminated them. "Y" Company, therefore, was able to push on at once towards its objectives—Canvas Trench, Canvas Redoubt, and Wine House. No. 9 Platoon was held up by machine-gun fire from Wine House but, with the assistance of a platoon of "X" Company and some men from No. 10 Platoon, forced the enemy to retire and gained its objective. Canvas Trench and Redoubt were taken without resistance and by 7 a.m. "Y" Company had secured all its objectives. Its total losses so far amounted only to one officer and twenty men wounded. No. 8 Platoon of "X" Company which was acting as moppers-up to "Y" Company, and had already dealt with several dugouts between the "Blue" Line and the Steenbeek, proceeded to clear Canvas and part of Capital Trenches and collected a further fifteen prisoners. The remaining platoons of "X" Company, No. 5 and part of No. 7, got rather too far to the right during the advance and joined "V" Company.

So much for the left companies.

"Z" Company—the right front company—reached the Steenbeek with but little opposition and in touch with the 1/5th South Lancashires on its right. Like "Y" Company it found the stream easily passable, but there was some delay in getting across and the barrage got away and could not be caught up. Soon after crossing the Steenbeek heavy machine-gun fire was encountered from the neighbourhood of Capricorn Trench and from the right flank, and it became necessary to advance by single section rushes under cover of the fire of the remainder. By this means considerable progress was made, but at heavy cost, and when at last the Company got near its objective—Capricorn Trench—it found that the wire had escaped the preliminary bombardment and no gaps were to be seen. In face of this obstacle and the machine-guns in the trenches a frontal attack was out of the question and the only hope of securing the objective was that a Tank should come along and break down the wire. " Z " Company accordingly took what cover it could and awaited developments.

The supporting company, " V," had suffered very severely during the shelling with mustard-gas on 21/22 July and the following nights and its total available strength for the attack was only 4 officers and 55 other ranks, amongst whom were no corporals and only 2 serjeants. Its numbers were further reduced by No. 4 Platoon being detached to act as moppers-up to " Z " Company. This platoon did good work in clearing gun-emplacements and dugouts north of the Grafenstafel Road near the Steenbeek. Eight prisoners were taken from the emplacements, and the occupants of the dugouts—who refused to give themselves up—were bombed out and bayoneted.

The other three platoons in support of " Z " Company reached the Steenbeek almost intact but then came under heavy machine-gun fire from Capricorn Trench and Spree Farm. Here a message was received from " Z " Company-Commander, 2nd Lieut. Mackay, the only officer unhit, that he was held up and required reinforcements. 2nd Lieut. B. P. Gallop, after a personal reconnaissance, took " V " Company up by section rushes until it, too, was checked by the uncut wire. Shortly afterwards Tank F 38—one of the two detailed to assist the Battalion—came in sight, and a message was sent back to it that its help was needed. At once it made for Capricorn Trench across which, after breaking a gap in the wire, it settled down to silence the enemy machine-gunners. Immediately afterwards it received three direct hits from a field-gun and was disabled. " Z " and " V " Companies followed the tank closely through the gap in the wire and entered the trench. A number of prisoners were taken here and in Capricorn Support but there was little real opposition. Two of the prisoners were Red Cross men and were kept to attend to our wounded, the stretcher-bearers of both " Z " and " V " Companies having become casualties. The greater part of the garrison of Capricorn Support tried to escape to the south, but ran into the South Lancashires and were captured by them. By 7-45 a.m. all the objectives of the right companies were in their hands.

The work of consolidation was now begun and—as in the

attack itself—the conditions on the left and right of the Battalion front were quite dissimilar and this operation, too, will, for convenience, be divided into two parts.

On the left, " Y " Company, as soon as it had reached its objectives, started to dig in and two strong-points were begun, one just to the north-east of Wine House and one in Canvas Redoubt. Owing to the broken condition of the ground due to the bombardment the latter could not be made, and portions of the original trenches of the redoubt were cleared and manned.

At 7-40 a.m. a further advance was made to secure the final objective. This task had been allotted to " X " Company, but its numbers were by this time insufficient and it was reinforced by No. 10 Platoon of " Y " Company. During this advance a party of sixty to seventy Germans was observed forming up east of Spree Farm, evidently in preparation for a counter-attack. Nos. 8 and 10 Platoons hurriedly lined Capital Trench and opened fire on them. Many were seen to fall and after several attempts to re-form the survivors broke and ran, providing some very pretty shooting as they made for cover. The consolidation of the final objective was now begun but was seriously hindered by machine-gun fire from Border House and by snipers firing from shell-holes who were very difficult to locate. A number of the Scottish were hit, but before long Tank F 36 came on the scene and disposed of the machine-guns in Border House, whose garrison bolted and were nearly all brought down. The tank then turned south to patrol the Battalion's front but stuck helplessly in the mud, signalled " out of action " and was abandoned by the crew, but Captain Philpots salved its Lewis-gun ammunition. The crippling of the tank gave fresh heart to the enemy snipers, who re-opened their harassing fire, but in spite of it a line was dug from north-east of Wine House towards Border House and posts were also established in Capital Trench. About noon enemy aeroplanes came over the position, flying very low, and evidently were able to locate exactly the disposition of the left companies for very shortly heavy and accurate fire was opened by 4·2 and 5·9-inch howitzers. The garrison of the strong-point north-east of Wine House was temporarily shelled out and joined No. 10 Platoon in Canvas Redoubt, but returned later to its own position.

The right companies, " Z " and " V," had orders to dig a strong-point east of Capricorn Support but, owing to the fact that both companies had already incurred severe casualties, this proved impracticable in face of the heavy machine-gun fire which was directed upon them from Capricorn Keep. The two officers left, 2nd Lieuts. B. P. Gallop and H. Mackay, decided therefore to make Capricorn Trench their main line of resistance and to establish forward posts in Capricorn Support, which was a shallow and poorly-constructed trench quite unsuitable for defence. Capricorn Trench had escaped the preliminary bombardment almost entirely and little work was needed to convert selected parts of it into a sound defensive line. The decision to consolidate in a ready-made trench was justified as the low-flying enemy aeroplanes which had easily located the new works on the left of the Battalion's front seem to have had difficulty in observing which parts of Capricorn Trench and Support were held by us, and the right companies were not seriously troubled by hostile shell-fire until 2 August.

Battalion Headquarters, as soon as the " Blue " Line was taken, moved in accordance with orders from the Wieltje dugout to Bossaert Farm. This proved to be a very unsuitable position and a headquarters was established instead in a shell-hole about 100 yards east of the Steenbeek.

About 10 a.m. the 164th Brigade troops passed through the Battalion on their way to attack the " Green " Line. Though much reduced by casualties they reached their objectives after heavy fighting, but a counter-attack which drove back the Division on their left, and another later which developed simultaneously against both their left and right flanks, compelled this Brigade to withdraw fighting to the " Black " Line, where as many as possible of the survivors were collected and kept to increase the garrison.

After the failure of the attack on the " Green " Line orders were received that the " Black " Line would now become the main line of resistance of the Division and must be held at all costs against counter-attack.

At 4 p.m. Battalion Headquarters moved forward again and occupied a strong-point, dug by the Royal Engineers, north of Wine House, in order to strengthen the garrison of what appeared the more exposed flank of the Battalion.

Late in the afternoon a considerable body of the enemy, estimated at about one thousand, was seen advancing in artillery formation over a ridge about a mile away. When they had approached to within 600/700 yards of our positions rifle and Lewis-gun fire was opened on them and they halted and attempted to dig in, but with the assistance of the Divisional Artillery they were dispersed.

At dusk the 1/5th Loyal North Lancashires, who had dug in on the " Blue " Line, came up close behind the Scottish and dug supporting-points which they occupied. The line now appeared strong enough to deal with any counter-attack which might be launched against it, but at about 9-30 p.m. a message was received that the 39th Division on the left was retiring and some anxiety was felt about the security of this flank. To cover it No. 12 Platoon sent out a strong patrol in front and also established a new post on the left towards St. Julien. It was not until dawn on 2 August that touch was again established with the 11th Sussex who had re-occupied their positions during the previous night.

31 July had been dry during the early part of the day and in the attack the men had had the advantage of firm ground over which to advance, but towards noon the rain came down in sheets and continued throughout the whole of the night and the next day. By the evening of 1 August the new trenches had filled with water and were falling in as there was no means of draining them and no revetting material to hold them together. It was impossible to allow the men to remain in them any longer and it became necessary to reorganize the line. All the men were brought back from the advanced positions on the left, and the German trenches in Canvas Redoubt and Trench were put in a state of defence, some posts still remaining in Capital Trench. Battalion Headquarters, which was flooded out of its strong-point near Wine House, moved to Capricorn Trench.

On both 1 and 2 August the enemy attempted to form up in front of the Battalion but was dispersed—before any actual attack could develop—by the harassing fire of the artillery which continually searched those areas where the preliminary concentration of troops was likely to occur.

Rations reached the Battalion on 2 August and were very welcome. Not that any man had actually gone short of food or water, but the stocks were beginning to run low. " Z " and " V " Companies were lucky enough to find in Capricorn Trench a large number of full soda-water bottles which had evidently formed part of the German trench-stores.

During the night of the 2nd the S.O.S. twice went up on the 39th Divisional front and the Battalion made ready to meet a counter-attack, but no action developed on its sector.

The Scottish were relieved by the 11th Inniskilling Fusiliers in the early hours of 3 August and moved back by platoons to Liverpool and Bilge Trenches. After resting during the day they went on the same night to Ypres and entrained for Vlamertinghe where they bivouacked.

The success of the attack demonstrated very clearly the value of the preliminary training which had been carried out at Esquerdes. Every man had in his head a mental picture of the ground over which he would advance and of the position of the objective of his own particular platoon and company. This familiarity on the part of all ranks with every detail of the attack was one of the principal factors in its successful issue. The enemy as he was forced back from each successive position deliberately left snipers behind him in shell-holes and hedges— and stout fellows they must have been. "X" Company combed two of them out of a tree with a Lewis-gun. Their duty was to pick off leaders. As a result the casualties amongst officers and senior N.C.O.'s were severe, and by the time the objective was reached several corporals and lance-corporals—in one case even a private—found themselves in command of platoons. If these men had not had an accurate idea of exactly what was required of them confusion and failure must have resulted. They all rose magnificently to the occasion and took charge of their men like seasoned commanders. Let us hear a little of what one corporal of "Z" Company has to say in his official narrative of his part in the business.

"3-50 a.m. Barrage opened. All section in fine spirits. "Gave strict instructions to same to pay strict attention to "orders. 3-51 a.m. Mount parapet and follow closely on "L.N.L. The whole platoon kept excellent line until making "L.R.B. Cottage. Was still then in direct touch with platoon "officer who gave orders to settle down until further orders. "3-56 a.m. Order from platoon officer to move forward. "Section still well in good command. Passed over front system. "Was in touch with platoon officer (now lost as regards time). "Clear of front system but think I am going too much to the "right. Come across enemy sniper in shell-hole shamming "death, with full equipment and rifle. Put sniper out and also "find another and shoot the same . . . a lot of casualties "occurring from machine-gun on right. Marked spot and get "into action with rifle-grenades. . . . Came up to platoon "officer. Same gave me right direction and gave me orders to "try my hand with resisting machine-gun. Call my squad "together—still intact. Get into ditch and make for machine-

" gun. Arrive at machine-gun, still under cover in ditch.
" Machine-gun still firing overhead. Arrive at machine-gun
" house minus squad. Was preparing to bomb machine-gun
" when South Lancs. bomber arriving simultaneously put him
" out (*how tiresome*). Asked had he cleared dugouts. No.
" Was then joined by ' Y ' Company bomber. Together we
" cleared two dugouts, 15 Bosches getting away from dugout in
" rear. Fire on same, dropping 7 or 8 between us. . . .
" Company then steadily going forward. . . . Get two
" prisoners out of near dugouts of Farm. Dressed wounded
" prisoner and South Lancs. man. Carry on to join Company.
" Came up with Company about 50 yards our side of Steenbeek.
" Carry on then in short rushes to objective. . . . My section
" then intact. Platoon officer casualty. Get into Capricorn
" Trench. Asked C.S.M. if anybody has got in touch on left.
" No. Collect bombing squad and work to left. Then in direct
" touch with South Lancs. on right. Work about 100 yards to
" left. Further progress impossible. Trench bashed in so far.
" Come back and report all clear but nobody in touch. Then
" go up right hand C.T. with squad. Reach Capricorn Support,
" thus making all objectives gained. . . . Arrange with South
" Lancs. officer for squad to work along road and meet me on
" left. Send down to Capricorn Trench for Lewis-gun. Get
" same into position and report back to Mr. Mackay. Front all
" clear. Enemy still holding Capricorn Keep. . . . Come in
" with Mr. Gallop fixing post at junction of Capricorn Support
" and C.T. Good posts established by officers along whole line.
" Get in touch with ' Y ' Company on left. Enemy reported to
" be holding Support Line to right. Collect squad again and
" work up same, Mr. Mackay accompanying same. . . . No
" enemy in Capricorn Support. Salve two Lewis-guns from
" Capricorn Support and made block and left sentries. . . ."

Quite a busy morning !

The casualties in the battle were—4 officers and 51 other
ranks killed or died of wounds, 8 officers and 172 other ranks
wounded, and 6 men missing. A heavy price to pay even for
such a success, but the Battalion had the satisfaction of
knowing that it had caused the enemy much heavier permanent
losses than its own and squared the long-overdue account for
Guillemont.

But there was one who gave his life in this action of whom
it can be said, without offence to the memory of the other
gallant dead—for they would understand and themselves be the
first to agree—that no punishment inflicted on the enemy could

ever be a just compensation for his loss. In the manner of his passing he overtopped even his own past record of courage and self-sacrifice, and the Bar to the Victoria Cross awarded to him posthumously was a fit reward only because there is no higher distinction. Captain Noel Godfrey Chavasse, while carrying a wounded man to his dressing-station early on 31 July, was himself severely wounded on the right side of the head. The other officers implored him to go back and have his wound attended to, but he refused. The next day he was again hit, this time on the left side of the head. Still he insisted on carrying out his duties and he did not confine his work to those men who were brought to the dressing-station he had established in a dugout in the captured German trenches. He repeatedly went out with stretcher-parties to the firing line in search of wounded and to dress those lying out, and he personally assisted in carrying in under heavy fire a number of badly wounded men who were found in the open. Though suffering intense pain he continued for two days to attend to casualties, and during this time he had no rest and very little food. At last, on the morning of 2 August, as he was dressing a wounded man, a shell pitched right into his dressing-station and he received a terrible wound in the body. He was taken at once to hospital at Brandhoek and an operation was performed, but his case was hopeless and he died on 4 August.

It is difficult to find words to express all that " The Doc's " life and example had meant to the Liverpool Scottish. There never was a man who was better loved by officers and men alike ; there never was a man who gave himself more unsparingly in the service of others. His bravery was not of the reckless or flamboyant type but the far finer bravery that sprang from his determination that nothing should stand in the way of whatever he considered his duty. More than once he was offered the less dangerous work at a Casualty Clearing Station or Field Hospital to which his long service as a regimental medical officer entitled him, but he preferred to remain with the men he knew and admired. The award of two Victoria Crosses—a distinction gained by only one other—was the official recognition of his work ; the Battalion's is in the hearts of those who served with him.

Major J. L. A. Macdonald received the Distinguished Service Order for his fine work during the action.

Military Crosses were awarded to Captain J. A. Roddick, Captain W. E. Philpots, 2nd Lieut. B. P. Gallop, and 2nd Lieut. H. Mackay—the four officers in command of the companies

Capt. N. G. CHAVASSE, V.C. (and Bar), M.C.

when the objective was reached—to whose skilful leading and determination the success was largely due.   A Military Cross, too, was awarded to Company-Serjeant-Major D. A. B. Marples who very ably organized the defensive flank on the left of the Battalion's sector, and thus secured the position until the troops of the 39th Division were able to get up into line with the Liverpool Scottish.

Distinguished Conduct Medals were won by Company-Serjeant-Major J. H. Amos, who, when he was told that all his officers had become casualties, took command of the company and by his inspiring example got it forward to its objective and was himself one of the first to enter the German trench; and by Private W. Marsden, who did magnificent work with his Lewis-gun during the advance and afterwards kept it in action until the Battalion was relieved though all the remainder of his section had been killed or wounded.

Military Medals were won by the following :—Serjeants G. Codling and A. Stanley, Corporals W. Daw and A. F. Butterfield, Lance-Corporals W. A. Stone, W. S. Carlisle, F. Spargo, H. Lockwood and A. J. Milnes (attached A.P.M.), and Privates E. D. Blackburn, W. H. McClelland, P. Quinn, J. Holland, D. Butcher, J. Davies, W. Webster, C. Martin, W. L. Hunter and H. Braid (166th Trench Mortar Battery). Privates E. Herd and J. R. Pollock were awarded Bars to the Military Medals they had won at Guillemont and Hooge.

The number of the rewards is a sufficient indication of the behaviour of the men in the attack itself and during the equally trying period of consolidation and holding on which followed it, but a special word must also be given to the administrative branch—the Stores and Transport.   Their work, if not so spectacular, was as efficiently done as that of the fighting troops. To carry ammunition by day and rations by night on pack-mules to the firing line over shell-torn and unfamiliar country was no light task, but it was performed without fuss and without hitch in spite of heavy shelling and not a few casualties.

THE LAST OF THE SALIENT

On 4 August the Scottish left Vlamertinghe for Poperinghe and thence marched to Lee and Esk Camps near *1917* Watou. After two days' rest they set out for Abeele, three miles south, where they again took train, and after a weary night in the inevitable cattle-trucks reached Audricq at 6 a.m. on the 7th. Another short march followed by a journey in motor-buses brought the Battalion to its destination, Zouafques, a village in the wooded valley of the St. Louis River and near the main road from St. Omer to Calais. The next day Major-General Jeudwine inspected the 166th Brigade and congratulated all ranks on their splendid work on 31 July.

During the early part of August drafts of 7 officers and nearly 500 men joined the Battalion, most of whom had still to undergo their baptism of fire. Fortunately the Battalion had a full month at Zouafques to get these new hands thoroughly shaken down into the companies and to train them for the next task for which the Division was ordered to prepare itself. For the sake of the old hands, too, it was as well that so long a period of preparation was possible, as the training carried out at Zouafques was rather different from any previously undertaken.

Amongst the documents captured from the enemy during the first stages of the Third Battle of Ypres were very important orders by General Sixt von Arnim, commanding the 4th Army, on the construction of defensive positions. The Germans had found during the Battle of the Somme that their system of defence—holding in great strength continuous lines of trenches and providing deep dugouts to shelter the garrison during bombardment—had proved a failure. The trenches, very conspicuous from the air, were an easy target for artillery, and the deep dugouts—as soon as the British troops had learnt to follow the protective barrage closely—were mere death-traps for the defenders, as the attackers were on top of them before they had time to scramble out into the open. All group commanders in the 4th German Army, therefore, were ordered to discard the old method and reorganize their scheme of defence on the following lines. Instead of the stereotyped front, support and reserve trenches, a new system consisting of isolated shell-hole posts in the forward areas with strong-points for machine-gun nests and counter-attack troops behind them had to be constructed. All these new works had to be made, as far as possible, difficult of observation from the air. Only in the reserve positions, one or perhaps two miles behind the forward posts, was a continuous network of trenches allowed and even these had either to be on the reverse side of a slope or sited in such a way that they would not easily be identified. It will be realized that not only was this new system much more elastic than the old but the centre of gravity of the defence was entirely altered. Instead of the main resistance being concentrated in the front line it was now transferred far to the rear, and the farther an attack penetrated the greater would be the resistance it had to meet. The work of the British gunners was made immeasurably more difficult. Whereas formerly they had, before an attack, carried out destructive bombardments on easily observed trenches, they would in future have to attempt to knock out a number of almost invisible posts scattered over a wide area of ground. That many would escape altogether was certain and the attacking infantry would find themselves committed to the task of dealing in detail with hidden points of resistance and of meeting local counter-attacks from unsuspected places. Truly the war was becoming more than ever a platoon-commanders' war, for it would be on their initiative and determination that success would depend against a defence of this nature.

These changes necessitated modifications in the British method of attack and the training at Zouafques, while it did not neglect fundamentals such as route-marching and musketry, was principally confined to practice in semi-open warfare, and particular attention was given to the sort of problem that might confront the platoon-commander. On all exercises umpires were present, whose duty it was to spring surprises on the platoon as it was advancing. In this way the officers and N.C.O.'s learnt how to deal at once with any emergency and to launch immediate local attacks on the supposed machine-gun nest which was holding them up, or make instant dispositions to smash up counter-attacks from unlooked-for quarters.

This training culminated in a Divisional exercise on 10 September, when the Liverpool Scottish acted as a skeleton enemy against an attack by the 164th and 165th Brigades.

There were many pleasant interludes during this period of hard preparation for serious business. Outstanding amongst these were the distribution of medals on 2 September, following a Brigade Church Parade, to those who had won them in the last battle, and a most successful Divisional Horse Show on the 6th, at which relief from the drab monotony of khaki was given by the presence of a number of civilians and of English nurses from the hospitals in the neighbourhood. Then, as Calais was only a matter of ten miles away, many men were granted twenty-four hours' leave to visit it. A pleasing jaunt but unsettling ! When a man's name is far down the leave-roster it does not do him good to stand on the heights above Calais and see the white cliffs of Dover shining on the horizon. Nor does it help him to bear his lot with patience when he sees on the crowded evening beach the stalwarts of the R.A.S.C. and R.A.M.C. promenading with their lady friends. The members of these efficient corps are every bit as necessary to the successful prosecution of war as is the fighting soldier, but the poor infantryman may be forgiven if, in moments of bitterness, he sometimes referred to them as " Base stiffs."

On 8 September Lieut.-Colonel J. R. Davidson went to England on leave. There the Liverpool Corporation claimed him and he returned to civilian life. Major J. L. A. Macdonald took over the Battalion. He had been in command during the fighting of 31 July to 3 August and the men had every confidence in him.

On 13 September the Scottish marched to Audricq and took train to Goldfish Château, between Vlamertinghe and Ypres. The next night they relieved the 2/6th Gloucesters in the line, two companies being in the front line and two with Battalion Headquarters in Call Reserve. There was nothing like a trench line in the forward areas, the men in the advanced positions holding a line of shell-hole posts and those in support occupying old German concrete dugouts and gunpits. The weather had been very wet and the condition of the ground was indescribable. The surface was one lake of liquid mud and to move from one place to another, especially at night, was a matter of great difficulty. The duckboard tracks were greasy with mud and water, and a man who slipped and fell off was sure of a soaking. If he was unlucky enough to fall at a place where the track spanned or skirted a shell-hole he ran a real risk of being drowned unless his friends got hold of him at once.

Here the Battalion was entrusted with the execution of a minor enterprise which, on such sodden ground, proved anything but easy. The enemy was holding several posts on the banks of the little river Hanebeek which were likely to prove troublesome to the left flank of the attackers when the time came for

THIRD BATTLE OF YPRES, 20 SEPTEMBER, 1917.

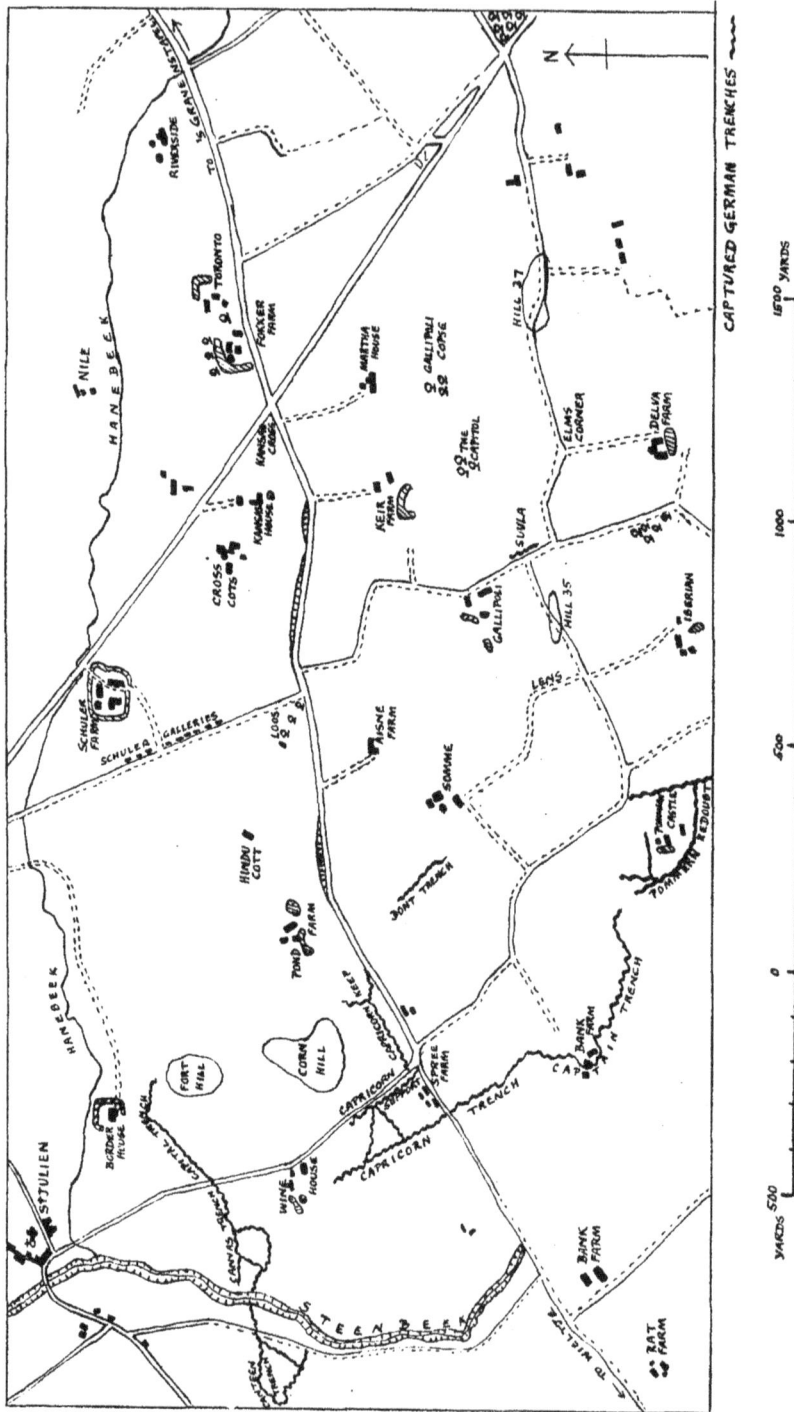

CAPTURED GERMAN TRENCHES

the Division to assault. " V " Company was detailed to capture
these posts, and on the night of the 15th sent out a strong patrol
to reconnoitre them and secure them if possible. As it was a
matter of some difficulty to locate even one's own posts in the
forward areas, it is not surprising that this patrol failed to
achieve its object. Nor was a second patrol the following night
any more successful, but a third attempt was made on the 17th
and the positions were taken after some fighting. Private
G. L. Jones distinguished himself by searching for four hours
that night and, though in full view of the enemy, for the whole
of the following day for a wounded officer and man who were
lying out, and received the Military Medal. Both were
eventually brought into our lines. Our casualties during these
three nights amounted to two men killed and one officer and
twelve men wounded.

In this little affair no prisoners had been taken but while
the raid was in progress two of the enemy were driven into one
of the Battalion's forward posts by the British artillery barrage
and provided useful identification.

On the night of the 17/18th the two companies in Call
Reserve were relieved and marched to L4 Post near Ypres,
where they were joined the next night by the remainder of the
Battalion.

While the 55th Division had been resting in the Recques
area two attempts had been made by other Divisions to continue
the advance, but both had failed, and except for a few minor
gains the line was substantially as it had been on 4 August.
The objective now given to the Division was that " Green " Line
which the 164th Brigade had taken but failed to hold seven
weeks before, and the attack was entrusted to the 164th Brigade
on the left and the 165th Brigade on the right, each brigade
having as immediate supports a battalion of the 166th Brigade,
the 1/5th Loyal North Lancashires and 1/5th King's Own
Royal Lancasters, respectively. The assembly position allotted
to these supporting battalions was the original German front
line, and behind them the remainder of the 166th Brigade—the
Liverpool Scottish and 1/5th South Lancashires—under their
own Brigadier, formed the Divisional Reserve.

On the night of 19 September the Battalion moved up in
heavy rain to its assembly position, Liverpool and Bilge
Trenches and Congreve Walk. It looked as though the weather
would be on the side of the enemy—and how many times the
elements seemed to take a fiendish pleasure in fighting against

K

us—but during the night the rain stopped and the day of the attack dawned fine but overcast. At 5-40 a.m. the protective barrage added its weight to the intense bombardment of the heavier guns which had been firing continuously since 3 a.m. the previous day, and the assaulting waves of the 164th and 165th Brigades went forward. At 11-30 a.m. the Scottish received orders to be ready to move at fifteen minutes' notice and at 2 p.m. two companies, " V " and " Z," under the command of Captain R. T. Ainsworth, were placed at the disposal of the 164th Brigade and ordered to take up a position in and about the British front line astride the Wieltje-Gravenstafel Road, and to hold it at all costs in the event of a counter-attack by the enemy breaking through the forward brigade. " V " Company established itself in front of Fort Hill, and " Z " Company on its right from the Wieltje-Gravenstafel Road to Somme. As these companies remained under the orders of the 164th Brigade until the Division was relieved it will be more convenient to follow their fortunes during the next few days and return to the Battalion itself afterwards.

" V " Company was disposed with two platoons—Nos. 1 and 3—in front of Fort Hill, No. 2 Platoon at Cornhill strong-point, and No. 4 in shell-holes immediately to the right of Hindu Cott. " Z " Company placed two platoons—Nos. 13 and 16—in shell-holes and old dugouts near Dont Trench on the south side of the Gravenstafel Road about 100 yards east of Capricorn Keep, and two—Nos. 15 and 14—to the left and right of Somme. The farmhouse which was Somme had been flattened by shell-fire, but the enemy had reinforced the cellar roof and turned it into a strong redoubt. No. 15 platoon-commander, who made it his headquarters, noticed that the steel rails which roofed the cellar were stencilled " Darlington, 1904," and felt safer !

By the morning of the 21st the 164th Brigade had consolidated its gains of the previous day and there was not the same risk of the enemy breaking through the line. The rôle of the two supporting companies of the Scottish was therefore changed, and they were ordered to be in readiness to deliver local counter-attacks on any part of the line where they might be required if the enemy secured a footing in the positions of the 164th Brigade advanced troops. About 6 p.m. a very heavy bombardment was laid down by the enemy and reports were received that he was seen to be massing for a counter-attack. This soon developed and was delivered with great dash but in only a few places did he break into the forward positions and he was quickly pushed out again by the troops on the spot. " V " and " Z " Companies were not called upon but after the attack had been repulsed some slight modifications were made in their dispositions. No. 3 Platoon of " V " Company moved forward to a new position about 100 yards to the rear and on the left of Schuler Galleries, and No. 1 Platoon which had been withdrawn earlier in the day to behind Fort Hill occupied the position vacated by No. 3 Platoon. The only alteration in " Z " Company's dispositions was that No. 15 Platoon was ordered to move to Aisne. Though Aisne was only a matter of a furlong away from Somme the fact that the move to it had to be carried out by compass-bearing is a fair illustration of the churned-up state of the ground and of the difficulty of keeping direction in such a maze of shell-holes over even such a short distance. A trench was dug on the left of the farm and the farmhouse itself which was in fair condition and gave good shelter was used to house the men off duty. It was a strongly-built place and seven direct hits from 8-inch shells which it received on the 23rd did no more than knock chips off it.

On the 22nd two platoons of the 2/6th North Staffordshires were placed at the disposal of Captain Ainsworth and dug in in the neighbourhood of Fort Hill.

With the exception of heavy shelling, particularly before dawn and at dusk, the remainder of the stay was without incident and these two companies were relieved on the night of 23/24 September by two companies of the 2/5th North Staffordshires and returned to Vlamertinghe. In spite of the heavy and accurate shelling casualties in both companies were miraculuosly light. The officers spoke in the warmest terms of the behaviour of the men, many of whom had not been under fire before. One act of gallantry must be set down. When No. 2 Platoon took up its position at Fort Hill it found in a shallow trench a Lancashire Fusilier badly wounded in the right arm. He had lost a good deal of blood and was so weak that he could not stand. Lance-Corporal Gilbride volunteered to take him to the dressing station and, carrying him over his shoulder the whole way, brought him safely there through very heavy shelling.

Now to return to the Battalion (less " V " and " Z " Companies) whom we left in Bilge and Liverpool Trenches.

20 September passed without incident until at 7 p.m. orders were received that the Scottish must be ready to move at a moment's notice. At 8-30 p.m. further orders came in that the Battalion was now attached to the 165th Brigade and shortly

afterwards the Commanding-Officer, Major J. L. A. MacDonald, was instructed to report with his men to Lieut.-Colonel Drew, commanding the 1/9th King's Liverpools, at Bank Farm. Here the Battalion was provided with guides and ordered to proceed to Hill 37 and (1) make a strong-point in rear of the forward positions and (2) get in touch with the front line and reinforce it where required. All went well until the column had passed Gallipoli about 12-40 a.m. Here the guides confessed that they were totally lost. As the ground was simply a mass of shell-holes and all landmarks had been obliterated there was nothing particularly surprising in this, clear starlight night though it was. The really surprising thing during the Third Battle of Ypres was that anyone ever found his way anywhere at night in the forward areas. There was nothing for it but to get the Battalion into what cover it could find and to reconnoitre. The Commanding-Officer and Captain A. G. Davidson set off to explore and in half-an-hour's time identified Elms Corner. The Battalion was then brought forward and ordered to consolidate shell-holes—" X " Company about Elms Corner facing east and " Y " Company about the south end of Keir Farm Dugouts facing north-east. Battalion Headquarters occupied shell-holes at Elms Corner.

The 21st passed quietly enough except for sporadic shelling but the number of enemy aeroplanes flying low over the position suggested trouble brewing. About 5 p.m. a message was received by visual from the advanced troops—the 1/5th South Lancashires—that the enemy was massing for a counter-attack, and the Scottish were ordered to reinforce the front line at once if the S.O.S. was sent up. Hill 37, the highest ground in the neighbourhood, was the key to the whole position. It had changed hands more than once the previous day and if the enemy intended to recover the ground he had lost it was essential that he should first retake the hill. At 6-30 p.m. he laid down a terrific barrage and the S.O.S. at once went up from Gallipoli Copse and Keir Farm. The Scottish immediately dashed forward, " X " Company on the right and " Y " Company on the left of the hill. It was as well that they had been forewarned to be ready to move instantly for within a few moments the enemy barrage came down on the positions they had just vacated. The low-flying aeroplanes had not wasted their time.

" X " Company advanced to within 100 yards of the front line and lay down in readiness to counter-attack. The South Lancashires, however, gave the enemy a rough reception and by 8 p.m. things were quiet again. Two platoons of " X " Company,

Nos. 5 and 8, were withdrawn to their original positions, while the remainder of the company, under Lieut. H. A. Bardswell, moved forward to the front line on the hill and reinforced the South Lancashires, who by this time were running very short of ammunition and also had had two Lewis-guns put out of action. They gave a warm welcome to Nos. 6 and 7 Platoons who were able to replace the damaged guns and hand over their spare bandoliers to the garrison.

" Y " Company was divided. Nos. 9 and 11 Platoons, under Lieut. C. M. Barber, advanced on the left of Hill 37 and took up a position on the left of the South Lancashires towards Gallipoli Copse which the 1/5th Loyal North Lancashires were holding. Nos. 10 and 12 Platoons, under Lieut. McCullough, moved half-left and lay down 50 yards behind Keir Farm to reinforce the Loyals. Like the South Lancashires they had beaten off the attack and, after a personal reconnaissance, Lieut. McCullough took his two platoons back to their shell-holes.

The remainder of the night and, for the most part, the 22nd were quiet, but the low-flying aeroplanes gave trouble by bombing and machine-gunning the support-positions. One attempt during the day at a counter-attack was smashed by the artillery but the movement of troops in the German lines gave Nos. 9 and 11 Platoons an opportunity to do some satisfactory execution. They were themselves subjected to a certain amount of sniping from the direction of Cross Cots but it was mostly ineffective. At dusk No. 9 Platoon moved to the left and occupied a strong point named the Capitol, where they were in direct touch with the 1/5th Loyal North Lancashires, and the Divisional line was then continuous throughout and connected up with the division on the right.

On the afternoon of the 22nd the Heavy and Divisional Artillery gave the troops a memorable display of fireworks by laying down, at 4 p.m. and 6 p.m., two intense practice barrages in which nothing could possibly have lived. The enemy's reply, heavy though it was, seemed a tame affair by comparison and caused no casualties.

The Battalion was relieved without incident at midnight on 22 September by the 2/6th North Staffordshire Regiment and after assembling at St. Jean proceeded on the light-railway to Goldfish Château.

Casualties during the battle amounted to eleven men killed and forty wounded and the Scottish counted themselves lucky to have got off so lightly.

Although there had been few opportunities for deeds of gallantry, six men particularly distinguished themselves and received the Military Medal—Serjeants J. Henshaw and G. Maxwell, Lance-Corporal M. Gilbride, and Privates H. Thompson, J. H. Donnelly and F. Child.

On 20 September for the first and only time throughout the war rations failed to reach the Battalion. It was not the fault of the Quartermaster's Stores or the Transport Section. In accordance with orders they delivered the rations at Wieltje Dugout and handed them over to the officer responsible for getting them forward to the troops. What happened to the carrying parties under his command is unknown. The officer lost his way—and perhaps his head—and the rations were never delivered. When, late at night, an urgent message was sent back to the Quartermaster asking what had become of them he and his Quartermaster-Serjeant lorry-hopped back to Wieltje Dugout from the transport lines and interviewed the wretched O.C. ration-parties. As he could not throw any light on the situation they took him with them and searched the countryside but not a bag could be found and, as a day's rations for a battalion cannot be conjured into existence at will, the men had to go hungry.

The Liverpool Scottish had now been in France two years and ten months of which time all but the odd ten months had been spent in or on the fringe of the Ypres Salient. It is believed that no other battalion in the Army can claim such a long period of service in what was generally admitted to be the worst portion of the whole front both as regards danger and discomfort. The Battalion was not disappointed to learn that its next tour of duty would be in a sector far from " Wipers."

EPÉHY, 30 NOVEMBER, 1917.

EPÉHY

1917

On 23 September the Battalion embussed at Vlamertinghe and went on to Watou where it was joined the following day by the two Companies—" V " and " Z "—which had been attached to the 164th Brigade and had spent an extra day in the line. On the 26th the move was continued and after a march to Proven a long train-journey southwards was begun which ended at 2 a.m. the next day at Miraumont, a town on the River Ancre five miles west of Bapaume. The Battalion immediately set out on foot eastwards and after five hours reached Beaulencourt, where it was billeted in wooden shacks. After resting for two days another easterly march, of fourteen miles, brought the Scottish to their destination, Villers-Faucon. The journey from Miraumont to the battle zone had been an interesting but terrible object-lesson in the destruction that war entails. The first stage had been over ground where the Battle of the Somme had raged twelve months before, and the second through country systematically stripped by the enemy during his great retreat in the Spring of 1917 of anything which might provide shelter or comfort for his pursuers. Every house and out-building had been destroyed, the orchards had been cut down and all streams and ponds had been poisoned or polluted. Not a thing was left intact or serviceable that might in any way have been of use to the British troops. The country was literally a desert for, of course, all the inhabitants had been evacuated. To find oneself in a part of France lacking *estaminets* was both novel and depressing.

The Battalion was not left idle long enough for the unpleasantness of its surroundings to affect its spirits for on the 30th it relieved the 15th Cheshires in the trenches in front of Epéhy.

The country was not unlike that around Rivière, but its ridges and hollows were more pronounced and it was intersected by a network of sunken roads. The Scottish held a front of 2,000 yards, too long to permit of anything like a continuous system of sentry-posts. Instead the forward platoons were concentrated in four localities, styled Ossus 1, 2, 3 and 4, connecting which there was a travel-trench, ungarrisoned and used simply as a means of communication. The right forward company had a platoon each in Ossus 1 and 2 and the other two at Holt's Bank—later they were moved to Kildare Post and Trench. Company-headquarters were at Lloyd's Bank. The left forward company similarly had platoons in Ossus 3 and 4 and the remainder with Company Headquarters in Pigeon Quarry. The support company was disposed with Company Headquarters and three platoons in Cox's Bank and one platoon in Pigeon Quarry, the reserve company was in a sunken road off Fallen Tree Road in front of Epéhy and Battalion Headquarters at the Adelphi. The siting of the trenches was unsatisfactory. From Ossus 1 there was a good field of fire and a clear view across the St. Quentin Canal towards the enemy's main line of resistance, the immensely strong Hindenburg Line, two miles away, but from the other front-line positions the garrisons could see little beyond their own barbed-wire entanglements, though the enemy's forward posts, on the west side of the Canal, were 700 to 1,000 yards from the Ossus line. The support positions of the right sub-sector were sited reasonably well but there had been little or no attempt to protect them with wire. The left supporting positions were thoroughly bad. Pigeon Quarry had only two exits, the narrow cart-track connecting it with the road behind and a goat-track up the side of the quarry which led to Wog Loop, a half-dug trench to the south of it. The quarry was a remarkable place and successive occupants had made it a really comfortable billet. It was very extensive and deep and a number of mine dugouts had been constructed below its eastern face which were fitted with bunks and were invulnerable to shelling. It boasted a bath-house with hot showers, most of the Battalion's cooking was done in it and the canteen was established in one of its dugouts. The draw-back from a military point of view was that owing to the scarcity of exits the occupants were bound to have a difficult time if they were compelled to attempt, under fire, to reach their battle positions in Wog Loop, but as the sector was a very quiet one this seemed an unlikely contingency.

The Battalion settled down in comparative peace to the dull routine of trench-warfare, and a programme of work was, by Brigade order, laid down which consisted almost entirely of trench-repair and maintenance. As the rainy season was approaching it was certainly desirable that the trenches should be put into such a state that they would be able to resist the weather, and much labour was expended on clearing the channels under the duckboards, digging sump-pits and revetting the fire-bays and communication-trenches. As things turned out the time would have been more profitably spent in digging and wiring strong-points behind the front line but there was a reason, which will appear later, why work on the rear positions was not allowed.

One curious thing about the Epéhy trenches was that they appeared to have attracted to them all the frogs in France. The Battalion had long looked on rats as a necessary evil but frogs were a new experience and nearly as unwelcome. By day they remained hidden in the trench drains and in out-of-the-way corners but at night they swarmed into the fire-bays and communication-trenches and became a general nuisance to all who had to walk the duckboards in the dark. To tread unexpectedly on a frog is disconcerting. It is as slippery as a banana-skin and makes an unpleasant popping sound if solidly stepped on which is distinctly unmanning. One hyper-sensitive subaltern when on trench-duty at night always insisted on his runner preceding him to clear the frogs from his path and when, one day, he found one in his newly-completed dugout he gave orders for the floor boards to be lifted and the frog removed before he would take possession. When his batman shortly afterwards produced the results of his labours, one hundred and fifty frogs in a sandbag, the subaltern was noticeably shaken and his friends declare that he has never been the same man since.

After relief by the 1/9th King's Liverpools on 13 October the Battalion spent ten days in reserve at Villers-Faucon. The usual training was carried out, and after the Brigade had been inspected by Major-General Jeudwine at Longavesnes on 19 October it took part the following day in a tactical exercise in semi-open warfare, of which Major-General Wright, of the United States Army, was an interested spectator.

The Scottish relieved the 1/7th King's in the same sector on the night of 28 October and began a tour of trench-duty which was to last for thirty-nine days. Such a long spell of duty would have been well-nigh impossible in the Salient but at Epéhy it was no great hardship, though the mental and physical inactivity imposed a severe strain on the spirits of the men. There was little shelling by the enemy, the trenches, thanks to the continuous work done on them, were dry and even in the front line every man when off duty had a bunk in a weatherproof shelter in which he could rest comfortably—when the lice which infested the dugouts would allow him. Regular inter-company reliefs and good feeding kept the men from becoming stale, and if they became tired of even such a varied menu as was provided by the Quartermaster there were always plenty of partridges for those who liked them and could hit them. The really good shots made a regular income by selling them to the officers at a franc a bird.

It was remarkable how little the lives and habits of the wild things were affected by the war. Dïd not Captain Cunningham once shoot a hare in no-man's-land at St. Eloi and were there not nightingales in Scottish Wood? Epéhy provided a novelty in the owl which settled on a Lewis-gun one night. This was an opportunity which Captain A. G. Davidson could not let pass and his intelligence report the following day read :—
" Last night the enemy's trained observer flew over to our lines
" and alighted on my No. 1 Lewis-gun. After a careful scrutiny of
" his surroundings and listening for some time to the conversation
" of the men he uttered a triumphant hoot and flew back to his
" own lines with the information obtained."

Battalion Headquarter officers were genuinely concerned at the inadequacy of the support positions on the left of the sector and the difficulty that would be experienced by the garrisons of Pigeon Quarry and Cox's Bank—which was merely a row of dugouts beneath the high easterly bank of a road—if they were called upon to man Wog Loop during a hostile attack. Permission was, therefore, sought of Brigade to concentrate work upon Wog Loop and the approaches to it but this was refused. The reason was not clear at the time but it was afterwards learnt that the Staff had in mind the great surprise attack opposite Cambrai and the simultaneous feint attacks which were to take place on 20 November and were anxious that the enemy should not see any new defensive positions behind the British front line which might indicate that there was no intention of advancing in that particular area and thus help him to discover what were the flanks of the attack proper. A suggestion that a tunnel should be dug from Pigeon Quarry to Wog Loop was also negatived for the time being, although this would have shown no surface alteration. It was not until 27 November that the Battalion was allowed to start the tunnel and to begin a defensive wiring programme and by then it was too late.

On 29 October the 55th Division took over an additional 2,500 yards of front at the northern end of the sector and was now holding a line almost seven miles in length with six battalions in the forward areas, two in support and one brigade in reserve.

It is outside the scope of this history to say more of the attack carried out on 20 November by the III, IV and VI Corps, with the co-operation of 380 Tanks and with four Cavalry

Divisions in reserve, than that it was a complete surprise to the
enemy and came within a hair's breadth of being as decisive a
success as it was spectacular. The right limit of the actual attack
was some miles north from the 55th Divisional sector, but the
Division was given the unpleasant task of making a holding
attack to engage the enemy's attention and reserves and to
deceive him as to the extent of the main operation. This was
carried out with great gallantry by the 164th Brigade against
two prominent features, the Knoll and Guillemont Farm,
opposite the Right Brigade sector and achieved its object. The
166th Brigade, on the left, co-operated by opening rapid fire from
its forward posts at zero-hour but otherwise took no active part
in the attack; 1,320 gas cylinders also were discharged against
selected areas in the German lines. On this brigade front the
enemy's reply was negligible and the Scottish escaped with
the loss of one man wounded. The resistance to the 164th
Brigade had, however, been severe and its casualties were so
heavy that it was withdrawn to reserve for reorganization and
its place was taken by the 165th Brigade which could not,
therefore, relieve the 166th Brigade in the line as was the original
intention. So far as relief within the Brigade itself was concerned the Scottish were at this time so much the strongest
battalion that there was no other that could have undertaken
the defence of the sector they held and their chances of being
relieved were therefore nil.

The Higher Command appear to have been convinced that
the great wedge driven into the enemy's line by the successful
attack to the north would compel him to adjust his dispositions
on its flanks and probably cause him to withdraw the troops
facing the 55th Division and the division on its left to new
positions in rear. The battalions in the line, therefore, were
ordered to be particularly vigilant and by constant patrolling
to keep in the closest touch with the enemy so that they might
be ready to move forward as soon as there was the slightest
suspicion that he had begun to withdraw. The Scottish night
and dawn patrols during the next week, however, consistently
brought in reports that the enemy was holding his forward
posts as usual and that the activity of his machine-guns against
no-man's-land during the night was no greater than was
customary. The only abnormal feature was that the amount of
movement heard behind his lines was much greater than it had
been before 20 November. This was confirmed by daylight
observers and might have been construed as preparation for
departure, though the fact that several hostile batteries were
seen taking up new positions hardly suggested withdrawal.

On 28 November a very decided change in the enemy's general attitude took place. The Scottish sector in the past had received very little shelling but on this day all the forward posts and the communication-trenches as far back as the Adelphi were at intervals subjected to fire from 4.2-inch howitzers.   The fire appeared to come from batteries which had not previously been active and the type of fire—airbursts with high-explosive shell—could mean one thing only, registration. A number of low-flying enemy aeroplanes, too, persistently reconnoitred the whole of the Divisional area.

Patrols that night still reported nothing unusual but the following day the registration was renewed, mostly by 77 mm. batteries on Targelle Valley and the posts in the vicinity and on the defences about Pigeon Quarry, but also by 4.2 howitzers on other points.   A heavy trench-mortar, too, spasmodically shelled the front line where it crossed Canongate but did no damage to trench or wire.

There was now not the least doubt in anyone's mind that an attack was imminent, and strict orders were sent out from Battalion Headquarters to all company-commanders that on no account must they dismiss their companies after morning stand-to unless they were satisfied that conditions were normal. They were also told that in the event of any enemy shelling whatsoever they must at once order their men to their battle positions.

The Divisional Commander was in entire agreement with the opinion of the officers in the trenches that an attack was coming and coming soon.   He personally reconnoitred the Divisional front and chose new positions for machine-guns from which they might be able to hold up any of the enemy who broke through the front line.   He had good cause to be anxious about the result of an attack in force.   Not only was his Division holding an unduly extended front but the greater part of his artillery and machine-guns had been taken from him and sent north to assist in the battle there.   It is believed that supporting the 166th Brigade there were only one 4.5-inch howitzer battery and one 18-pounder gun.

Some modifications in the general dispositions of the Division were also contemplated and the Liverpool Scottish were ordered, on the 29th, to send officers to reconnoitre the sector held by the 1/5th South Lancashires with a view to taking over from them at the earliest possible moment but, as will be seen, there was no time to carry out this relief.

On the night of 29/30 November the dispositions of the Division were :—

On the left the 166th Brigade with the 1/5th South Lancashires, 1/5th Loyal North Lancashires and Liverpool Scottish from left to right in the front line and the 1/5th King's Own Royal Lancasters in support.

On the right the 165th Brigade with the 1/6th, 1/5th and 1/7th King's Liverpools in the front line and the 1/9th King's in support.

The 164th Brigade was in Divisional reserve with the 1/4th Loyal North Lancashires—less one company at St. Émilie—at Vaucelette Farm, about two miles due west from Pigeon Quarry, the 2/5th Lancashire Fusiliers in Villers-Faucon and the remainder at Tincourt.

The Liverpool Scottish dispositions were as set down earlier in this chapter with " Z "—less one platoon—the left front, " V " the right front, and " Y " the support company. Two platoons from the company of the 1/5th King's Own in Limerick Post were also at the disposal of Lieut.-Colonel Macdonald for counter-attack purposes, but " X " Company, except for a strong Lewis-gun post near " V " Company's headquarters in Lloyd's Bank, was detached from the Battalion and was in Brigade reserve under the direct orders of the Brigadier-General. " Z " Company was below strength, as one of its platoons from Pigeon Quarry had been sent back a day or two before to the Divisional Reinforcement Camp to act as a demonstration platoon.

On the morning of 30 November the dawn patrols returned at 4-30 a.m. and reported that the enemy was unusually quiet. At 5 a.m. the Divisional Artillery opened a slow rate of fire against selected portions of the enemy's front line. This continued for an hour and provoked no reply whatever. The Battalion, which had stood to arms at 5 a.m., was ordered to stand down at 6-30 a.m. as the situation appeared perfectly normal. At 7 a.m. an intense barrage was opened by the enemy on all trenches and areas which he had registered on the two previous days. The S.O.S. was at once sent up by the forward companies and was repeated from the Adelphi by light signals and by wire. Almost immediately all telephone lines forward from Battalion Headquarters were broken by the shelling and as the enemy appeared to be using smoke-shell against the Pigeon Quarry area the visual station there could not be seen. From that time no messages were received from either " Z " or " Y " Companies. Four men, three of them wounded, got back to

Battalion Headquarters but it was not until after the war that anything was known of what had happened to these two companies. As their disappearance materially affected the fighting on the remainder of the Battalion's front it will be as well here to describe their doings.

The enemy's plan appears to have been to effect a quick break-through in great force on the front of the division on the left of the 55th and then to widen the gap by a flank attack on the 55th Division assisted by a simultaneous frontal attack all along its front.   The plan at first succeeded.   He quickly penetrated the front of the Division on the left—which also had a long line to hold with little artillery support—and part of his forces then turned south. The 1/5th South Lancashires, attacked both in flank and rear, disappeared to a man although they first put up a stout resistance.   The 1/5th Loyal North Lancashires fared little better when their turn came, but some of them succeeded in escaping to the south-west. This rapid rolling up of the battalions to the north of them left the flank of the Liverpool Scottish entirely exposed.

The bombardment on the Battalion's front continued without a break until 8 a.m. and was particularly violent on the positions, both front and support, on the left of the sector.   The support platoons in Pigeon Quarry, one each of " Y " and " Z " Companies, succeeded in getting out and into Wog Loop where they halted to reorganize before going on to reinforce the front-line posts. They were much harassed by low-flying enemy aeroplanes which attacked them both with machine-gun fire and bombs. A bomb from one of these aeroplanes had already destroyed a Lewis-gun team of " Z " Company which was occupying an enlarged shell-hole behind Wog Loop and which had attempted to bring the gun into action against them. Wog Loop, which was in parts only six inches and nowhere more than two feet deep, afforded poor cover and numerous casualties were suffered. The two officers, 2nd Lieuts. Gulick and Lowe, after sending runners forward—none of whom succeeded in getting through— to find out if the front line had been attacked, decided to push on. They had great difficulty in getting through a new belt of barbed-wire which had been put out in front of Wog Loop the previous night and by the time Ossus 4 was reached only 2nd Lieut. Lowe and 10 men were left, the remainder had all been killed or wounded. The barrage now lifted and the enemy was seen advancing over the high ground in front of Ossus 1 and 2.   No direct attack developed on Ossus 4 and fire was therefore brought to bear on the right flank to assist the defence there. The barrage had been particularly heavy on Ossus 3 which covered the Targelle valley. The post on the south side of the valley had been entirely obliterated and that on the north had fared little better. The destruction of the defences there had far-reaching results, as will be seen later. Meantime the enemy had broken through on the Battalion's left and was heard bombing his way along towards Ossus 4. A few moments later sounds of heavy firing and bombing were heard from the direction of Pigeon Quarry and the officers, after a consultation, decided that as the front line would soon be entirely surrounded the best thing to do was to attempt to reach the quarry and endeavour to hold it. This they set out to do but came under the fire of a machine-gun posted about the north-east corner of the quarry which forced them to turn north and seek what shelter they could on Canongate. While they were trying to locate this gun a large body of the enemy appeared behind them on the bank of the road and they had no choice but to surrender. Three officers and about 20 men, some of them wounded, were all that were left of four platoons. They were allowed to collect their wounded and then taken back to the German lines.

The three platoons of " Y " Company in the support dugouts at Cox's Bank were responsible for the garrisoning of Wog Loop and also a small trench on the south side of the road running east along the Targelle Valley. So heavy was the bombardment on Cox's Bank that the company-commander, Captain A. T. Salvidge, decided that to attempt to reach the battle-positions would entail too great a sacrifice of numbers and he therefore temporarily kept his men where they were in the hope that a lull in the shelling would give him a chance to get them forward later on. He posted a Lewis-gun team in a shell-hole on top of the bank to give warning of any approach of the enemy. This Lewis-gun did good work until it was knocked out. The first news that the front line was broken was brought by a number of gunners who, with their officer, came running down the Targelle Valley. They were the teams of two howitzers which were in action in a small quarry between Cox's Bank and the front line and which were firing not on the Divisional front but far to the north of it. These men reported that the enemy was close behind them and were kept by Captain Salvidge to strengthen his company. Almost at once the enemy appeared and while an attempt was being made, from the impossible position in which " Y " Company found itself, to deal with this flank attack another body of the enemy attacked from the north and took the company in rear, driving it back into its dugouts where the survivors were trapped and taken prisoners.

The "Z" Company headquarter details who, with the Battalion snipers and engineers, formed the garrison of Pigeon Quarry, put up a great fight. The first news they had of the breaking of the front line was brought by Serjeant Moody who managed to get back, wounded, from Ossus 3. A little later some stragglers and wounded—including 2nd Lieut. Gulick, carried in by Company-Serjeant-Major Gilbart—from Ossus 4 and Wog Loop came in and reported heavy machine-gun fire from both flanks. The wounded were taken for shelter to a dugout half-way up the chalk face of the quarry and shortly afterwards the few uninjured men were compelled to take refuge in the same dugout from the fire of two machine-guns which the enemy had posted on top of Cox's Bank. From this dugout the small party resisted for a long time all attempts to subdue them. Some Germans who had succeeded in entering the Quarry were forced— by long-range rifle-fire from the Scottish Battalion-headquarter details near the Adelphi—to seek cover behind a small cottage in the Quarry immediately to the north of the entrance. Here they were dealt with by the remnant of "Z" Company in the dugout. A number of the enemy, too, after taking Cox's Bank attempted to advance to the west. They, too, were held up and many accounted for. At last the enemy succeeded in getting on to the edge of the Quarry immediately above the dugout and by dropping bombs into the entrance kept the defenders quiet until other Germans worked their way along the goat-track to the dugout and forced the little garrison—only two of whom were unwounded—to surrender.

The wiping-out of these two companies left the remainder of the Battalion with a completely exposed flank and added immeasurably to the difficulties of holding an inadequately pre-pared and already undermanned position.

When the S.O.S. was sent up at 7 a.m. the two platoons of "V" Company in Kildare Post, according to their orders laid down in the Defence Scheme, at once counter-attacked towards Ossus 1. On reaching it they found that no enemy attack had developed and, leaving one platoon under Serjeant F. C. Pugh to reinforce the front line, Lieut. C. M. Barber withdrew the other to Dados Loop. At 8 a.m. the enemy attacked in great strength but was held up by uncut wire and by the fire of the platoons in Ossus 1 and 2 who did great execution. They reported later that the Germans came on in eight waves and that it was impossible to miss them. The platoon in Dados Loop opened fire on the enemy who were attacking the Bird-Cage on the front of the 1/6th King's, but Catelet Road and Ossus Wood

Road were both in dead ground from Dados Loop and down these the enemy advanced very quickly, the Lewis-gun team responsible for looking after this flank having been knocked out by a shell. About 8-30 a.m. two runners from the 1/6th King's reported to Lieut. Barber that the enemy had occupied Holt's Bank and was pushing on across Sprint Road. This officer at once disposed his platoon astride Sprint Road facing south to protect the right company from this out-flanking movement. About the same time the enemy was seen to be advancing in strength south from Cox's Bank, and Captain R. T. Ainsworth, commanding " V " Company, disposed his company-headquarter details from Lloyd's Bank across Sprint Road facing north to resist this threat to his left flank. The platoons in Ossus 1 and 2 meanwhile continued to hold the enemy on their front and also, by firing over the back of the trenches, helped to check those who were trying to work round behind them. A great deal of the credit for the magnificent defence put up by these front-line posts must be given to Serjeant F. C. Pugh who, by his energy and personal example, gave a splendid lead to all the garrison.

At 8-30 a.m. the enemy attacked Kildare Post from the south and west and forced an entry, and about the same time another hostile party reached Fallen Tree Road in rear of Kildare Trench and succeeded in entering it. This party was quickly bombed out by the garrison of Limerick Post and a small group from Kildare Post, under Serjeant Crane, whose work deserves special mention. The enemy left several dead in the trench and one prisoner, who was at once sent back to Brigade Headquarters. Kildare Trench, between Fallen Tree Road and a point about 80 yards from Kildare Post, was then manned by the remnants of the garrison of Kildare Post.

The right company was now almost entirely surrounded and the forward platoons were reduced to a total strength of about thirty. Captain Ainsworth therefore ordered a withdrawal to the high ground running south from the Adelphi. This was successfully carried out at about 9-30 a.m. but several men, including Serjeant Pugh, were hit in crossing Sprint Road, which was being swept by machine-gun fire from the neighbourhood of Cox's Bank. What was left of these platoons of " V " Company then joined up with Battalion Headquarters and formed a defensive flank to the south.

Battalion Headquarters, consisting of 6 officers and 51 other ranks—orderly room staff, runners, cyclists, cooks, batmen, signallers, wireless operators and police—had been occupying the Adelphi which was an unfortified position. As soon as the

L

bombardment opened at 7 a.m. the garrison deployed on the high ground about 50 yards east of the Adelphi and bombs and ammunition were issued. A block was constructed and manned in Kildare Lane. Shortly after 8 a.m. a large body of the enemy, estimated at from two to three battalions, was seen to be advancing in extended order westwards over Honnecourt Spur about Canongate and Fawcus Avenue, and rapid fire was opened on them at 1,300 yards' range. Part of this force turned south to attack Pigeon Quarry and Cox's Bank in rear and the remainder pushed on rapidly along the valleys running west from Pigeon Quarry, but were held up by the fire of the Adelphi garrison. Casualties were also inflicted on the enemy surrounding Pigeon Quarry and some were seen to turn and run away northwards. As he advanced the enemy constantly fired white Vérey lights to show his artillery the position of his forward troops. At 9-20 a.m. the enemy attempted to advance against the Adelphi from behind the ridge to the north of it 350 yards away but was driven back with heavy loss. He continued, however, to receive reinforcements from the Pigeon Quarry direction, and as he was able to form up in dead ground at close range the menace to the left flank became serious. A platoon of the 1/5th King's Own Royal Lancasters from Limerick Post was ordered to counter-attack, covered by rapid fire from the Adelphi garrison. Some of the Lewis-gun team of this platoon—including the No. 1—were immediately hit but Lieut. T. G. Roddick, Assistant Adjutant of the Scottish, dashed forward and single-handed brought the gun into action. By this daring act he drove the enemy back for several hundred yards. The relief was only temporary, however, and the situation was becoming impossible. Already three officers and twenty other ranks had become casualties and ammunition was running short. The Commanding-Officer therefore ordered a withdrawal to Kildare Trench and this was accomplished by 10-40 a.m., Battalion Headquarters being established at the south-east corner of Limerick Post.

The situation at this time was as follows :—The 1/5th King's Own were still in occupation of Meath and Limerick Posts and the Liverpool Scottish—about 90 strong—were holding Kildare Trench from Limerick Post to the point near Kildare Post named above. No touch could be obtained with any other troops either to north or south. The position of the enemy was uncertain but he was known to be round both flanks and to be in possession of the sunken road portion of Kildare Post.

The ammunition supply in Limerick Post was adequate but

in Kildare Trench it was insufficient and a message was sent to Brigade asking for it to be replenished. Shortly afterwards 2nd Lieut. Provan, 1/5th Loyal North Lancashires, arrived with a small party of men, ten of whom were at once sent back to Brigade for ammunition and on their return were kept to strengthen the garrison.

At 12-30 p.m. enemy reinforcements, estimated at about one battalion, were seen moving westward over the Honnecourt Spur and a little later another large body was observed farther north moving towards Villers-Guislain. It was now obvious that the enemy had penetrated a considerable distance to the left rear and at 1 p.m. the Commanding-Officer and Captain J. A. Roddick decided to carry out a personal reconnaissance to try and learn the exact situation. After going about 300 yards west down Kildare Lane they found a Vickers-gun firing over the north parapet at the enemy about 500 yards away and being itself engaged by hostile machine-gun fire. No other British troops were seen and on arriving at Parr's Bank they found the enemy in occupation of the dugouts 200 yards from the eastern end of it and approaching Parr's Bank itself. On their way back to the firing line they learnt that the enemy was in possession of Meath Post which he had attacked from the north-west.

The defence was now somewhat reorganized. Captain J. A. Roddick was ordered to take command of Limerick Post and Lieut-Colonel MacDonald took over Kildare Trench which had previously been put under the command of Lieut. T. G. Roddick. The garrison of Kildare Trench was hard pressed. The S.A.A. and bomb store had been destroyed by a direct hit and ammunition was scarce. Portions of the trench were enfiladed by machine-gun fire from Kildare Post and though this was partly subdued by rifle-grenades casualties were suffered. At 2-15 p.m. the enemy began an attack against the left rear from the direction of Parr's Bank and rapid fire was opened on him. He was supported by machine-gun fire down Fallen Tree Road from the east which caused several casualties at the junction of this road with Kildare Trench. Ammunition was now so short that many of the garrison were forced to use German rifles and cartridges. The only Lewis-gun could not be kept in action as there was no S.A.A. for it. At 3-15 p.m. the enemy attacked down Fallen Tree Road in strength and succeeded in entering that portion of Kildare Trench between the road and Kildare Lane. An attempt to dislodge him failed. This cut off the garrison of Kildare Trench from Limerick Post. For some time rifle-fire was kept up against the enemy about Fallen Tree Road in rear and such rifle-grenades as could be used—many of the rods would not go into the rifles owing to the barrels being over-heated—were directed against the machine-guns and snipers in Kildare Post, but further effective resistance was hopeless and Lieut.-Colonel MacDonald at 3-20 p.m. sent a message to Brigade that he intended to withdraw fighting at dusk and form a defensive flank to the 165th Brigade on the right. Its position was doubtful but men in khaki had been seen about No. 12 Copse.

The reasons for this withdrawal given in the Battalion's official account of the action were :—

No ammunition.
No field of fire.
Wire negligible in front.
No wire in rear.
Looked down on from Kildare Post.
No food or water.

They would appear to be sufficient !

At 4-5 p.m. flank guards each of one N.C.O. and six men crawled out, suffering one casualty on the way, and five minutes later the withdrawal was begun in small parties. It was carried out without interference and posts were established about 800 yards in rear, from Fallen Tree Road to a copse on high ground about 700 yards south-east. The copse was placed in a state of of defence, patrols were pushed out to flank and rear and touch was obtained with the 165th Brigade on the right in the vicinity of No. 12 Copse.

Captain J. A. Roddick when, at 1-45 p.m., he took command of Limerick Post had at his disposal a garrison consisting of 4 officers and 90 other ranks of the 1/5th King's Own Royal Lancasters, 2 officers—Captain Ferguson and Lieut. C. M. Barber—and 25 other ranks of the Liverpool Scottish Head-quarter details and one officer and some details of the 1/5th Loyal North Lancashires. There were three Lewis-guns in service-able condition and a good supply of ammunition and bombs.

The first task was to put the post into a proper state of defence and three bombing-blocks were constructed, one in Kildare Lane in rear of the position, one in Kildare Trench at the entrance to Limerick Post and one in the communication-trench leading to Meath Post. There was already a block in Kildare Lane towards the Adelphi. Captain Roddick then reorganized the garrison to cover all the approaches to the position, informed the men that they were surrounded and

ordered them to resist to the last.　They fully realized the
situation and their determination and courage were beyond
praise.

At 3-15 p.m. the enemy, after offering the garrison surrender
which was, of course, refused, made a determined simultaneous
attack from north, west and south but was repulsed with heavy
loss after severe hand-to-hand fighting.　He did, however,
succeed—as has been told above—in cutting off Limerick Post
from the garrison of Kildare Trench.　He then made repeated
efforts to drive in the bombing-blocks but had no result to show
for the many casualties which were inflicted on him.

At 4-15 p.m. another attack was launched by the communication-trenches from Meath Post and the Adelphi and from the
rear, but again the enemy got a rough reception and achieved
nothing.　For some time after this he was inactive and this
welcome lull in the fighting was used to issue one-third of the
reserve-rations and water as the men had had nothing to eat
all day.　A jar of rum three-parts full was a providential find
and it, too, was issued.

At 6-15 p.m. two volunteers from the 1/5th King's Own
were sent back to Brigade Headquarters with a verbal message
regarding the situation.　They succeeded in getting through as
did two further volunteers from the Liverpool Scottish two
hours later.

Except for desultory rifle and machine-gun fire and a few
faint-hearted reconnoitring patrols to find out if the defenders of
Limerick Post were still fighting, the enemy contented himself
with defensive measures until 2-45 a.m. when he brought up
Granatenwerfer and two light trench-mortars and registered with
them by the aid of Vérey lights.　At 3-30 a.m. after thirty
minutes' intense bombardment he launched an all-round attack
which was again repulsed with the heaviest punishment, but the
trenches had been seriously damaged by the trench-mortar fire
and eighteen of the garrison were casualties.　It was clear that
as soon as daylight came the enemy would obliterate the trenches
at his leisure and Captain Roddick therefore decided to evacuate
the position and try to reach the British lines.　After consultation
with Captains Bennett and Keene, of the 1/5th King's Own, the
following scheme was decided upon :—

(*a*) A Lewis-gun to be pushed out beyond the barbed-wire
to cover the gap at the south-west corner by which the garrison
was to withdraw.

(*b*) All ranks to report to Captain Roddick at this point and go out in parties of fifteen, each under an officer, the first party to carry bombs and, if necessary, clear a way across Kildare Lane.

(*c*) The guards at the bombing-blocks and the teams of the remaining two Lewis-guns, under Captains Bennett and Ferguson, to remain at their posts until all the remainder were clear. The signal for them to leave to be one Vérey light—the only one left—fired from the point of exit.

(*d*) The route to be followed after evacuation to be half-left across Kildare Lane and then down the valley south of Fallen Tree Road.

All were clear without interference at 5-5 a.m. and the little force, with its wounded, moved off across country in artillery formation with a screen of scouts fifty to sixty yards ahead. No resistance was encountered and the British lines were reached at 5-45 a.m.

The defence of Limerick Post was specially mentioned in Sir Douglas Haig's Despatch on the battle. Again, at a banquet given in his honour at the Town Hall, Liverpool, on 6 July, 1919, he singled out this dogged resistance as one of the outstanding feats of arms performed during the war by Liverpool and Lancashire troops. Every member of the garrison played his part heroically but there is no question that the driving force behind the stubborn defence was the personality and consummate leadership of Captain J. A. Roddick. Three things may truly be said to have disorganized and limited the scope of the enemy's attack on the 55th Divisional front, the stand at Limerick Post, a particularly gallant defence and counter-attack by the 1/4th Loyal North Lancashires at Vaucelette Farm 1,000 yards to the north-west, and the determined and sustained resistance by the 1/6th King's Liverpools at the Birdcage.

" X " Company which, it will be remembered, was in Brigade reserve had been split up. Two platoons had been detached and were occupying a reserve position behind the 1/5th King's Liverpools, a mile and a half to the south. The front line here was not broken in the attack nor were the flanks exposed and consequently these two platoons never became involved in the fighting. The remainder of the company—less the strong Lewis-gun post supporting " V " Company—under Captain A. G. Davidson, was occupying the reserve dugouts at the Willows, a short distance in front of Epéhy, and was at the disposal of Major Anderson, commanding the 1/5th King's Own Royal Lancasters. On the alarm being given, Captain Davidson reported to Major Anderson and received orders to take his men forward some 150 yards and to line the top of a rise, to the south-east of Fourteen Willows Road, which commanded two valleys running westwards from the trenches towards Epéhy. When this position was reached the party came under heavy machine-gun fire but the men quickly dug cover for themselves with their entrenching tools though not before one serjeant and five men had been killed and four others wounded. The enemy never penetrated far enough to attack the position held by " X " Company but the company, from its commanding position, made its presence felt. It was able to enfilade Kildare Lane which the Germans were seen to be converting into a fire-trench, evidently as a defensive flank to their operations farther north, and Serjeant Henshaw with the only Lewis-gun not only considerably delayed the work but did great execution on the workers. He claimed 250 and his estimate was probably not very wide of the mark.

There was one other detachment of the Scottish which took part in this action. As soon as it was known that the enemy had broken the front line, orders were sent to the transport officer, Captain R. W. Johnson, that all available men at the transport lines at Villers-Faucon should report as soon as possible to Brigade Headquarters and a party of about 70, under Lieut. G. L. D. Hole, was hurriedly marshalled. This party, which was made up of " Z " Company's demonstration-platoon, tailors, butchers, sick and men returned from leave or courses, reached Brigade Headquarters at the Willows at about 10 a.m. after a gruelling march, during which it encountered, particularly in Epéhy, more shelling by 5.9-inch howitzers than was pleasant. On reporting to the Brigadier the party was split up into three groups which, after carrying out special tasks—wiring, carrying ammunition, etc.—took up positions about Fourteen Willows Road and to the north-west towards Vaucelette Farm and filled in the gaps in what was to become the new line of resistance.

The night of 80 November—1 December passed quietly, and advantage was taken of the darkness and the inactivity of the enemy to reorganize the defence and to get all the men well dug in and the position consolidated in readiness for the attack which it was fully expected would be renewed as soon as daylight came. The enemy, however, had had enough and contented himself with consolidating his gains of the previous day. About 9 a.m. a counter-attack was launched by British and Indian Cavalry, dismounted, in conjunction with two companies of the 1/5th King's Own Royal Lancasters. The Indians, who attacked through the Scottish front, at first drove the enemy before them and succeeded in reaching Limerick and Kildare Posts, but there encountered barbed-wire and heavy machine-gun fire and were compelled to fall back. The remainder of the day was uneventful except for spasmodic shelling of the new positions. In the afternoon Brigadier-General Lewis was wounded. Lieut.-Colonel MacDonald took command of the Brigade and handed over the Battalion to Captain J. A. Roddick.

The Liverpool Scottish were relieved at 4 a.m. on 2 December by the 9th Leicestershire Regiment, of the 110th Brigade, and marched back to billets at Tincourt, the pipe-band helping them along for the last five miles.

The casualties in this action as first given were :—11 men killed or died of wounds, 1 officer and 67 other ranks wounded, and 9 officers and 435 other ranks missing, but later it was learnt that of the missing 1 officer and 90 men had been killed. The remainder, as time went on, turned up as prisoners in Germany, a large number wounded and in hospital. These losses were severe but they were light in comparison with those inflicted on the enemy.

Military Medals were awarded to Serjeants A. Baybut, D.C.M., T. E. Whitby and F. W. M. Crane, Corporal G. Thomas, Lance-Corporals J. Plant and R. G. Jones, and Privates G. Stephens, H McCracken, B. Metcalfe, E. Schless and F. Tweedale, and to Private J. R. Pollock a second Bar.

Captain J. A. Roddick was recommended for the Distinguished Service Order and two other officers for the Military Cross but the decorations were not awarded, the comment of the higher authorities being that although the work of these officers was admired they had only done their duty. Had such a high standard been insisted upon throughout the war the number of officers decorated in the British Army would have been considerably less.

It was unfortunate that the enemy should have chosen St. Andrew's Day for his attack. All preparations had been made for a special dinner and the necessary haggis, whiskey and rum were already stored in Pigeon Quarry and fell into the enemy's hands. From the behaviour of some of the Germans later in the day it was evident that they had not wasted time in sampling the liquid part of the feast. The whole of the canteen stock of the value of about 1,100 francs was also lost, and if the attack had taken place in the evening instead of in the morning the piano would have gone, too, for it had been intended to finish off the celebration with a smoking concert in the Quarry.

REST, REORGANIZATION AND A NEW SECTOR

The Liverpool Scottish remained three days at Tincourt, where reinforcements of 2 officers and 40 other ranks *1917* joined them. On 4 December Brigadier-General R. J. Kentish, D.S.O., arrived from England to take command of the Brigade and Lieut.-Colonel Macdonald rejoined the Battalion. The next day the Battalion moved to Flamincourt and on the 8th took train to Aubigny, ten miles north-west of Arras, and from there marched to Izel-lez-Hameau. Three days later it set out on foot for its destination, Beaumetz-lez-Aire, which was reached on the 14th, the intervening nights having been spent in billets successively at Bailleul-aux-Cornailles, Tangry and Crépy. In spite of the long spell of trench life which they had just experienced the men stood the march—about thirty miles—remarkably well.

Beaumetz-lez-Aire, twenty miles due west of Béthune, was an unattractive village in the midst of bleak rolling country and had little to recommend it to troops. The billets were poor and the nearest place of any size was Fruges, a sleepy country town four miles away. There was so little spare accommodation that the strict rule regarding the closing of the *estaminets* between certain hours was relaxed by Brigade order and authority given for them to remain open all day so that the men might have somewhere to read and write.

A regular programme of training was quickly drawn up, but first it was necessary to do a certain amount of navvying as there were no facilities near the village for musketry practice. Miniature ranges were soon made and a shallow valley selected suitable for a rifle-range where shooting, up to 500 yards, could be safely practised. Firing-points and butts were constructed by the companies, and targets and target-frames made by the pioneer section. A field at the eastern end of the village, also, was levelled for football.

After these preliminaries the Battalion settled down to hard work. Five days a week the training was under battalion arrangements but on the sixth day the Brigade assembled at a point some three miles from Beaumetz-lez-Aire and received instruction from the Brigade Commander with the assistance of a demonstration-platoon which he trained personally. After the morning's Brigade-training the men returned to billets under the Adjutant and the officers remained behind for tactical exercises. Brigadier-General Kentish, whose previous appointment had been Commandant of the Senior Officers' School at Aldershot, was a born instructor and these days were of great benefit to officers and men and enjoyed by all.

Nine officer reinforcements had reported for duty shortly after the Battalion arrived at Beaumetz-lez-Aire, but there was no sign of a large draft of men to replace the Epéhy casualties and some reorganization within the Battalion became imperative. "X" Company had come out of the battle with comparatively few losses but "Z" and—particularly—"Y" Companies were at little more than cadre strength. They therefore each received thirty men from "X" Company as a nucleus of experienced men to stiffen the new drafts when they should arrive. The company spirit had always been keenly—perhaps too keenly— encouraged in the Liverpool Scottish and no company had it in greater measure than "X." It was a sad day for the exiles when they were transferred but they were sportsmen and did their best to make their new companies at least the equal of the old.

On 16 December three inches of snow fell and a hard frost set in which lasted almost without a break for several weeks. The clean ground and crisp air gave conditions ideal for training and very rapid progress was made. Special attention was paid to musketry and practice in rapid-wiring, and interest was stimulated by numerous competitions not only in the Battalion itself but in the Brigade and Division. In the Battalion musketry competitions on the miniature range "Y" Company won four out of the six events, while on the large range "X" Company won the platoon competition under Army Rifle Association conditions—the platoon advancing on an objective by section rushes and providing its own covering fire. This platoon afterwards was placed second in the Brigade competition. In the Brigade rapid-wiring, "X" Company won the inter-company competition and the Pipe Band that for what was styled the Permanent Wiring Party. "X" Company afterwards represented the Battalion in the Divisional inter-company competition and gained second place. The team completed its task—fifty yards of double-apron fencing with a fixed quantity of wire and pickets—before any of the others but lost points because it exceeded the prescribed distance by twelve yards and as a result the fence was not steady enough.

Christmas dinners—rissoles, stew with potatoes and vegetables, Christmas puddings, fruit and nuts, beer, *citron* and tea—were served in the local recreation-room and dance-hall, which was gaily decorated with paper lanterns and garlands specially sent out from England, and the companies finished off the evening by adjourning to the *estaminets* near by for speeches and smoking concerts for which there was never a lack of talent. The usual presents were sent out from the officers' wives and friends, far too many for the shrunken Battalion, and two hundred of them were sent on to the 2nd Battalion at Elverdinghe.

Early in the New Year an appeal was made throughout the Army for funds to assist Sir Arthur Pearson's Home *1918* for Blinded Soldiers and Sailors and the Scottish belied the national reputation by subscribing more than a third of the total sum contributed by the Division.

On 29 January the Brigade was inspected by the Corps Commander and afterwards Brigadier-General Kentish pinned the newly-issued 1914 ribbon on the breasts of all those entitled to wear it. As the Scottish were the first battalion in the Brigade to go to France they, of course, predominated on this parade and numbered sixty-five out of a total of about eighty. Not the least proud memory of a proud day for the nineteen-fourteeners was the " eyes-right " they received from the whole Brigade as it marched past them after the ceremony.

About this time an important and beneficent innovation was introduced in the British Expeditionary Force. Long service at the front imposed a considerable strain, varying with the individual, both on nerves and general health, and a system was inaugurated whereby officers—and soon afterwards warrant-officers, N.C.O.'s and men—who either had two years' continuous service in the line or were suffering from strain, or even for very urgent private reasons, were allowed, if recommended by their commanding-officer, to return to England for six months on what was called substitution leave, their places being filled by others of the same rank from the draft-finding units at home. Four officers of the Liverpool Scottish—Captains A. G. Davidson and R. T. Ainsworth and Lieutenants B. P. Gallop and G. T. McCullough—were chosen, on account of long service in France and Belgium, to be the first to benefit under this new scheme and later several of the old hands amongst the men also were released for a time from active service. It may be mentioned at this point that others had in the past enjoyed a privilege somewhat similar though for a very different reason.   All Territorials who were serving at the outbreak of war were allowed, when their four years' engagement terminated, either to take their discharge or to re-enlist in the same unit after one month's leave in England.   This did not apply, of course, to those who joined after the outbreak of hostilities as the period of their enlistment was three years or the duration of the war, and in any case the privilege, so far as discharge was concerned, became a dead letter when conscription was introduced.   To their credit nearly all those of the Liverpool Scottish who were qualified to benefit under this arrangement chose the month's leave and not discharge.

Towards the end of January it was found necessary to reduce the number of infantry battalions in the Expeditionary Force owing to the impossibility, with the depleted man-power of the British Isles, of keeping service units up to strength and at the same time retaining sufficient reserves in England for home defence.   In the 55th Division one battalion was removed from each brigade and sent off on 31 January to be amalgamated with its second-line unit in the 57th Division at Armentières.   From the 166th Brigade the 1/5th Loyal North Lancashires were the unlucky battalion chosen to go, and from the other brigades the Liverpool Irish and the 1/9th King's Liverpools.   The reduction could not, of course, be made simultaneously in all Divisions and it was not until April that the 57th Division sent to the senior Division those battalions which it had decided to eliminate, one of which was the 2nd Battalion of the Liverpool Scottish.

Drafts of 5 officers and 129 other ranks reached the Scottish during January but when the period of rest ended and the Battalion, on 9 February, once more turned its steps towards the trenches, it was still far below strength.   After a march of six miles to Westrehem the Battalion went into billets for the night and the next day tramped fourteen miles to Lapugnoy, four miles west of Béthune.   Very few men fell out on this march but " Y " was the only company to reach its destination with a full complement and was duly congratulated in Battalion Orders.   It is interesting to note that on this march the men formed up in threes instead of fours because many of the roads were very narrow and even on the main roads the camber of the pavé was frequently so pronounced as to make walking a painful business for the outer files.   The experiment was a great success.

After two days of cleaning up and inspections the Battalion was placed temporarily under the orders of the 164th Brigade

FESTUBERT-GIVENCHY SECTOR 8, APRIL, 1918.

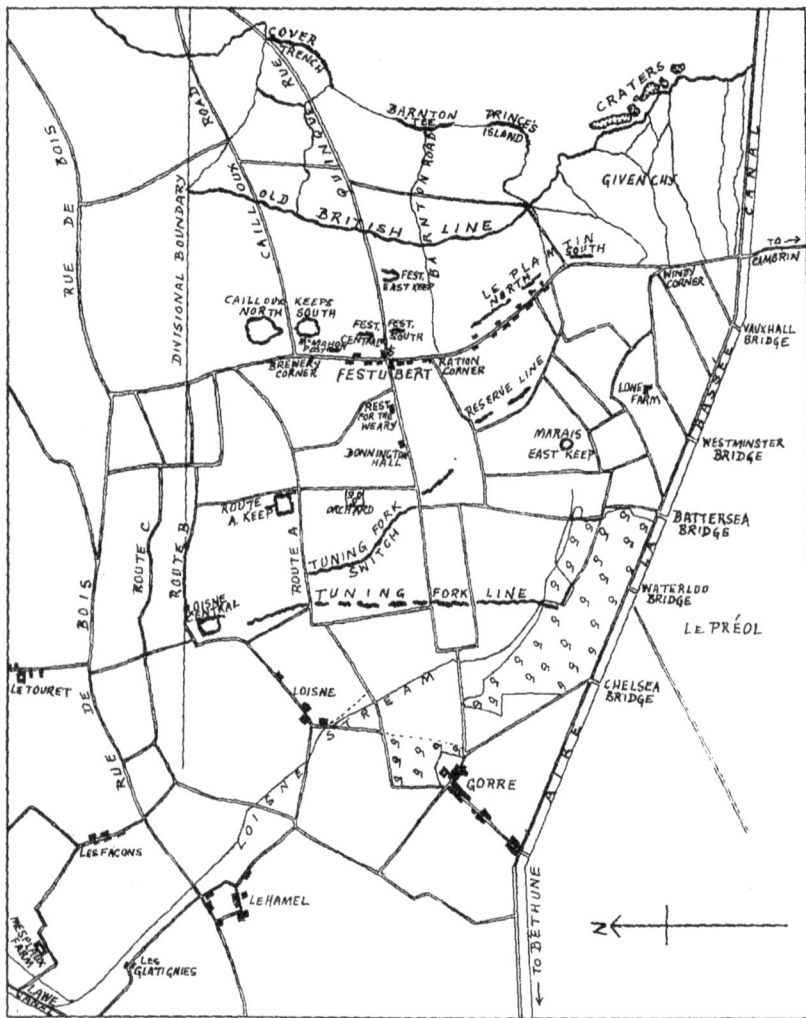

YARDS 1000 500 250 0 1000 2000 YARDS

BRITISH TRENCHES
WOODS

Commander and moved up to Verquin, two miles south of Béthune. Here the officers spent a day reconnoitring the back areas and rear defences of the new sector and on the 14th the Battalion went forward again into Brigade reserve at Le Préol, a pretty little village set in low-lying wooded country close to the Aire—La Bassée Canal and about two miles from the front line. Here for more than a week final preparations were made for the, return to trench life. Company parades, practice alarms, lectures by the Commanding-Officer to the officers and N.C.O.'s and by the company-commanders to their men, tactical schemes for officers under the Divisional Commander, working parties of various descriptions, and further reconnaissance of both forward and back areas by officers and N.C.O.'s amply filled up the days until the 25th, when the Battalion, under the command of Major J. A. Roddick—Lieut.-Colonel Macdonald having proceeded to England on one month's leave—relieved the 1/7th King's in the trenches in front of Givenchy.

The sector which the Division had taken over had a frontage of about three miles and extended from just south of the La Bassée-Cambrin Road, south of the Canal, to Cailloux Road beyond Festubert to the north of it. There was high ground south of the Canal and as far as Givenchy but beyond this village the ground fell away both to the north and west and much of it was marshy. As a consequence the trenches on the right and on the left of the Divisional sector were of entirely different types. From in front of Givenchy to the southern boundary they were deeply dug and the support and reserve positions contained many mine dugouts. In the Cambrin sector there were even several tunnels from the support to the front-line trenches. On the whole of this portion of the front there had been great mining activity and the opposing forces were separated from each other, except immediately to the north and south of the Canal, by craters of which, as at St. Eloi, each side held its own lip by a succession of saps run out from the front line proper. Some of these craters were enormous. Red Dragon, the largest of them, was more than one hundred yards long and fully fifty feet deep. The front line itself here was practically continuous and was strongly held. On the left of the Divisional front the trenches were very different. The ground was too marshy to permit of deep digging—or, luckily, mining—and the front and subsidiary lines consisted entirely of breastwork defences. Nor was the front line continuous. Prince's Island, Barnton Tee and Cover Trench were all isolated localities with several hundred yards of unoccupied ground separating them from each other and from the posts to the right and left, and each of them was connected by its own communication-trench with the support trench, the Old British Line.

Since the fighting in the spring and summer of 1915 there had been no movement forward or back on this part of the front and the defences, therefore, were highly organized, with numerous supporting points and subsidiary lines. The left Brigade sector is the one which chiefly concerns the Scottish and a glance at the map will show the scheme of defence. Behind the advanced posts there was the support trench, the Old British Line, which had been the front line before the attack at Festubert in 1915. In rear of it was the Village Line, the main line of resistance, a succession of strong-points from Le Plantin South to Cailloux North Keep. Behind this again were the reserve lines, the Tuning Fork Switch and the Tuning Fork Line. All the trenches, as might be expected after such a long period of stationary warfare, were in fairly good condition and were well protected by wire, even as far back as the Tuning Fork Line.

The country bore few of the sinister scars of war and, except in the forward zone, the damage from shelling was wonderfully light. Cuinchy and Givenchy had been severely pummelled and were little more than heaps of rubble, but villages like Cambrin and Festubert, only a mile from the front line, still boasted roofed houses and were used to billet supporting troops. Cambrin even had one tiny shop which carried on a furtive but profitable business in delicacies not included in the army bill-of-fare. Farther back again the countryside was practically unspoilt, all the villages were inhabited, the woods at Gorre and Le Préol showed none of those jagged stumps of shell-riven trees that betoken counter-battery work, and the roads and tracks were free from those pitfalls for the unwary, water-filled shell-holes. Béthune, the hub of the sector, was a busy town in which places of refreshment and amusement, ranging from a first-class restaurant, an excellent officers' club, a well-stocked Expeditionary Force Canteen and several cinemas to others of a more dubious character, catered for every taste and every pocket.

The sector which the battalion had taken over on 25 February included Prince's Island and the crater-posts in front of Givenchy, with their support positions. The enemy was quiet but the company-commanders, owing to the shortage of men and the inexperience of many of the new officers, had a trying time and all of them fell foul of the Brigadier-General. " X " Company, which was holding Prince's Island, had an unpleasant experience which did not help to clear the atmosphere. This position, as has been told, was composed of breastwork defences, and though the parapet was sound there was little or no parados. There was, therefore, no protection against the blow-back of any shells and trench-mortars which pitched behind the trench and, in fact, some men were hit in this way. Captain J. McSwiney, who had inspected his wire-entanglements the first night in the line and found them fairly adequate, decided that the most urgent work to be done on his bit of front was to build a parados and this was taken in hand energetically, with the approval of the Brigadier-General. Major-General Jeudwine inspected the trenches on 2 March and, on learning that trench-building and not wiring was the scheme of work, announced that he had given orders that all companies in isolated posts should concentrate exclusively on wiring during this tour of duty and that " X " Company would remain in the line until it had put two new double-apron fences completely round Prince's Island. As the wiring-order had never reached the Battalion from Brigade— though the Major-General did not know this—" X " Company's feelings were rather those of the small boy who is whipped for something his elder brother has done while the elder brother looks on with his hands in his pocket. It took three nights' work by the whole company to complete the task and cost it one officer and one man wounded as well as an extra day in the line after the remainder of the Battalion had been relieved.

On relief by the 1/7th Kings on 4 March two companies were billeted at Ferme-du-Roi, a large farm near Béthune on the north bank of the Canal, and the third company with Battalion Headquarters in Gorre where they were joined the next day by " X " Company.

It had long been obvious to the General Staff that the enemy, reinforced by the divisions set free from his Eastern front by the collapse of Russia, would make a supreme effort early in 1918 to force a quick decision before the arrival of the American troops turned the scale of numbers against him. Where the blow would fall could not be predicted with any certainty but prisoners captured by units of the 55th Division were unanimous in saying that an attack was imminent on the La Bassée front. A most elaborate defence scheme was prepared by Division laying down the action to be taken in the event of alarm and defining the positions to which every platoon in the support and reserve battalions should move. The code-word BUSTLE was to be the signal for the scheme to be put into operation. Shortly afterwards another code-word, PORT, was issued involving an entirely different set of dispositions and was to be used only in the event of the attack falling on the Portuguese, immediately to the north of the Divisional sector, and their requiring support. On 7 March about 5-20 a.m. a heavy bombardment fell on the front-line trenches and the Battalion stood to arms and took up its "bustle" positions in the Tuning Fork area. The shelling gradually died down and the Battalion returned to billets, but this false alarm had been of untold value in familiarizing the men with the approaches to and situations of those positions which they were shortly to have to occupy in real earnest. The Divisional front at this time had been shortened by the relief, by another division, of the brigade south of the Canal, and all three brigades were now concentrated to the north of it.

On 8 March "V" Company relieved in the front line a company of the 1/5th King's Own, withdrawn to train for a raid which it was to carry out a few days later. On the 12th the Battalion relieved the remainder of the 1/5th King's Own in the left sector and found itself next to the Portuguese whose flank post in the Old British Line dovetailed with the flank post of the Scottish, each, that is, having a post in the other's portion of the trench.

The Battalion during this tour was commanded by Major W. M. Phillips, of the 1/5th King's Own. Major Roddick had taken his own and the company-commanders' troubles to Major-General Jeudwine with satisfactory results but it was obvious in view of the somewhat strained relations with the Brigade-Commander, that he could not continue to command the Battalion, and he left for England on substitution leave with a recommendation to the Senior Officers' School, Aldershot, in his pocket. Major Phillips handled a delicate situation with great tact and none of the officers would have complained if he had taken over the command permanently.

The chief interest of this tour of duty was the elaborate preparation for the raid by the 1/5th King's Own. From 14 March the 4.2-inch howitzer batteries of the Divisional Artillery carried out daily shoots with instantaneous fuse on the enemy's wire opposite Cover Trench and each night the Scottish scout section inspected the effect of the fire and reported the position and extent of the gaps made. These were then kept open by the fire of the Lewis-guns from Cover Trench which sprayed them with bullets at frequent intervals throughout the night to prevent the enemy from sending out parties to repair the damage. Naturally this programme annoyed the Germans, and their retaliatory fire against the British trenches was heavy and caused the Scottish several casualties. The raid finally came off on the night of 16/17 March and was an entirely bloodless affair. The raiders found—as the Scottish scout officer, 2nd Lieut. G. N. Rome, had predicted—that the Germans, warned of the coming raid by the wire-cutting, had withdrawn their men from the front line. Not one of the enemy was seen nor a machine-gun nor even a rifle, and the only trophy brought back from the German trenches was a ship's bell which had evidently been used as a gas gong. " Y " Company, from whose trenches the raid was made, was a trifle apprehensive that it might feel the full weight of the counter-bombardment especially as orders had been received that only a skeleton garrison consisting of the numbers one and two of the Lewis-gun teams should be left in Cover Trench and that the remainder of the two platoons there should be withdrawn to Richmond Trench or any other suitable trench close at hand until the raid was over. Fortunately, although the enemy shelling was brisk enough, no shells fell in Richmond Trench and " Y " Company got off scot-free as, indeed, did the raiders themselves. The only British casualties were some unfortunate members of the team of a Stokes-mortar supporting the raid who were injured, two fatally, by the premature explosion of one of their own shells. It was bad luck that a raid so carefully prepared, and carried out, as it was, with great dash by the King's Own should yield no useful result.

The Battalion was relieved at mid-day on the 17th by the 1/7th King's Liverpools and, after taking up its " bustle " positions for practice *en route*, went into Divisional Reserve, two companies being at Le Hamel and two with Battalion Headquarters at Mesplaux Farm.

About this time Army issued a cordial invitation to a limited number of subalterns to spend a few days at Army Headquarters, partly for rest and relaxation and partly to see how the Staff carried on the good work. Not to be outdone in hospitality the Liverpool Scottish issued a general invitation, in identical form but with rather different phraseology, to all Staff Officers to visit them in the trenches. History does not relate if this document was ever actually circulated amongst the Staff but there can be little harm in reproducing it here.

It is proposed that during the winter months Corps and Army Staff Officers should be given an opportunity of staying with officers of the line for a few days at a time. The primary object of the scheme is to improve the relations of the line officers and the Staff and to bring these officers into closer touch. A further object is to give Staff Officers an occasional rest and recreation.

The following entertainments are provided by the line officers and will be placed at the disposal of guests :—

1. A visit to the grottos of Givenchy.
2. Clock Golf in the Canadian Orchard.
3. Nightly pyrotechnic displays by King Manoel's Own accompanied by the roll of Hindenburg drums.
4. Mudbaths in Prince's Island.

As Mackensen Trench and Red Dragon Crater are so near Officers will be privileged to join Rome's personally-conducted tours in no-man's-land. Comfortable wire-beds and even baby elephants will be provided, and Officers who wish to ride will be provided with free passes on the trench-tramway—last man on the tram to return it to the dump.

It is thought also that Staff Officers would considerably benefit by seeing the work at platoon headquarters and would learn much that is new and interesting to them. Each of these Officers would be made a guest—that is, a non-paying member—of one of the company-officers' messes.

The company-commanders are very anxious to try the scheme and would be glad of an early answer. Come and see us !

Pont Fixe is *so* bracing.

(Sgd.) W. P. BASKET,
Comdg. 2nd Mudshire Regt.

It was well known to the General Staff that the great German offensive was imminent but there was still no definite indication of where it would be launched. No risks were taken on the 55th Divisional front. The reserve troops were under orders to be ready to move at one hour's notice except between the hours of 5 a.m. and 9 a.m. when the time allowed was only thirty minutes. To ensure a quick start if the alarm came at the dangerous time—dawn—the Battalion's usual routine was varied and reveillé put forward from 6 a.m. to 4 a.m., with a corresponding alteration of "lights-out" to 8 p.m. Only ten per cent. of the men were allowed passes to Béthune in the evenings, and the days were largely filled with lectures and reconnaissances, particularly of the "port" positions.

On 19 March Major D. C. D. Munro, M.C., D.C.M., 1st Battn. The Gordon Highlanders, arrived from England and assumed the duties of second-in-command. He was just in time to say good-bye to the only officer who had served continuously with the Battalion since it went to France, the Quartermaster, Captain A. C. Jack, who went off on the 20th for a well-earned tour of duty in England. There never was a better Q.M. than " Jolly," and the Battalion hardly seemed the same without him. His place was taken by Hon. Lieut. and Quartermaster G. T. Coulson, 9th Bn. Durham Light Infantry, who so absorbed the atmosphere of the Liverpool Scottish that before he parted from them the following year he had learnt to swing the kilt with the best.

On 21 March the storm broke on the front of the 3rd and 5th Armies, the southern portion of the British line. The sweeping success of the German attack there which came near to decisive victory compelled the dispatch of more and more fresh divisions to take the place of those battered almost out of existence, and dangerously denuded the remainder of the front of its reserve troops. In these circumstances it seemed very probable that the enemy, as soon as the progress of his main attack was slowed down, would launch a new attack on some other part of the line in the hope that he might stop the flow of reserves to the south and that by a supreme effort there he might then succeed in his real object, the splitting apart of the British and French armies. There were many indications—registration by new batteries, reports from prisoners of rumours of an early offensive on the La Bassée front, etc.—that trouble was brewing for the 55th Division and steps were taken to make even more perfect the scheme of defence and to familiarize all ranks with it. At 10 p.m. on the 25th the Battalion received orders to be prepared to move at midnight at which hour the code-word " bustle " was received. The companies at once moved off and all were reported in position by 3 a.m. Everything remained quiet and the Battalion expected an early message that it might return to its billets and breakfasts. The Major-General had other ideas, however. He himself, with Brigadier-General Kentish, visited every platoon and satisfied himself that each was in its proper place and that every officer and man knew who was in front and on the flanks—and where; the position of reserve ammunition and bomb-stores; and all the hundred and one details connected with the fighting of a defensive battle. It was not until 12-30 p.m. that permission was given for the Battalion to dismiss.

This was the first parade of the Liverpool Scottish under the command of Major Munro, Major Phillips having rejoined his own battalion on the 25th.   The Scottish should always be grateful to Brigadier-General Kentish for one thing, that he applied specially for Major Munro to be sent out from England to command them.   The Battalion never had a more competent, sympathetic or—incidentally—fearless commanding-officer nor one who more jealously looked after the interests of the officers and men under him.

The steady absorption of reserves into the fighting in the south meant that the divisions in those portions of the line where the position was still normal were called upon to extend the length of front they were holding.   On 26 March the Battalion received a warning order that the 166th Brigade would take over a brigade sector south of the Canal in the near future.   Reconnaissances of the Cambrin locality were carried out the same afternoon, and the next night the Battalion went by motor-bus to Annequin and marched up to the Village Line in the Cambrin sector where it relieved the 1/6th North Staffordshires, of the 137th Brigade.   The following night the Scottish relieved companies of the 1/5th South Lancashires and 1/5th King's Own in the right sub-sector, " V " and " X " Companies taking over the front line and " Y " and " Z " Companies remaining in support in the Village Line.   " Y " Company joined the other companies in the front line the next night.

The economy campaign was at its most acute stage at this time and the Battalion received orders that all work which it undertook should be completed as far as possible with materials salvaged from between and in front of the British trenches. Search parties were sent out nightly by all the companies and the material they found was collected at the Battalion dump. It is illustrative of the appalling waste which went on in the Army that during the ten days which were spent in these trenches it was never once necessary to requisition pickets or barbed-wire from Brigade.   In addition to the normal renewals and repairs to the wire protecting the front-line posts a complete new belt of double-apron fencing, put up in front of the support line along the whole length of the Battalion's sector, was made entirely with salvaged materials.

There was one curious feature in the Cambrin sector which the Scottish had not met with elsewhere.   One of the dugouts in the support line was fitted up as a chapel and here on Easter Sunday, 31 March, a number of men attended divine service and received communion.   On weekdays it served as a reading and writing-room.

The necessity for up-to-date knowledge of the situation on all parts of the front was urgent and Corps were insistent in their demands for prisoners. Always ready to oblige, 2nd Lieut. G. N. Rome decided to do what he could to satisfy them. By nightly patrols with his scouts he had located the positions of all the enemy's advanced posts on the Battalion front and he determined to try and surprise one of them and capture the garrison. On the night of 2/3 April he went out with a party of twelve scouts, slipped through between two of the German advanced posts and struck one of their communication-trenches from the support to the front line. Here he posted three of his men to protect his rear. Another three he placed close to the post he intended to raid. With the other six men he then started to work his way up towards the post from the rear. At this moment a German was seen walking up the communication-trench towards the post but as the patrol was not in a good position to take him he was allowed to go on. Rome decided to wait and, if the man came back, to try and capture him. He posted his men along the top of the communication-trench and himself got into it and sat down in a latrine just off the trench. Very soon the man was heard returning. Rome waited until he was near and then jumped out and called on him to surrender. The man shouted, then turned and ran for his life back towards the front line. Rome, after firing two shots which missed, proceeded to chase him. After going about fifty yards the German fell at a turn in the trench. Rome promptly fell on top of him and, as he continued to shout at the top of his voice, hit him on the head with the butt of his revolver. By this time the general racket had wakened up every German post in the vicinity including the one chosen for the raid. The men in it looked over the top to see what was happening and two of them were promptly shot at about ten yards' range by the three men who had been left to watch the post. While this was taking place the prisoner had been hoisted out of the trench and carried about fifty yards to a flank where he was laid down until he recovered consciousness. He soon came round and proved very docile. Rome then got his patrol together and, leading his prisoner by the hand, made his way back to the British line, eventually entering the trenches of the Battalion on the left of the Scottish. None of the patrol received so much as a scratch.

The prisoner turned out to be an ideal one from the point of view of the Intelligence Department. He was an armourer-serjeant's assistant who had been sent up to the trenches with a supply of oil for the machine-gun posts. As he spent most of his time at Provin, some miles behind the line, he was in a position to give information about troop movements which would not have been within the knowledge of the ordinary trench soldier, and the particulars he gave when interrogated of the battalions holding the line, their rest billets and system of reliefs were exceedingly valuable. He had heard rumours for some weeks of an impending attack on the La Bassée front but said there were no signs of its taking place in the immediate future. That it did take place within a week is rather an illustration of the rapidity with which the Germans could move guns and troops from one part of the front to another than a reflection on the veracity of the prisoner who was too cowed to be deliberately misleading.

This raid, surely one of the most original and impertinent of the whole War, brought congratulations to Lieut. Rome from the Corps Commander downwards. He was awarded the Military Cross and one of his scouts, Corporal K. Helliar, the Military Medal.

Patrolling was vigorously carried on each night during this tour. None of the enemy was encountered in no-man's-land but one patrol, close to the enemy's wire, was fired on by a machine-gun and had several bombs thrown at it. It was lucky to get away with the loss of only one man wounded.

The Battalion snipers, too, were active and had the satisfaction of killing two of the enemy in a post from which they themselves had been fired on.

From the beginning of April there had been a very marked increase in the enemy's shelling and in the activity of his aeroplanes, which one day succeeded in bringing down five British observation balloons. It was becoming increasingly evident that there was something in the wind, especially when the Battalion after being relieved on the night of 7 April by the 2nd King's Royal Rifles, 2nd Brigade, 1st Division, was shelled, mostly with gas, all the way along the Béthune Road almost as far as Beuvry. The enemy had previously done very little harassing fire on the back areas at night.

The Scottish spent the night of 7/8 April at Beuvry and Le Quesnoy and on the 8th crossed the Canal and went back to their old billets at Le Hamel and Mesplaux Farm. This change of quarters was of supreme importance as the next chapter will tell.

If the 166th Brigade expected a few days' rest it was disappointed, for it received orders to relieve a Portuguese brigade in the trenches. The relief was to take place on 9 April but there was a thoroughly good reason why it was not carried out.

THE BATTLE OF GIVENCHY—9 APRIL, 1918

About 3-30 a.m. on 9 April a severe bombardment was opened by the enemy on the back areas, Le Hamel *1918* and Mesplaux Farm receiving their full share of it. The men at once were roused and fell in in battle order. Packs were stored and an extra bandolier of S.A.A. issued to each man. Though it was pitch dark there was surprisingly little confusion but the Adjutant, Captain T. G. Roddick, started the day well by running out of the farm-house and taking a header into the midden.

Orders to move to " bustle " positions were received at 4-35 a.m. and it was clear to all that this was no practice alarm.

The writer, acting second-in-command, was sent on to Le Hamel to see that the order had reached " V " and " X " Companies and found on his arrival that they were already moving off. The battle positions of these two companies were—" V " to the Tuning Fork Line between the Tuning Fork North Road and Route A, " X " to the Tuning Fork Switch and Route A Keep. They reached their positions with the exception of the platoon of " X " Company which should have occupied Route A Keep. This platoon got a heavy shell right into it on the way through Gorre, which practically wiped it out and killed its officer, 2nd Lieut. J. E. Moffat. In the light of after events this was the one platoon which could least easily be spared as Route A Keep, which became one of the key positions of the action, was left ungarrisoned, except for a handful of the 1/6th King's, and was captured by the enemy from the rear.

" Y " and " Z " Companies, with Battalion Headquarter details, had a gruelling time. The barrage was very fierce where the road from Le Hamel by Les Glatignies crossed the Lawe Canal and there was a large proportion of gas shell in it. The Companies cut the corner and went over the open to avoid this barrage and had trouble in negotiating several belts of barbed-wire and in crossing the Loisne Stream. They were greatly hindered by having to wear their box-respirators most of the way. " Z " Company was lucky enough to reach its position, the Tuning Fork Line between the Tuning Fork North Road and Route A, with only one casualty, but " Y " Company had some men hit as it was leaving Mesplaux Farm and more on the march. Half of "Y" Company reached its place in the Tuning Fork Switch after working across from Loisne in front of Gorre Wood and then up the Tuning Fork North Road. The other half of the Company chose to go via Loisne and Route A, and on reaching the Tuning Fork Line found the trenches to the north of Route A unoccupied. Realizing that they should already have been manned by another battalion, 2nd Lieut. J. Monkhouse ordered his men into them to fill the gap until the situation became a little clearer. Battalion Headquarters was established in a house at the junction of the Tuning Fork North Road and the road behind the Tuning Fork Line, but as this house had already been badly knocked about a move was made to the trench itself.

In spite of the shelling and a heavy ground-mist which in places reduced visibility to a matter of a few yards all were reported in position by 7-30 a.m.

The Lewis-gun limbers had a very unpleasant time. They were compelled to stick to the roads and therefore had to face the worst of the shelling. Thanks to the determination of the drivers and the Lewis-gun N.C.O.'s they all got through and delivered their loads to the carrying parties sent from the companies to meet them.

The enemy's bombardment continued without a break for some hours, the Tuning Fork area and the Tuning Fork Line itself being among the principal targets. As there were two companies of the 1/6th King's Liverpools in the Tuning Fork Line with "V" and "Z" Companies, the congestion was considerable and made the task of attending to and removing the wounded a very difficult one. To ease things a little Nos. 1 and 2 Platoons of "V" Company were moved to the trench between the Tuning Fork North and South Roads. The trenches themselves suffered badly and altogether it was a trying morning, especially when the enemy turned on a 14-inch gun which twice missed, by feet only, the firebay which Headquarters were using. It is said that at times like these a man's mind turns to the more serious things in life and this is borne out by the following extract from the official narrative of a platoon serjeant—"I "thought of the 26 eggs we had bought the night previous "and which would be gone by now".

The entire lack of any news of what was happening in the front line did not help matters. Not a single message was received from Brigade the whole morning but gradually rumours spread that the Portuguese had been attacked and that the enemy had got clean through.   If true that meant an exposed left flank and a very grave outlook.

At noon all troops in the Tuning Fork locality came under the orders of the 165th Brigade Commander, and under the immediate command of Lieut.-Colonel J. B. McKaig, D.S.O., the Commanding-Officer of the 1/6th King's.   Soon after, reports were received that the enemy was attacking the Village Line and that the Portuguese were retiring.

Lieut.-Colonel Munro was anxious to find out the exact position of affairs on the left flank and, after patrols which he had sent out had brought him purely negative information, set out himself to reconnoitre.   He found Loisne Central unoccupied and a battery of 6-inch howitzers and an 18-pounder battery in position in rear, unprotected and with the enemy only 350 yards away. He at once ordered " Z " Company to move from the Tuning Fork Line and occupy Loisne Central, the platoons of " Y " Company in Tuning Fork Switch were brought back to the Tuning Fork Line north of Route A to join the remainder of the company, and Nos. 1 and 2 Platoons of " V " Company moved up from the Tuning Fork Line to reinforce " X " Company in the Tuning Fork Switch.   " Z " Company established contact with " A " Company, 1/5th South Lancashires, which had dug in in rear and to the left of Loisne Central.   All these changes in disposition were carried out between 3 p.m. and 6 p.m. and greatly strengthened the left flank.

About 2 p.m. the mist lifted and both " X " Company in Tuning Fork Switch and " Y " Company in the Tuning Fork Line got a sight of the enemy 5/600 yards away in the neighbourhood of Route A Keep.   Rifle and Lewis-gun fire was opened on him with good effect.   This was the first definite information that the Keep was in German hands but the lack of knowledge as to how strongly it was held, the weak artillery support available and the shortage of men precluded the hazarding of an immediate counter-attack against it.

It was particularly noticeable throughout the day that the reply of our artillery to the German bombardment was negligible but this was hardly to be wondered at.   The gun-pits, like the trenches, were nearly all built up and not dug in and it had been a fairly easy matter for the enemy to locate and register most of them before the attack.   As a result, when the bombardment began a large part of the Divisional Artillery was knocked out before it had had a chance to reply.   Those guns which were undamaged did great work.   One 18-pounder in the

Tuning Fork Line between the North and South Tuning Fork Roads continued in action all day in spite of the most determined attempts by the enemy to silence it.

The shelling died down towards evening and the night of 9/10 April was quiet. The chance was taken to do what repairs were possible to the damaged trenches and wire. Patrols were sent out to keep in touch with the enemy and " X " Company was ordered to establish a post—afterwards known as Orchard Post—at the north-east corner of an orchard west of the road from Route A Keep to Tuning Fork North Road, to frustrate any attempt by the enemy to get between the Village and Tuning Fork Lines. The night passed without incident except that a German gave himself up to " Z " Company in Loisne Central.

It may be as well here to set down very briefly the situation on the remainder of the Divisional front.

The attack first fell on the Portuguese at 8 a.m. and their line was quickly broken. At 9 a.m. the enemy assaulted the 55th Division in great strength all along the front. The 164th Brigade, which held the right sector from the Canal to Givenchy, after severe fighting, was able to report at nightfall that it was holding the whole of its line, even the crater posts, nor was it ever dislodged in the days that followed. The 165th Brigade in the left sector had had a punishing day. In the mist the enemy had filtered through between the front posts and taken them in rear and, following the collapse of the Portuguese, the Old British Line had been turned and attacked both from flank and rear. Posts both in the front and Old British lines had continued to hold out long after they were surrounded and when all hope of rescue had gone, but so far as its general line was concerned this Brigade was forced back to its main line of resistance, the Village Line from Cailloux Keep North to Le Plantin South. From this line it could not be driven out in spite of repeated assaults by the enemy. Of the 166th Brigade the Liverpool Scottish and two companies of the 1/5th South Lancashires had been attached to the 165th Brigade and the remainder of the South Lancashires to the 164th Brigade. This left only the 1/5th King's Own Royal Lancasters and the 166th Trench Mortar Battery under the Brigade-Commander, Brigadier-General R. J. Kentish, to form the defensive flank made necessary by the retirement of the Portuguese. Before the day was over the three Divisional Field Companies Royal Engineers, Nos. 419, 422 and 423, part of the Divisional Pioneer Battalion

the 1/4th South Lancashires, a machine-gun company of the
11th Tank Battalion from the 1st Division south of the La
Bassée Canal, the 1/4th Seaforth Highlanders of the 154th
Brigade, 51st Division, and, later, the 1st Battalion
Northumberland Fusiliers of the 9th Brigade, 3rd Division, all
came under the orders of the 166th Brigade and formed a line
from Loisne in a north-westerly direction to beyond the Lawe
Canal 1000 yards north of Mesplaux Farm. This composite
force was attacked in strength on the 9th and succeeding days
but held its line intact, though its left was forced to fall back
to Mesplaux Farm to conform with a withdrawal by the Division
on its left.

As examples of the rapidity and ease of the enemy's advance
on the Portuguese front it may be noted that by 2-30 on the
afternoon of the 9th German patrols had reached Robecq, five
miles west by north of Mesplaux Farm, and one German officer
who was captured farther north stated that his company, which
was in the second phase of the attack, was given Merville as
its objective and that he led it there in fours without once
requiring to deploy and without a shot being fired at it. Merville
was seven miles behind the front line.

At 6 a.m. on the 10th the enemy attempted to attack Loisne
Central and also to work round the left flank but was easily
repulsed with heavy loss. He tried again a few hours later with
no better succees. " Z " Company's Lewis-guns fired about
2,000 rounds each during these skirmishes and, judging by the
numbers of empty cases in the firebays, the riflemen, too, had
not been idle. " Y " Company continued throughout the day
to get excellent sniping practice at the Germans in the Route A
Keep locality.

At dusk a determined attempt was made by the enemy to
cut off Loisne Central between which and " Y " Company's
trench to the south there was a gap of 300 yards. A party of
about 60 of the enemy waded along a ditch which ran through
this gap and succeeded in getting behind the trench undiscovered.
They were then seen by " Z " Company officers' cook, who had
got out of the trench to collect firewood. He gave the alarm
and before the Germans could establish themselves, as seemed
their intention, in the gunpits behind, they were attacked by a
party of " Z " Company and a platoon of the 1/5th South
Lancashires and, after hand-to-hand fighting, practically wiped
out. Twenty-five dead and wounded were counted and sixteen
prisoners, five of them wounded, and two machine-guns were
captured. Those who succeeded in breaking away came under

the fire of No. 12 Platoon of " Y " Company as they made for
their own lines and more casualties were inflicted on them.
After the failure of this daring effort the enemy gave up trying
to capture Loisne Central.   An attack seemed imminent the
following morning as the whole Tuning Fork area received
thirty minutes' hurricane bombardment but no infantry action
followed.

Some changes in dispositions had taken place on the 10th.
The two platoons of " V " Company were moved from the
Tuning Fork Switch to " Rest for the Weary," where they made
a position for themselves in old gunpits.   A company of the 13th
King's Liverpool Regiment, 9th Brigade, was placed at the
disposal of the officer commanding the Tuning Fork locality and
two platoons of this company were sent forward to the Tuning
Fork Switch with two platoons of the 1/4th South Lancashires
which had been occupying the Tuning Fork Line south of the
Tuning Fork North Road.

On the 11th " Z " Company—now under the immediate command of Major W. V. Pilkington, commanding two companies
of the 1/5th South Lancashires—was greatly troubled by a field-
gun which continually fired on Loisne Central at point-blank
range.   Every hit brought down part of the parapet and
casualties were frequent.   To obtain relief the company dug a
new trench in rear and when this was completed the gun caused
no further loss.   That night a patrol of the enemy blundered
on to the wire in front of " Z " Company's position.   A Lewis-
gun opened fire and one of the patrol was left on the wire,
wounded.   He was brought into the trench but died shortly
after, though not before he had volunteered the information that
an attack might be expected at dawn on the 12th.   The Heavy
Artillery was warned and at dawn all farm-houses and places
where the enemy was likely to form up were shelled.   No
attack developed.

On the afternoon of the 11th the enemy had attacked the
165th Brigade and succeeded in capturing Festubert East Keep
and both the Cailloux Keeps.   He was immediately counter-
attacked and Festubert East Keep—easily—and the Cailloux
Keeps—after hard fighting—were retaken so that by 7-30 p.m.
the whole line had been re-established.   This fighting had further
depleted the already weak garrison of the Village Line and on
the night of 11/12 April several changes in dispositions were
made.   Liverpool Scottish Battalion Headquarters moved forward to Festubert and took over from the 1/5th King's
Liverpools, and " Y " Company—whose place on the Tuning

Fork Line was taken by a company of the 1/6th King's—and a company of the 13th King's relieved the 1/5th King's and two companies of the 1/6th King's in the Festubert area.   One company and two platoons of the 13th King's already in the area stood fast.   On completion of relief this force, under the command of Lieut.-Colonel Munro, occupied the following positions :—

"Y" Company, Cailloux Keep South and McMahon Post.

One company, 13th King's, Festubert East Keep, Cailloux Keep North and two cottages on the Festubert-Brewery Corner Road.

One company, 13th King's, Festubert Central and Festubert South.

Two platoons, 13th King's, in shell-hole positions forming a defensive flank west of the Cailloux Keeps.

"V" and "X" Companies remained in the Tuning Fork locality and came under the orders of the officer commanding the 13th King's Liverpools.   "Z" Company continued to garrison Loisne Central.

It was decided that the time was now ripe to try and retake Route A Keep and remove the menace to the left flank which the enemy's occupation of it constituted.   The task was given to "X" Company of the Liverpool Scottish and "D" Company of the 13th King's and zero-hour was fixed for midnight.   During the day the position was registered by 60-pounders, 18-pounders and trench-mortars.   "D" Company was given as its objective the Keep itself and "X" Company a strong post which the enemy had established in some ruins immediately south of the Keep on the other side of Route A.   After taking this post "X" Company was ordered to support the attack on the Keep if necessary.

At 11 p.m. "X" Company moved forward to its assembly position and, as soon as the barrage opened, extended to two paces and advanced to within fifty yards of the objective.   When the barrage lifted the men rushed in and took the enemy completely by surprise, killing five and capturing nine and one machine-gun.   By 12-10 a.m. "X" Company had consolidated the position and was ready to go on to the Keep if required.   Sounds of fighting in the Keep continued until 1-30 a.m. and as no messages had been received Captain J. R. McSwiney went forward to reconnoitre.   He found that both "D" Company's officers were casualties and that only the southern end of the Keep had been captured. The company was rather disorganized and had run out of bombs. After hurriedly sending back for four boxes of bombs which he had kept in reserve Captain McSwiney issued them to the forward posts whom he ordered to hang on until more bombs were brought up. A party was sent off to the Tuning Fork Switch for these and on its return at about 2-30 a.m. Captain McSwiney, with some of his N.C.O.'s, organized several bombing parties of 1 N.C.O. and 5 men each and sent them forward, supported by other parties of 6 men to mop up and to guard dugout entrances. Little resistance was met and by 3-30 a.m. the whole of the objective was in our hands. " D " Company was then reorganized and the Keep put in a state of defence.

At 4-45 a.m. the enemy made a weak attempt to recapture the Keep from the east but was easily beaten off. Captain McSwiney then handed over to three officers of the 18th King's who had been sent up as reinforcements.

In connection with this counter-attack a curious incident took place. Lieut.-Colonel Munro with 2nd Lieut. G. N. Rome visited the Keep at about 4 a.m. and, finding everything satisfactory, started to walk back, with their two runners, to Festubert by the road running east. Soon after leaving the Keep they ran into a party of ten Germans. So close were they that the Colonel actually hit one man across the head with his cane before turning to join the others in a dash for safety. Luckily the Germans lost their heads and instead of using their rifles threw bombs which were quite ineffectual though the Colonel did get a number of small superficial wounds in the back. By the time they remembered their rifles the party was out of sight but 2nd Lieut. Rome had the bad luck to get a bullet through the hand. On arriving back at the Keep, Colonel Munro warned Captain McSwiney that a counter-attack was being prepared and the task of the garrison was made easier for them.

A patrol of "Y" Company from Cailloux Keep South brought in a wounded German warrant-officer in the early hours of 13 April. He had been wounded during the attack on the 11th and had been found by a patrol the same night but as he begged to be left where he was on the chance that his own side might find him he was given food and water and allowed to remain. The next night he was very weak and " Y " Company sent him down to Battalion Headquarters on a stretcher. While he was lying outside the dugout waiting to be sent away another German, who had just walked over from his own lines and given himself up, was brought in. It did one good to see the undisguised contempt of the warrant-officer, exhausted and suffering though he was, for the little skrimshanker.

On the night of 13/14 April further changes in dispositions were made. "Z" Company was relieved by the 1/5th South Lancashires and took the place of "D" Company, 13th King's, in Route A Keep; "X" Company took over Festubert East Keep and Festubert South, "V" Company occupied Festubert Central and the shell-hole positions west of the Cailloux Keeps and the party of "Y" Company in McMahon Post moved to Cailloux Keep North, its place being taken by Battalion Headquarter details.

The next two days passed without special incident, but Festubert was heavily shelled at intervals by 5.9 and 8-inch howitzers. There had been in the Festubert area several artillery observation posts, concrete towers built inside houses and, of course, invisible until the houses were blown away. The enemy had already destroyed three of these—at Brewery Corner, MacMahon Post and Ration Corner—but there was one still standing just outside Battalion Headquarters near the Festubert cross-roads, and this seemed to be the German gunners' target. The shelling made the headquarters dugout a very noisy place, to say the least of it. One shell burst under the dugout occupied by the batmen and blew the floor up to the ceiling. By rights they should all have been killed but except that one sprained his ankle none of them was any the worse.

The Battalion was relieved on the night of 15/16 April by two companies of the 1st Gloucestershires and one of the 1st South Wales Borderers, 1st Division, and after marching to Beuvry by platoons climbed into motor-buses and reached its billets at Raimbert, a mining village eight miles west of Béthune, at 4 a.m.

So ended a strenuous week which cost the Battalion 2 officers and 57 other ranks killed or died of wounds, 8 officers and 127 other ranks wounded, and 1 officer and 5 other ranks missing, afterwards reported killed.

The decorations won were numerous. Lieut.-Colonel D. C. D. Munro received the D.S.O., and his Adjutant, Captain T. G. Roddick, the Italian Silver Medal for Military Valour. Military Crosses were awarded to Captain J. R. McSwiney and 2nd Lieut. L. A. Davey who were responsible for the attack on Route A Keep, and to 2nd Lieut. T. W. Pilkington who took command of " Z " Company when Captain H. Mackay, M.C., was killed and by whose fine leadership Loisne Central was successfully held. A bar to the Military Cross was awarded to Captain J. E. Rusby, M.C., the medical officer attached to the Battalion, who did sterling work for the wounded. The Scottish were always lucky in their doctors. Distinguished Conduct Medals were won—by Corporal G. Jordan who, in the attack on Route A Keep, was the first to reach " X " Company's objective; he then worked his way round the flank and overpowered a machine-gunner who was holding up the main attack; his coolness and daring materially contributed to the success of the operation and saved the attackers many casualties; by Lance-Corporal A. Haynes who, in " Z " Company's action at Loisne Central, did extraordinarily fine work ; in the hand-to-hand fighting he killed several Germans with the bayonet and when, in the general melée, he had no room to use the bayonet, fought them with his fists; he took two machine-guns and brought them back with him ; and by Corporal J. Frost who, as N.C.O. in charge of the transport, brought the rations safely through each night on roads that were continually shelled ; on two occasions his horse was killed under him but he carried on and got the transport forward. Three men, Serjeant F. W. M. Crane, Corporal P. Quinn and Lance-Corporal J. Plant, received bars to the Military Medal, and the Military Medal was awarded to Serjeant W. Rushton, Corporal R. J. Lowes, Lance-Corporal J. V. Short and Privates F. Settle, W. Ellison, E. Penlington, F. S. Coward, E. Wright, T. R. Hoyle, G. Marsh, F. Walker, T. V. Edwards, W. C. Veevers, J. McLoughlan and J. T. Ryder.

The work of the Transport and Quartermaster's Stores throughout the battle was beyond praise. Their task was a difficult one. Shelled out of Mesplaux Farm they first moved to a field behind Locon, losing one wagon on the way which was recovered at night after the Orderly Room Serjeant, W. G. Bromley, and some of the pipers had made a special journey to it to rescue secret documents and the Battalion's typewriter. From there, for a time, all available men were rushed up to a position east of Locon where they were ordered to line a hedge and to hold on to the last if attacked. On relief they followed the transport to Hinges, two miles west of Locon, where the night of the 9th was spent. The next move had to be made in a hurry when Hinges was shelled and they withdrew to Chocques, three miles south-west. From there, too, they were shelled out and went on to Lapugnoy and afterwards to Raimbert when the Battalion came out of the line. In spite of all these wanderings they never failed to get rations up to the Battalion at night—and ample rations, 35 to 40 bags to a company—though the work was complicated by their having to deliver to two or three dumps owing to the Battalion's being split up and attached piecemeal to other units. There was even rum, sufficient for at least one issue per night and made doubly necessary because the men had left their greatcoats behind at Le Hamel and Mesplaux Farm and suffered a good deal from the cold.

The Battalion runners, too, deserve special mention.   The buried cable from Festubert to Gorre was the only line not broken by the bombardment on 9 April and practically all communication had to be carried out by runner. The way in which all the runners discharged their duties without complaint in the heaviest shelling and even after they were almost too tired to stand excited the admiration of everyone.

The 55th Division is believed to be the only Division which, attacked in force during the enemy's offensive in the Spring of 1918, held its line intact, and it was the means of preventing the coal-mining area, of which Béthune is the centre, from falling into German hands. 9/16 April was a glorious week in the history of the Division and the Scottish can claim to have done their share in making it so.   Though they were never involved in such severe fighting as fell to the lot of the 164th and 165th Brigades, their defence of Loisne Central and their capture and retention, with the 13th King's, of Route A Keep made the line safe at one of its most vulnerable points and provided the firm pivot necessary to the formation of the defensive flank.

There is no doubt that the practice which the Battalion had had in taking up its " bustle " positions was a very important factor in securing the victorious result of the battle.   Not only the officers and N.C.O.'s but all the men knew exactly where they had to go and the best way to get there and this knowledge undoubtedly saved a great deal of time and prevented confusion. The Major-General's foresight in insisting upon these practice " stand-to's " which, as can be imagined, were very unpopular, had its due reward.

The enemy was unlucky in choosing 9 April for his effort. If he had attacked the previous morning he would have found the 166th Brigade south of the Canal where, indeed, he expected it to be on the 9th for from captured documents it was learnt that his gunners had guaranteed that this brigade would be prevented by their shelling of the bridges from crossing the Canal to assist the remainder of the Division.   Certainly the

N

Brigade's task would have been made immeasurably more difficult if it had had to cross the Canal under heavy shell-fire, and the result might very well have been that, when it did succeed in crossing, it would have been too late to play the part it did in defending the flank of the Division. Again, had the enemy postponed his attack one day he would have met the 166th Brigade in the trenches of the right portion of the Portuguese sector. Possibly he would not have succeeded in breaking through there, but there would still have been a defensive flank to be formed farther north and no reserve brigade to form it.

All the gear—blankets, packs, etc.—which had been stored at Le Hamel and Mesplaux Farm was recovered later unharmed except that some light-fingered gentry had been through a few of the packs. There was, however, one serious loss, the sausage-making machine, which must have taken the fancy of the battalion which had been occupying Mesplaux Farm. An appeal was sent to Liverpool to which, as usual, Colonel Forbes Bell gave immediate attention and within a month a new machine reached the Battalion.

Eight officer reinforcements joined the Battalion at Raimbert amongst whom was Major R. Cunningham, M.C., who took over the duties of Second-in-Command.

No training on a large scale was attempted and company parades were the rule, the time being devoted to cleaning up and refitting. On 19 April Major-General Jeudwine inspected and addressed the Battalion. The men were as pleased with him as he was with them and gave him a great reception.

Any hopes that a long rest might be anticipated were dispelled when orders were received on 20 April that the 166th Brigade would return to the Givenchy area the same night and be attached to the 1st Division. The 1st Division had been heavily attacked on 18 April in front of Givenchy. After severe fighting, during which he suffered appalling losses, the enemy was thrown back, but he succeeded in taking and holding the front-line trenches including the crater-posts. There appeared every prospect that the attack would be renewed and the 166th Brigade was sent up to be handy if required.

After a motor-bus journey the Battalion spent one night in billets at Verquin and the next evening, the 21st, relieved the 1st Gloucesters in the defences in front of Gorre, " X " and " Y " Companies being in trenches in Gorre Wood and " V " and " Z " Companies farther forward in the southern portion of the

Tuning Fork Line. That night a new trench was begun behind the Loisne Stream, east of Gorre Wood.

At 4 a.m. on the 22nd the enemy opened a hurricane bombardment on Loisne and Route A Keep and in the attack which followed succeeded in retaking the Keep. Later in the day word was received that the 2nd Battalion Liverpool Scottish from the 57th Division would join the 1st Battalion for amalgamation. The 2nd Battalion arrived in the early hours of the 23rd and immediately took up positions in the trenches as follows : " A " Company in the new trench behind the Loisne Stream, " B " Company in the Turning Fork Line, " C " Company in the Tuning Fork Switch, and " D " Company in the vicinity of Windy Corner. This opportune arrival of a fresh battalion warranted the immediate preparation of a counter-attack on Route A Keep by troops from the scanty reserve, " X " Company, under 2nd Lieut. L. A. Davey, M.C., with a platoon of " Z " Company, was chosen to carry out this work, zero-hour being fixed at 4 a.m. on the 24th. It seemed hard on " X " Company to ask it to attack the Keep for the second time but it was the only company which had a real knowledge of the ground.

At 3-30 a.m. the five platoons, about 130 all ranks, moved off and took up their position in extended order about 150 yards from the enemy, facing north. At 3-55 a.m. the Heavy Artillery and 18-pounders, assisted by machine-guns, laid down a barrage on a line in front of the Keep immediately south of Route A. Five minutes later the heavies lifted to the Keep itself and the men moved forward. At 4-5 a.m. the 18-pounders also lifted to the Keep and the attackers dashed in to secure the road which they did, capturing a machine-gun and killing five Germans who apparently were a covering party for wiring operations which were being carried on in front of the Keep itself. Without a pause the platoons went on and in spite of uncut wire and heavy machine-gun fire forced an entry into the Keep and were soon in possession of the whole objective.   Ten prisoners were taken and three machine-guns, one of which was turned on those of the enemy who had escaped and were running for safety. The fighting had been bitter and up to this time casualties amounted to approximately fifty. The platoons were at once reorganized to meet a counter-attack but none was made, the enemy contenting himself with steady shelling of the Keep throughout the day which caused a further twenty casualties, curiously enough all slightly wounded. The bombardment became intense at midnight but no action followed and at 1 a.m. on the 25th the garrison was relieved by " D " Company of the 2nd Battalion from Windy Corner, and went back to hutments near Brigade Headquarters.

Success in this lively little action was only won by the splendid determination of the men, who were admirably led by 2nd Lieut. L. A. Davey. He received a Bar to the Military Cross he had won a fortnight before. A Military Cross, too, was awarded to 2nd Lieut. T. J. Price who, though mortally wounded in front of the Keep, refused attention and continued to cheer his men forward to the assault.

A Bar to the Distinguished Conduct Medal was well earned by Serjeant A. Baybut who, as usual, was fearless in carrying out his duties as Medical Serjeant; he went forward through a very heavy enemy barrage to tend the wounded, German as well as our own, and by his gallant behaviour saved many lives; he also rushed out of a trench to the assistance of some officers and men who had been buried in a dugout, and worked with unremitting energy, in spite of continuous shelling, until all but two were rescued; his contempt of danger and his splendid example were an inspiration to all. The Distinguished Conduct Medal was awarded to Serjeant D. McRae who, when his platoon-commander became a casualty, took command and led the platoon with great skill; he entered an enemy post and attacked from the rear a machine-gun that was holding up the main attacking party which was then able to advance without further loss; his very gallant behaviour undoubtedly greatly helped in the capture of the Keep.

The following received the Military Medal—Serjeants S. McKay and R. Bell, Corporals L. Cottam and J. Dixon and Private J. Selby.

On the night of the 25th, units of the 137th Brigade, 46th Division, took over the left portion of the 55th Divisional front and both the 1st and 2nd Battalions of the Liverpool Scottish moved to new positions. "A" and "C" Companies relieved two companies of the 1/5th South Lancashires in the front line from Barnton Road to Le Plantin South, "B" and "D" Companies joined "V" Company in the Windy Corner locality, "Y" Company occupied a strong-point, Marais East Keep, south of Estaminet Corner, and "Z" Company was withdrawn to Le Préol. Except for intermittent shelling and several false alarms of enemy attacks the next two days were quiet so far as the Scottish were concerned, but they heard with considerable interest that the enemy had retaken Route A Keep on the evening of 26 April. He was turned out again two days later by troops of the 46th Division and thenceforward the Keep, which had changed hands eight times since 9 April, remained in British possession.

Both Battalions were relieved on the night of the 27th, the 1st by the 1/7th and the 2nd Battalion by the 1/6th King's Liverpools, and marched back to billets at Labourse, a large village three miles south-east of Béthune.

The casualties during this second half of the Battle of Givenchy totalled 2 officers and 24 other ranks killed and 50 men wounded. Nearly all of these casualties were incurred during the recapture of Route A Keep.

THE SECOND BATTALION

AT HOME

As for the remainder of the time which the Liverpool Scottish
spent in France and Belgium the 1st and 2nd Battalions
1914 were combined to form one unit, it will be convenient
at this stage to set down the doings of the 2nd Battalion
at home and abroad.

Briefly stated, its history is one of monotony and disappointment. The Battalion was made up of the best type of recruit
and leavened with a fair sprinkling of wounded and invalided
men from the 1st Line. No finer material could have been wished
for and the Battalion asked nothing better than to be allowed
to show as soon as possible that it could hold its own in the field
in any company. Instead, however, of being sent overseas when
its training was completed it found that, with all the other
second-line units of the West Lancashire Division, it was required
for home defence, and for upwards of two years it marked time
in England. More than once warning orders to be prepared to
go abroad were received and the men were given final leave
but it was not until the early months of 1917 that the Division
at last went to France. On arrival it was sent to hold a quiet
sector in front of Armentières and remained there until the
autumn. The Division then took part in one of the final attacks
of the Third Battle of Ypres but the Liverpool Scottish had little
chance to distinguish themselves as their Brigade was in reserve.
There followed another spell of trench-warfare in the old sector
and then came the order to amalgamate with the 1st Battalion.
Notwithstanding its undoubted efficiency, therefore, thanks to
a home-training such as few battalions received, the 2nd Line
of the Liverpool Scottish, during its stay in France as a separate
unit, was never called upon to take part in a major engagement
but had the exasperation of seeing its energies dissipated and its
numbers frittered away in costly minor enterprises and by the
normal wastage of trench-warfare. But all the dreariness and
drudgery could not weaken its spirit as the 1st Battalion quickly
found when the amalgamation took place.

In September, 1914, the Military Authorities decided to raise
second line units of the Territorial Force. Captain A. Fairrie
was sent to Liverpool from Edinburgh to enrol recruits for the
Liverpool Scottish and shortly afterwards Captain W. H.
Maxwell and Lieut. G. B. L. Rae joined him to assist in the

formation of the new battalion. There was no difficulty in finding the men and it was not long before the Battalion was up to strength. For some time the men slept at their own homes and training was carried on daily, usually in Newsham Park. The only permanent-staff instructors available, Colour-Serjeant A. T. Thacker and Serjeant J. M. Forsyth, were busy men for almost the whole of the work of instruction in recruits' drills and musketry fell on their shoulders. Their services then and throughout their connection with the 2nd Battalion merit special mention.

Early in November the home service contingent and the foreign service details, who had been left behind at Tunbridge Wells when the 1st Battalion went overseas, returned to Liverpool and joined up with the 2nd Line. Lieut.-Colonel Wm. Nicholl took command of the new unit with Captain Fairrie as his Adjutant and, in the middle of the month, a move was made to Blackpool, where the men were billeted in houses in the Albert Road area. On the day before the Battalion left for Blackpool the King's and Regimental Colours were handed over to the Lord Mayor for safe keeping in the Town Hall.

The Battalion remained at Blackpool, with occasional detachments at Fleetwood, until 28 February, 1915, *1915* and was then transferred, with the remainder of the South Lancashire Brigade, to Tunbridge Wells where the next three months were spent.

Up to the end of its stay at Tunbridge Wells the 2nd acted as draft-finding unit to the 1st Battalion. Four drafts in all, totalling about 600 men, were sent out and the numbers were made good by further recruiting. Towards the end of May, however, the rôle of the 2nd Battalion was changed. It was no longer called upon to furnish drafts but became a permanent complete unit of the West Lancashire Division. A special draft-finding unit, the 3rd Battalion, was formed at Weeton, near Blackpool, consisting of a training staff and 200 men under Major D. A. Campbell. A summarized account of the work of the 3rd Line will be found in the Appendix.

The Battalion at this time presented a rather nondescript appearance on parade. The demand for uniform far exceeded the supply, owing to the rapid expansion of the Army, and battalions, like the Liverpool Scottish, with a distinctive dress fared worse than those which wore the stereotyped khaki. Though most of the men were clad in the regulation Forbes tartan kilt many had to be content with khaki kilts, and some even had to put up with tartan trews. This difficulty, of course, gradually righted itself.

After an uneventful stay at Tunbridge Wells the 2nd Battalion, on 1 June, set out by route-march to Ashford, in Kent, a two days' journey, one night being spent in bivouacs at Cranbrook. Three weeks later those ineligible or not passed fit for active service—about 300 in all—were detached from the battalion and went off, under the command of Lieut.-Colonel Nicholl, to Norwich where, with details of other Lancashire Regiments, they were formed into the 49th Provisional Battalion, a home-defence unit. The command of the 2nd Battalion was taken over by Major A. Fairrie, with Major W. H. Maxwell Second-in-Command, and Hon. Lieut. D. D. Farmer, V.C., Quartermaster. Lieut. Farmer, who had been one of the colour-serjeant-instructors on the permanent staff before the War, had gone to France as Regimental-Serjeant-Major of the 1st Battalion and was posted from it to the 2nd Battalion when he received his quartermaster's commission. A year later he was appointed Adjutant, and Bandmaster G. W. Mansbridge became Hon. Lieut. and Quartermaster.

Ashford, an important railway centre, was the target of a Zeppelin raid on 17 August. Nineteen incendiary bombs were dropped, some of them unpleasantly near headquarters, but the only casualties reported were two sheep killed.

The rifle-shortage had been acute ever since the outbreak of war and Japanese rifles, for drill purposes only, had been issued to the Battalion at Blackpool. These were withdrawn at Ashford and replaced by Lee-Enfields, but only of the old long pattern. The short Lee-Enfield was not given to the Battalion until shortly before it went to France.

A further move was begun on 22 August and occupied four days. The Battalion bivouacked successively at Harrietsham; Clare Park, West Malling, near Maidstone; and The Wilderness, near Sevenoaks; and finally arrived at Oxted where it went into a canvas camp in Tandridge Park. This camp had been occupied for some time by other units and the Scottish quickly discovered that their predecessors had not taken away all their belongings with them. It was not until all the palliasses and clothing had been stoved that the trouble was overcome and the experience was not relished by men who, up till then, had been sleeping in clean and comfortable beds in private houses.

The work done by the Battalion at Oxted consisted principally of digging trenches in the chalky soil on the heights at Woldingham as part of the London Defence Scheme.

Only two incidents of note need be recorded of the stay at Oxted, a Zeppelin raid which did no damage and a tremendous gale early in October which brought down most of the marquees and some of the bell tents but did not disturb the Regimental-Quartermaster-Serjeant, J. Tweedie, who was found peacefully asleep amid the wreckage of his store-tent.

The Scottish left Oxted on 23 October to take up winter quarters at Maidstone. The last night in camp was a convivial one and the men thought it rather like hitting below the belt when they were turned out at 11-30 p.m. for a practice alarm. Everything passed off smoothly, however, and there were no regrettable incidents. Perhaps the officers had been celebrating too.

After a night in bivouacs at The Wilderness, Maidstone was reached on the 24th and the men were billeted on the inhabitants in the neighbourhood of the Tonbridge Road.

The Scottish remained at Maidstone for nearly seven months. Besides the normal training the Battalion repeatedly practised the occupation and relief, by day and night, of trenches which it had dug on Boxley Hill. Special training, also, was given to a number of recruits who had arrived from the 3rd Battalion.

The Social side of things was not forgotten. Many members of the Brass Band had not gone overseas with the 1st Battalion and they formed a nucleus round which Bandmaster G. W. Mansbridge built up a really excellent instrument. Frequent concerts were given in the Corn Exchange which were greatly appreciated by the townspeople and the troops. Dramatic and variety entertainments, too, were regularly given by parties from other units and the men could not complain of lack of amusement in their spare time.

The Agricultural Hall was requisitioned as a dining hall for the Battalion and here on Christmas Day the men had their dinner of turkey and plum-pudding. All the carving and waiting was done by the officers and serjeants.

Shortly before the Battalion left Maidstone there was a curious departure from the usual order of things when *1916* a large draft was sent to the 3rd Line for final training before being passed on for service overseas with the 1st Battalion. This was the exception which proved the rule and was the last occasion on which the 2nd Battalion acted as a draft-finding unit.

The Battalion left its "cushy" billets at Maidstone on 12 May, and two days later, after one pouring wet night in bivouacs at Charing and a second at Chilham, went into a canvas camp at Littlebourne, four miles south-east of Canterbury. The whole Division, now styled the 57th, was concentrated in the neighbourhood of Canterbury and on 16 May was inspected, at Westbere, by Field-Marshal Sir John French to whom had been given the responsibility of organizing the defence of Britain against invasion. He insisted that two complete divisions of trained troops, to be chosen by himself, should be retained in England for home defence and he was so impressed with the appearance of the 57th Division that he at once selected it as one of the two.

The Battalion fired a musketry course at Sandwich between 22 and 26 May and afterwards, as a plague of gnats was making the camp at Littlebourne unbearable, moved to Scotland Hills near Fordwich, one mile nearer Canterbury. Here two more inspections took place, the first by General Sir William Robertson and the second by General Sir Francis Howard. From here, too, the Battalion marched to Canterbury Cathedral to attend the memorial service for Field-Marshal Lord Kitchener. It was a strange coincidence that the 1st and 2nd Battalions of the Liverpool Scottish should each have taken part in ceremonial parades connected with the deaths of the two great Field-Marshals, Lord Roberts and Lord Kitchener, who jointly had brought the South African War to a successful end.

In July the 57th Division was transferred from Canterbury to Aldershot and on the 16th the Liverpool Scottish entrained for Mytchett where they remained under canvas for more than two months. This was a busy period. Two full musketry courses were fired on the Pirbright ranges, much practice in the science of trench-warfare was put in on Frith Hill where a complete system of trenches had been dug, and inspection followed ceremonial inspection with monotonous regularity. The first of these, a Brigade affair, was held on 26 August by Brigadier-General G. C. B. Paynter, D.S.O., Scots Guards, who had a few days before taken over command of the 172nd Brigade from Brigadier-General A. L. Macfie, V.D., an old friend and an ex-commanding-officer of the Liverpool Scottish. General Macfie had commanded the Brigade for more than a year and the Battalion said good-bye to him with real regret. Field-Marshal Sir John French inspected the Division for the second time on 19 September and this was a full-dress rehearsal for a still more important inspection on the 23rd when the Division, under the command of Major-General R. G. Broadwood, marched past His Majesty the King on Laffan's Plain. With His Majesty were the Earl of Derby, Field-Marshal Sir John French and General Sir Archibald Hunter.

In spite of all these martial activities time was found for other pursuits. From 15 to 20 August the men were given training leave, the third they had had since the Battalion was formed. During their absence a tremendous rain-storm flooded the camp and kept the camp-guard occupied. Very successful Regimental Sports were held in Mytchett Farm Field, and boating, in craft of all shapes and sizes, on the Aldershot-Basingstoke Canal was a popular evening entertainment for the troops which often ended in shipwreck, happily with no fatal results.

On 29 September the Battalion once more changed its address and moved into Blackdown Barracks where it was housed in huts and in the married quarters. The usual training was continued except during one fortnight when the Battalion was lent to the Senior Officers' School, Aldershot, for demonstration purposes and received high praise from the 'Commandant, Brigadier-General R. J. Kentish, D.S.O., whom it was to know more intimately later on in the 166th Brigade.

Early in 1917 rumours, more persistent and circumstantial than ever before, were circulated that the Battalion *1917* would really see active service in the near future. Rumour became certainty when steel-helmets and gas-masks were issued. All the men, too, again repeated the Oath of Allegiance before their company-officers. By the end of January the Battalion was fully equipped and ready for war-service and in February, with the other units of the 57th Division, the 2nd Line of the Liverpool Scottish left England. Shortly before the departure of the Division H.R.H. The Duke of Connaught visited every unit, on behalf of His Majesty the King, and wished it good-bye and good luck.

An advance party consisting of Captain E. W. Bird and four other officers with fourteen N.C.O.'s left Blackdown Barracks on 1 February. Their experiences will be dealt with in the next chapter. On the 16th the Battalion's transport with Lieuts. E. Duckworth and A. Jowett and 83 other ranks, under the command of Major W. H. Maxwell, sailed from Southampton for Havre and reached Bailleul on the 19th. The Battalion itself set out by train to Southampton on 18 February. Fog caused a delay of two days and on the 20th the Battalion was

marched on board the s.s. *La Marguerite*, an old acquaintance
as any who sailed from Liverpool to Llandudno before the war
will remember. For some reason unexplained the men were
marched ashore again and, after a night in one of the rest-camps
near the town, re-embarked on two other transports, the right-
half Battalion under Lieut.-Colonel Fairrie and the left under
Major R. H. D. Lockhart. Havre was reached the following
morning and the Battalion entrained at once for Bailleul. It
arrived there at 11 p.m. on the 23rd and set out to march to
its immediate destination, Estaires, where it went into billets
in the town at 3 a.m. on the 24th.

THE ARMENTIÈRES SECTOR AND
" DICKY'S DASH "

1917

The advance party reported on 4 February to the Head-quarters of the 1st Brigade, New Zealand Expeditionary Force, and the same night went into the trenches in the Bois Grenier sub-sector where it was attached to the 2nd Canterbury Battalion. Although many individuals in the Liverpool Scottish, both officers and men, had already seen active service they were none of them up to date in the elaborate routine of trench-warfare and the object of sending parties in advance to live with the troops which the 57th Division would shortly relieve was, of course, to familiarize a certain number of leaders with the sectors which their battalions would take over and to ensure continuity of method and of work after the New Zealanders had gone out.

The Liverpool Scottish advance party was most cordially received by the 2nd Canterburys and the three weeks which it spent in the line and in reserve with them would have left no regrets behind if it had not been for one unlucky experience. On the night of the 18th 2nd Lieut. I. I. McGillvray, a Cameron Officer attached to the Scottish, and Serjeant F. Tyson went out with a patrol of the Canterburys. The patrol was ambushed in no-man's-land and the only men who got back to the British trenches were two wounded privates. 2nd Lieut. McGillvray and Serjeant Tyson were both killed. It appears that patrols were in the habit of leaving the trenches always by the same route and that, in course of time, the Germans discovered this and sent men out to lie in wait with results only too successful. Accidents of this sort may occur in any battalion if continued immunity from disaster is allowed to breed carelessness but this accident, for which they considered themselves responsible, so upset the New Zealanders that they voluntarily left behind, when they were relieved, several of their men to show the Scottish any known danger points and to help them in every possible way.

The advance party rejoined the Battalion at Estaires on 24 February.

While at Estaires all members of the Battalion were passed through a specially constructed chamber filled with poison-gas, to test the reliability of their gas-helmets. This operation had other uses besides the purely technical one of proving that the helmets were sound. The man who learns by experience that he is fully protected even in a dense concentration of gas is not likely to lose confidence in himself or in his helmet if he afterwards has the unpleasant experience of watching a cloud of chlorine rolling towards him from the enemy's trenches.

On 26 February the Liverpool Scottish, 30 officers and 836 other ranks, relieved the 2nd Canterburys in the Bois Grenier sub-sector and to those men who had been with the 1st Battalion when it first went into the trenches the contrast between the two reliefs must have been arresting. At Kemmel there had been a furtive scramble over muddy fields in the middle of the night; at Bois Grenier, thanks to the long communication-trenches, the Battalion strolled comfortably into the line in broad daylight and found, not the miserable burrows which did duty as trenches during the first winter, but a highly organized system of front, support and reserve lines, linked together by numerous communication-trenches. The trenches themselves—or breastworks, rather, for it was impossible to dig down into the low-lying marshy ground—were in good repair, dry and floored with duckboards. The front line was peculiar in that it had a parados only at those parts of it which were garrisoned. Between these posts there was merely a sandbag barricade with a duckboard track behind it. As the front taken over by the Battalion was more than 2,000 yards, the front line was only thinly held and the posts were few and far between. The duty of visiting these posts at night was not a congenial one as there were long stretches of unoccupied breastwork between them. This point will be dealt with later.

The sector which had been allotted to the 57th Division extended from Laventie through Fleurbaix to Chapelle d'Armentières, a distance of some seven miles. This was an exceptionally long divisional front even for a quiet part of the line. The 170th (North Lancashire) Brigade—2/4th and 2/5th King's Own Royal Lancasters and 2/4th and 2/5th Loyal North Lancashires—held the southern sub-sector, the 171st (Liverpool) Brigade—2/5th, 2/6th, 2/7th and 2/8th King's Liverpools—the centre, and the 172nd (South Lancashire) Brigade—2/9th and 2/10th King's Liverpools and 2/4th and 2/5th South Lancashires—the northern sub-sector. It will be noticed that the grouping of the infantry battalions in the brigades differed from that of the 55th Division. In the 57th they were grouped in the same way as in the pre-war West Lancashire Division.

o

The hub of the divisional sector was Armentières, a town of nearly 30,000 inhabitants. Although at its eastern end it was within rifle-shot of the German trenches, Armentières had suffered surprisingly little damage. It was full of civilians who carried on their normal business as though the war were a thousand miles away instead of at their doors. Some of the factories were working and it was said that, unknown to the enemy, they were getting their electric power from Lille, seven miles away behind the German lines, and that a French engineer at the Lille electricity works was responsible for this impudent subterfuge.

During the seven months which the Division spent in the Armentières sector the 172nd Brigade continually held the Bois Grenier—Chapelle d'Armentières sub-sector. The usual routine of the Liverpool Scottish was eight days in the trenches in front of Bois Grenier or Chapelle d'Armentières followed by eight days in support at Streaky Bacon and La Rolanderie Farms or, sometimes, in Erquinghem-Lys which may be described as the Battalion's base for it contained the Quartermaster's stores and in its cemetery the Scottish buried their dead.

The Battalion quickly settled down to trench-life and began, by active patrolling at night, to learn its way about in no-man's-land and to make itself familiar with the position of the German posts.

On 21 March Lieut. A. S. Darroch and 2nd Lieut. J. Darroch took out a silent raiding-party of one serjeant, J. E. Moss, two corporals and four men and, after cutting a gap in the German wire, entered the trench which proved at that point to be unoccupied. The raiders waited for some time in the hope of intercepting a patrol but as no one came along they moved to their left up the trench until they heard voices and were challenged from the firebay next to the one they had reached. As they did not reply to the challenge a stick-bomb was thrown over the traverse at them and slightly wounded Lieut. A. S. Darroch. The raiders at once replied and, after they had bombed the post thoroughly, made their way back to their point of entry without interference. They were heavily fired on as they recrossed no-man's-land but reached their own trenches without further casualties.

This was only one of several occasions on which the enemy's lines were entered and the Scottish soon gained a reputation for daring and useful patrol work. Both Lieut. A. S. Darroch and his brother were later awarded Military Crosses and Serjeant

J. E. Moss a well-merited Distinguished Conduct Medal for consistent good work and fine leadership on patrol.

A night raid, on more ambitious lines than that recorded above, was attempted shortly afterwards in which each unit in the 172nd Brigade was represented. The Liverpool Scottish contributed one officer, Lieut. J. H. Mennie, 4th Camerons attached, three N.C.O.'s and eight men for the raiding party itself and Lieut. J. C. Belford to act as adjutant and liaison officer to the officer in charge of the raid, a company-commander of the South Lancashires. A fortnight was spent in practice on dummy trenches representing that part of the enemy's lines which was to be entered and all details were most carefully worked out. The raid had the usual object, to do damage and take prisoners, but it was also made the occasion for an experiment with new equipment which the higher command wished to test. There was issued to each man a breast-plate of steel, jointed to allow freedom of movement, and a fibre cape which covered the neck and shoulders and had a turned-up collar attached to it to protect the head and face. This fibre was said to resist shrapnel and bomb splinters. The Scottish, like the others, were dressed in khaki with all regimental badges and distinguishing marks removed, to make identification difficult if any of the raiders fell into the enemy's hands. As was usual in night raids the men had blackened faces.

Zero-hour was at 10 p.m. on 10 April and promptly at that time the artillery and trench-mortars, which had been bombarding the German trenches, lifted and formed a box-barrage round the area to be attacked. The raiders then made their assault, their flanks guarded by two Lewis-guns posted in no-man's-land. The raid was a complete failure. The Germans had evidently been expecting it and opened a murderous fire not only from their trenches but from the borrow-pit in front of them. It is doubtful if any of the raiders succeeded in entering the enemy's line. They were hampered by the experimental equipment and the parties which had been responsible for laying bridges across the barbed wire could not carry out their task. It was a much diminished party which eventually got back to the British trenches.

Two of the Liverpool Scottish received the Military Medal for particularly gallant conduct, Serjeant R. Hartley and Lance-Corporal A. S. Getty. They found Lieut. Mennie lying wounded in the borrow-pit in front of the German line and fought off the enemy while they attempted to get him away. He was, however, wounded again, and mortally, by a bomb and they had to leave him.

A week later the 171st Brigade attempted a raid with similar results. After it was over Lieut. P. Carnelly with four of the Liverpool Scottish went out to look for wounded. Though they searched the ground for some hours they found none and had to content themselves with bringing in a dead man and a wire bridge.

About this time the Scottish said good-bye with great regret to Lieut.-Colonel A. Fairrie who was recalled to England on attaining the age-limit for commanding-officers. The 2nd Battalion was very much his child; he had served with it from the day it was formed and its efficiency was due in no small measure to his keenness and ability. His place was taken by Major E. L. Roddy, Cheshire Regiment.

On 20 April the Battalion was sent to Bac-St-Maur, nearly four miles from the line, for three weeks in Brigade reserve. There was not much rest about this break in trench duty for a great deal of work was done in the digging of reserve-trenches, but at least it was a change of surroundings. At Bac-St-Maur, Major E. G. Thin, from the 3rd Battalion, reported for duty and the Scottish were in hopes that he might be given command but to his disappointment and theirs he was appointed second-in-command of the 2/9th King's Liverpools.

Shortly after the return of the Battalion to the trenches an incident occurred which illustrates the risk run by visiting-patrols at night in the front line where there were long unoccupied stretches of travel-trench. On 16 May Captain A. MacD. Doughty and eight men were on their way from one post to another when bombs were thrown on to the duckboard track immediately in front of them. No one was hit and the patrol at once replied with bombs and rifle-fire, ineffectively as it turned out, for when the ground was searched no enemy dead or wounded were found but only a few stick-bombs and a German cap. The patrol was lucky. It would not have got off scot-free if the Germans had not thrown their bombs too soon. Other battalions had had similar experiences, not always with such tame results, and as a consequence orders had been issued that visiting-patrols in the front line at night should never consist of fewer than one officer and six men.

As a reprisal for this attempted ambush the Scottish, ten days later, sent out a fighting patrol of 2 officers, 2 serjeants and 36 men with orders to enter the enemy's trenches and bring

" DICKY'S DASH."

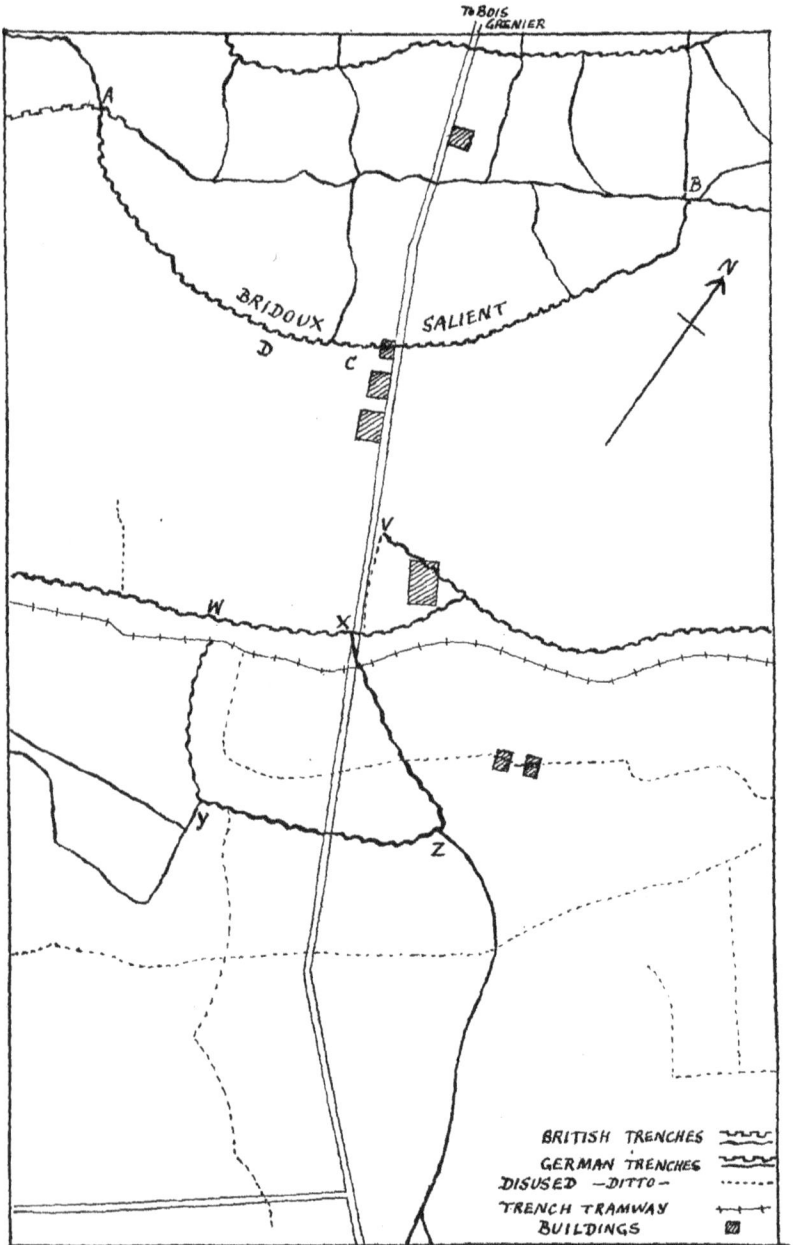

To BOIS GRENIER

A

B

BRIDOUX SALIENT

D

C

N

V

W

X

Y

Z

BRITISH TRENCHES
GERMAN TRENCHES
DISUSED —DITTO—
TRENCH TRAMWAY
BUILDINGS

YARDS 100   50   0   100   200   300 YARDS

back prisoners. The enemy, however, proved to be very much on the alert. While the patrol was still fifty yards from the German wire a searchlight was turned on to it, and at once three machine-guns opened fire. The patrol reached its own lines again with a loss of two men killed, one officer, 2nd Lieut. R. McKinnell, and eight men wounded, one of whom afterwards died. The two dead men and all the wounded were brought back to our trenches.

Portuguese troops made their appearance in the divisional sector on 14 June when the 12th Regiment relieved the 2/9th King's Liverpools in the trenches. A Company of the Liverpool Scottish was put into the subsidiary line behind them until they settled down. Later 80 of them were attached to each Company in the line for instruction. The men were a fine sturdy lot but their officers did not appear to take much interest in them or in what they did. The enemy was not long in discovering that they had arrived and he promptly shelled a battalion of them out of its billet, a laundry on the road between Erquinghem and Armentières. It was inevitable, of course, that the man in the ranks should waste no time in inventing a nickname for them and they became and remained the " Pork and Beans " in spite of an Army Order forbidding the use of a phrase which might offend allied susceptibilities, though nothing derogatory was intended. Indeed it is rather a compliment than otherwise to have the dignity of a nickname conferred on one by the British Tommy but other nations cannot be expected to appreciate his unique point of view.

Early in June the Scottish were ordered to begin training a company for a daylight raid—afterwards known as " Dicky's Dash "—the first to be attempted in the 57th Division. " C " Company, Captain A. P. Dickinson, which had won the silver bugle for the best company in the Battalion, was chosen but the other company-commanders' protests were so loud that it was decided to toss for it. " C " Company won and was sent to billets in Erquinghem to spend three weeks in practising the attack in dummy trenches representing the enemy's position, specially constructed with the help of aeroplane photographs.

The part of the enemy's line selected for the raid lay on the extreme right of the Bois Grenier sub-sector, opposite to a disused trench in the British front line known as the Bridoux Salient. The objects of the raid were to destroy as many of the enemy as possible and to bring back identifications and booty. Zero-hour was fixed for 3-5 p.m. on 29 June.

During their training very careful attention was given to every detail which might help the men in the raid. In addition to the actual rehearsals in the practice-trenches, they received numerous lectures on what had been learnt, from air-photographs, of the enemy's dugouts, machine-gun emplacements, etc., and parties were sent up to the line at night to patrol the ground and learn its features. The rest of the Battalion also had its share in the preparation. The Bridoux Salient, which was unoccupied except for one listening-post, had been filled with barbed-wire and its parapet had fallen in many places. As it was chosen for the point of assembly of the raiding party the parapet of the front line proper was tunnelled through at A and B to allow the men to enter the salient, the parapet of the salient itself was repaired where it did not give cover from view and the barbed-wire was cleared sufficiently to leave a free passage from one end to the other. All this work was carried out as unobtrusively as possible so that the enemy might have no previous warning of the raid. There remained one task, the cutting of gaps in the barbed-wire entanglements in front of the salient to let the raiders out into no-man's-land. Two of these were made, at C and D, and were cut at an angle so as to be inconspicuous from the enemy's trenches. This work was left until the last and the gaps were not completed until the night before the raid. All the preparation was done well, but at a price. On the night of 27/28 June the enemy suddenly opened a chance bombardment on the salient and of the three killed one was Captain Alan Cookson, "D" Company's commander, who had been superintending the work. After spending the first winter with the 1st Battalion he had been posted to the 2nd Line and it had no more capable officer nor one who was more popular with his men. Seven others were wounded by the shelling, amongst them Lieuts. E. H. Hollins and W. Sergeant who were two of the officers of the raiding party and had been out with a reconnoitring-patrol. Their places in the raid had therefore to be filled at short notice.

"C" Company's 4 officers and 161 other ranks, marched out from Erquinghem between 10 and 11 p.m. on 28 June to Crombalot Farm, on the western outskirts of Bois Grenier, where they spent the night in barns. If any proof is needed that the men were in good fettle and not troubled by nerves, the fact may be mentioned that one platoon "slept in" the next morning long after reveillé. Dinners and a tot of rum were served at 11 a.m. and before noon Mills and P bombs had been issued and the company was ready to move off. At 1 p.m. it set out for the front line by sections at 200 yards' interval, Nos. 10

and 12 Platoons by Hudson Bay Avenue, a communication
trench in the sector of the battalion to the west of the Scottish
and Nos. 9 and 11 Platoons by Shaftesbury and Tramway
Avenues, two main communication-trenches to the north of the
Bridoux Salient. On reaching the front line the half-companies
turned inwards and entered the salient from opposite ends. By
2-30 p.m. all were in position, Nos. 9 and 11 near gap C., and
Nos. 10 and 12 near gap D.

The section of the enemy's position—front line, communication-trenches and support line—which the raiders were to attack
is enclosed on the sketch-map between the letters W, X, Z
and Y. Each platoon was allotted a definite task. No. 12
Platoon was ordered to cross the enemy's front line at W, move
down the communication-trench to Y, block the trench at that
point and then turn along the support line towards Z to join
up with No. 11 Platoon which would be undertaking an exactly
similar programme by way of X and Z. These two platoons were
called the right and left communication-trench parties. Behind
them Nos. 10 and 9 Platoons were ordered to capture and
occupy the front line between W and X, to make blocks at
these points and to keep the way clear for the withdrawal of
the forward parties. One section of No. 9 Platoon under Lance-
Serjeant J. H. Collins was given a special duty. Its task was
to enter the " nose " between X and V and to mop up that
part of the trench in order to protect the left flank from possible
enfilade fire.

The raid was to be carried out in three phases on a rigid
time programme. During the first phase, two minutes, the men
were to leave their assembly position and get across no-man's-
land under cover of the barrage on the enemy's front line.
In the next phase five minutes was allowed for the assault on
the front line and the advance of the communication-trench
parties, while the barrage lifted to the support line. The
third phase, when the hardest fighting might be expected, was
to last for twenty-three minutes during which time the support
line was to be attacked and the whole area cleared of the enemy.
Finally the signal for withdrawal was to be given by bugle and
whistle in the enemy's trenches and the British front line.

There was no preliminary bombardment but the German
barbed wire was cut by medium trench-mortars from dawn to
8 a.m. on the 29th and, as the Intelligence Officer was not
satisfied that it was sufficiently destroyed, by 18-pounders during
the morning, using 106 fuse. While the raid was in progress the
heavy artillery fired on selected points in the enemy's lines and

a flight of the Royal Flying Corps co-operated by bombing his trenches on the flanks of the position. A box-barrage, too, was laid down by machine-guns round the raided area and other machine-guns were detailed to cover the flanks.

At 8-5 p.m. the barrage opened and the men filed out through the gaps at C and D, extended in no-man's-land and moved forward in two waves at 25 yards' interval, Nos. 12 and 11 Platoons in front. They were played across by Piper T. Wilson who continued to play until his pipes were smashed. No-man's-land was crossed without a casualty and the men lay down before the enemy's front line and waited for the barrage to lift. The artillery was marvellously accurate but one or two men, who had got too close to the barrage, were hit.

At 8-7 p.m. the second phase began, the barrage lifted to the support line and the raiders dashed in. They had no trouble whatever with the barbed wire. The enemy was quick to man his parapet in the front line when the shelling stopped and the trench was not entered without hard fighting. 2nd Lieut. A. Jowett, lent by " A " Company, was killed here. He exchanged revolver shots with a German officer and killed him but was himself immediately struck by two bombs. No quarter was asked or given on either side and the struggle which followed was savage in the extreme. The only party which was not heavily engaged was the section of No. 10 Platoon detailed to form a bombing-block at W. It met little opposition and did the work allotted to it without interference. The party of No. 9 Platoon responsible for the bombing-block at X met considerable resistance, especially in the trench behind the " nose." After a bombing fight, all the enemy there were killed. The Lewis-gun with this party disposed of an enemy post on the left flank and the bombing-block was established. A deep dugout with a heavy steel door was found in this vicinity. Just as the door was being closed a P bomb was thrown in and many Germans rushed out. Ten or twelve were killed with the bayonet and two prisoners were taken but as they refused to get over the parapet they were disposed of. While this melée was going on, a number of the enemy escaped from the dugout by another exit and made off by the communication-trench down which No. 11 Platoon had gone towards the support line. The remainder of Nos. 10 and 9 Platoons, between W and X, also had their share of fighting. After a general bombing affray they rushed in and bayoneted all Germans found in the trench. Those who had taken refuge in the three concrete dugouts in this stretch of trench were ejected with P bombs and killed as they emerged. These platoons reported that the artillery fire had been most effective and had cost the enemy many casualties.

At 3-12 p.m. the third phase began. No. 12 Platoon, the right communication-trench party, had great trouble in finding the communication-trench as it had been almost obliterated by the shelling. This delayed the platoon and it was unable to carry out the full programme but what it had time to do was done thoroughly. Its bombers ejected a body of Germans from shell-holes where they had taken shelter and its Lewis-gun, mounted on the parados of the front line, wiped out the survivors as they ran. This Lewis-gun also knocked out a hostile machine-gun which had been mounted in the support-trench south from W. No. 12 Platoon, too, reported that the barrage had caused the enemy losses.

No. 11 Platoon, the left communication-trench party, found its communication-trench little damaged and reached Z without serious opposition, half the men going by the trench and half over the open. Two prisoners were sent back by this platoon who bolted when they got to the front line. Both were killed before they had crossed the tramway. A bombing-block was established at Z and No. 11 Platoon turned along the support line. At once fighting developed and the platoon became heavily engaged. An officer who was seen to be directing the enemy's resistance was killed and a German who was coolly mounting an automatic rifle in the support line was shot. The platoon bombed its way along the trench and completed its task.

The withdrawal signals, at 3-35 p.m., were clearly heard and the raiders started to make their way back from the German trenches, taking three prisoners with them. By this time the enemy had begun to shell the Bridoux Salient and no-man's land and several men were hit. Unluckily, two of the prisoners were killed by the shelling and the third broke away from the escort and took cover in a shell-hole. He was shot by other members of the company during the withdrawal.

The retaliatory shelling on the Bridoux Salient had, of course, been expected and the men had received orders to take cover in ditches in no-man's-land on the flanks of the salient and not to return to the front line until dusk, or earlier if things were quiet enough to allow them to do so. These ditches had been carefully reconnoitred beforehand and their position pointed out to the men at lectures during the training for the raid. Those who obeyed this order and remained in the ditches avoided the worst of the shelling but a number of men who ran straight back

into the salient were killed or wounded, as were about a dozen
of a platoon of " A " Company which had been sent up to
support the raid and to garrison the Bridoux Salient while it
was in progress.

It was unfortunate that it had not been possible to bring
in any prisoners but, this apart, " C " Company had done all
and more than all that was asked of it and had given the enemy
such a handling as he was not likely to forget. Messages were
received from the Corps and Divisional Commanders congratulating the company on its fine work. Officers of other units, too,
who had watched the raid from the flanks were full of admiration for the behaviour of the men and one observer in an artillery
observation-post reported that " they went across in magnificent
style."

" C " Company had indeed made a name for itself and for
the Battalion but at a heavy cost.   The company and the
supporting platoon of " A " Company lost between them 15 other
ranks killed or died of wounds and 48 wounded, besides 3 officers
and 32 other ranks missing. The officers, 2nd Lieuts. A. Jowett,
L. C. Blencowe and D. G. McLaren, and 23 of the men were
afterwards known to have been killed. These figures speak only
too plainly of the grimness and bitterness of the fighting.

In such an engagement there must necessarily be many acts
of outstanding determination and bravery. They did not pass
unnoticed as the list of numerous decorations awarded shows.

Two men won the Distinguished Conduct Medal : Serjeant
L. S. Welbon who, at the head of his men, attacked an enemy
counter-attack, bayoneted three and dispersed the remainder,
was the first to enter the enemy trench and, though wounded,
remained at his post until all his party had withdrawn ; he set
a splendid example throughout : and Private G. Sammons who,
though shot through the neck, kept his Lewis-gun in action until
he was wounded a second time, and later brought it back to our
lines himself after all his team had become casualties ; he
displayed remarkable pluck and determination.

Military Medals were awarded to Corporal C. B. Cluer,
Lance-Corporals A. H. Lester and J. E. Davis and Privates
C. H. Quayle, S. Ritchings, H. Stone and W. G. Lawson, who all
distinguished themselves by acts of conspicuous bravery.

Captain A. P. Dickinson, in spite of his repeated appeals,
was not allowed to go over the top with his company but had
to remain in the British lines at raid-headquarters. He had been

responsible for the smooth organization of " Dicky's Dash " as
well as for the actual training of his men, and the Military Cross
which he received was no more than his due.

The enemy's *moral* was good and he fought well.   The only
sign of panic in his ranks was that when the raiders entered his
front.line a party broke from the support line and ran away over
the open.   They were dealt with by the machine-guns of the
aeroplanes.   Otherwise he fought with great coolness and again
and again tried to mount machine-guns in his support line.   These
were as frequently knocked out by the forward Lewis-guns of the
raiders which did excellent work.

It is impossible to say with accuracy what the enemy's
casualties were but, at a most conservative estimate, there were
60 to 70 dead in the trenches which were attacked, besides a
number wounded, and he must also have suffered from the
bombing of the Royal Flying Corps and the shelling of the
howitzers on the flanks of the attack.

On the night of 6/7 July the enemy raided a part of the line
held by the 2/5th South Lancashires and must have been not a
little surprised to find the trenches tenantless.   The explanation
was that an aeroplane photograph taken a few days before had
shown what appeared to be practice-trenches in a field near
a village used by the Germans as a billet for reserve troops.   On
investigation these trenches were found to be an exact copy of
a portion of the British line and it was obvious that a raid was
being prepared.   It was especially important at that time, three
weeks before the opening of the Third Battle of Ypres, that the
enemy should be prevented from securing prisoners from the
examination of whom he might glean information which would
help him to guess that an attack was coming and where it would
fall.   The South Lancashires, who were holding the threatened
area, were therefore ordered to evacuate it on the first sign that
the raid was imminent.   The enemy's trench-mortars, as soon as
they began to cut the barbed-wire, advertised the fact that the
raid was about to begin and the garrison withdrew hurriedly and
left the Divisional Artillery to deal with the raiders.   The South
Lancashires got off lightly but the Scottish were caught by the
protective barrage, which the Germans put down on the flanks
of their attack, and lost four killed and twenty wounded.

In July the volume of artillery fire increased on both sides
and on the night of the 21st Armentières, which had escaped so
long, was subjected to a heavy bombardment, probably retaliation for the British shelling during the Battle of Messines the

previous month, when many of the guns were in Armentières itself. A large proportion of the 3,000 shells which came over that night was of the new mustard-gas type and casualties were numerous both in the ranks of the 57th Division and amongst the civilians, who were ordered to evacuate the town. The shelling was renewed on the 22nd and continued intermittently until the 29th, when the bombardment was particularly severe and between 6,000 and 7,000 gas shells fell in the town. The Scottish, who were occupying the Chapelle d'Armentières sector, had a number of casualties but other units in the Division had such serious losses that the usual system of reliefs was dislocated and, as a result, the Scottish spent three weeks at a stretch in the line.

The British Army at that time was using, in addition to the Stokes-gun, a trench-mortar which threw a heavy shell, popularly known as the "flying-pig." It made a very satisfactory noise and no doubt did serious damage when it landed in the right spot, but the mortar was erratic in range and direction and when it was firing at a part of the line where the enemy's trenches were close to ours the garrison of the front trench was usually withdrawn to avoid accidents. The "flying-pig" was probably as unpopular with the British as with the German infantry, and the Scottish were not pleased when they heard that a shoot had been arranged on 10 August during which they would evacuate Orchard Post, a small salient which jutted out towards the enemy's lines and the supporting line behind it. The garrison withdrew according to orders and the "pig" got to work. The counter-bombardment which the Germans laid down seemed exceptionally severe—it cost the Battalion one man killed and seventeen wounded—but the reason for it was clear when the men returned to Orchard Post and found that an enemy raiding party had come across in their absence. The raiders had, of course, failed to secure any prisoners but they had taken a Stokes-gun away with them. The officer responsible for having left it behind when Orchard Post was evacuated must have spent a most enjoyable five minutes explaining its loss to his commanding-officer.

On the night of 27 August three strangers arrived in the front line from no-man's-land. One was very badly wounded and died soon after and one was too weak to talk but the third man was exceedingly voluble in a language that no one had ever heard before. They turned out to be Russian prisoners who had been working close behind the German lines and had managed to make their way across the trenches unseen until, in scrambling through the barbed-wire entanglements, they attracted the attention of a sentry whose shot cost one of them his life.

In September the 57th Division was relieved by the Welsh Division and taken out of the line for a rest and to train for active operations. The Scottish handed over their trenches on the 17th to the 17th Royal Welch Fusiliers and went back to billets in Estaires. The next day they moved on to Bas Rieux, on the outskirts of Lillers, where they spent a rainy night in bivouacs and on the 19th marched nine miles farther west to Flechin which was to be their home for a month.

The Battalion took a trophy with it from Bois Grenier as a memento of the sector. In a little tower, high up above Moat Farm, hung a bell. The farm and the tower were shell-damaged and rickety and the bell looked as if it might crash into the courtyard at any unexpected moment. The public-spirited Company-Serjeant-Major W. E. Cole averted what might have been a nasty accident by climbing up to the tower and perilously bringing the bell with him to the ground. Battalion Headquarters claimed it and it became a sort of mascot. It afterwards figured prominently in a strange episode which will be described in its proper place.

ALARUMS AND EXCURSIONS

Flechin is a quiet village in a fertile valley and the rolling country round about is all arable land. The harvest *1917* had just been gathered and billeting was difficult as all the barns were full of farm produce but the Battalion was fairly comfortably housed, part at Flechin and part at Boncourt, a smaller village about a mile away.

Training was at once begun, largely in attack-practice, in which the transport and quartermaster's-stores personnel had a share for they were exercised in taking rations across country on pack-mules. The mules were not accustomed to the work and did not take kindly to it and the companies got a good deal of quiet amusement from the frequent tussles between man and beast. On the whole the work done each day was not too long drawn out and, as duties and fatigues were cut down to a minimum, the men had plenty of spare time in which to explore the pleasant countryside. Blackberrying parties were popular.

Brigade sports were held at which one event was a beauty competition open to all ladies in the Brigade area. The prize was won by a British gunner disguised, above and below, in the latest Parisian fashions. If the General had his suspicions when he presented the prize he kept his own counsel.

On 8 October the 57th Division was inspected at Auchy-au-Bois by Sir Douglas Haig. It was a bitterly cold day, with torrential rain which soon drenched everyone to the skin. As usual at these affairs, the troops were on parade long before the hour of the inspection and when the turn of the Scottish came for the march past the pipers were so cold that their fingers would not function at all and the Battalion was played past by the band of the 2/9th King's Liverpools.

The Scottish left Flechin on 18 October and, after a long march of nearly twenty miles, bivouacked for the night at Coinperdu, five miles from St. Omer. The march was unnecessarily lengthened owing to the Battalion's losing its way in the Forêt de Clairmarais and being forced to make a wide detour. A motor-bus journey the next day brought the Battalion to Proven, four miles north-west of Poperinghe. The weather was atrocious and the men arrived at Proven soaked to the skin. It was not encouraging to find that, instead of going into billets or into a dry hutment-camp, they were expected to live in tents on ground that was little better than a muddy marsh. A week was spent under these miserable conditions and the men were not sorry when the Battalion set out for Elverdinghe on the 26th and reached camp, tents again, in the early hours of the following morning.

The Third Battle of Ypres, begun three months before, was still raging and the 57th Division was ordered to attack at Langemarck. Each Brigade in turn was to take part in the attack and the 170th Brigade duly went over the top on 30 October. The work it did proved the value of the Division as a fighting and not merely a trench-holding unit. The Brigade gained ground and held on with the utmost determination but the weather was appalling and, as any further attempt to advance until conditions improved would have meant useless sacrifice of men, the orders of the 171st and 172nd Brigades were cancelled.

The Scottish had moved up on 2 November from Elverdinghe through Langemarck to support positions, " C " and " D " Companies in Eagle Trench, 1,000 yards north-east of Langemarck, " A " and " B " in shell-holes 1,200 yards in advance of them. Two nights later the Battalion was relieved by the 2/4th South Lancashires and took over the front line from the 2/9th King's Liverpools. There was, of course, no trench line. " A," " B " and " D " Companies which were in the advanced positions were given company localities—Requête, Besace and Gravel Farms— in front of which they held a line of shell-hole posts roughly two miles north-east of Langemarck with Houthulst Forest on the left. It was a significant fact that at 5 a.m. on the 5th, the zero-hour of the cancelled attack, the enemy artillery opened a heavy barrage on what would have been the jumping-off line.

The Ypres Salient was a nightmare in winter even when things were reasonably quiet. In the winter of 1917/1918, with almost daily fighting added to the normal discomfort, it was altogether beyond words. The rain and the incessant shelling had turned the ground into a veritable morass and the duck-board tracks, which were constantly shelled, were the only possible means of approach to the forward positions. To attempt to move over the open was to run the risk of getting bogged and many men were, in fact, drowned in the water-logged shell-holes. The Scottish were not sorry that they were only called upon to spent twenty-four hours in the front line. Their burden was made a little heavier than it need have been by the British guns which shelled them heartily, an additional risk not infrequently to be faced after an attack over country with few landmarks, before the new line has been accurately plotted on the maps.

The Scottish were relieved by the 2/4th South Lancashires and returned to Elverdinghe. The losses during the three days at Langemarck were 9 men killed and 34 wounded. The rôle of the Battalion had been entirely passive but it had put in useful work, particularly on one misty morning when the bodies of 150 British and a number of German dead were buried and identifications forwarded to the proper quarter.

After its gruelling at Langemarck the 57th Division was again sent to the back areas for rest and training, and the Scottish left Elverdinghe by train on 7 November for Audricq whence they marched to billets at Zutkerque, a small town eleven miles from Calais and near the Calais/St. Omer road. Here, for a month, the Battalion was exercised and again special attention was paid to practice in the attack, an unpleasant omen for men who had just seen the Salient under winter conditions. Any foreboding of bad times to come did not prevent the Battalion from enjoying its rest and St. Andrew's Night was celebrated in accordance with national tradition—the 1st Battalion at Epéhy was observing the festival in another manner. Leave to Calais was granted on a liberal scale and many men took the chance of getting away for a time from battalion routine.

On 2 December Lieut.-Colonel Roddy left the Battalion. It was unfortunate that circumstances connected with his leaving, which need not be discussed here, involved the departure, not long afterwards, of Major W. H. Maxwell whom everyone had hoped to see promoted to the command of the Battalion. The general disappointment was to a certain degree lessened by the appointment, ten days later, of Lieut.-Colonel W. L. Brodie, V.C., M.C. (Highland Light Infantry), to the command. He soon proved himself an able and considerate commanding-officer and under his strong guidance the Battalion more than maintained its reputation. This gallant officer was killed in 1918 while commanding his own battalion.

There were persistent rumours that the Division would remain in the Audricq area until after Christmas and the Scottish took thought for the morrow and made arrangements to ensure that the dinners should be up to standard. An option was secured on all the turkeys at the surrounding farms and brick ovens were built but this gastronomic foresight was wasted for on 10 December the Battalion was sent by train to Herzeele, twenty miles farther east. After a week there in comfortable billets and amongst really friendly inhabitants—the two did not always go together—the Battalion moved another stage towards the war and took over two hutment-camps—Larry and Émile—at Elverdinghe, where it remained another week. The guns on both sides ceased fire on Christmas Eve and Christmas morning but the Scottish were not allowed long to enjoy the atmosphere of peace and goodwill for they were ordered, on the afternoon of Christmas Day, to march to Boesinghe where they relieved the 2/6th King's in the dugouts in the Canal Bank. It was an awkward flitting as the Christmas mails were exceptionally heavy and the men had to carry their parcels as well as the usual impedimenta of the infantry soldier.

On the 29th the Scottish relieved the 2/9th King's in the front line at the south-west edge of Houthulst Forest, the forward posts being a line of German pill-boxes. The weather was cold, dry and clear and the forest was a weird place at night in the brilliant moonlight. The trees, with their fantastic shadows, brought a sensation of eeriness hard to overcome and startlingly intensified, as one walked through the wood, by the sudden sight in a clearing of a life-size Calvary, picked out in every detail by the moon's frosty light.

The Battalion was not called upon to take the offensive during this tour of duty though the 2/5th South Lancashires, of the same Brigade, attacked successfully on the night of 30/31 December and advanced their line 200 yards.

On the left of the Liverpool Scottish was the 1st Battalion, Queen's Own Cameron Highlanders. This was the first time, since the affiliation, that the Scottish had met the Camerons and they seized the chance of getting to know their parent unit. The company-commander of the left company is reported to have finished the whiskey at the nearest Cameron company-head-quarters on Hogmanay but as there was very little of it no harm was done to the officer himself or to the good-feeling with the Camerons.

The Scottish were relieved on 2/3 January by the 7th Battn. The Buffs and, after assembling at Boesinghe, went *1918* on by train to Elverdinghe. The next day another rail journey brought them to Bailleul and from there they marched to Hollebecque Camp, Steenwerck.

The work done by the Battalion at Steenwerck was principally wiring strong-points in the reserve line which was being con-structed there, and all along the British front, in readiness for

P

the expected German attack later in the year.   As the real Christmas Day had been spoilt by military duty, the men got their dinners and presents on 10 January which was made a holiday.

On the 13th the Scottish returned to the familiar Armentières sector and occupied the subsidiary line at Erquinghem. On the 18th they moved up and relieved the 2/5th King's in the front trenches of the Houplines sub-sector, with their left on the River Lys. This was an uncomfortable period. The trenches were full of water, the weather was bitterly cold and conditions generally could scarcely have been more miserable.

For the next month the Battalion carried on the old dull routine, occupying either the Houplines or L'Épinette sub-sectors and spending a few days periodically in support, or in reserve at Hollebecque Camp. One bright spot early in February was the arrival of Major E. G. Thin from the 2/9th King's to take over the duties of second-in-command.

On 15 February the Battalion went out to rest at Neuf Berquin, a very hard rest as a great deal of work had to be done on the digging of reserve trenches which, incidentally, were of little use when the enemy made his great drive through the Portuguese during the Battle of the Lys in April as there were no reserve troops to occupy them.

In the middle of March the 1st Battalion was at Mesplaux Farm, near Locon, only six miles from Neuf Berquin. A lorry was borrowed and a number of officers and men were given leave to visit their friends in the 2nd Line. With the exception of a visit paid by Lieut.-Colonel J. R. Davidson to the 2nd Battalion soon after it arrived in France this was the only occasion on which the members of the two units had been able to meet as the battalions had never been near enough to each other. There were many happy reunions of old friends and only the return of the 2nd Battalion to the forward area at Fleurbaix on 20 March and the German attack in the south on the 21st, which stopped all leave, prevented a continuation of these cheery meetings.

The Scottish took over the front line before Fleurbaix on 26 March and little thought that this was to be their last tour of duty in trench-warfare as a separate unit. It is interesting to note that at this time the 55th and 57th Divisions were separated from each other only by the Portuguese but it is idle to speculate on the course which the Battle of the Lys might have taken if the 57th Division had remained in the sector until 9 April.

Perhaps the result would have been the same but it seems a pity that the 57th Division missed by only a few days the chance of sharing with the 55th Division the honours of that anxious but glorious day.

The transport-lines and quartermaster's-stores of the battalion holding the Fleurbaix sector were at Croix-du-Bac, four miles away. This meant a long walk each way for the company-quartermaster-serjeants when they went up the line at night with the rations, and the Scottish transport officer, Captain E. Duckworth, offered them each a mule to ride. Only one, Stanley Menin, took advantage of the offer but even he asked to be excused after the first night when his mule reached home two hours before him.

On the last day of March the Scottish received orders to hand in to stores at Estaires all blankets and superfluous kit as the 57th Division was under orders to move to the south and to travel light. It was to be a "flying" division for use in emergency wherever it might be required. The Scottish left Fleurbaix the same night and marched thirteen miles to Haversquerque, near St. Venant. The next day they marched through the Forét de Nieppe and entrained at Steenbecque for Doullens. A march of seven miles northwards brought them to Sus-St.-Leger on 3 April.

There now began a bewildering series of marches and countermarches, all within an area eight miles long and three miles broad. The Scottish moved successively to Sombrin on the 5th, Famechon on the 8th, back to Sombrin on the 12th, to Pas on the 13th and finally, on the 16th, to Hénu. The orders for dress were changed with nearly every move, one day steel helmets were the fashion, the next balmorals, and the object appears to have been to delude the enemy's air scouts into the belief that a large concentration of troops was taking place on the right flank of the great wedge he had driven into the Allied line.

There were one or two incidents during this coming and going which should be recorded.

On the 6th Major Thin once more left the Battalion and took command of the 2/9th King's Liverpools. His fine work with them later on resulted in his gaining the Distinguished Service Order. His place in the Scottish was filled by Major S. Ball of the 2/4th Loyal North Lancashires.

When the Battalion arrived at Pas on the 13th there was a hostile demonstration by the villagers which almost became a riot. They had seen, on one of the limbers, the Battalion's

mascot bell and were convinced that it had been looted from a
Church. At length the parish priest was found and, after explana-
tions, he was able to calm his flock and the incident closed with
mutual expressions of esteem.

On the 17th the Division was allocated to Army reserve and
ordered to hold itself in readiness to attack.   The objective
allotted to the 172nd Brigade was to the east of Fonquevillers and
to the Scottish a line roughly southwards from les-Essarts to a point
east of Fonquevillers. This line was reconnoitred by the officers.

On 19 April instructions were received for the transfer of
the 2/10th Battn. The King's Regiment (Liverpool Scottish)
from the 57th to the 55th Division and the next day they set
off in 'buses for Auchel, seven miles from Béthune.   Farewell
messages were sent by Major-General Barnes and Brigadier-
General Paynter with highly complimentary references to the
Battalion's work in the 57th Division and good wishes for the
future.   An Irish battalion, with pipers, took the place of the
Scottish in the 172nd Brigade.

The Battalion marched three miles to Burbure and after a
night there went on, on the 22nd, to join the 166th Brigade at
Gorre. The remainder of the 2nd Battalion's history as a separate
unit has already been described in the chapter on the Battle
of Givenchy.

So ends the story of the 2nd Line. It is a story of duty well
and cheerfully performed and, if it contains little that is spectacular, success or disaster, it does at least show that a battalion
destined for the most part to live a life of drudgery and inaction
can still gain an enviable reputation for reliability and keenness.
What chances it had to distinguish itself the Battalion grasped
eagerly and the men proved in "Dicky's Dash" that they had that
fighting spirit which would have carried them through to great
things if they had been called upon to take part in any major
engagement.   Thanks to its long home training the interior
economy of the Battalion was exceedingly efficient and there can
have been few units in which every link in the chain of responsibility from the colonel downwards was so sound and the
subordinate commanders knew and fulfilled their duties so well.
On the sports side the Battalion ranked high and the 172nd Brigade
Football Cup presented by Brigadier-General Paynter, which is
now at Fraser Street, is a permanent reminder of this fact. The
Battalion had no concert party of its own but the 57th Divisional
Concert Party, an exceptionally good one, included four members
of the Liverpool Scottish, Grey, Firth, Gordon Browne and
Ralph Collis.

THE COMBINED BATTALIONS

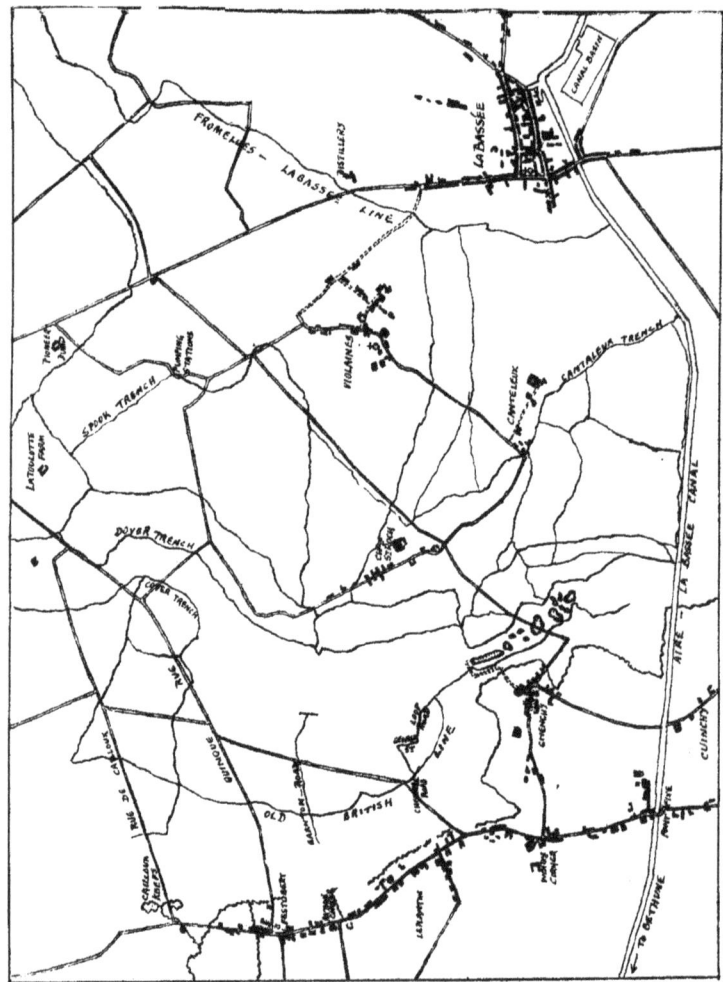

FESTUBERT—GIVENCHY SECTOR, MAY—AUGUST, 1918.

THE END OF TRENCH WARFARE

On 28 April the enemy shelled Labourse and caused some casualties in the 2nd Battalion. For greater safety both *1918* battalions moved the next day to a hutment-camp at Vaudricourt, two and a half miles south of Béthune, and here on 30 April the official amalgamation took place. The battalions were drawn up facing each other and Brigadier-General Kentish welcomed the 2nd Battalion in a very happy speech.

Eighteen officers and 299 other ranks of the 2nd Line were drafted into the 1st Battalion, the men, as far as possible, being transferred to corresponding companies—" A " to " V," " B " to " X," etc. A composite party of 9 officers and 49 other ranks was made up from both battalions and sent off to act as instructional staff to the American Army which was rapidly assembling in France for final training and the remainder of the 2nd Line men, for whom there was no room on the establishment of the 1st Battalion, went first to the Divisional Reinforcement Camp at Allouagne and afterwards to the Base, Étaples, where they were used both for fatigues and demonstration work. They were not transferred to other units but were specially reserved to provide drafts for the 1st Battalion as necessity might demand. The surplus officers of the 1st and 2nd Lines were posted to the famous 51st (Highland) Division.

On 2 May the Battalion, once more up to effective strength, returned to the trenches and took over the Festubert sector from the 1/7th King's Liverpools. It is not necessary to write separately of the successive tours of trench-duty during the summer of 1918. The Scottish invariably returned to the left brigade sector which was divided into the Festubert and Le Plantin sub-sectors. The normal routine was four days in the front line and close support in one sub-sector, four days in support in the positions near to and in the southern part of the Tuning Fork Line and four days forward in the other sub-sector followed by six days' rest at Vaudricourt or, occasionally, Drouvin. Always on relief from the trenches the Battalion took up its " bustle " positions where it remained until after dawn the following morning. On many occasions, too, the Battalion was ordered to leave behind two half-companies as bridge-head guards at Vauxhall and Westminster Bridges. This duty was not unpopular as the men, nominally being on rest, were seldom turned out for work and it was pleasant to bathe in the canal or to sun oneself on the towpath. The dugouts were roomy and comfortable, meals were regular and the area was not often shelled. In many respects the bridge-head guards were better off than the rest of the Battalion at Vaudricourt for besides escaping the march to and from camp they avoided such troublesome distractions as kit-inspections and company-parades.

The 55th Division was still holding the same length of front north of the Canal as before the Battle of Givenchy but owing to the great re-entrant in the British line to the north the angle of the sector was changed. The left boundary of the 55th Division was now a line drawn from immediately north of the Cailloux Keeps south-westwards through the Tuning Fork North Road where the Tuning Fork Switch Line crossed it. Beyond that line was the 46th (North Midland) Division.

The defences of the sector were adjusted to meet the new conditions. The Village Line, which had become the front line, was strengthened and a continuous trench dug from MacMahon Post towards Route A Keep with a branch forking off from behind Brewery Corner and joining up with the southern end of Cailloux Keep North. A network of support and communication-trenches was dug in the neighbourhood of Donnington Hall and Rest for the Weary and this system connected the Festubert defences with the Tuning Fork Switch Line. An immense amount of work was done on the new main line of resistance which was a continuation southwards of the Tuning Fork Switch Line through Estaminet Corner and the Reserve Line. Behind it machine-guns were concentrated in section or sub-section posts and farther back strong-points were strengthened or constructed to pin down the enemy if he should succeed in breaking the main line. One of these, Lone Farm, was turned into a miniature fort with shell-proof concrete rooms, It bristled with machine-guns and concealed an anti-tank 18-pounder gun.

Early in May it was learnt from prisoners and other sources of information that the enemy was preparing another large-scale attack on the Givenchy front. A German who wandered into " Z " Company's trenches on 6 May said that the attack might be expected within two or three days. Harassing fire at night by the Divisional and Corps Artillery on the roads behind the enemy's lines, and on his back areas generally, was redoubled and on 8 May a shoot with aeroplane observation was carried out on an enormous dump of shells which he had for some time been accumulating at Salomé, one and a half miles east of La Bassée. This shoot was entirely successful. One shell scored a direct hit on the main dump and exploded it along with the smaller dumps surrounding it. A personal reminiscence may convey something of the magnitude of the explosion. The writer was sitting at tea in the Transport Officer's billet at Houchin when suddenly the house rocked and there was an ear-splitting crash which seemed to originate somewhere in the village. Thinking that a new giant British howitzer had been brought up and had just fired its first shot from a position unpleasantly close to the billet the members of the little tea-party decided to go out and try to find the gun and reason with the gunners, but on reaching the door saw a heavy pall of black smoke hanging in the eastern sky which told its own tale. As the crow flies Houchin is nearly eleven miles from Salomé.

It was known that against all the rules of war the Germans were employing British prisoners for work on the Salomé dump and it was feared that many of them must have lost their lives when it was blown up. By a strange coincidence the writer recently met one of these prisoners and was told that as the explosion took place during meal-time none of them was hurt, but several had been killed or injured a few days before by an aeroplane bomb which fell on their billet. This prisoner was rather peevish about the success of the shoot. The rush of air from the detonation knocked him off his feet and as he was carrying his day's ration of soup at the time he had to go hungry for twenty-four hours. The fact that the destruction of the dump probably was one of the main causes of the abandonment of the intended attack did not impress him !

Though the attack never came, rumours that it was impending continued to be current for some weeks and the persistence of the enemy's shelling and the constant patrolling by his low-flying aeroplanes, which frequently harassed the men in the trenches with machine-gun fire, appeared to foreshadow active operations. It was, no doubt, the expectation of hard fighting which gave rise to a very pleasant innovation. As has been told already, units which were detailed to take part in an attack were ordered to leave behind a nucleus round which a new battalion could be built up if casualties were overwhelming. This system was now applied to units going into the line for ordinary tours of trench duty and a proportion of officers, N.C.O's and specialists was left out. These battle details, as they were called, were expected to do a fair amount of training but they were not overworked and the few days' respite from the trenches was a privilege greatly appreciated by all ranks. To begin with, the battle-details were billeted at Labourse but when the enemy made things too hot there they were taken right back to Allouagne, five miles west of Béthune, where all was peace except for an occasional high-velocity shell from a long-range gun.

May saw the beginning of the Battalion Concert Party and a first-class party it was with a quite admirable pianist, Daniells. Attractive pierrot costumes and a collection of music, grave and gay, were sent out from Liverpool. The members of the party were permanently excused trench-duty and by diligent rehearsal they soon settled down into an excellent team and were in great demand with the other units in the Brigade as well as with their own battalion.

On 7 June Colonel R. Campbell gave his well-known lecture on the Bayonet, always a good show and perhaps better than usual on this occasion as his P.T. Serjeant assistant was the famous Jim Driscoll. This lecture was followed by a Brigade Fête in the beautiful grounds of Vaudricourt Château.

A curious incident took place during the next trench-tour of the Battalion. The dawn-patrol on 11 June brought in with it three Portuguese prisoners who had succeeded in escaping and were working their way across no-man's-land to the British lines when the patrol ran into them. They had been lucky in being able to slip through the German line of posts unobserved and luckier still not to be mistaken for enemies when the patrol met them.

The second half of June was remarkable for an epidemic of influenza. The symptoms were severe headache and high temperature but the attack, though sharp, was short and lasted only a few days. Corps Routine Orders, indeed, referred to it as " Three Day Fever." Most of the Scottish were infected and more than two hundred had to be evacuated to hospital. As a result the Battalion was unable to leave out any battle-details when it returned to the trenches on 26 June. The Germans had had a very similar epidemic in May and it was commonly reported that the shortage of men through sickness was one of the principal reasons for the cancellation of the much-advertised attack on the Givenchy front. It was a curious fact that if one side suffered from an epidemic of an infectious disease the other side was certain to catch the infection sooner or later. Probably prisoners were the germ carriers.

The enemy's shelling throughout May and June had been very

troublesome and was responsible for almost the whole of the Battalion's casualties during this period, 4 officers and 79 other ranks killed or wounded. Amongst those killed was that fine company-commander, Captain Alan Dickinson, M.C., who had confirmed with the 1st the reputation he had made with the 2nd Battalion. The headquarters of the support battalion near Battersea Bridge was a favourite target and it was here on 29 June that the Scottish for the first time made the acquaintance of the German instantaneous fuse. The British gunners had been using a similar fuse—the 106—for some months and most effective it was. The ordinary high-explosive shell which penetrated a certain distance before detonating had little lateral effect in the open and a man lying down would escape injury nine times out of ten even if the shell landed within a few feet of him. The instantaneous fuse was another matter entirely. So sensitive was it that a shell fused in this way would detonate even on contact with water, and on ordinary ground the lateral effect was extraordinary. There was no shell-hole to show where the shell had pitched, only a blackened circle on the surface of the ground. It was very galling to find that the enemy had been able to copy—without doubt from the examination of shells abandoned during the great retreat in the Spring—one of the most useful inventions of the War.

On 12 July a Brigade Horse-Show was held in Vaudricourt Château grounds. The cup for the best aggregate of points was won by the 1/5th King's Own Royal Lancasters, the Scottish, who won first place for water-cart, light draft and company-commanders' horses and second for cooker, being bracketed second with Brigade Headquarters. The horse-show was followed by jumping and tent-pegging competitions and altogether it was a most enjoyable day. It is probable, however, that the proceedings had been observed by the enemy for the next morning a salvo of 4.2-inch high-velocity shells suddenly arrived on the road behind the huts and the shelling continued at intervals until 9 p.m. The Battalion spent the night in trenches near the Camp. Luckily there were only four casualties, one of them Major R. Cunningham, M.C., who was wounded in the arm. His place was taken the following month by Major J. Gray, M.C., 1/4th Royal Scots.

On 14 July, after a Brigade Church Parade, the Major-General distributed the decorations won in the Givenchy battle.

A new form of entertainment was provided on 19 July when

the Battalion headquarter-details held aquatic sports at Waterloo Bridge. The programme was :—

AQUATIC SPORTS.

H.Q. 10th (Scottish) Battn. King's Liverpool Regiment, 11 a.m. July 19, 1918, in the

MANCHESTER SHIP CANAL.

1. Sprint—60 yards.
2. Diving—(*a*) Neat
      (*b*) High Leap ⎱ Each man has three dives.
      (*c*) Back ⎰
3. Long Swim—from Pier to Pier.
4. Floating Race.
5. Swimming under Water.
6. Relay Race—Police and Runners v. Signallers and Cyclists.

Dress to be Worn—Identification Discs.

Prizes : 1st Prize, 5 francs.   2nd, 100 cigarettes.

The events were judged by Lieut.-Colonel Munro and there was a very large entry but unfortunately the names of the successful competitors have not been preserved.   These sports were organized by Father Pike, the Roman Catholic Chaplain to the Brigade. He had been captured by the enemy during the Battle of Cambrai and repatriated as a non-combatant but insisted upon rejoining the Division in France. The Scottish were fortunate in having him attached to them. He was tireless in his work for the men both in and out of the line and it was only after being directly ordered to do so that he consented to live at Battalion Headquarters and not in the trenches when the Battalion was in the line.   No Padre set a finer example of militant Christianity than Father Pike and in his constant and selfless thought for the comfort of   the   man   in   the   ranks   he,   more   than   any   other, approached the standard of Captain Chavasse.

The summer months of 1918 were remarkable for the activity and success of the daylight patrols carried out by the scouts and snipers under the leadership of 2nd Lieut. B. Rathbone who had succeeded 2nd Lieut. Rome as Scout Officer. The rank growth of vegetation in no-man's-land made it possible for men to creep undetected from shell-hole to shell-hole between the trenches and in this way very valuable information was obtained of the positions of the German posts.   On 26 July Rathbone decided to attempt to rush one of these posts from the rear.   He, in the lead, succeeded in getting under the protecting barbed-wire and had started to work his way round behind the post when he came face to face with a German also on a crawling expedition. Rathbone got his shot in first but the report alarmed all the posts in the neighbourhood and machine-guns started to chatter. Rathbone, on the wrong side of the German wire, was in a very awkward predicament. All patrols wore overalls—as the kilt was an unsuitable dress—and there was always the risk that anyone captured in this garb might be shot out of hand as a spy as he was not wearing a recognized uniform. The only thing to do was to make a bolt for it and this Rathbone did. Thanks to his being a fine athlete he was able to hurdle the barbed-wire and get to earth in a shell-hole before a machine-gun could be switched on to him. By dint of great patience and skill the patrol eventually reached its own trenches, its only casualty one man slightly wounded. Several attempts were made later to cut out isolated posts but the barbed-wire proved too great a handicap. On many occasions, however, the patrol was able to shoot the sentry and there can have been little enthusiasm in the German ranks for the duty of garrisoning the forward positions. The usefulness of the work done by these patrols was recognized by the award of the Military Cross to 2nd Lieut. Rathbone and Military Medals to Privates N. Tanner of the scouting section and R. Burton of the snipers.

On 20 July one company of the 36th Northumberland Fusiliers was attached to the Battalion for instruction and spent twenty-four hours in the trenches, one platoon with each company. This battalion was one of the units of a Division of B 1 category men who had not hitherto been considered fit for service in the line but were now to be used to hold quiet sectors and thus permit fighting divisions to be withdrawn for rest and training. Their medical category did not, however, prevent these B1 men from giving a good account of themselves in the final advance.

On 8 August both the party of the Scottish which had been detached as training staff to the Americans and the surplus men of the 2nd Battalion—274 other ranks—from the Base arrived at the Divisional Reinforcement Camp. Many of these were at once drafted into the Battalion and the rest remained behind for special duty. The 2nd Line details had earned a good name at Étaples for work and discipline which was all the more creditable as they had had no officers with them but had carried on under their own Warrant Officers and N.C.O.'s.

By the middle of August the enemy's great effort had spent itself. Both in the north and south counter-attacks had wrested from him much of the ground he had won in the spring and early summer and the initiative had now passed from his hands for ever. It was time for the 55th Division to improve its position and make ready for the day when it would be called upon to advance. The first necessary step was to retake the crater-posts and high ground at Givenchy which had been in the enemy's hands since 18 April in spite of more than one attempt to dislodge him. This operation was successfully carried out with small loss on 24 August by the 164th Brigade. Two counter-attacks were beaten off and the whole of the crater-posts and the Old British Line as far north as Cheshire Road were recaptured and held and a line of posts established two hundred yards east of the craters. The Scottish took no active part in the attack but were ordered to send up two platoons at night to assist in the consolidation and in wiring the new positions. The next night " Z " Company took over part of the Old British Line captured the previous day.

The Battalion lost another company-commander on 29 August when Captain H. T. Whitson was severely wounded by a shell and died a few days later in hospital. He was one of the officers who originally went to France with the 1st Battalion and had already been twice wounded. Those who knew " Whitty " will realize what the loss of such a cheerful and capable optimist meant to his company and to the Battalion.

Towards the end of August reports were received from other parts of the front that the enemy was starting to withdraw and, on the 30th, units of the 46th Division, on the left, found that he had retired from in front of them and were able to advance their line considerably. Orders were at once sent out from 55th Divisional Headquarters that the battalions in the trenches should keep in the closest touch with the enemy and be ready to go forward immediately if he showed signs of retiring. The next day the Scottish were able to establish a new post in the Old British Line eighty yards north of Cheshire Road and no attempt was made by the enemy to turn them out. In the early hours of 2 September there were definite indications of a withdrawal. The battalion scouts at once went out but failed to make contact with the enemy. A platoon of " Z " Company then moved forward and occupied George Street and Loop Road. A platoon of " X " Company also advanced and was able to occupy the Old British Line as far as Barnton Road. Patrols which were pushed out found no sign of the enemy but no further advance could be attempted as the Battalion was due for relief by the 1/7th King's the same night. After relief the Scottish returned to Vaudricourt Camp where, the next day, they heard that the 165th Brigade had been able to occupy Dover Trench which had been the German front line opposite Cover Trench before 9 April.

The Battalion returned to the line on 8 September and relieved the 1/7th King's Liverpools in the old German front and support trenches in the left sub-sector.   There was no further withdrawal by the enemy during the next ten days and his guns were active against his old trenches. He had left behind a variety of booby-traps in his dugouts—innocent-looking boxes of bombs which exploded when moved and similar unpleasant-nesses—and, though most of these were detected and avoided or rendered innocuous, there were some accidents in one of which a lance-corporal and six men of " V " Company were badly burned.

On 13 September the 166th Brigade dispositions were changed. One of the forward battalions was withdrawn and the Brigade then had one outpost, one support and one reserve battalion, the Scottish being the support battalion. In the course of the next week several minor operations were successfully undertaken.   On the 16th the Division on the left—now the 19th—took La Toulotte Farm and the next day the 55th Division's right Brigade cleared the enemy out of Canteleux Trench.   On the 20th the 1/5th South Lancashires captured Spook Trench and the Pumping Stations in co-operation with the 19th Division who reached the main La Bassée road.   The enemy was still offering considerable resistance and was not prepared to let these successes go unchallenged.   By a counter-attack on the 22nd he drove back the Gloucesters immediately on the left of the Scottish who had now become outpost battalion again.   To conform with the situation " X " Company was compelled to withdraw two platoons which fell back to a position in front of La Toulotte Farm.   The same day a Lewis-gun post of " V " Company under Lance-Corporal E. C. Stanley was attacked simultaneously from two sides by hostile parties each twelve strong.   Stanley and his men at once opened fire on one of the parties and dispersed it.   The other party had by then approached to within bombing range but, hurriedly switching his section's fire round, Stanley forced this party also to retire in disorder.   For their coolness and bravery against odds Lance-Corporal Stanley and Privates R. E. Underwood and A. J. Townley received the Military Medal. Serjeant P. Quinn, M.M., of " V " Company, also had his share of excitement.   He ran into a German patrol but managed to shoot the officer and get away untouched.

The Scottish were relieved on 23 September and went back by train to billets in Béthune. After the usual period of training and a fierce series of inter-company football matches the Battalion returned to the line on 29 September and relieved the 1/5th King's Liverpools as support battalion. During its tour of duty the 165th Brigade had pushed on and captured Pioneer Dump, the Distillery and portions of the La Bassée road all of which it had held against an immediate counter-attack. This operation was carried out by the 1/6th King's Liverpools.

The dispositions of the Scottish were—two companies in the Old British Line and two in the old German support line. The officers of the forward companies on the morning of 2 October were astonished to see through their glasses troops advancing eastwards over the open towards the crest of Aubers Ridge, three miles to the north. If the Germans no longer held the ridge they could not hold La Bassée and it was no surprise when a message was received from Brigade at about 5 p.m. that the enemy was retiring, that the outpost battalion had set off in pursuit and that the Scottish should at once move forward and occupy the position vacated by the outpost battalion.

The great advance had begun.

THE FINAL ADVANCE, OCTOBER—NOVEMBER, 1918.

3 October, Hocron ; 17 October, Allennes ; 18 October, Seclin ; 19 October, Grande Ennetières ; 20 October, Bourghelles ;
21 October, Froidmont ; 9 November, Gaurain-Ramecroix ; 10 November, Villers-Notre-Dame ; 11 November, Attre.

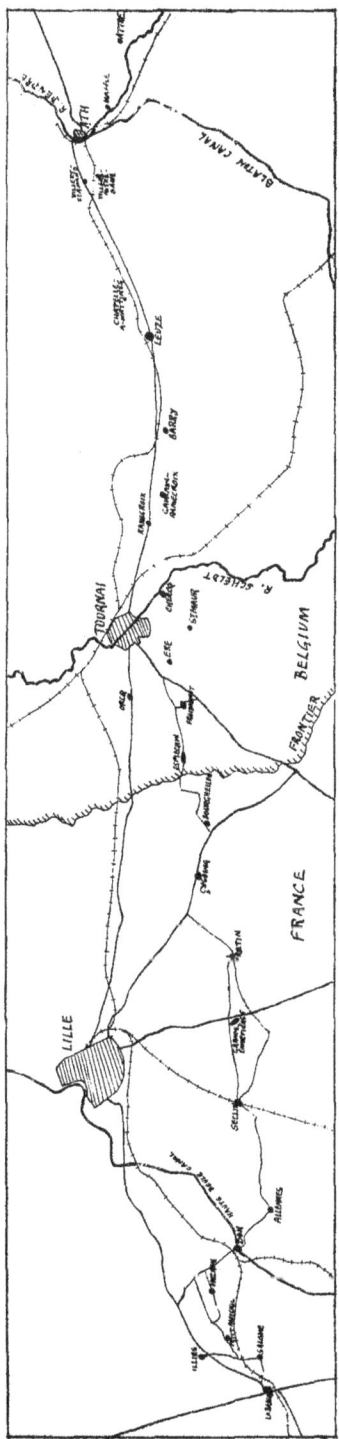

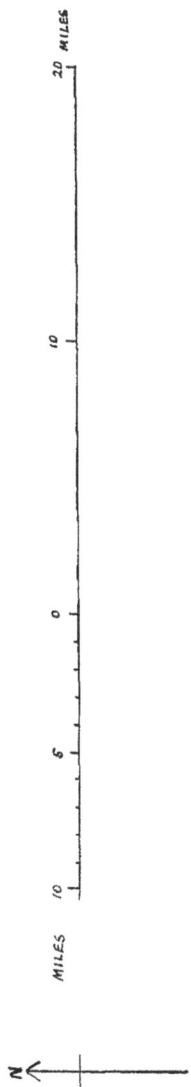

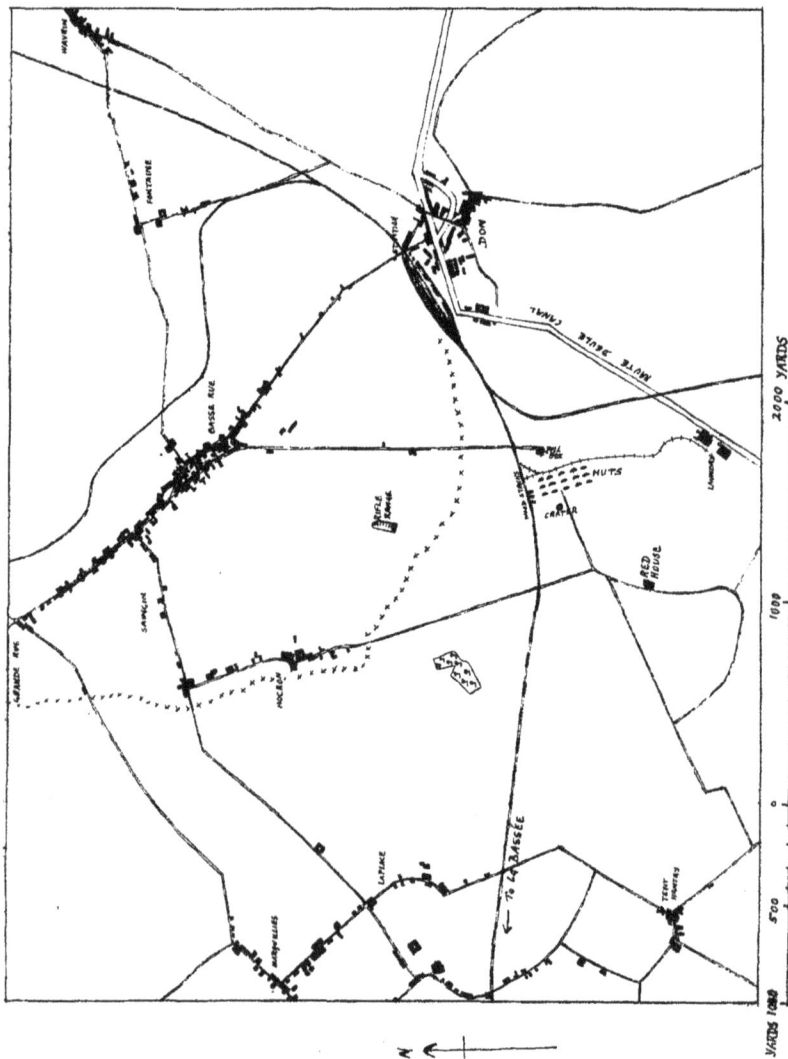

DON.

HAVEN
FONTAINE
CASSÉ RUE
GRANDE RUE
SAMPIGNI
MOREAU
MARQUILLES
LATANE
TENT SQUARES
RIFLE RANGE
PULL BOX
HUTS
CRATER
RED HOUSE
UNNAMED
HAVTE DEULE CANAL
TO LABASSÉE

N ←

YARDS 1000   500   0   1000   2000 YARDS

THE FINAL ADVANCE

Early on the morning of 3 October the Battalion advanced to the La Bassée—Fromelles Line and soon afterwards *1918* moved on via Illies to the neighbourhood of Petit Moisnil. It was a curious sensation to be marching in column-of-route over ground which had been in the enemy's hands for four years and very satisfactory to notice how unpleasant his life had been made for him by the British heavies. The line of burnt-out motor-lorries on the main road from La Bassée to the north, the battered dugouts behind the cemetery and the unburied horses on the road outside Illies were visible proofs of the effectiveness of the harassing fire on the back areas. But apart from the damage wrought by the British guns the Germans themselves had deliberately helped to turn the country-side into a wilderness before they retreated and, as far as possible, they had made the main roads and the railway unfit for traffic. At regular intervals these roads had yawning holes in them which prevented the passage even of horse-drawn vehicles, and in the middle of the railway track systematically every eighty yards a shell had been buried and then exploded electrically or with a time-fuse. To make the railway still more useless and difficult to repair a slab of gun-cotton had been wired to the side of the rails at every join. When the gun-cotton was detonated there was not one individual rail that was unbroken. Booby traps, too, abounded, a favourite one being to remove a strip of pavé from one side of a road to the other, bury two or three big shells base downwards and lay a plank over them with its under-side just clear of their noses. When the plank was covered over with dust it was not easy to detect and the first vehicle which crossed it pressed it down on to the shells. The vehicle then ceased to function and there was another fine hole in the road. " Y " Company had a very lucky escape from a booby-trap of this sort. When approaching Petit-Moisnil by a farm-track through a field the company had to cross a stream by a wide plank-bridge. All got safely over and no trap was suspected but when a motor-lorry crossed the same bridge later in the day the weight on its rear wheels exploded the hidden shells beneath the bridge. The back end of the lorry was thrown right over the bonnet and the driver must have been surprised to find he had suffered nothing worse than a broken arm.

229

Q

At dusk the Scottish became outpost battalion and relieved the 1/5th King's Own on a line running roughly north and south through Hocron. The King's Own had been able to advance some four miles unopposed until in the late afternoon their right company exchanged shots with enemy machine-guns posted close to the La Bassée—Don railway and was held up.

The Scottish had " Z " Company and one platoon of " Y " south of the railway and the remainder of " Y " Company, " X " and " V " Companies to the north of it, the whole front covered amounting to about 3,000 yards. The relief was completed without difficulty and, soon after, orders were received from Brigade to continue the advance and, if possible, get across the Haute Deule Canal, a tall order as it had been learnt from prisoners that the enemy intended to make a stand behind the Canal.

It should be explained that the rôle of the Fifth Army, of which the 55th Division was now a part, was to pursue the enemy and keep him on the move but not to atempt anything in the nature of a serious attack, for which there were neither men nor guns to spare, if he took up a defensive position and showed that he meant to put up an obstinate resistance. In the event of such a situation being encountered, therefore, there was nothing to do but to wait until successful attacks and the pushing back of the enemy on other parts of the front compelled him to withdraw opposite the Fifth Army also, when the pursuit would again be taken up. This should be kept in mind as it has an important bearing on the operations which shortly took place in front of Don.

In the early hours of 4 October the companies pushed on and when dawn broke " Z " Company had dug in just to the east of the continuation of the Hocron road south of the railway, " Y " Company had two platoons on this road astride the railway while " X " and " V " Companies had advanced through Basse Rue and turned south-east, " X " between the diverging roads and " V " to the east of the road from Basse Rue to Don Station, the general line of posts of these two companies being roughly 800 yards from Don. The only company which had had any fighting was " Z," one of whose patrols had run into a German machine-gun post on the Hocron road and captured the gun after killing one of the team. Two platoons of " Z " Company had been compelled to fall back from the farthest point reached as the enemy opened the Canal sluices and flooded all the low-lying land in the neighbourhood of the laundry and to the south of it. These platoons, which had been within 200 yards of the laundry, were washed out of their positions and retired to the vicinity of the red house on the road behind.

The night's advance amounted to about 1,000 yards on the right and 2,000 yards on the left of the Battalion's front.

By 9 a.m. on the 4th every platoon had reported its position except one, No. 10 Platoon of " Y " Company, and the company-commander set out with a runner to look for the lost sheep. After more than an hour's searching of the countryside he came to the conclusion that this platoon must have got into the German lines and been captured, and was walking back to Battalion Headquarters in Hocron to report when he met Lieut.-Colonel Munro with two runners some 500 yards north of the La Bassée railway and midway between the Hocron road and the road running south from Basse Rue. This group stood in the open for several minutes while the officers discussed the situation and was presently joined by a runner from No. 10 Platoon who had previously lost his way and had had to return to his platoon-commander for fresh directions. During all this time there was no sign of life from the enemy, though the little group must have presented an easy and tempting target, and the only conclusion that could be reached was that the Germans had gone. " Y " company-commander left with No. 10 Platoon's runner to see where the missing men had got to while Lieut.-Colonel Munro went off to get the right companies on the move again. The Colonel found Nos. 9 and 12 Platoons of " Y " Company and told them to get forward but as soon as they began to advance heavy machine-gun fire was opened on them and, after they had both suffered a number of casualties and it was clear that they had no chance of getting on, they were ordered back to their starting point and told to try again later, if possible.

So far from having retired the enemy had shown himself very much on the spot. Apparently he did not object to individuals or small groups strolling about the countryside, in fact they were of the greatest possible assistance to him because they showed him the exact positions of the forward platoons, but he would not allow anything like an organized advance—as Nos. 9 and 12 Platoons had found to their cost.

Their losses did not prevent these platoons from making another attempt an hour later. This time they managed to advance 400 yards or so but they were an easy mark for the six machine-guns on the railway-embankment in front of them and casualties were so heavy that Serjeant Cassidy, commanding No. 12 Platoon, took the remnant of his men—six besides himself, two of whom were wounded—for shelter in between two of the wood-stacks at the side of the railway, and Lieut. H. J. White with No. 9 Platoon, after halting amongst the huts to reorganize and making another attempt to get on, withdrew what was left of his platoon—Corporal G. E. Antrobus, the acting platoon-serjeant, and four men—to a bomb-crater to the west of the huts.   These platoons' troubles were not over by any means.   A low-flying British aeroplane spotted the No. 9 Platoon survivors in their bomb-crater and, mistaking them for the enemy, turned the 18-pounders on to them.   The shelling lasted an hour and a runner had to be sent back to get it stopped.   When the British guns gave up the German 4.2-inch howitzers began and, though no shells fell in the crater, they were too near to be pleasant.   Then in the late afternoon the enemy, who had seen No. 12 Platoon disappear into the wood-stacks, put a machine-gun barrage down each side of them to keep the sentries quiet and a raiding party walked down the railway, concealed from any other posts by the thick hedges at each side of the line.   When this party reached the wood-stacks the barrage stopped and the first warning Serjeant Cassidy and his men had of anything wrong was the sudden arrival of several Germans, armed with bombs and revolvers, who invited them to put their hands up.   They were in a trap and, with no chance of resistance, surrendered and were taken away.   The two wounded men with Serjeant Cassidy had made an attempt to escape earlier in the day.   One succeeded in getting away untouched but the other was shot dead as he tried to cross the railroad.

About dusk, No. 9 Platoon sentry caught sight of a small body of Germans on the railway to the left rear.   No doubt they were covering the men who were raiding No. 12 Platoon.   Fire was at once opened on them and they disappeared but Lieut. White, fearing that his little post might be surrounded when darkness fell, decided to withdraw immediately to his original position on the road.   Heavy machine-gun fire was opened as soon as the men showed themselves, and before they got back to the road Lieut. White and one man were wounded.   This reduced No. 9 Platoon to a total strength of a corporal and three men.   In No. 12 Platoon the only men who escaped injury or capture were a lance-corporal and two men who had been with a section which advanced up the north side of the railway and had succeeded in getting back to their position on the Hocron road when the attack was broken up.

Altogether this was " Y " Company's day.   No. 11 Platoon, which had been left behind in reserve at La Place, was ordered, about mid-day, to move forward and take up a position in the old German miniature rifle-range. The platoon advanced in artillery formation and came under machine-gun fire before it reached the Hocron road. The rest of the way the men had to get forward by section rushes but Serjeant J. S. P. Burns, the platoon-commander, handled them so cleverly that he got them through a thick belt of wire and up to their objective with only one casualty. This man was mortally wounded when within a few yards of safety and, unfortunately, Private T. Palmer, who had at once gone back and bandaged him under heavy fire, was himself killed when he attempted to carry out a stretcher to get him away.

The events of the day proved conclusively that the enemy had every intention of disputing the crossing of the Canal and that to dislodge him from his strong position was beyond the power of infantry unsupported by artillery. It was therefore surprising, to say the least of it, to receive orders from Brigade about 8-20 p.m. stating that the Canal bank was the next day's objective and adding that the Battalion was to cross the Canal if possible.

The only possible chance of success was to make a night-attack and try to get amongst the enemy machine-gunners before they realized what was happening. Orders on these lines were at once prepared by the Commanding-Officer but, as every minute was precious, no time was wasted in drawing up an elaborate scheme. " V " and " X " Companies were ordered to work in co-operation on the left, and " Y " and " Z " Companies on the right. The company-commanders were left to make their own plans but all were told that they must reach their objective, the Canal bank, by 5-30 a.m.

The action which followed falls naturally into two parts :—

" V " and " X " Company-commanders, whose headquarters were in Basse Rue, worked out their scheme together and decided to attack with two platoons each and to keep the remainder in reserve in houses immediately south of Basse Rue. Lieut. C. A. White, commanding " X " Company, was responsible for the attack itself and Captain R. T. Ainsworth, commanding " V " Company, remained with the reserve platoons to receive reports from both companies and to deal with any situation which might arise.

" X " Company advanced with a platoon on each side of the road from Basse Rue to Don Station. All the houses along the road were searched, but no enemy was seen until the Company had got forward some 500 yards to a point where the road crossed a deep ditch and the bridge which spanned it was blocked with barbed wire.   Stick-bombs were thrown from across the bridge and in the faint light of dawn, which was just breaking, several Germans were seen running back and into a large house twenty yards away.   A Lewis-gun was at once brought into action against them but the farther advance of both platoons was stopped by flooded and swampy ground and by the ditch itself. The platoon under Serjeant P. Quinn, M.M., south of the road, was ordered to dig in in front of the ditch and the men scratched head-cover for themselves with their entrenching-tools. The platoon under Lieut. W. R. Douglas, north of the road, found natural cover behind an earth rampart at the edge of the swamp. These platoons had both suffered several casualties but they managed to hang on to their positions throughout the day, though continuously tormented by sniping, to which they could not reply effectively, from the windows of houses towards Don Station. Lieut. White managed to find an officer of the Trench-Mortar Battery to whom he explained the situation. A Stokes-gun was brought into action and, with its first shot, hit the house from which most of the snipers were shooting.   They ran for safety, covered by fire from other houses, but the respite was only a short one as the Germans immediately opened fire with a trench-mortar whose second shot knocked out the Stokes-gun. The snipers then returned to the house and resumed their rifle-practice.

" V " Company's platoons advanced to the north of " X " Company with their left astride the branch railway and quite in the air as no contact could be made with the troops of the division on their flank.   They had a succession of skirmishes of a hide-and-seek nature with Germans who were holding houses close to the railway but they gradually pushed on until they were finally held up by heavy fire about 150 yards from the main railway-line. Their casualties had been numerous but they dug in and held their ground all day, though, like " X " Company, they had to submit to a galling fire from snipers whom they could not counter.

These two companies carried out a fine piece of work.

" Y " and " Z " Company-commanders were farther afield than the others, the former in a concrete dugout south-east from the rifle-range and close to the road south from Basse Rue, the latter on the road about 300 yards west from the Red House. In the pitch-darkness and over unfamiliar ground it was no easy task to find, in open country, company headquarters which had been established only a few hours before. No blame can be attached to the runners—who were picked for their bump of locality and "guts"—for the late arrival of the orders. They reached "Y" Company-commander at 3-15 a.m. and Captain A. G. Davidson, commanding "Z" Company, half-an-hour later. There was thus a quite insufficient interval between the receipt of the orders and the time when the attack had to be launched for these two officers to collaborate effectively, especially as they were a mile apart. Each, when he got his orders, sent out patrols to see what was in front of him and worked out his plan independently of the other. They met eventually at 4-15 a.m. in the red house north-west of the laundry and discussed their plans. Captain Davidson had arranged that his company, which was then holding a front of about 700 yards from the neighbourhood of the red house named north to the railway, inclusive, should attack with three platoons—one up the railway and two in the open to the south of it—and make good successively the light railway, the branch railway and the Canal bank. To help this operation "Y" Company-commander promised to try and send a platoon down the road running south from Basse Rue, to turn the enemy's position and guard "Z" Company's flank. "Y" Company's participation in the action which followed was soon over and is quickly told. The company-commander, on returning to his headquarters found that his patrol had come in with the news that the belt of wire—indicated on the map by a line of crosses—was very broad and dense and quite impassable. A squad of men with wire-cutters was at once sent out to cut a gap. When this was finished and No. 10 Platoon, which had dug in astride the road south from Basse Rue and about 100 yards north of the belt of wire, was ordered to advance, it was after dawn. As soon as the sections left their trenches and began to make their way towards the gap machine-gun fire was opened on them and, as it was obvious that no one would get through the wire uninjured, the company-commander ordered the platoon back to its position. So much for "Y" Company.

"Z" Company's attack went famously for a while. No. 15 Platoon, which had been ordered to advance up the railway, bolted an enemy machine-gun team from the wood-stacks, and Nos. 14 and 16 Platoons, on its right, reached the light railway without a shot being fired at them and surprised the Germans in the forward posts there who ran for their lives. After a short halt for re-organization No. 15 Platoon attempted to continue its advance but was driven back. No. 14 Platoon, after going three-parts of the way to the branch railway, came under fire from its embankment and, following an exchange of shots, was thrown back. No. 16 Platoon reached the branch railway with little opposition and some men, on the extreme right, even crossed it and approached the Canal bank. The failure of " Y " Company to get forward and the withdrawal of No. 15 Platoon had, however, left the flank exposed and both Nos. 14 and 16 Platoons were compelled to fall back to the light railway.

Captain Davidson at once organized a fresh advance. He started his reserve platoon, No. 13, up the railway-line and sent a strong Lewis-gun section, of an N.C.O. and eight men from No. 16 Platoon, to attack the pill-box between the light and branch railways. No. 13 Platoon could make no headway at all and the Lewis-gun section, most gallantly led by Lance-Corporal Claridge, was destroyed before it had covered 200 yards. Claridge himself was killed and all his men except one wounded.

An attempt was then made to dig in behind the light railway but it was now daylight and the enemy was fully alive to the situation. He opened heavy fire with his machine-guns and Nos. 14 and 16 Platoons were ordered back behind the first line of huts where again they tried to dig in.

About this time a party of the enemy appeared on top of the branch-railway embankment. Fire was at once opened on them and they moved off northwards. After an interval of comparative quiet—except that any movement at once drew fire—the enemy, about 10 a.m., put down a heavy machine-gun barrage under cover of which he was able to re-occupy his old positions on the light railway. From here he threw bombs over and between the first row of huts and kept " Z " Company's two platoons occupied while he made his preparations for a final assault. At last, half-an-hour later, the enemy opened a heavy barrage with high-explosive shells along the road from the red house to the railway and sprayed the huts with fire from his machine-guns which he had moved to new positions. Under cover of this fire his attacking party was able to work round on the left and take Nos. 16 and 14 Platoons in flank and rear. Only six escaped, the two platoon-serjeants and four men who had been behind a hut in rear of their platoons. They managed to get back to the road and, on their way, collected a Lewis-gun team of No. 15 Platoon which had been posted on the right of the position to watch the flank. So ended a sorry day for " Z " Company.

The Brigadier-General, about a fortnight later when the enemy was once more on the run, attempted to reconstruct on the ground " Z " Company's part in the action and, on quite insufficient evidence, apportioned the blame for the loss of the two platoons to an entirely wrong quarter. The truth was that, as " Y " Company's experience on the 4th had proved that the enemy could not be dislodged without careful preparation, the order to advance on the 5th should never have been given.

The Battalion was relieved at dusk on 5 October by the 1/5th South Lancashires, who wisely did not attempt to occupy the most advanced positions, and went into reserve, with Battalion Headquarters and two companies at Marquillies, one company at Hocron and one at Petit Moisnil.

The two days and nights in the outpost position in front of Don had cost the Scottish 1 officer and 19 other ranks killed, 4 officers and 55 other ranks wounded and 45 men missing. All the missing, except those 5 men of " Y " Company already mentioned who had been taken prisoners, were from " Z " Company and it was not until after the war that anything was known of their fate. Of the 40, 6 had been killed, 19 wounded and 15 were unwounded prisoners. These losses were at once made good by a draft of 129 men from the Divisional Reinforcement Camp and the arrival of 4 officers from England.

Many individual acts of gallantry were brought to the notice of the higher authorities and the following decorations were awarded :—

The Military Cross to 2nd Lieut. Hugh Henderson who, while patrolling with two men in front of " V " Company's position on the night of 4/5 October, encountered an enemy patrol of one officer and twelve men. The officer called on him to surrender but he, with his two men, at once opened fire and drove off the enemy patrol. He then completed his reconnaissance and brought back information of the utmost value.

The Military Medal to Serjeant J. J. Ashcroft, " X " Company, who, in the attack on 5 October, covered the advance of his company by the skilful use of his Lewis-guns and also carried in a wounded man under heavy fire ; and to Corporal E. Grist, " V " Company, who, with only two men, rushed forward and drove the Germans out of a house from which they had been holding up the advance. The Military Medal was also awarded to Corporal G. E. Antrobus who, as acting platoon-serjeant, had given an inspiring example of courage to his men when " Y " Company was trying to get forward on the morning of 4 October.

The Battalion remained in the Marquillies area until 12 October when the 164th Brigade took over the left sector from the 166th Brigade which went into divisional reserve. The Scottish were sent back to Béthune where they found excellent billets. Their period in brigade reserve had been uneventful except for occasional shelling, often with gas, of the villages where they were housed.

Only three days were spent in Béthune and the time was principally devoted to reorganization and company-training. On the 15th the Battalion Concert Party gave a splendid performance. It had been strengthened by the inclusion of new talent and very hard work had been put in at rehearsals. The result was a much more ambitious and homogeneous programme and the troupe justifiably blossomed out into the dignity of a high-sounding title, the " Kinky Roos " (Quinque Rue's).

On the night of the 15th orders were received that the Battalion should be prepared to move early the next morning and at 6-30 a.m. it set out by light railway to Illies and from there marched to the Marquillies area.

During the past four or five days there had been indications that the enemy was about to begin a further withdrawal but he had still stubbornly resisted any attempt to drive him from the Don bridge-head. Troops of the I Corps, immediately south of the 55th Division, had, however, succeeded in crossing the Canal and on the 15th the advance-guard battalions of the 164th and 165th Brigades pressed on and captured most of the enemy's positions west of the Canal. At night the 1/5th King's Liverpools forced a crossing at Don and occupied the village and the next day the enemy was again in retreat hotly pursued by the 164th and 165th Brigades.

On the 17th the 166th Brigade moved forward. The Scottish marched to Allennes where they spent the night and went on next morning to Seclin.

So far no civilians had been found in any of the villages and the enemy had left in his wake evidence of his determination to destroy what he could not hold. Much of the destruction was wanton and malicious. The inhabitants of Seclin had been evacuated a week earlier and all their houses had since been looted. Drawers and cupboards had been ransacked and whatever was not worth carrying away had been tossed aside. The litter in the rooms and in the streets was like a nightmare of spring-cleaning. Nor was the damage confined to goods and chattels. Many of the larger houses and villas had been gutted by fire and the church, with its tower, blown up. Seclin, which must have been a pretty town a few days before, looked as if it had been struck by lightning.

The next morning sudden orders to move cut short a lecture by the Brigadier-General to the officers and N.C.O.'s of the Brigade, and the Scottish marched three miles to Grande-Ennetières. Here, for the first time, civilians were found in the village and here too there had been none of the deliberate destruction for destruction's sake that had been so evident up to this point. The enemy was running so fast that he had no time nor thought for anything except saving his neck by making for his next line of resistance as quickly as possible.

The march the following day through Frétin and Çysoing to Bourgelles, seven miles farther east, was a triumphal progress. All the villages were *en fête* and decorated with bunting and national and allied flags which the inhabitants had somehow managed to hide from the Germans during the occupation. The streets were lined with cheering, laughing, hysterical people who hardly knew what to do to express their joy at the sight of British troops after four years of the hated *boches*. They mobbed the men as they marched along, shaking hands, embracing them and covering them with paper streamers. The Scottish, the first kilted battalion these people had seen, caused great excitement and as for the Pipe Band, it never before had such an enthusiastic audience.

Up to this date, 20 October, the advanced brigades had experienced no serious opposition but their further advance on the 21st was hotly resisted and it was clear that the enemy intended to make a stand on the line of the River Scheldt. An outpost line was established by the forward battalions of these brigades running east of St. Maur—east of Ere—west of Orcq and the same night the 166th Brigade was ordered forward to relieve the 165th Brigade. The Scottish took over from the 1/7th King's Liverpools as support battalion in Froidmont. On the march from Bourgelles the Franco-Belgian frontier was crossed near Esplechin. The great industrial district of France, of which Lille is the centre, was at last clear of the enemy.

The next few days passed without special incident but the enemy shelling was troublesome, particularly at night, and on the 25th all civilians were ordered to leave Froidmont. On the western outskirts of the village there was a large charity home for aged and destitute folk and it was pathetic to see these old people turned out of their comfortable quarters and sent off, the hale on foot and the infirm in ambulances, to a safer area.

On 25 October the Scottish became outpost battalion and relieved the 1/5th South Lancashires in front of St. Maur and Ere where they remained for six days. Here again the shelling was regular and irksome though only four actual casualties were suffered—one man killed and three wounded. A number of men, however, were affected when the enemy, in the early hours of 30 October, drenched St. Maur and the vicinity with mustard-gas and many had to be sent back to the dressing-station for attention.

The Scottish were interested spectators of a thrilling air-battle on 30 October. A German pilot in a single-seater fighter boldly attacked a flight of British scout-machines at about 5,000 feet. He was shot down in flames almost immediately but jumped clear of his machine. After falling like a stone for a considerable distance he was seen to be working at some ropes attached to his body and, all at once, a parachute opened above him. He landed safely a few yards from one of " V " Company's posts and was taken prisoner. Parachutes had long been part of the equipment of the observers in observation-balloons who frequently had to jump for it when their " sausages " were destroyed above their heads but the Flying Corps was not so equipped nor, up to that date, was it known that the Germans were giving their pilots this protection.

The Battalion was relieved on the 31st and went back to billets at Esplechin. Late that night news was received that Turkey had signed an armistice and the next day that Austria had capitulated. The end was in sight.

During this period of rest the " Kinky Roos " gave excellent performances on three successive nights, each time with a complete change of programme. The professional help which those old Bensonians, Lieuts. B. St. J. Rathbone and James Dale, had given to the troupe at rehearsal was evident in the creditable representation at one of these concerts of a scene from " Othello."

The Battalion relieved the 1/5th South Lancashires in support at Froidmont on 5 November. The position was unchanged and the enemy still held his forward posts west and south of Tournai. His withdrawal had now been so long delayed that orders were received from III Corps that it would be necessary for the Division to attack, in co-operation with the 16th Division on the right, and force the crossing of the Scheldt. As a preliminary to this operation, plans were drawn up for an attack by the 165th and 166th Brigades with a limited objective, the west bank of the river. Before this plan could be carried through, however, it was found, on the morning of the 8th, that the enemy was withdrawing. He was energetically followed by the outpost battalions, 1/6th King's Liverpools and 1/5th South Lancashires, which reached the Scheldt during the afternoon in spite of opposition from machine-guns on the eastern bank. The Scottish meantime had moved forward to Ere in readiness to join in the pursuit. Later in the day news came through that the Germans had been given until 11 a.m. on 11 November to accept terms for an armistice dictated to their plenipotentiaries by Maréchal Foch.

The same night the two battalions named crossed the Scheldt on bridges erected by the 419th and 422nd Field Companies, R.E., the enemy having destroyed all the permanent bridges. Little opposition was met and by 3 p.m. the final objective was reached, just beyond Barry, 7 miles east of Tournai.

III Corps had ordered, a short time before, that in the event of the enemy's retiring to a considerable distance from Tournai a mobile and self-contained force should be formed and kept in readiness to act as advanced-guard to the Division. This force, under the command of Brigadier-General Stockwell, C.M.G., D.S.O., was made up of 164th Brigade Headquarters; a squadron of the Divisional Mounted Troops, King Edward's Horse; a Cyclist company; a battery of 18-pounders; the 2/5th Lancashire Fusiliers; a Field-company, R.E.; a section of the West Lancashire Field Ambulance and various oddments. It passed through the outpost battalions at 4 p.m. and took up the pursuit.

The Scottish left their billets at Ere at 9 o'clock on the morning of 9 November and, after crossing the Scheldt by the temporary bridges, marched on to Ramecroix, where the men fell out for dinners, and in the afternoon to Gaurain-Ramecroix where they were ordered to billet for the night. The first civilians were met on the outskirts of Chercq and for the rest of the day the same enthusiastic and emotional welcome was experienced as had been given to the troops when they crossed the Belgian frontier.

The following day the Battalion moved off at 8-30 a.m. and marched, with the 1/5th King's Own Royal Lancasters, to Barry in column-of-route, helped along by the Pipe Band and the Band of the King's Own. At Barry the Brigadier-General held a conference of all officers and platoon-commanders and gave them the day's news—that the Kaiser had abdicated and left for an unknown destination with " Little Willie," that the

Americans had taken Sedan and that the Germans in that district were abandoning stores and guns. The march was then continued and a halt was made for dinners half-a-mile east of Leuze. In Leuze, a town of some 6,000 inhabitants, the troops received perhaps the most wonderful reception of the whole advance. The entire population turned out to see them, of course, even the nuns and monks. The streets were hung with flags and archways of flowers. Not content with this display and with shouts of " *Vive les Anglais*," " *Vive les Écossais*," the people forced gifts on the men—flowers, cigarettes, coffee, anything they had—to prove their gratitude for their deliverance from the invader. After dinners the Pipe Band was sent back into the town to play and dance and, even if they did not altogether appreciate the wild and barbaric music, the good folks of Leuze were polite enough to pretend they liked it. The dancing, at any rate, was something they could understand and there was nothing uncertain about their applause.

In the afternoon the Scottish became advanced-guard to the 166th Brigade and, after passing through the 1/5th South Lancashires, took up an outpost line three miles east of Leuze, with Battalion Headquarters at Chapelle-a-Wattines. At 4-30 p.m. a further move was ordered and the companies marched independently another three miles to a position on the high ground a mile or so from Ath. Battalion Headquarters was established at Villers-Notre-Dame. As advanced-guard the Scottish had attached to them one battery of the 276th Brigade, R.F.A.; one section of the 55th Machine-Gun Battalion; one section of the 170th Tunnelling Company, R.E., and one section of the 166th Trench Mortar Battery.

During this period of his retreat the enemy had done no damage to the villages but had contented himself with blowing up the main road from Tournai to Ath at selected points where it would be most inconvenient and difficult to repair. The Royal Engineers and Pioneer Battalion, however, with civilian help, soon had everything shipshape again, and transport and guns were little, if at all, delayed.

By the evening of the 10th " Stockwell's Force " had reached the Dendre River, north of Ath, and the Blaton Canal, south of the town, but was then held up as the enemy was covering the bridges into Ath with machine-guns. Orders were issued by Division that if the passage was not forced by the advanced-guard during the night the 165th and 166th Brigades were to attack south and north of the town the next day. A conference of all commanders was arranged for 9 a.m. at Villers-St.-Amand to draw up a plan. At 7 a.m., however, the 2/5th Lancashire Fusiliers, by a splendid piece of work, drove the enemy from the southern of the two bridges, before he had time to blow it up, and occupied the town. The mounted troops immediately passed through and continued the advance with little resistance.

Lieut.-Colonel Munro went to the conference as arranged but while the scheme of operations was being discussed a message came through from Divisional Headquarters at Barry that hostilities would cease at 11 a.m. and that troops would stand fast at that hour on the most easterly ground reached.

The other officers of the Scottish, meanwhile, were waiting at Battalion Headquarters for the return of the Colonel with news of what was in store for them. Instead of the expected operation orders for the attack they received a visit from the Commanding-officer of the 55th Machine-Gun Battalion who told them that he had seen the official news that the armistice had been signed. Troops and civilians at once went mad. All the church bells in the district were set ringing, the Pipe Band marched and counter-marched up and down the village street through crowds of cheering Jocks and excited natives and the riotous scene would have made Donnybrook Fair seem like a prayer-meeting.

The War was over.

ATH, BRUSSELS, ANTWERP, HOME AGAIN

When the first burst of enthusiasm was over the Scottish fell in and marched to Ath, with " Y " Company as *1918* advanced-guard. After a halt of a quarter-of-an-hour by the Church where the townspeople gave them a tumultuous reception, the companies moved on again and took up an outpost line east of Attre, three miles south-east of Ath. Picquets were placed on all the roads to prevent civilians going east, a necessary precaution as it was not certain that the war might not break out again and until that danger was past it was wiser to check any possible flow of information at its source. No one quite knew, either, what spies the enemy might have left behind during his retreat.

For several days a steady stream of released British prisoners passed through the posts, singly and in groups. They had been turned adrift to fend for themselves as soon as the armistice was signed and were wearily plodding on towards the west knowing that sooner or later they would find friends. The appearance of these men, unkempt, ragged, half-starved and dull-eyed, told more of the suffering they had undergone than they themselves could ever tell. Their joy at finding themselves once more amongst kindly folk was pitiful but many were too spent to realize that they were free and their troubles over. The inhabitants had done what they could for these waifs as they passed through the villages, but they were hard put to it to feed themselves and had little to spare for others.

On 12 November the villagers at Attre turned out in force to celebrate St. Martin's Day. A procession was formed in the square and, with an effigy of the Kaiser in its midst and led by the Scottish Pipe Band and the Village Band, marched round the Château grounds and back to the square where the effigy was burnt with due solemnity while the Church bells rang a knell and the Pipers played a lament.

On the 14th Major-General Jeudwine went round the outpost line and brought back the war atmosphere by ordering that the men should put on their " tin-hats," which they had discarded, and also wear their small-box-respirators in the alert position.

The next day the Battalion was relieved by the 1/5th King's Own Royal Lancasters and went back to billets at Ath, " V " Company and half " Y " Company in a factory and the remainder in houses.

The Scottish remained at Ath for a month and were joined there by drafts of 150 other ranks from the Divisional Reinforcement Camp and 570 from England. These, with a number of officers who had also arrived, brought the strength of the Battalion up to the remarkable total of 54 officers and 1,735 men.

During the early part of its stay at Ath the Battalion provided parties daily to repair the damage done to the railway by the Germans. The Royal Engineers had been able to get a single-line service going within a week of the armistice but it was some time before the track was fit to take normal traffic. Apart from this work, company or battalion parades were held each morning and the men were left to themselves for the rest of the day for sport or recreation.

To make the transition easier and to prepare the men for their return to civil life educational classes were instituted throughout the Division and all the teachers were found in the ranks of the Division itself. The classes in the Scottish were in the charge of Lieut. C. A. White who had a sound teaching staff under him. The response on the part of the men was not at first encouraging but within a month 295 pupils were going to school daily and getting real profit from their instruction. Most of the men only needed a refresher course to get their brains attuned to commercial pitch and for these teachers were found in the following subjects : English, French, Spanish, shorthand, book-keeping, advertising, invoicing, salesmanship, commercial subjects generally and science, theoretical and applied. A small percentage of the men, however, required purely elementary education and for these was provided a beginners' course in mathematics, English, history and geography. Those who were manual workers attended special classes with the Battalion or at Division in such subjects as building construction, electric lighting and power, mechanics and machine drawing. Others, such as fitters, turners, blacksmiths, divers, chemists, printers and motor mechanics, were sent to courses at Army workshops while the men with no trade were allowed to attach themselves to the various groups in the Battalion who had their own skilled work to do—the tailors, carpenters, pioneers, shoemakers and blacksmiths.

The men were keen students and periodical tests showed how

R

much they benefited from the training. Fifteen entered for the 1st Class Army Certificate and studied the special subjects laid down in addition to taking the general commercial classes. All those who took advantage of the educational scheme were excused other parades.

Sport in all its branches was now taken up more seriously than had been possible while the war was claiming everyone's first thoughts. A Brigade Soccer League was started and the Scottish, to find the best talent available, arranged a series of inter-platoon and inter-company matches. The team which was picked after these trials was quite first-class and was never beaten while the Battalion was at Ath. A second team was also chosen which was little inferior to the first. The Rugger players also got together a useful side under the captaincy of Captain T. G. Roddick. Cross-country running was popular and, after an inter-company race won by " Y " Company, a battalion team was picked and trained for more serious competitions later. The boxers settled down to strict training to such good effect that on 28 November in the Brigade competition they beat the much-fancied 1/5th King's Own into second place by 42½ points to 41 and won the Cup presented by Brigadier-General Kentish. Members of the Battalion teams were all excused parades.

The " Kinky Roos " took over a real theatre in the Rue de Spectacle and gave performances two or three times a week besides visiting villages in the neighbourhood to play to other units.

A few incidents during the stay at Ath must be briefly recorded.

On 17 November Major-General Jeudwine, Brigadier-Generals Stockwell and Kentish and all officers of the 166th Brigade, with the Civil Authorities of Ath, attended a solemn Commemoration Service in the Church. It was a most impressive ceremony and concluded with the Belgian, French and British National Anthems.

On St. Andrew's Night the officers dined at the Hotel Duquesne. The Divisional Band was in attendance and played an excellent programme. The dinner was almost ruined by the non-arrival of the haggis which the Mess-president had ordered from Edinburgh. Luckily the Padre, Revd. Major Morrison, came to the rescue with two haggises which had been sent out to him personally. Forty-eight officers sat down and the same number got up. The evening is believed to have ended in the hospitable Divisional " C " Mess.

The warrant-officers and serjeants, with sixteen guests, also celebrated the feast of St. Andrew. They were entertained by members of the " Kinky Roos " and other artistes and exhibition dancing by the pipers.

On 2 December a meeting was held in the Theatre to discuss the formation of a 55th Divisional Comrades' Association. Major-General Jeudwine presided over a large gathering of representatives, of every rank, from each unit in the Division and, after a long discussion, it was decided to form an Association forthwith. Anyone who had served with the Division during the war was eligible to join and the annual subscription was fixed at one shilling or one franc. Those who wished to do so could become life-members on payment of thirty shillings or forty francs. The objects of the Association were to perpetuate the war-time spirit of comradeship, to assist those who might experience hard times in civil life, to look after the welfare of the dependants of the fallen and to arrange re-unions of members. An executive committee was formed, with Canon Coop as Chairman, to organize the enrolment of members. The Association has since splendidly justified itself, through its officials, by what it has done for those members who have had to seek its assistance and has kept alive the spirit of interdependence and fellowship which was always a marked characteristic of the 55th Division.

On 7 December the Scottish, with all other units of the Division, took up a position on the main road from Ath to Leuze and were inspected, informally, by the King. His Majesty, with whom were the Prince of Wales, Prince Albert, General Birdwood and other distinguished people, was given a rousing reception. The original intention had been that the parade should be a ceremonial one and the Scottish were detailed to find the Guard of Honour. All the men chosen for the Guard had either a decoration or the 1914 ribbon and, after a few days' hard training under the Regimental-Serjeant-Major, D. A. B. Marples, M.C., their drill was faultless. It was somewhat of a disappointment, therefore, when the arrangements were altered.

On 10 December muster-parades by companies were held to issue ballot-papers for the general election. The company-offices were used as polling-booths. No political speeches were allowed and it cannot be said that any great interest or party feeling was shown but most of the men recorded their votes.

The same day the first batch of men—ten coalminers—left for demobilization. There was at first, before the demobilization scheme was thoroughly understood, considerable resentment amongst those with long service at the front when they found that some men who, perhaps, had never heard a shot fired were to be demobilized before them. Lectures by officers sent to units by G.H.Q. and by others made the scheme clear—key-industries men first and then, as far as possible, according to length of service—and did much to clear the air. The difficulty was finally overcome by the system inaugurated whereby men could volunteer for another year's service, of which a large number of the Battalion took advantage.

While on the subject of discipline a word may be said about the 570 men who had arrived from England after the armistice. Many of these men had volunteered for service early in the war but had been kept at home on work of national importance, and many of them had been in sheltered trades and were only called up for service as the teeth of the comb were set closer together. A large proportion of them, therefore, had seen no fighting at all and it would not have been surprising if they had not taken kindly to strict military discipline. It was greatly to the credit of these men that they very soon settled down as useful members of the Battalion, and to that of the old hands that they so quickly taught their new comrades what was expected of them. Crime was rare—there were, for instance, only three cases of desertion during the year which the Battalion spent in Belgium after the armistice—and it was only at long intervals that prisoners appeared at Battalion Orderly Room.

The 55th Division had originally been selected for duty with the Army of Occupation on the Rhine but these orders were cancelled and instead the Division was sent to Brussels to take up winter-quarters. The move began on 15 December and for the Scottish was a matter of extreme difficulty. After deducting those at courses, on leave or in hospital, the actual strength of the Battalion was 1,497, all ranks, and it was beyond the capacity of the ordinary battalion transport to move the kit for such a number. When a whole division is on the move every vehicle is fully loaded and it was only after much flustered coming and going that extra lorries were secured to take the surplus kit. To help out the commissariat department four German field-cookers were commandeered.

The move—about 35 miles—took three days and the Division was quartered in the southern suburbs of Brussels. The Scottish were stationed at St. Job, a residential suburb on the Waterloo road some five miles from the centre of the city. All the billets were excellent, the townspeople were anxious to do all they could to help, and the Scottish looked forward with considerable pleasure to the prospect of spending some months in first-class quarters and within easy reach of all the attractions and amusements which a large city, unspoilt by the war, could offer them. They were not disappointed.

The Scottish remained at St. Job until the beginning of March and enjoyed every minute of their stay. After *1919* morning parade or school, for the educational classes were continued, the men were free and all of them had permanent passes to visit Brussels from 2 to 9 p.m. Late passes, too, were given on a liberal scale. These privileges were seldom abused and the general behaviour of the men when in the city soon made the Battalion popular with the natives who showed their appreciation by their friendliness and kindness to all ranks. It is certainly true of all the officers and probably so of the men that they had never experienced such warm-hearted hospitality. Before long nearly every member of the Battalion had a choice of several houses where he knew he would be a welcome guest any time he cared to call. It was natural, of course, that after four years under the heel of the Germans the population should be anxious to show their gratitude to the men who had helped to free them but the attentions of the good people of Brussels went far beyond that. It was difficult to return the hospitality which was showered on the Battalion but the officers did what they could by asking all their friends to a Ball at the Taverne Royale on 21 January. More than 200 were present and the affair was a great success, particularly the foursome reels which were encored until one officer, at any rate, wished he had been born an Englishman.

Within the Battalion itself, too, the fact of being in more or less permanent quarters made it possible to run the social side of things on a battalion basis and not by companies only as had always been a necessary rule when the Scottish were resting between periods of trench-duty. A Battalion Officers' Mess was opened on Christmas Eve in one of the fine houses on the hill above St. Job and a week later—Hogmanay, an appropriate festival—the ceremony of opening a Serjeants' Mess was performed by the Commanding-Officer with the formalities proper to the occasion.

The problem of serving Christmas Dinners to such a huge battalion was solved by seeking permission, which was readily granted, to use the local School. " V " and " X " Companies dined on Christmas Day, " Y " and " Z " on Boxing Day, and about 800 men sat down each night. After dinners were finished

the tables were cleared and removed and the men danced with
their lady friends to the strains of the Divisional String
Orchestra. These dances proved so popular that others were
afterwards held under company arrangements.

Soon after the Armistice a party had been sent to England
to bring out the King's and Regimental Colours. As many of
the men had never seen them a Battalion parade was ordered
on the morning of Boxing Day and the Colours, uncased, were
taken from Headquarters Mess to the new Officers' Mess. This
was practically the only ceremonial parade by the Battalion
during the stay at Brussels but one very important and impressive parade was held on 3 January when the whole Division
marched past the King of the Belgians, with whom were the
Duke of Teck, the Earl of Derby and the British Ambassador.
The route was through the lovely Bois de la Cambre and the
salute was taken at the top of the Avenue Louise. In addition
to the 28 officers and 850 other ranks who took part in the
march-past the Scottish provided 5 officers and 250 men to line
the road near and at the saluting base. The Battalion received
warm congratulations on its general turnout and marching.

Much could be written of the activities of the Battalion in
the sphere of sport but a few sentences must suffice. The Soccer
team was uniformly successful whether it played against other
units or civilian teams. Four of its members were chosen for
the 55th Division side and two, Serjeant Quinn, M.M. and
Corporal Valentine, later played for the British Army of Occupation team. In the first round of the Army of Occupation Cup
the Scottish beat the 1/6th Cameron Highlanders by three goals
to two after two drawn games had been played, but were knocked
out in one of the later rounds. The cross-country team was
beaten in the Brigade Race by the 1/5th King's Own Royal
Lancasters though the Scottish had the first and third men home.
In the Divisional race on 11 January the Battalion entered two
teams of one officer and 29 men each and again finished as runners-
up to the 1/5th King's Own. Private Beattie repeated his previous
success by finishing first. A team later competed in the Corps
and Army cross-country runs and was placed third on each
occasion. Beattie was third man home in the latter race. In
the Divisional Boxing Tournament the Battalion was represented
by two competitors in the feather-, light-, welter-, and middle-
weights, and by one, Private Parker, the Divisional Champion, in
the heavy-weights. After eliminating rounds the finals were held
on 20 January and the Scottish won the Cup presented by Major-
General Jeudwine with a score of 35 points. The 1/5th King's

Own were second with 32 points. Teams of officers and other ranks were sent to Lille to take part in the Army Championships and returned on 15 February with seven cups. The officers won the Officers' Team Prize. 2nd Lieut. P. Broadhurst was the winner of the heavy-weights and Captain A. MacD. Doughty and 2nd Lieut. T. D. J. Finlayson were runners-up in their weights. Owing to a misunderstanding about the weight limits several of the men found that they had to fight in a class above their normal. Private Stokes was one who suffered in this way but he proceeded to win the welter-weights. He later represented the Army as a light-weight at the Imperial Tournament and was the winner of his weight.

On 9 February the Battalion received a very welcome reinforcement, a Brass Band of 32 musicians. They were nearly all under-age boys who had been drafted to the Reserve Battalion. Their playing reflected the greatest credit on Band-Master Davidson who had taught and trained them.

As the Scottish had in all 1,085 men who were eligible for retention, either because they had volunteered for an extra year or had been called up after 1 July, 1918, and so could not claim immediate demobilization, application was made for the Battalion to remain, as a unit, in the Army of Occupation. This application was granted and the Battalion was ordered to Antwerp to take charge of an Embarkation Camp designed to receive the cadres of units from the Rhine as they passed through on their way to England for demobilization. Brigadier-General R. J. Kentish was appointed Commandant of the new camp.

On the 26th an advance party of 50 men under Lieuts. T. A. Roberts and R. Aitken proceeded to Antwerp to prepare a hut-ment camp. The Battalion followed at the end of the first week in March.

The Camp was situated on a large area of waste ground enclosed on three sides by docks and was about two miles from Antwerp itself. The general layout of the camp and the system of carrying out the duties which fell to the Battalion were decided by Brigadier-General Kentish who had a genius for organization and who was thus largely responsible for the subsequent smooth working of the camp. To him should be given a fair share in the compliments which the Scottish frequently received from the commanding-officers of units which passed through their hands.

Cadres, with their transport, arrived by train. The transport, guns, etc., were unloaded, manhandled to the quay and put aboard waiting steamers. The personnel were received into the camp where they waited until a sufficient number, 600 to 1,000, had assembled to make a ship-load. Then they embarked for England. From the time they arrived in Antwerp all duties were taken over for them by the Liverpool Scottish and everything was done that could be done to make their stay comfortable and amusing. If they wished to see the town, there was a fleet of lorries waiting to take them there and bring them back again. If they preferred to remain in camp, there were a Y.M.C.A. Hut, an Expeditionary Force Canteen and a Camp Theatre in which the entertainments ranged from variety performances by the Battalion Concert Party to serious concerts gladly given by Belgian artistes, some of whom were principals at one or other of the Opera Houses in Antwerp. For a time, too, one of Miss Lena Ashwell's excellent parties gave a season of plays in the Camp Theatre. Of course there was a football ground.

It will be realized that the duties of the Scottish were many and varied. Everything was arranged on the best Trade Union lines. Whether his job was to unload trains, to act as a waiter in a dining hall, to be a camp policeman or to tend the camp incinerator each man knew exactly what his hours of work were and that only in very exceptional circumstances would he be called upon to put in overtime. The result was clockwork efficiency and a contented battalion.

The strength of the Battalion was steadily reduced by the departure of those marked for demobilization and by the end of May there were not enough men left—though the Battalion was still about 1,100 strong—to cope with the work of running the camp. A reinforcement of a company of the Sherwood Foresters from the Rhine helped things, as did a draft of 140 Liverpool Scottish—the remnant of the 3rd Battalion—which arrived on 29 June. The Sherwood Foresters were relieved the following month by 6 officers and 200 men of the Leicesters and they in turn by a similar number of Royal Fusiliers in August.

On 11 June the Scottish said good-bye to one of the very few who had served with them continuously during their whole period of war service, Captain R. W. Johnson, M.C., the Transport Officer. Originally a Lance-Serjeant in the transport section, he had received his commission in the spring of 1916. He was offered substitution leave at the beginning of 1918 but refused it as he preferred to see things through to the end with the Battalion. He sailed to England on the *Sicilian*, incidentally the last occasion on which troops went by sea direct from Antwerp. Afterwards they were passed on by train to Boulogne.

During their stay in Antwerp the Scottish were several times called upon to provide detachments to participate in combined marches through the city with Allied troops—the Americans and French each had a Base Camp at Antwerp and of course there was a Belgian garrison. These outings, which invariably finished with a march-past in the Place de Meir, were very good fun and roused tremendous enthusiasm in the town. In spite of the difficulty of finding time for rehearsals the marching and drill of the men were consistently excellent and they always compared very favourably with the detachments of other nationalities, though the French Chasseurs were a particularly smart body of men and their march-past, almost at a trot, was beautifully done.

On two occasions the Scottish took part in ceremonial of a different nature.

On the first of these, in March, 100 men paraded to show respect to the remains of twenty-three Belgians who had been condemned and shot by the Germans for suspected or actual espionage and buried outside the town. Their bodies were exhumed and, escorted by a large number of troops, taken first to the Cathedral for a short service and afterwards to the Cemetery where they were reburied in consecrated ground.

The second occasion, on 6 July, was a purely British one. The case of Captain C. A. Fryatt of the s.s. *Brussels* will still be vividly recalled by many readers. His ship was torpedoed and he himself was taken on board the submarine and handed over to the German military authorities. After a travesty of a trial he was sentenced to death—for the alleged crime of having tried to ram the submarine—and was buried at Bruges. When arrangements were made to remove his body to England for decent burial the Liverpool Scottish were given the honour of escorting it to the destroyer which had come to Antwerp to receive it. Lieut. A. McF. Cram with eight serjeants as pallbearers went to Bruges and brought the coffin to Antwerp. It was received at the station by a guard of honour of 100 Liverpool Scottish and 25 Leicesters, and then, at the slow march and led by the Pipe Band and Brass Band, the party set off through the town to the River. On arrival at the landing-stage, close to the Steen, a short service was held and then, as the coffin was taken aboard H.M.S. *Orpheus*, the band of the Chasseurs sounded the French Last Post and the troops remained at the Present as the ship cast off and moved away down the River.

Battalion Sports were held on 19 July and a large number of visitors attended.   During the tea interval a terrific thunderstorm broke over the camp and the meeting had to be postponed as the track was under water.   The sports were eventually carried through on 9 August in beautiful weather and " Z " Company won the inter-company shield presented by Lieut.-Colonel Munro.

The usual routine was continued until the end of October by which time all those units not retained in the Army of Occupation had returned to England and the camp at Antwerp was no longer required.   Early in November the Liverpool Scottish themselves were ordered to prepare for demobilization and their popular Commanding-Officer, Lieut.-Colonel Munro, left them to rejoin his own Regiment, the Gordon Highlanders.   After the ordnance stores had been shipped direct to Southampton the whole battalion entrained on 7 November for Cologne and went into a rest-camp the following afternoon.   From there everyone except the cadre and the band was sent home to be demobilized. The band was to have gone too but Major Lockhart managed to persuade Rhine Army G.H.Q. to allow it to accompany the unit.

On the afternoon of 9 November all that was left of the Liverpool Scottish set off by train to Calais, Major R. H. D. Lockhart, T.D., in command, Captain C. A. White his Adjutant, Lieut. H. Cooper, the Transport Officer, the cadre of 80 men, the band, the Colours, the band instruments and twenty tons of baggage.   After a night in Calais and a foul channel-crossing of five and a half hours, the unit reached London at 5 p.m. on the first anniversary of Armistice Day, went on to Liverpool by the 9 p.m. train and arrived at Lime Street, where it was met by Lieut.-Colonel G. A. Blair, T.D., and Private J. R. McCullagh, at 3 a.m. on the 12th.   After the men had been given a meal which had been arranged for them at a near-by café, they were dismissed until noon.   Within the next two or three days all had been demobilized except Major Lockhart and Captain White. They spent a fortnight on clerical work connected with the demobilization of the Battalion, tidying up loose ends generally and waiting for news of the arrival of the ordnance stores.   On 29 November they gave up hope of ever hearing what had become of the stores, went to Prees Heath and were demobilized by Lieut.-Colonel Adam Fairrie, T.D.

It was fitting that the Liverpool Scottish should be brought home by two men who had originally gone out with the 1st

Battalion, Major Lockhart in command of " H " Company and Captain White as a full private. It was fitting too that the officer who demobilized them should himself be a very old member of the Scottish who had commanded the 2nd Battalion in England and France.

APPENDIXES

APPENDIX I

THE THIRD BATTALION.

The 3rd Battalion was formed at the end of May, 1915, to act as the draft-finding unit for the 1st and 2nd Battalions. Major D. A. Campbell was appointed to command with Captain C. B. Glynn as his Adjutant and Regimental-Serjeant-Major A. T. Thacker, promoted Honorary Lieutenant, his Quartermaster. A training staff was selected from the officers and N.O.C.'s of the 2nd Battalion and these, with 200 of the latest recruits, moved to a canvas camp at Weeton, three miles from Blackpool on the Kirkham road. All the 3rd line units of the West Lancashire Division were concentrated in this area under the command of Colonel Grattan.

The facilities for training were, to begin with, very inadequate. Practice trenches had to be dug and equipment for use in musketry and bayonet-fighting improvized from the materials readiest to hand. These difficulties gradually passed away and a programme of training was organized to such good purpose that on 3 September seventy-eight men were sent off as reinforcements to the 1st Battalion.

Towards the end of October the weather made a transfer to winter quarters imperative and the Battalion moved to billets at Blackpool, the men in St. Chad's Road and the officers in the Belsfield Private Hotel, near South Shore. Two months later the Battalion was transferred to North Shore, the men to Albert Road and the officers to the Clifton Hotel. Changes in organization also took place; Lieut.-Colonel E. G. Thin, wounded, and Captain G. B. L. Rae, invalided, from the 1st Battalion became Commanding-Officer and Adjutant.

Blackpool, healthy though it was, was not an ideal training centre. The areas available for training were few and congested and the recruits had to receive most of their instruction on the promenade where the presence of interested civilians was a handicap, though Serjeant Herd never allowed this to cramp his style. With men less keen the progress must have been slow but all were willing to learn and anxious to go overseas at the earliest possible moment. That nine drafts totalling 800 men were trained and sent out to France within six months is proof that the instructors were competent and the men triers.

On 16 February, 1916, the Battalion Soccer team won the Northern Command Championship, beating the 3/5th Loyal North Lancashires in the final after a fine game.

In May and June the 3rd line units of the West Lancashire Division moved to what proved to be their home for the rest of the war, a group of first-class hutment camps at Park Hall, between Oswestry and Gobowen. Except that the camp lay in a broad, shallow valley, which made it too hot in summer and very wet in winter, no fault could be found with it. The huts were good, there was plenty of room and the training areas were a great improvement on Blackpool, especially Brogyntyn Park on the slope of the hills towards the Welsh border.

At Park Hall Camp, with the men always at hand instead of being split up two or three to a billet, it was possible to lay down a very much more rigorous training-programme without imposing any hardship. A word may be said here of the system adopted in the Battalion.

There were four companies, of which " A," " B," and " C " were reserved for recruits, while " D " was composed entirely of returned-service men, either recovering from wounds or sickness and on light duty, or passed fit for active service and waiting their turn for draft. On arrival from the Depôt, Fraser Street, a recruit was posted to " A," " B " or " C " Company and drew his kit from the stores. For a fortnight or so his company-commander saw him only at the pay-table or kit-inspection for he was taken in hand by special instructors while he was learning foot drill, saluting and squad drill. When he was sufficiently proficient in these he paraded under his company-commander and for a month or six weeks his time was occupied with arms drill, elementary musketry, extended-order drill, physical jerks, bayonet fighting and platoon drill. He was also taught something of bombs and practised throwing. His next stage was intensive musketry training for which he paraded under the musketry officer and his experts. This period lasted about four weeks and ended with a classification course at Frant. The man then joined the special draft company and in it he learnt company drill and was given his final polish. He also tested his small-box-respirator in the gas-chamber and visited the bombing-school at Oswestry where he threw live bombs. He was then ready for the G.O.C.'s inspection and to take his place on the list of those available for draft. Of the many lectures to which he listened one of the most important, the History of the Battalion, was always given in the first few days of his service by the Regimental-Serjeant-Major, a lecture no one was better qualified to give than "Bill" Flint, whose regimental number was 10.

Fourteen weeks was the normal time allowed to prepare the raw recruit for draft but in times of stress this was reduced to twelve weeks. It would have been impossible to secure anything like efficiency in such a short time if the instructional staff had not been thoroughly expert, each in his own subject. Where all were good it is perhaps unfair to mention individuals but some names stand out; Serjeant Alec Finnie who was responsible for the recruits' training, Captain E. B. Monkhouse, who was in charge of musketry training, and Captain T. G. Roddick who, as draft-commander for nearly two years, turned out draft after draft which, in drill and general smartness, would have done credit to any peace-time Regular battalion. All drafts were re-inspected at the Base Camp in France and, if not up to the required standard, were kept for further instruction before being sent to join their battalions. The Scottish soon established a reputation for satisfactory drafts, so much so that on one occasion when Company-Serjeant-Major W. E. Rae reported his arrival with a draft of 50 men at the Orderly Room of the Base Camp, Étaples, the Adjutant said to him "Who are you? "Liverpool Scottish? You needn't bother about an inspection. "Your drafts are always first-class."

One rule which was early laid down in the 3rd Line was that no fit officer or N.C.O. should remain permanently on the instructional staff. As soon as a substitute had been trained to fill his place he was transferred to the waiting list for service overseas. This undoubtedly was for the good of the Battalion, and the reproach could not be levelled at it which some units deservedly incurred, that men who had never seen active service were kept in soft jobs at home. With one or two legitimate exceptions—for reasons of health—all the instructors in the 3rd Line were returned-service men.

All the drafts which were trained by the 3rd Battalion did not reach the Liverpool Scottish in France. During the Battle of the Somme, when casualties were unprecedented, men were sent haphazard to whichever battalion needed them most. In this way drafts of the Scottish were sent to the 1/5th, 1/9th and 13th King's Liverpools, 2/4th Gloucesters and 21st Manchesters. Sometimes they were allowed to retain the kilt, sometimes not. The draft of 200 which joined the 13th King's

S

not only kept the kilt but was formed into a separate company. This draft was in three attacks in the space of a few days and very few were left afterwards.

The quality of recruit, of course, varied. When the volunteer well was running dry and those who had attested under the Derby Scheme were called up, a number of curious old gentlemen joined the Battalion. It was incredible how soon exercise and an open-air life made them ten years younger and in the end they became better soldiers than many of their juniors. The conscripted men, too, surprised everyone by the way they settled down cheerfully to army life. Some of them found the sudden transition from a well-paid job with all home comforts to army pay and fare a little trying, but the grumblers were soon brought to a proper frame of mind. Probably the company-serjeant-major's retort to one of the latter, who complained that his tea was cold, " No wonder, my lad, it's been waiting for you for " two years," was used in other battalions besides the Scottish, though original humorists like Gilbart are rare. Another type of recruit was the conscientious objector. Some of them undoubtedly had sincere scruples against the taking of life under any circumstances and, while one could not agree with them, one could at least respect their point of view. A few of these men, who were quite prepared to help the common cause and to risk their own lives, were trained in specialist duties, such as stretcher-bearing and signalling, which would lessen the probability of their having to use their rifles. The other sort of conscientious objector, who sheltered himself behind his alleged principles, received very different treatment. Legally he was protected, under severe pains and penalties, from bodily violence, but there were many ways in which his life could be made miserable within the law—and, when no one was looking, outside it. One of these specimens, a professional cyclist and boxer, probably still remembers vividly the manhandling he received outside the orderly room from a hefty returned-service man who broke away from the ranks of the draft which was taking him back to France and relieved his feelings very satisfactorily.

The men's pay-accounts were for long a source of worry to them and to their company-commanders. The Pay Office at Preston, owing to the enormous expansion in the number of accounts which it had to keep and the difficulty of training a growing staff of clerks—for a time women were employed—who had little or no knowledge of book-keeping, soon reached a state of chaos. In almost every case, at any rate so far as the returned-service men were concerned, the balance shown in a man's pay-book was different from the balance which Preston said was correct.   Usually the mistake was in Preston's favour.   One wounded serjeant, who had failed to get his particular tangle straightened out by correspondence, went to the Pay Office to settle the matter personally.   He was first offered £10 in full settlement.   When he refused this the offer was increased to £15 and he finally accepted £21 and started again with a clean sheet.   This is a typical illustration of the go-as-you-please system which passed for book-keeping.   The old story about adding in the date is no fairy-tale.   Things reached such a pitch that Captain Rae arranged for the transfer of Quartermaster-Serjeant Bubbins from the Record Office to the Liverpool Scottish and he was appointed quartermaster-serjeant of the returned-service company.   This transfer had admirable results, and Bubbins was able to recover hundreds of pounds for the men. When something like order had been reached the accounts were kept accurate by sending the company-quartermaster-serjeant of each company, or his clerk, to Preston once a month to check the balance of every man.

After the Irish Rebellion, Easter, 1916, it appeared likely that all the men in the Division who were sufficiently trained would be sent over to Ireland.   A composite battalion was formed in each brigade from those who had reached the ready-for-draft stage and fully equipped with transport and stores.   This force was frequently inspected and was ready to move at short notice but was never used.   The Scottish did, however, see something of the rebels, several hundred of whom were in a prisoners' camp at Frongoch, Bala.   An officer with 25 other ranks of the Scottish, all returned-service men, spent ten days conducting batches of these prisoners from Frongoch to Wormwood Scrubs or Wandsworth Prisons in London, and taking back parties of those who had already been tried, on alternate days.   In London the troops were billeted at Chelsea Barracks, where the Guards treated them royally, and all thoroughly enjoyed the holiday.

Like the 2nd Battalion, the 3rd Line suffered from the rifle shortage and the early drafts were armed with the old long rifle. D.P. long Lee-Enfields and, later, Japanese rifles were for a long time used for arms drill and bayonet fighting and it was not until the third year of the war that the men were armed from the start of their service with the S.M.L.E.

Some changes in the administrative personnel of the Battalion took place in the winter of 1916/17.   Shortly before Christmas Captain Rae left to return to France and his place as Adjutant was taken by Captain F. Holland. A few months later Lieut.-Colonel Thin also returned to active service. There was some misgiving amongst the officers when they heard that Lieut.-Colonel Adam Fairrie, from the 2nd Battalion, was to be the new commanding-officer for he had something of a reputation for barking and biting! Their fears proved groundless for within a very short time Colonel Fairrie satisfied himself that he had taken over a well-organized and well-run show, and that it would not be necessary to use the whip.

The 3rd Battalion was never without a Pipe-Band which Pipe-Major John Mackay managed to keep up to effective strength in spite of the periodical loss, on draft, of his more experienced players. " Pipey," one of the most lovable men who ever served in the Liverpool Scottish, was not only a great piper himself and an ex-champion of the North but had a wonderful gift of teaching and the way in which, in a few months, he could turn very raw material into efficient pipers was little short of miraculous. When the 2nd Battalion went overseas those of its Brass Band who were unfit for active service joined the 3rd Line. Later they were transferred elsewhere and Band-Master Davidson took in hand the training of the Band of youngsters which was such a success later in Antwerp.

There were a number of under-age boys at Oswestry who were not allowed to go overseas until they reached the age of eighteen. Some of them, by giving a false age when they enlisted, had already been in France and had been sent home when they were found out—the youngest of the three brothers Law, by the way, spent his sixteenth birthday in the trenches at Kemmel in 1914. They were all collected into " A " Company under Captain A. B. Johnson Houghton and were largely used for demonstration work. They were a lively party and took some handling. Many of them afterwards received commissions.

After the amalgamation of the 1st and 2nd Battalions, which resulted in the formation of a special battalion reserve at Étaples, the demand for reinforcements from Oswestry was dormant for the last six months of the war and the numbers of the 3rd Line rose to nearly 1,300. After the armistice, Park Hall Camp was vacated. Colonel Fairrie went off to Prees Heath as Commandant of the demobilization camp and the Battalion was split up. 570 men were sent to the 1st Battalion and the remainder were transferred to Ireland where, at Kinsale, they were attached to a Battalion of the Argyle and Sutherland Highlanders. Most of the men had been conscripted late in the war and had seen no active service. The Kinsale Camp was an uncomfortable one, not designed for winter-quarters, and there was endless trouble in getting supplies of clothing, particularly boots, for the men. Little training was attempted and the officers, only eight or nine in all, concentrated their attention on keeping the troops fit and cheerful in which they were wonderfully successful. No one was sorry, however, when demobilization began in the middle of January. Within a few months the 3rd Battalion of the Liverpool Scottish had ceased to exist.

APPENDIX II

THE DEPÔT.

The command of the Depôt, 5, Fraser Street, was given to Lieut.-Colonel G. A. Blair, when he returned to England from the 1st Battalion in November, 1914, and he remained in charge to the end in spite of constant ill-health and frequent suffering. What it cost him to carry on only he himself knows. That he permanently wrecked an already over-strained constitution by his work in the service of the Battalion is a fact which the Liverpool Scottish should not forget. His duties in connection with recruiting and as keeper of the Battalion's records were arduous enough but he added enormously to them by the scrupulous attention he paid to the claims made upon him by the relatives and friends of the men who were serving overseas. Especially was this so in the case of those seeking news of the killed, the wounded and the missing, and there are many who will still remember gratefully his kindly help and unfailing sympathy. Officers and men on leave, too, always received a friendly welcome from him at Fraser Street and he liked nothing better than to talk with someone newly returned from the front who could give him the latest news of the Scottish and their doings.

There was other work to be done at the Depôt, the administration of the funds subscribed by generous friends and the organization of the supply of whatever comfort or necessity the 1st and 2nd Battalions demanded. This work was voluntarily undertaken by Colonel C. Forbes Bell and to it he devoted every moment that he could spare and many that he could not. In the course of the war upwards of £4,000 passed through his hands and every penny of it was wisely spent—on clothing, general comforts, medical comforts and parcels for the prisoners of war. The Battalion was indeed fortunate in having such a competent provider as its first Commanding-Officer and his ungrudging labours in this connection, which have already been mentioned earlier in this book, have won for him a very special place amongst those who have rendered outstanding service to the Liverpool Scottish.

APPENDIX III

NOMINAL ROLL SERVICE SECTION
SOUTH AFRICA, 1902.

Watson, J., Lieutenant.
Saunderson, W., Serjeant.
Rice, W. J., Corporal.
Johnstone, T. A., Bugler.
Balfour, R., Private.
Cowie, T., Private.
Duthie, W. H. Private.
Grierson, D., Private.
Hadden, G., Private.
Hughan, S. G., Private.
Ingram, R., Private.
Kerr, W., Private.
Lea, H. S., Private.
Mowat, W. G., Private.
Mitchell, J., Private.
McDougall, D., Private.
McLaren, R., Private.
Nield, J. C., Private.
Pontet, H., Private.
Watson, J., Private.
Watson, J. H., Private.
Whitten, G. R., Private.

APPENDIX IV

NOMINAL ROLL, 1st BATTALION, 1 NOVEMBER, 1914.

Blair, G. A., Lieut.-Colonel.
Davidson, J. R., Major.
Thin, E. G., Major.
Twentyman, A., Captain.
Anderson, A. S., Captain.
Lockhart, R. H. D., Captain.
Dickinson, R. F. B., Captain.
Campbell, D. A., Captain.
Harrison, F., Captain.
Macleod, D., Captain.
McKinnell, B., Lieutenant.
Dickinson, G. F., Lieutenant.
Renison, W. J. H., Lieutenant.
Bingham, D. A., Lieutenant.
Turner, F. H., Lieutenant.
Graham, J., Lieutenant.
Cunningham, R. D., Lieutenant.
Whitson, H. T., 2nd Lieutenant.
Gemmell, K. A., 2nd Lieutenant.
Cookson, A., 2nd Lieutenant.
McGilchrist, A. M., 2nd Lieutenant.
Doughty, A. MacD., 2nd Lieutenant.
Gemmell, A. A., 2nd Lieutenant.
Holland, F., 2nd Lieutenant.
Kendall, P. D., 2nd Lieutenant.
James, C. P., Captain and Adjutant (Argyle and Sutherland Highlanders).
Chavasse, N. G., Lieutenant (R.A.M.C.).
Jack, A. C., Hon. Lieutenant and Quartermaster.

2544 Abernethy, W. C., Private.
2850 Ackerley, R., Private.
3193 Adams, L. W., Private.
8517 Adams, S. S., Private.
8143 Ainsworth, R. T., Private.

3783   Aitken, A., Private.
3105   Aldcroft, W. H., Private.
2750   Alderson, C. R., Private.
2502   Alexander, J., Private.
2526   Allan, W. B., Private.
2850   Allen, J., Private.
3081   Allman, J., Private.
2109   Almond, J. B., Private.
1820   Almond, S., Serjeant.
 998   Amos, J. H., Serjeant.
1080   Anderson, F., Corporal.
2651   Anderson, H. S., Bugler.
1874   Anderson, J., Corporal.
2839   Anderson, J., Private.
1656   Andrews, W. F. A. Quartermaster-Serjeant.
2599   Annersley, E. B., Private.
3090   Archer, J. C., Private.
3191   Arkle, B., Private.
3774   Arkle, W., Private.
3192   Armstrong, F. J., Private.
3190   Armstrong, J. G., Private.
3138   Armstrong, W. D., Private.
3188   Ashcroft, J. G., Private.
3890   Askew, H. F., Private.
3195   Atherton, F., Private.
3189   Atkins, S., Private.
2212   Atkinson, G. W., Corporal.
2358   Austin, G. E., Private.
2703   Bailey, A., Private.
2509   Bailey, H., Private.
1942   Bailey, R. C., Private.
3079   Bain, J. M., Private.
2604   Baker, A., Private.
3129   Baker, G. G., Private.
3206   Ball, C. A., Private.
2782   Ball, H., Private.
2756   Band, G. L., Private.
2515   Banner, F. S., Private.
3043   Barber, J. C., Lance-Corporal.
3917   Barber, K., Private.
3205   Barker, C. G., Private.
3505   Barker, H. B., Private.
2439   Barker, H. E., Lance-Corporal.
3213   Barker, P. D., Private.
3214   Barnett, H., Private.

3116 Barnish, L. Private.
3010 Bartlett, G., Private.
2593 Barton, E., Private.
1608 Barton, S., Lance-Corporal.
2688 Basnett, R. J., Private.
2361 Baybut, A., Acting-Drummer.
3216 Bayly, C., Private.
2924 Beach, J. T., Private.
3204 Beck, J., Private.
3012 Beckett, A., Private.
2989 Bedlington, H., Private.
2331 Belgrove, J. G., Private.
2217 Bell, F., Private.
3209 Bell, H. H., Private.
2418 Bell, N., Private.
3211 Bellis, A. H., Private.
2505 Benbow, W., Private.
2518 Bennie, M., Private.
1610 Benson, J., Serjeant.
2656 Berry, S. J., Private.
2801 Berry, T. G., Lance-Corporal.
3527 Billington, E. Private.
2735 Binns, A., Private.
1751 Black, W., Lance-Corporal.
2747 Blackmore, H., Private.
1590 Blackwood, T., Private.
2033 Blakeston, S. W., Corporal.
2445 Bland, J., Private.
3802 Blyth, M., Private.
2387 Blythe, A., Private.
2862 Boocock, H. J., Private.
3509 Bothamley, H., Private.
1981 Boulton, W. J. D., Serjeant.
2466 Bowler, C. H., Private.
3158 Boyd, P. J., Private.
3196 Boyle, A., Private.
3198 Boyle, C., Private.
1540 Bradshaw, A. W., Serjeant.
3203 Bradshaw, W., Private.
2379 Breckenridge, E. P., Private.
3771 Breeze, J. A., Private.
1943 Bridden, H. C., Private.
2082 Briggs, J., Corporal.
3070 Briggs, R., Private.
2878 Broad, A. H., Private.

3215	Broadbent, E. P., Private.
2885	Bromley, R., Private.
3206	Bromley, W. S., Private.
2722	Brooks, A. E. Private.
3055	Broomhall, A., Private.
2991	Broster, J. O., Private.
2002	Brown, J., Lance-Corporal.
1827	Brown, J. S., Private.
1605	Brownbill, J. F., Private.
3207	Brownlie, J. N., Private.
2450	Buchan, W. K., Private.
3186	Buchanan, A., Private.
3117	Bullen, W. F., Corporal.
2828	Burley, A. J., Private.
2484	Burley, R. B., Private.
3032	Burnell, G. C., Private.
3039	Burnett, J. F. E., Private.
3102	Burrell, K., Private.
3208	Burrows, T., Private.
2580	Butcher, W. G. R., Private.
2600	Caldwell, L. A., Private.
2605	Callander, R. J., Private.
2412	Callie, D. S., Private.
3520	Cameron, C., Private.
2836	Campbell, A., Acting-Piper.
686	Campbell, J. K., Serjeant.
3065	Campbell, J. R., Private.
2608	Campbell, R. D., Private.
2639	Campbell, R. T., Drummer.
2932	Campbell, W. S., Private.
3229	Cane, L. O., Private.
2451	Carnelly, R. D., Private.
3225	Carr, D., Private.
3130	Carruthers, S., Private.
1586	Carter, M., Lance-Corporal.
3524	Case, F. E., Private.
3518	Catterall, P., Private.
3153	Chaddock, H. B., Private.
3033	Charters, J., Private.
3512	Cheney, J. W., Private.
2992	Chubb, G. A., Private.
2933	Citrine, A., Bandsman.
2893	Clarke, P. W., Private.
1895	Clarkson, H., Serjeant.
3218	Cleaver, C. T., Private.

3001	Clements, J. B., Private.
3156	Coddington, C. E., Private.
2763	Cogan, J., Private.
2213	Cole, C. V., Private.
2430	Cole, J. R., Private.
3106	Collier, J., Private.
2474	Collins, S. E., Private.
3234	Collins, W. S., Private.
3224	Comberbach, E. S., Private.
2705	Constantine, C., Private.
3075	Cooke, C. N., Private.
3898	Cooksley, H. J., Private.
2693	Cooper, J., Private.
2896	Corey, A., Private.
2255	Corkhill, C. V., Private.
1043	Corlett, A. E., Lance-Serjeant.
2591	Cornes, T., Lance-Corporal.
2729	Costain, W. E., Private.
3222	Costello, J., Private.
2889	Cottam, A. F., Private.
3239	Cottam, L., Private.
2784	Cottam, W. D., Private.
2744	Courtney, J. W., Private.
3236	Cowderoy, H., Private.
2922	Cox, C., Private.
2480	Coyle, S., Private.
8231	Coyne, T., Private.
2499	Craig, J., Private.
2791	Creer, J., Private.
2867	Crooks, J., Private.
3219	Crosbie, R., Private.
3073	Crosby, J. J., Private.
2980	Crosett, W. H., Private.
1570	Croston, D., Drummer.
2305	Culton, J. M. C., Private.
3787	Cunningham, J., Private.
3233	Cunningham, J. A., Private.
3133	Cunningham, T. H., Private.
2225	Currie, C. D., Serjeant.
2286	Curtis, W. A., Lance-Corporal.
2119	Cutts, H. A., Private.
2807	Dalton, G. S., Private.
2391	Dalzell, W. O., Bugler.
3885	Darroch, J. C., Private.
2230	Davenport, W. H., Private.

3142 Davey, G., Private.
2552 Davey, H., Lance-Corporal.
3008 David, J. E., Private.
2975 Davidson, A. G., Lance-Corporal.
1580 Davidson, C., Lance-Corporal.
2590 Davies, D. B., Private.
1829 Dawkins, R. D., Corporal.
3247 Day, A. H., Private.
805 Dean, W., Lance-Corporal.
2311 Denard, D., Private.
3255 Denton, S., Private.
2676 Dewar, J., Private.
3104 Dickinson, J. A., Private.
3256 Dixon, H. O., Private.
2890 Dobbin, H., Private.
3077 Dodd, E., Private.
2681 Dodd, J. F., Private.
3249 Dodd, R. W., Private.
3250 Donaldson, J. J., Corporal.
2856 Donaldson, W., Private.
2519 Donnelly, F., Bugler.
2957 Dorman, W. M., Private.
2796 Douglas, B., Private.
3062 Douglas, P., Private.
3041 Dow, F. N., Private.
3179 Drummond, W. A., Private.
2265 Drury, H. G., Private.
1198 Duff, J. S., Serjeant.
2597 Duffey, J., Private.
1062 Duguid, J. M. G., Private.
3059 Dumbell, H. C., Private.
2370 Dumbreck, W. V., Corporal.
3068 Dun, L. F., Corporal.
2913 Duncan, H. B., Private.
1842 Duncanson, A. W., Serjeant.
611 Dunham, J. W., Colour-Serjeant.
3241 Dunlop, G. H., Private.
2360 Dunn, G. A., Private.
162 Dunnett, W., Serjeant.
2194 Dunning, J. W., Private.
3182 Dunt, A. H., Private.
3180 Earl, G. G., Private.
2446 Eaton, A. H., Private.
3570 Edgar, E., Private.
1551 Edgar, F., Serjeant.

3258	Edgar, M. G., Private.
1193	Edgar, S. G., Corporal.
2654	Edgar, T., Drummer.
8011	Edmunds, P., Private.
2982	Edwards, A., Private.
3178	Edwards, H. L., Private.
2812	Egan, H. L., Private.
3260	Ellick, C., Private.
2488	Ellis, H., Private.
2524	Ellis, R., Private.
3263	Ellison, D. C., Private.
3257	Ellison, F., Private.
3259	Evans, O., Private.
2961	Evans, P., Private.
2959	Fardo, F. G., Private.
2986	Farmer, D. D., V.C., Serjeant-Major.
2935	Farquhar, H., Private.
3757	Faulkner, E.'J., Private.
2884	Faulkner, H. C., Private.
2900	Fennah, A., Private.
3146	Ferguson, A. K., Private.
2462	Ferguson, G., Private.
693	Ferguson, Geo., Serjeant.
2880	Ferguson, J., Private.
3266	Ferguson, J., Private.
2749	Fernihough, W., Private.
2916	Finlay, C., Private.
2266	Finnie, A. T., Lance-Serjeant.
2408	Fisher, H., Lance-Corporal.
3061	Fitton, W., Private.
2553	Fletcher, H., Private.
1033	Flett, D., Serjeant.
10	Flint, W. G., Colour-Serjeant.
2757	Foden, A. F., Private.
3274	Forbes, D., Private.
2891	Forbes, W., Private.
2500	Forshaw, A., Private.
2202	Forshaw, H., Private.
3265	Forster, A., Private.
2837	Forster, A. M., Private.
3267	Forster, T. M., Private.
3772	Forsyth, G. W. G., Corporal.
2554	Foster, J., Lance-Corporal.
3508	Foster, J. L., Private.
2880	Fothergill, A. W., Private.

2687 Fothergill, J. L., Private.
1908 Foulkes, J. S., Lance-Serjeant.
2929 Foulkes, W., Private.
3054 Francis, J. E., Private.
3268 Francis, T., Private.
1667 Fraser, A., Private.
3269 Fraser, K., Private.
2602 Fraser, L., Private.
2578 Frayne, E., Private.
3272 Frazer, J. C., Private.
2222 Freeman, A., Corporal.
2949 Freyer, A. R., Private.
2951 Frost, J., Private.
3264 Fyfe, F. A., Private.
3002 Gardiner, E., Private.
514 Gardner, R., Serjeant-Cook.
3097 Garner, F., Private.
2892 Garner, J., Private.
3596 Garvie, D., Private.
3287 Garvie, H., Private.
3276 Gaskell, W., Private.
3288 Gattens, C., Private.
2527 Gavin, G. A., Private.
2585 Gavin, J. J., Private.
3275 Geen, G. A., Private.
2479 George, W. H., Private.
3533 Gibbins, S. G. R., Private.
3279 Gibson, J., Private.
3283 Gibson, S. G., Private.
3161 Gibson, W. H., Private.
2163 Gilbart, B., Serjeant.
2884 Gilbart, G. A., Private.
3280 Giles, C., Private.
85 Gillanders, H. S., Colour-Serjeant.
1410 Gillespie, A., Serjeant.
2435 Gillespie, A., Private.
3127 Gillespie, R., Private.
2095 Gledsdale, A., Lance-Corporal.
2052 Glen, H. J., Private.
2896 Glendinning, A., Private.
156 Glendinning, W. C., Lance-Corporal.
3165 Golding, A. J., Private.
2467 Gordon, C. A., Private.
2569 Gordon, S. R., Private.
2525 Gorton, G. A., Private.

2400	Graham, D., Private.
1619	Graham, R. L., Private.
3181	Grant, D., Private.
1087	Grant, J. D., Colour-Serjeant.
2603	Grant, J. G., Private.
2351	Grant, L., Serjeant.
2815	Gray, H., Private.
1705	Greaves, C., Private.
2511	Green, C. L., Private.
3282	Green, H. A., Private.
3277	Green, W. J., Private.
3019	Greenhalgh, T. C., Private.
2610	Greenup, J. G., Private.
460	Grierson, W., Serjeant.
2818	Griffiths, W. M., Private.
2203	Hall, F., Serjeant.
2631	Hall, H. J. L., Private.
2354	Hall, W., Private.
3124	Halsall, H. S., Private.
2917	Halton, R. A., Private.
2573	Hampson, H. N., Piper.
3308	Hardman, W., Private.
2898	Hargreaves, W. C., Private.
2539	Harper, P. H., Private.
2551	Harris, C., Private.
2985	Harris, P. T., Private.
3159	Harrison, H. J., Private.
3304	Harrison, R. P., Private.
3294	Hay, J. M., Private.
2662	Hayes, R., Private.
2495	Haygarth, J., Private.
3291	Haygarth, J. H., Private.
3303	Hayward, W. S., Private.
3314	Heald, H., Private.
2993	Heald, H. S., Private.
2307	Heaton, E., Private.
3049	Heenan, H. S., Private.
1853	Helliwell, T., Private.
3599	Hempshill, J. W., Private.
3680	Henderson, D., Private.
3305	Henery, G. T., Private.
3838	Herbert, H., Private.
3112	Heywood, J., Private.
2768	Heywood, R., Private.
2868	Higgins, H., Private.

2440	Hignett, H. N., Private.
2581	Hill, J. P., Private.
2882	Hill, R. E., Private.
2322	Hinton, G. N., Private.
3302	Hobbs, H. B., Private.
3761	Hocking, J., Private.
1523	Hodgson, B. H., Private.
2927	Hodgson, W. H., Private.
2738	Hogg, A., Private.
3310	Holland, A. J., Private.
1144	Holliday, J., Serjeant.
3147	Hollins, E. H., Private.
1356	Holmes, T. A., Private.
2806	Holmes, W. A., Private.
2431	Holt, A., Private.
3040	Hood, N. C., Private.
2611	Hooson, W., Private.
2792	Hopley, A., Private.
2870	Hopwood, F. C., Private.
3790	Hornsby, J. P. S., Private.
2894	Horrocks, R., Private.
3312	Houston, T. H., Private.
3298	Howarth, W. W., Private.
3134	Howells, D. C., Private.
2837	Hoyle, E. V., Private.
2299	Hughan, C., Private.
2443	Hughes, G. F., Private.
3307	Hughes, J., Private.
3309	Hughes, L. E., Private.
2491	Hughes, R., Private.
1680	Hughes, R. D., Private.
2968	Hughes, T. M. S., Private.
3290	Hulatt, C. R., Private.
2282	Hulme, W., Private.
3137	Hume, W., Private.
3293	Humphries, J., Private.
2477	Hunt, H., Private.
2883	Huntriss, G. H., Private.
2835	Hurley, T., Private.
2826	Hurton, A., Private.
3301	Hutchieson, R. M., Private.
2886	Ince, J., Private.
2362	Inwood, G., Private.
3315	Irvine, C. S., Private.
1682	Irvine, W. H., Private.

T

2494	Irving, H. R., Private.
2914	Irving, J., Serjeant.
2871	Ison, C. H., Private.
2268	Izzett, G. D., Private.
1447	Jack, H., Corporal.
2777	Jackson, W. A., Private.
3318	James, W., Private.
2493	Jamieson, A., Private.
2416	Jardine, J. D., Lance-Corporal.
8914	Jennings, S., Colour-Serjeant.
1806	Jessop, A. C., Private.
2652	Johnson, A., Private.
2612	Johnson, C., Private.
3317	Johnson, F., Private.
1808	Johnson, R. W., Lance-Serjeant.
3323	Johnston, D., Private.
3092	Johnston, G., Private.
2859	Johnston, S. R., Private.
1573	Johnston, T., Private.
2016	Johnstone, E., Lance-Corporal.
1797	Johnstone, J. H., Lance-Corporal.
3322	Jones, A., Private.
3321	Jones, F. C., Private.
2342	Jones, H. R., Private.
1538	Jones, J. D., Serjeant.
3325	Jones, M. V., Private.
3791	Jones, S. F., Private.
3326	Jones, T. F., Private.
2507	Jones, W., Private.
3118	Jowett, A., Private.
3333	Kay, N. B., Private.
3327	Keen, P., Private.
2701	Keith, C. McD., Private.
1574	Kelly, W. F., Private.
3331	Kemp, T. H., Private.
3091	Kennedy, A. G., Private.
1490	Ker, D., Serjeant.
3335	Kerr, A. M. D., Private.
3037	Kerr, A. W., Private.
2271	Kerr, H. H., Private.
3334	Kerr, W., Private.
2780	Kershaw, J. G., Private.
3099	Kirkman, R., Private.
2465	Kirkness, J. W., Lance-Corporal.
3120	Kirkpatrick, G. P., Private.

2839 Kitson, G., Bugler.
2557 Kitwood, H. F., Private.
3341 Lace, V., Private.
3340 Lamb, J., Private.
1792 Lamont, A., Lance-Corporal.
2937 Lancaster, F. W., Private.
2627 Langford, G. F., Private.
2872 Large, N., Private.
2853 Latham, G. A., Private.
3020 Latham, R. L. E., Private.
2798 Latta, J., Private.
3093 Laurence, G. W., Private.
3350 Laurie, J., Private.
1904 Laurie, J. A., Private.
2653 Law, G., Private.
2793 Law, J. W., Private.
2831 Law, L. R., Private.
3738 Law, P., Private.
3337 Lawler, H., Private.
1282 Lawson, E. G., Lance-Corporal.
3345 Laybourne, J. O., Private.
2454 Leach, J. D., Lance-Corporal.
2785 Leach, M. T., Private.
3338 Leach, R., Private.
2817 Leatherbarrow, A. L., Private.
3177 Lee, F., Private.
2682 Lee, W., Private.
3882 Leeke, F. W., Private.
2381 Leghorn, W. E. G., Private.
2429 Lever, H. V., Private.
3342 Light, D. A., Private.
2333 Lindop, G. H. B., Private.
2843 Lindsay, T., Private.
3042 Lindsay, R. C., Private.
1691 Little, G., Private.
2532 Little, R., Private.
2876 Little, R., Private.
2709 Little, W. A., Private.
2177 Littler, C., Serjeant.
2106 Lloyd, A. B., Private.
2664 Lloyd, F. C., Private.
3349 Lloyd, J. R., Private.
2711 Lorimer, D., Private.
2512 Lotz, J. B., Private.
3655 Loudoun, C., Private.

2766 Lowe, P., Private.
3018 Lowes, R. J., Private.
2197 Lyon, C., Private.
3336 Lyon, T. A., Private.
2065 Lyon, W. M., Lance-Corporal.
3028 McAdam, J. C., Private.
3695 Macalister, A., Private.
2587 McArthur, H., Private.
2977 McArthur, T. A., Private.
3377 McAuley, H., Private.
3811 McAughty, A., Private.
8375 McCaskill, W., Private.
2428 McClellan, J., Private.
1444 McColl, D. K., Colour-Serjeant.
3145 McConnan, G., Private.
3384 McCormick, I. J., Private.
2503 McCoy, C., Private.
2838 McCubbin, J., Private.
1566 McCulloch, J. R., Private.
2746 McDonald, A., Private.
3385 McDonald, A., Private.
2675 McDonald, D., Private.
2910 McDonald, G. W., Private.
2912 McDonald, R., Private.
2226 McDonald, R. A., Lance-Corporal.
2444 McDonald, W. G., Private.
3378 Macdermott, B., Private.
1774 McEwan, C., Serjeant.
862 Macfarlane, J., Private.
3379 McFarlane, W. A., Private.
3087 Macfie, R. A. Scott, Colour-Serjeant.
1302 Macfie, J. P., Lance-Corporal.
2575 MacGlasson, J. J., Private.
3382 McHarrie, F., Private.
3078 McIntosh, D. A., Private.
2566 McIntyre, D., Private.
2540 McIntyre, J. I., Lance-Corporal.
3376 McIver, D., Private.
3383 McKay, C. A., Private.
1415 McKay, C. R., Private.
2390 Mackay, L. A., Acting-Piper.
3380 McKay, S., Private.
475 McKay, W. G., Quartermaster-Serjeant.
2930 McKenzie, R. A., Private.
2586 McKenzie, R. G., Private.

3381	McKnight, J., Private.
2405	McKune, H., Private.
2628	McMillan, P., Private.
1530	McMinn, G., Private.
3098	McNab, G., Private.
2934	McNaught, J., Private.
2968	McPherson, D., Private.
2947	McQuilliam, F., Private.
3076	MacSwiney, B. F., Private.
2789	MacSwiney, J. R., Private.
3352	Mace, S. G., Private.
1758	Mack, M., Lance-Corporal.
2568	Maitland, C., Private.
3361	Manning, J., Private.
3358	Maries, C. H., Private.
2528	Marmion, H., Private.
3355	Marmion, L. J., Private.
2063	Marples, D. A. B., Serjeant.
2567	Marston, J. W., Private.
3163	Mason, C. R., Private.
2193	Mason, G., Private.
1766	Massey, H. H., Private.
3356	Mathieson, H. M., Private.
3366	Maycock, L. B., Private.
2374	Mayor, F., Private.
2800	Melville, J., Private.
2314	Menin, S., Corporal.
1519	Merry, W. H., Corporal.
3539	Metcalf, A. C., Lance-Corporal.
3354	Metcalfe, J. W. L., Private.
3359	Meyer, S., Private.
3367	Mill, L. B., Private.
2473	Miller, A. E., Private.
3353	Milligan, F. R., Private.
2689	Mills, W., Private.
2152	Mitchell, A. H., Private.
2964	Mitchell, T. P., Bugler.
2357	Mitchell, W., Private.
2819	Mitchell, W. H., Private.
2953	Mittlestiner, J. Private.
2392	Molten, S. R., Bugler.
2740	Montague, W. C., Private.
3030	Montgomery, H. B., Private.
2642	Moore, H., Private.
3789	Moore, J., Private.

2737	Moore, J. W., Private.
2588	Moreland, K., Private.
2571	Morley, A., Private.
2517	Morris, A. M., Private.
2369	Morris, C., Private.
2717	Morris, E. W., Private.
3068	Morris, V. L., Private.
2741	Morris, W., Private.
2759	Morton, Ed., Private.
2990	Morton, Ernest, Private.
3372	Morton, G. D., Private.
2510	Moss, F. S., Private.
2948	Mowatt, F. R., Private.
2841	Muir, G., Private.
3754	Muirhead, J., Private.
2251	Mulligan, G., Private.
8851	Munro, F. W., Private.
3863	Munro, T., Private.
2699	Murch, B. J., Bugler.
2349	Murray, J., Private.
3000	Murray, J., Private.
3860	Murray, W., Private.
3362	Musson, T. M. B., Private.
2478	Myles, W. A., Lance-Corporal.
2530	Neale, R. K., Private.
2484	Needham, E. W., Private.
2252	Needham, F., Private.
1687	Nelson, J. Lance-Serjeant.
2790	Nethercote, F., Private.
3391	Nevin, A., Private.
8390	Nevin, J. A., Private.
3674	Nevin, T., Private.
2402	Newman, J., Private.
3388	Newton, F. W., Private.
2487	Nichol, W., Private.
2858	Nicklin, F., Private.
3046	Nisbet, J. C. T., Private.
2625	Norman, J., Private.
3387	Norman, J. J., Private.
2315	Oakley, R., Private.
3395	O'Brien, K., Private.
8542	Ogden, A. H., Private.
1609	Ogilvie, E. S., Private.
1269	Ogilvie, H. H., Corporal.
2142	Ogilvy, C. K., Private.

2614	Ogilvy, J., Private.
3894	Oliver, A., Private.
3393	O'Neill, J., Private.
2645	Orme, S., Private.
1294	Ormisher, C. W., Private.
3396	Other, E., Private.
1813	Owen, T. H., Serjeant.
1860	Owens, E. S., Lance-Serjeant.
2938	Owens, S., Private.
3115	Oxenbauld, M., Private.
2623	Pape, J., Private.
3829	Parker, C., Private.
3404	Parker, H., Private.
2753	Parker, H. S., Private.
2813	Parkinson, P. W., Private.
2687	Parry, A., Private.
3899	Parry, W., Private.
3408	Parry, W. F., Private.
2725	Paterson, J. S., Private.
3407	Paterson, T., Private.
2555	Patterson, F., Private.
3745	Patterson, H. A., Private.
2998	Patterson, J., Private.
1720	Patterson, J. G., Serjeant.
2780	Pattison, H. E., Private.
3586	Peacock, T. W., Private.
2944	Pearson, J., Private.
2955	Pearson, W. G., Private.
3897	Peers, L. S., Private.
2779	Pendleton, W., Private.
3677	Pepper, R., Private.
3187	Perrin, W., Private.
2997	Phillips, G. W., Private.
3027	Philpots, W. E., Lance-Corporal.
2712	Phipps, F., Private.
1514	Pilkington, W. F., Private.
3410	Plant, N., Private.
3401	Plevin, K., Private.
3406	Pollexfen, G. B. Private.
3024	Pomeroy, J. P., Private.
2800	Pooley, P., Private.
2022	Pooley, R., Private.
2706	Potter, A. T., Private.
3514	Potter, W., Private.
3029	Powell, C. H., Private.

2811	Preacher, J. R., Private.
2665	Prenton, C. W., Private.
1948	Prescott, F. S., Private.
2395	Preston, J. S., Private.
2669	Pringle, C., Private.
2794	Pritchard, J. J., Private.
2720	Proudfoot, G. A., Private.
3109	Pruden, W., Private.
2795	Pryor, E., Private.
2421	Pulford, E. G., Private.
3400	Purton, G. L., Private.
2267	Qualtrough, E. W., Private.
3154	Quiggin, P. M., Private.
3412	Quinzey, T., Private.
2258	Quirk, H., Bugler.
3057	Rae, C. T., Private.
1982	Rae, W. E., Private.
2624	Raffle, E. L., Private.
3425	Randall, W. O., Private.
2915	Rannard, G., Private.
2657	Rathbone, W., Private.
3148	Rawlins, B. L., Private.
3784	Rawlinson, E. E., Private.
2829	Rawlinson, J., Private.
2666	Reed, F. D., Private.
1371	Renfrew, G., Private.
2428	Reppke, J., Corporal.
2946	Reynolds, S., Private.
2607	Richards, J., Private.
1568	Richardson, Geo., Corporal.
2986	Richardson, R. B., Private.
3429	Richardson, W., Private.
2617	Richman, S., Private.
2848	Rigby, A., Private.
3430	Rigby, A., Private.
3420	Rimmer, E. H., Private.
3896	Rimmer, F., Private.
3128	Rimmer, G. F., Private.
2543	Ritchie, A. D., Private.
3897	Robb, F., Serjeant.
3431	Robb, H., Private.
1422	Roberts, A., Private.
2814	Roberts, J. H., Private.
3416	Robertson, A. F., Private.
1828	Robins, T., Serjeant.

2131	Robinson, T. A., Lance-Corporal.
3427	Robinson, H., Private.
2438	Robinson, W. J., Private.
3124	Rockliffe, S., Private.
3119	Roddick, T. G., Private.
3414	Roe, J. L., Private.
3423	Rogers, F., Private.
3047	Rogers, H., Private.
2772	Ross, E. M., Private.
2852	Ross, J. C., Private.
2987	Rowatt, R., Private.
2297	Rowlandson, T. E., Lance-Corporal.
2272	Russell, G., Private.
3413	Russell, J., Private.
3417	Rutherford, G. E., Private.
3022	Rutherford, R. F., Private.
3516	Rutherford, T. H., Private.
3084	Ryalls, H. D., Private.
3455	Samson, C. R., Private.
3433	Sanderson, A., Private.
3438	Sandham, J., Private.
2844	Saunders, H., Private.
2486	Savage, A. M., Private.
3125	Sayce, R., Private.
1405	Scaife, H. G. R., Corporal.
2417	Schofield, A., Private.
2577	Scott, A. J., Private.
1640	Scott, J., Private.
2489	Scott, O., Private.
3475	Segrave, G., Private.
3454	Semple, J. R., Private.
2919	Settle, F., Private.
3443	Seward, W., Private.
1744	Sharp, T., Private.
1237	Shaw, W. R., Private.
2923	Shennan, J. K., Private.
2999	Shennan, T., Private.
2621	Shepherd, C., Private.
3441	Shimmin, T. G., Private.
3456	Simpson, A. N., Private.
3515	Simpson, W. A., Private.
3056	Sinclair, J., Private.
920	Sinclair, P. J., Lance-Corporal.
2820	Skinner, A. A., Private.
3349	Slade, C., Private.

2382	Sloan, T. A., Private.
3013	Sloss, W., Private.
2649	Smith, A., Private.
3431	Smith, C., Private.
2294	Smith, J., Private.
3080	Smith, P. J., Private.
3531	Smith, R., Private.
3435	Smith, T. W., Private.
3763	Solloway, T., Private.
2244	Somerville, W. B., Private.
3064	Spalding, H., Private.
3817	Spenser, G. A., Private.
3448	Spicer, R. S., Private.
2802	Spiers, J. T., Private.
2809	Spiers, R., Private.
2444	Sproat, D. E., Private.
2767	Sproston, W., Private.
2408	Stainton, H. H., Private.
2475	Stark, W. W., Private.
3446	Starkie, P., Private.
2753	Staveley, H. S., Private.
1515	Steeper, W. H., Serjeant.
3442	Stewart, R. E., Private.
3798	Stitt, J. A., Private.
2644	Stockham, H. E., Private.
184	Stoddart, J., Serjeant-Piper.
2188	Stoddart, J., Drummer.
2376	Stoddart, J. P., Piper.
3450	Stone, H. R., Private.
1079	Strang, D. B., Serjeant.
3511	Stuart, C. E., Private.
2570	Stuart, C. F., Private.
3439	Stubbs, E. W., Private.
3434	Sullivan, F. S., Private.
2425	Sullock, E. A., Private.
3510	Sunderland, W. B., Private.
2426	Sutherland, G., Private.
2210	Symons, E. H., Private.
3466	Taylor, D. G. A., Private.
1703	Taylor, D. W., Private.
2201	Taylor, G., Bugler.
3009	Teague, B. E., Private.
2595	Teare, A. F., Private.
2227	Tebb, C. D., Private.
3478	Thomas, A. E., Private.

3470	Thomas, E., Private.
2715	Thomas, F. W., Private.
2714	Thomas, G., Private.
1563	Thomas, H. E., Private.
2589	Thomas, L., Private.
3467	Thomas, S. N., Private.
1225	Thompson, J. E., Lance-Corporal Piper.
3160	Thompson, S. G., Private.
3762	Thomson, A. E., Private.
2650	Thomson, D. H., Private.
1890	Thomson, J. C., Corporal.
3769	Thomson, P. J., Private.
2736	Thrower, H., Private.
2199	Tibbells, W. T., Corporal.
2422	Tillotson, R. B., Private.
2732	Tinsley, T. S., Private.
3474	Toby, S., Private.
3463	Toft, W. S., Private.
3088	Tombs, J. S. McK., Private.
2572	Tomkinson, J. M., Private.
2317	Toolan, W. B., Private
2696	Tracey, W. K., Private.
2694	Trench, F., Private.
3469	Truby, C., Private.
2432	Tulloch, J., Private.
3462	Turner, F., Private.
2971	Turner, H. J., Private.
1046	Turner, R. T., Corporal.
2279	Turnock, A. J., Private.
629	Tweedie, J. G., Colour-Serjeant.
2219	Tweedie, J. P., Drummer.
3810	Twiss, T. H., Private.
3472	Tyrer, H. L., Private.
3476	Tyson, F., Private.
3486	Tyson, R. G., Private.
3480	Vance, A. P., Private.
3016	Vaughan-Roberts, R. W., Private.
3006	Veitch, D., Private.
3067	Veitch, G., Private.
3479	Vickers, W., Private.
3768	Waddall, J. D., Private.
2559	Wain, E., Private.
2718	Wakefield, L. E., Private.
3679	Walker, G. H., Private.
1418	Walker, J. T., Serjeant.

3498   Wallace, E. S., Private.
2708   Wallace, J. S., Private.
2399   Wallace, W., Private.
2866   Ward, C. F., Private.
3497   Ward, E., Private.
2382   Ward, G. P., Private.
3487   Ward, J. S., Private.
2879   Ward, S., Private.
2288   Ward, W. F., Corporal.
3495   Wareing, J. E., Private.
3481   Waterhouse, F., Private.
3176   Waters, K. R., Private.
2748   Watkinson, J. B., Private.
2873   Watterson, E., Private.
2874   Watterson, J. W., Private.
2085   Watterson, R., Lance-Corporal.
3489   Watts, F. W., Private.
3135   Waugh, J., Private.
3167   Weatherhead, A., Private.
3496   Weaver, H., Private.
1328   Weir, D. H., Lance-Corporal.
3493   White, C. A., Private.
3066   White, J. P., Private.
3175   Whitford, R. F., Private.
3035   Whitney, J. H., Private.
2979   Wiglesworth, G., Private.
2928   Wilde, C. E., Private.
2529   Williams, D., Private.
3110   Williams, F., Private.
2995   Williams, J. E., Private.
2323   Williams, J. J., Bugler.
3052   Williams, J. R., Private.
3131   Williamson, A., Private.
3074   Williamson, T. C., Private.
2954   Williamson, T. H., Private.
3107   Wilmot, G., Private.
3499   Wilson, C. A., Private.
3888   Wilson, D. A., Private.
1226   Wilson, H., Private.
2278   Wilson, J., Private.
2707   Wilson, J. W., Private.
3488   Wilson, P. S., Private.
3482   Wilson, T., Private.
3828   Wilson, W. E. P., Private.
3490   Windsor, R., Private.

3598   Wishart, R., Private.
3503   Wishart, W. A., Private.
3500   Wix, H., Private.
2821   Woodburn, J., Private.
1383   Woodward, J., Private.
1650   Woolfall, G., Private.
3502   Wright, G. A., Private.
3597   Wright, J. E., Private.
2415   Wright, N. G., Private.
2655   Wright, W. H., Private.
2827   Wyatt, F. E., Private.
3152   Wylie, M. P. K., Private.
3060   Yardley, L. P., Private.
2861   Yeo, H. C. J., Private.

ATTACHED FOR WATER DUTIES,

FROM 2nd WEST LANCS. FIELD AMBULANCE R.A.M.C., T.F.

903   Haygarth, E. G., Corporal.
1544   Delaney, J., Private.
1494   Garnham, F., Private.
1439   Griffiths, F., Private.
1215   Strange, C. E., Private.

ATTACHED FOR TRANSPORT DUTIES,

FROM A.S.C., T. & S. COLUMN, WEST LANCS. DIVN.
SOUTH LANCS. BRIGADE.

711   Byrne, F., Driver.
     Daniels, S., Driver.
129   Edwards, H. C., Driver.
1352   Stockton, J., Driver.
116   Welby, W., Driver.

APPENDIX V

HONOURS AND REWARDS.

BAR TO THE VICTORIA CROSS.
Captain N. G. Chavasse, V.C., M.C. (R.A.M.C.).

THE VICTORIA CROSS.
Captain N. G. Chavasse, M.C. (R.A.M.C.).

COMPANION OF THE MOST DISTINGUISHED ORDER OF ST. MICHAEL AND ST. GEORGE.
Lieut.-Colonel J. R. Davidson.

COMPANIONS OF THE DISTINGUISHED SERVICE ORDER.
Lieut.-Colonel D. A. Bingham.
Major J. L. A. Macdonald (H.L.I. attached).
Major D. C. D. Munro, M.C., D.C.M. (Gordon Highlanders attached).
Major G. B. L. Rae.
Major J. A. Roddick, M.C.
Lieut.-Colonel E. G. Thin.

COMPANION OF THE ORDER OF THE BRITISH EMPIRE.
Lieutenant A. J. Graham.

BAR TO THE MILITARY CROSS.
Lieutenant L. A. Davey, M.C.
Captain J. E. Rusby, M.C. (R.A.M.C.).

THE MILITARY CROSS.
Captain B. Arkle.
Lieutenant F. L. Arnold.
Captain N. G. Chavasse (R.A.M.C.).
2nd Lieutenant R. V. Clark.
Lieutenant A. S. Darroch.
Lieutenant J. Darroch.
Lieutenant G. B. Davey.

2nd Lieutenant L. A. Davey.
Captain A. G. Davidson.
Captain A. P. Dickinson.
Lieutenant W. Fairclough.
2nd Lieutenant B. P. Gallop.
2nd Lieutenant H. Henderson.
Lieutenant T. Houston.
Lieutenant J. Hunter.
Lieutenant R. W. Johnson.
2nd Lieutenant H. Mackay (4th Q.O. Cameron Highlanders
    attached).
Captain B. McKinnell.
2nd Lieutenant R. McNae.
Captain J. R. McSwiney.
Company-Serjeant-Major D. A. B. Marples.
Captain G. D. Morton.
2nd Lieutenant J. G. Muir.
Lieutenant W. E. Philpots.
2nd Lieutenant T. W. Pilkington.
2nd Lieutenant T. J. Price.
2nd Lieutenant P. St. J. B. Rathbone.
Captain H. J. Rice (R.A.M.C.).
Captain J. A. Roddick.
2nd Lieutenant G. N. Rome.
Lieutenant F. M. Scott.
2nd Lieutenant J. Tennant (4th Q.O. Cameron Highlanders
    attached).

BAR TO THE DISTINGUISHED CONDUCT MEDAL.
Serjeant A. Baybut, D.C.M., M.M.

THE DISTINGUISHED CONDUCT MEDAL.
Corporal F. M. Aldritt.
Company-Serjeant-Major J. H. Amos.
Corporal A. Baybut.
Private F. F. Bell.
Private T. C. Duckworth.
Corporal J. Frost.
Lance-Corporal A. Haynes.
Private W. W. Howarth.
Corporal G. Jordan.
Private C. A. Latham (attached to 166 M.G. Company).
Private D. A. Little (attached to 172 T.M. Battery).
Private W. B. McCann.
Serjeant D. McRae.

Private W. Marsden.
Serjeant J. E. Moss.
Lance-Corporal W. E. Pennington.
Private G. Sammons.
Private W. Short.
Corporal S. Smith.
Serjeant L. S. Welbon.

SECOND BAR TO THE MILITARY MEDAL.
Private J. R. Pollock, M.M.

BAR TO THE MILITARY MEDAL.
Serjeant F. W. M. Crane, M.M.
Private E. Herd, M.M.
Corporal J. Plant, M.M.
Private J. R. Pollock, M.M.
Serjeant P. Quinn, M.M.

THE MILITARY MEDAL.
Private J. Anderson.
Lance-Corporal T. Anderton.
Corporal G. E. Antrobus.
Private A. Arkle.
Serjeant J. J. Ashcroft.
Private B. G. Barnshaw.
Private J. Barton.
Serjeant W. A. Baughan.
Serjeant A. Baybut, D.C.M.
Serjeant R. T. H. Bell.
Company-Quartermaster-Serjeant J. Benson.
Private E. D. Blackburn.
Lance-Corporal G. Bond (attached to 166 T.M. Battery).
Private H. Braid (attached to 166 T.M. Battery).
Serjeant J. Briggs.
Private R. Burton.
Private D. Butcher.
Private T. B. Butler.
Corporal A. F. Butterfield.
Lance-Corporal W. S. Carlisle.
Corporal D. Carr.
Private F. Child.
Corporal C. T. Cluer.
Serjeant G. Codling.
Private J. V. Conway.
Corporal L. Cottam.

Private F. S. Coward.
Lance-Corporal C. D. Cowie.
Serjeant F. W. M. Crane.
Private J. Cushnie.
Private J. C. Darroch.
Private J. Davies.
Private J. E. Davies.
Corporal W. Daw.
Corporal J. Dixon.
Private J. H. Donnelly.
Private T. V. Edwards.
Private W. Ellison.
Private W. Fauldes.
Private H. Fildes.
Private Wm. Fitton.
Lance-Corporal A. F. Foden.
Private J. Furlong.
Lance-Corporal A. H. George.
Serjeant W. H. George.
Private A. S. Getty.
Lance-Corporal M. Gilbride.
Private G. A. Gorton.
Corporal F. L. Gresty.
Corporal E. Grist.
Lance-Serjeant R. Hartley.
Private W. Hayes.
Corporal K. Helliar.
Private J. Henderson.
Serjeant J. Henshaw.
Private E. Herd.
Private A. E. Hodgson.
Private J. Holland.
Private T. R. Hoyle.
Private W. L. Hunter.
Private A. Jones.
Private G. L. Jones.
Lance-Corporal R. G. Jones.
Private T. Jones.
Private H. Kellet.
Serjeant J. Kelly.
Private G. Large.
Private W. H. Lawson.
Private A. H. Lester.
Private S. Levy.
Lance-Corporal H. N. Lewis.

U

Lance-Corporal H. Lockwood.
Corporal R. J. Lowes.
Private W. H. McClelland.
Private H. McCracken.
Company-Quartermaster-Serjeant R. A. Scott Macfie.
Serjeant S. McKay.
Private J. McLoughlin.
Private G. Marsh.
Private C. Martin.
Serjeant G. Maxwell.
Private B. Metcalfe.
Lance-Corporal A. J. Milnes (attached to A.P.M., traffic).
Private S. Mullock.
Serjeant E. W. Needham.
Private J. O'Hara.
Lance-Corporal W. C. Parker.
Private J. S. Parkinson.
Company-Quartermaster-Serjeant T. Patterson.
Private E. Penlington.
Private J. Pirie (attached to 166th Brigade H.Q.).
Lance-Corporal J. Plant.
Private J. R. Pollock.
Private C. H. Quayle.
Private P. Quinn.
Private S. Ritchings.
Serjeant W. Rushton.
Private J. T. Ryder.
Private E. Schless.
Private J. J. Scott.
Private J. E. Selby.
Private F. Settle.
Lance-Corporal H. Shillitoe.
Lance-Corporal J. V. Short.
Serjeant W. Sloss.
Lance-Corporal F. Spargo.
Serjeant A. Stanley.
Lance-Corporal E. C. Stanley.
Private G. Stephens.
Private N. Stone.
Lance-Corporal W. A. Stone.
Private N. Tanner.
Private C. Taylor.
Private W. Taylor.
Corporal G. Thomas.
Private H. Thompson.

Serjeant P. J. Thomson.
Lance-Serjeant J. Thornton.
Private W. A. Tinniswood.
Lance-Corporal J. M. Tomkinson.
Private A. J. Townley.
Private F. Tweedale.
Private R. E. Underwood.
Private W. C. Veevers.
Private F. Walker.
Private J. L. C. Wallace.
Private J. M. Watson.
Private W. Webster.
Serjeant T. E. Whitby.
Private D. Williams.
Private J. T. Winstanley.
Private E. Wright.
Corporal W. E. Wyse.

THE MERITORIOUS SERVICE MEDAL.

Serjeant F. S. Bramwell.
Serjeant W. G. Bromley.
Company-Serjeant-Major W. E. Cole.
Private B. A. Denny.
Company-Serjeant-Major J. J. Donaldson.
Regimental-Quartermaster-Serjeant J. W. Dunham.
Private J. H. Humphreys.
Private R. Little.
Serjeant A. S. Lloyd.
Company-Serjeant-Major W. G. Mackey.
Private W. Ritchie.
Staff-Serjeant W. R. Shaw.
Private M. Squires.
Company-Quartermaster-Serjeant W. V. Temple.
Serjeant E. P. Ward.
Company-Serjeant-Major L. P. Yardley.

BELGIAN CROIX-DE-GUERRE.

Corporal R. Dutton.
Serjeant J. McArdle.

FRENCH CROIX-DE-GUERRE.

Serjeant S. McKay, M.M.
Private W. Short.

ITALIAN SILVER MEDAL FOR MILITARY VALOUR.

Captain T. G. Roddick.

MENTIONED IN DESPATCHES.

Company-Serjeant-Major J. H. Amos.
Captain A. S. Anderson.
Lieutenant B. Arkle.
2nd Lieutenant A. H. Bellis.
Serjeant H. S. Bennett.
Company-Quartermaster-Serjeant J. Benson.
Private T. G. Berry.
Lieutenant E. W. Bird.
Private E. W. Burns.
2nd Lieutenant P. Carnelly.
Corporal D. Carr.
Regimental-Serjeant-Major L. H. Carter.
Captain N. G. Chavasse.
2nd Lieutenant J. B. Clements.
Lance-Corporal J. P. Colston.
Serjeant A. G. Colter.
2nd Lieutenant R. H. Cooper.
Hon. Captain and Quartermaster G. T. Coulson (D.L.I. attached).
2nd Lieutenant G. E. Cowie.
Captain A. M. Cram (Q.O. Cameron Highlanders attached).
Lieutenant R. D. Cunningham.
Private J. C. Darroch.
Major J. R. Davidson.
Captain W. A. Davidson.
Captain R. F. B. Dickinson.
Major F. W. M. Drew (South Lancashire Regiment attached).
Company-Serjeant-Major J. W. Dunham.
Corporal W. Dunn (attached to 166 T.M. Battery).
Corporal R. Dutton.
Lance-Corporal C. Elliott.
Lance-Corporal W. S. England.
Captain D. D. Farmer, V.C.
Lieutenant G. Ferguson.
2nd Lieutenant E. K. Glazebrook.
Lieutenant J. Graham.
Private S. J. Harrison (attached to 172 T.M. Battery).
Lance-Corporal N. J. Heckle.
Hon. Lieutenant and Quartermaster A. C. Jack.
Captain C. P. James (Argyle & Sutherland Highlanders attached).
Regimental-Serjeant-Major S. Jennings.

2nd Lieutenant R. W. Johnson.
Private A. Jones.
Serjeant P. Law.
2nd Lieutenant F. T. B. Lyon.
2nd Lieutenant G. T. McCullough.
Regimental-Quartermaster-Serjeant R. A. Scott Macfie.
Company-Quartermaster-Serjeant W. Mackay.
Hon. Lieutenant and Quartermaster G. W. Mansbridge.
Captain T. E. Moffet.
Lieutenant A. McL. Morris.
Private C. P. Moss.
Lance-Corporal F. S. Moss.
Major G. B. L. Rae.
Serjeant W. Rathbone.
Captain J. A. Roddick.
Captain T. G. Roddick.
2nd Lieutenant G. N. Rome.
Captain J. Sillavan.
Lance-Corporal W. Slack (attached to A.P.M.).
2nd Lieutenant E. W. Stubbs.
Company-Quartermaster-Serjeant W. V. Temple.
Hon. Captain and Quartermaster A. Thacker.
Major E. G. Thin.
Lance-Corporal J. M. Tomkinson.
2nd Lieutenant L. G. Wall.
Private J. L. C. Wallace.
Serjeant E. P. Ward.

APPENDIX VI

ROLL OF HONOUR.

Roger Ackerley.
George Ackers.
Sydney Stephen Adams.
Ernest Addison.
James William Aitchison.
Joseph Aldred.
Samuel Rowland Allan.
Albert Victor Allen.
Alfred Allen.
Herbert Allen.
Walter Allen.
Hugh Stanley Allison.
Andrew Anderson.
Andrew Stewart Anderson.
James Edward Anderson.
John Anderson.
Joseph Anderson.
Thomas Colin Anderson.
Arthur Armstrong.
Frank Armstrong.
Charles Melbourne Arrowsmith.
William Ash.
Joseph Ashcroft.
William Ashcroft.
Charles Norman Ashton.
Fred Ashworth.
James Douglas Askin.
Christopher Basil Astley.
Jack Audsley.
Percy John Auger.
Charles Bailey.
Frederick Bailey.
Rawston Calmady Bailey.
Charles Baker.
Charles Alfred Baker.
Thomas Baker.
George Ball.
Lawrence Ball

Thomas James Ball.
William Ball.
Robert Bamford.
Thomas Benjamin Bamford.
Charles Banks.
Frederick Banks.
Frederick Sydney Banner.
John Christian Barber.
Edward Martin Bardgett.
Hamilton Ainsworth Bardswell.
Frank Barker.
Stanley Barker.
Tom Barlow.
Frederick William Barney.
Herbert Barron.
John Barrow.
Joseph Barrowclough.
Thomas Walter Barry.
A. Gordon Bartlett.
William Bate.
Colin Bayly.
William Edward Bebbington.
Clifford Beecroft.
Joseph Fuber Beecroft.
Thomas Belfield.
John George Belgrove.
Alexander Bell.
Herbert H. Bell.
Percy W. Bell.
Granville Clayton Bennett.
Thomas Bennett.
Edward Bentley.
Harold Benton.
Abraham Bernstein.
Arthur Louis Berry.
Harry Betteley.
Arthur Charles Bettens.
Alfred William Bevan.
John Anderson Bingham.
Stanley Birch.
Alfred Birchall.
Joseph Birchall.
George Trevor Bird.
William Black.
Edwin Duncan Blackburn, M.M.

Robert Henry Blair.
George Blake.
Lawrence Cave Blencowe.
Matthew Blyth.
Harry Boardman.
Thomas Boardman.
Robert Bond.
Alexander Booker.
Henry Robert Bothamley.
Harold Boulton.
John Arthur Bowen.
Percy Gernon Boyd.
James Boylan.
Colin M. Boyle.
Norman Bracher.
Joseph Bradley.
Alexander Greig Bradshaw.
James Simson Branthwaite.
Jonathan Brayton.
Ernest Pearson Breckenridge.
George Brellisford.
James Alfred Brewer.
Walter Bridson.
Fred Britton.
David Broadfoot.
Frank S. Brockbank.
Arthur Ernest Brookes.
Benjamin Woodrow Brown.
Charles Brown.
Morton Brown.
Waldran Brown.
William Cyril Brown.
William Cecil Brownell.
Isaac Rowlandson Brownrigg.
Alan Buchanan.
Archibald Charles W. Buck.
John Buckingham.
Hugh Bulger.
William Francis Bullen.
George Burgess.
G. Cuthbertson Burnell.
Albert Burns.
Andrew Burns.
Harry Lowe Burrows.
John James Burrow.

Alfred Fallows Butterfield, M.M.
William Butterworth.
James Adamson Bywater.
Harold Joseph Cain.
Albert Henry Caine.
Robert John Callander.
William Nelson Callister.
Thomas Stewart Cameron.
John Campbell.
Richard D. Campbell.
William Henry Campbell.
Edgar Candlish.
Joseph Candlish.
Arthur Cannell.
Alfred Cannon.
Frederick Cardwell.
Alexander Carrick.
Thomas Carrington.
Sidney Carruthers.
Reginald Carter.
Stanley Raymond Carter.
William Henry Carter.
Francis Edward Case.
Percival Catterall.
Harold Cawthra.
Harry Barton Chaddock.
Walter Chalmers.
Walter Champness.
William Charnley.
Noel Godfrey Chavasse, V.C. (and Bar), M.C.
Norman Cheetham.
Albert Chesters.
Fred Child, M.M.
Andrew Christie.
George Alfred Chubb.
Arthur Citrine.
Horace Claridge.
Fred Sumner Clark.
Joseph Clark.
Gilbert Clarkson.
James Clarkson.
Alfred Clayton.
Charles George Clayton.
George Clayton.
Thomas Clayton.

Walter Oswald Cleaver.
Hubert Clegg.
Joseph Edward Clegg.
Sidney Cleverley.
Percival George Cliff.
Oliver Close.
George Clotworthy.
James Cluness.
George Wallace Coates.
George Henry Cockayne.
Charles Ernest Coddington.
James Hunter Coke.
Matthew Hutchinson Cole.
George Coleman.
John Henry Collins.
Frederick Ernest Collinson.
Frank Alfred Collumbell.
William Edgar Collumbell.
John Percy Colston.
Martin Connor.
Charles Constantine.
Arthur Conway.
William Francis Conway.
Benjamin Cook.
Alan Curtis Cooke.
Francis Cooke.
Martin Denis Cooke
Thomas Cooke.
Alan Cookson.
Wilfrid Coop.
Herbert Cooper.
Thomas Cork.
Oliver Henry Cormack.
Donald Corson.
Edward Corteen.
Edward Corrin Costain.
William Edward Costain.
Martin Costello.
Walter Reginald Costine.
John Cottam.
William Arthur Cotterill.
Donald Cowie.
Alfred Cecil Cox.
William John Coy.
Douglas Crabb.

John Craig.
George Craige.
James Craven.
Edwin Crawford.
Charles Cregeen.
Harold Reginald Crighton.
Alfred John Croft.
Joseph Henry Crompton.
Andrew Crone.
Robert Singleton Cross.
Robert Cunningham.
William Currie.
Frederick Edward Dale.
William Hunter Dale.
George Stanley Dalton.
David Daniel.
Percy Dannit.
Charles Davidson.
Cyril Davidson.
John Philip Davidson.
Alfred Davies.
Dan Henry Davies.
Edward Davies.
James Davies.
Richard Davies.
Robert Davies.
Trevor Victor Davies.
William Davies.
William Arthur Gordon Davies.
George Davis.
Lewis Dawes.
Richard Donald Dawkins.
James Dawson.
Thomas Dawson.
Charles Dean.
Thomas Dean.
Bernard Dempsey.
Alan Peile Dickinson, M.C.
Ronald F. Bickersteth Dickinson.
Ronald Arthur Campbell Dickson.
Thomas Augustas Dickson.
Victor Dillon.
Ernest Dixon.
Henry Dobbin.
Sydney Archibald Dobbs.

Joseph Docherty.
Ernest Dodd.
Adrian Kingsley Dorrity.
Alfred Wilson Douglas.
Harry Douglas.
Robert Llewellyn Douglas.
William Robertson Douglas.
John Joseph Dower.
Benjamin Ducker.
Herbert Duckworth.
William Duckworth.
David Duffy.
Leslie Finlay Dun.
Frederick William Dunbabin.
Charles Duncan.
James Duncan.
Kenneth W. Allan Duncan.
Charles Dundas.
Christian D. Hamilton Dunlop.
Alfred Dunn.
Ernest George Dunn.
Patrick Dunn.
Stephen Durney.
William Richard Duxbury.
Paul Eagle.
Hubert Earle.
Leonard Eaves.
William Basil Ecroyd.
Frank Maxwell Edgar.
Edward Edwards.
James Harold Edwards.
Thomas Egan.
Charles Moody Ellick.
Arthur Samuel Elliot.
Edward Ellis
Herbert Charles Ellis.
Richard Arthur Ellis.
James Ellison.
Charles Hassall Ellwood.
William Thomas Emerton.
Wilfred English.
Elias Evans.
Frank Griffith Evans.
Harry Evans.
James Collingwood Evans.

Oswald Evans.
Ralph Evans.
George Farrimond.
James Farrington.
George Ferguson.
William Kermode Ferguson.
William Fernihough.
John Fielding.
John Finchett.
Alexander Finlay.
Noel Finucane.
Amos Fisher.
Harry Fisher.
Joseph Leo Fishwick.
James Fitzsimons.
Clarence Fleming.
George Kay Fleming.
Charles William Fletcher.
David Flett.
Fred Ford.
Stanley Robert Foreman.
Albert Forster.
Robert Forsyth.
James Foster.
John Logan Foster.
Thomas Matthew Foster.
William Charles Foster.
James Leslie Fothergill.
Horace Fox.
Leslie William Fox.
James Fraser.
John Fraser.
Wallace Fraser.
James Craig Frazer.
John Thomas Freeborn.
Arthur Freeman.
Maurice William Frith.
Robert Frizzel.
Leonard Richard Furnise.
Stanley Gambles.
Frederick Gandy.
Henry Gardner.
David Garvie.
James Johnson Gavin.
William James Geddes.

Thomas Gee.
Kenneth Alexander Gemmell.
Arthur Henry George, M.M.
Edward George.
Frederick Richmond George.
William Gibb.
Stanley G. Reginald Gibbins.
Henry Gibbons.
Gilbert Gibbs.
Sydney George Gibson.
Vernon Gibson.
Martin Gilbride, M.M.
George Arthur Gill.
Harvey Sisson Gillanders.
William Gillespie.
Arnold Gledsdale.
Alfred Ernest Gleig.
Harold Glenn.
Frederick William Glover.
William Albert Glover.
Edgar William Godwin.
John Alexander Goldrop.
William Good.
John Gorton.
James Henry Mortimer Gosson.
John Graham.
James Gibson Grant.
Lamont Grave.
Archibald William Gray.
Harry Gray.
James Haining Gray.
Peter Gray.
John Thomas Greenhalgh.
John George Greenup.
Thomas Greenwood.
Henry Harvey Greep.
Richard Greer.
John McCurdy Gregg.
Albert Gregory.
William Gregory.
Evan Frederick Griffiths.
Stanley Thomas Griffiths.
William Madoc Griffiths.
William Stanley Griffiths.
Archibald Campbell Grossart.

Douglas Buchanan Grossart.
Frederick Claude Grosvenor
Thomas Herbert Grundy.
Herbert Hayes Gunning.
Robert Forman Guthrie.
James Hadfield.
Frederick Hall.
Matthew Hall.
Edward Halsall.
Ernest Hampton.
Hubert Hand.
Ratcliffe Handley.
George Thomas Hankey.
George Hanmer.
John William Harding.
George Hargreaves.
Arthur Harrison.
John Archibald Harrison.
Thomas Harrocks.
Louis Hart.
John Eddy Hartley.
Leo Hartley.
Sydney Smith Hartley.
Willis Hartley.
John Frederick Hasler.
John Eric Haugh.
John Hawkins.
Robert Hawkins.
Matthew Haygarth.
Wilfrid Stanley Hayward.
Henry Heald.
Kenneth Helliar, M.M.
Cyril Norman Helsby.
John Henderson.
Graham Thornton Henery.
Ernest Herd.
John William Hesketh.
Harold Hewitt.
John Heywood.
James Hickman.
William Borthwick Hiddlestone.
Geoffrey Lea Higgins.
Harold Higgins.
Joseph Higgins.
Percy Higgins.

Geoffrey Hawksley Hill.
Rowland Edwin Hill.
Samuel Denys Hillis.
Frank Hindle.
George James Hoare.
Denton Hobbs.
Henry Bedo Hobbs.
Joseph Hocking.
Robert Hodges.
Reginald Hodgson.
John Hendon Hogg.
Leonard Brocklesby Holford.
Thomas Holmes.
William Arthur Holmes.
Eustace Addison Holt.
Edward Hood.
Frank Hooley.
Henry Herbert Hornby.
James Horne.
Joseph Horner.
Stanley Horner.
John Henry Horsley.
William Houghton.
Charles Houldsworth.
Charles John Joseph Howard.
William Howarth.
Vincent Hoyle.
David Hughes.
Eric Coulthard Hughes.
John Granville Hughes.
Robert Hughes.
Thomas Mathieson Sprott Hughes.
William Henry Hughes.
Walter Hume.
Cyril Cholmeley Humphreys.
James Andrew Legg Hunter.
George Joseph Hussey.
Robert McQueen Hutchinson.
Richard Huyton.
Edward Ingham.
George Stuart Inwood.
James Irvine.
William Harold Irvine.
Thomas Jackson.
Walter Alexander Jackson.

William Henry Jackson.
John Benjamin James.
William James.
Alick Jamieson.
John Jardine.
Joseph Jardine.
John William Jarrett.
Frederick Gustave Jarvis.
Roy William Jenkins.
William Jennings.
John Alfred Jillings.
Ernest Frederick Johns.
Harold Johnson.
Robert Johnson
George Johnston.
Thomas Johnston.
Charles Johnstone.
James Thomas Johnstone.
Joseph Johnstone.
Samuel Johnstone.
Alfred William Jones.
David Owen Jones.
Edward Thomas Jones.
Harold Jones.
John Jones (1538).
John Jones (359023).
Robert Owen Jones.
Spencer Robert Jones.
Thomas Frederick Jones.
William Jones (2507).
William Jones (357073).
William Arthur Jones.
William George Jones.
Alan Jowett.
Arthur Jowett.
Harold Frank Roe Juler.
Frederick William Jump.
William Jump.
Eli Kafkevitch.
Harry Kaye.
Walter Elder Keill.
George Keith.
Victor James Kelley.
William Reid Kellie.
James Kelly.

Robert Kelly.
Percy Dale Kendall.
Stanley Hayne Kennedy.
Charles Arthur Kennett.
William Kenolty.
Joseph Stanley Kershaw.
Maurice Kershaw.
Thomas Henry Kewn.
Clement Robinson Keyworth.
Robert Henry Kiddle.
James Kilburn.
William James Killip.
Hugh Kincaid.
John Abbott King.
Arthur Reginald Kingsley.
John J. Kinnish.
Alexander Kirk.
John Kirk.
Samuel Kirkwood.
Herbert Frederick Kitwood.
Arthur Knowles.
Duncan Laing.
Thomas Lamb.
Ronald Stuart Lamont.
James Bennett Lane.
Victor Large.
John Richard Larkey.
Adrian Percy Latham.
William Latham.
David Henry Laverty.
William John Lavin.
Robert Lawrenson.
Edward Gemmell Lawson.
Alexander Laylee.
Barnett Lazarus.
Arthur Leslie Leatherbarrow.
William Joseph Lee.
Benjamin Leece.
Richard Leech.
Vyvian Bisset Leitch.
Henry Leonard.
John Leslie.
Neil Letheren.
Frank Ernest Lewis.
Thomas Lewis.

Sydney J. Liddle.
Leslie Frank Lima.
Simon Lindsay.
Roland Little.
Alfred Livingstone.
Daniel Trevor Penllyn Lloyd.
George Evan Lloyd.
Richard John Lloyd.
Thomas William Lloyd.
George Arthur Lockley.
Hubert Arthur Lodge.
Elliott Longley.
Frederick Kaighin Looney.
Ernest Lord.
David Lorimer.
Charles Loudoun.
Wilfred Henry Lovell.
George Robbie Low.
Charles Samuel Lowe.
Edward Lowe.
William David Lowe.
William Bowyer Lowndes.
Alexander Lunt.
George Lutas.
Brodie Lyon.
John Lyon.
Samuel Ignatius Lyon.
James Cameron McAdam.
Robert James McAdam.
Henry McArthur.
Thomas McAteer.
Charles McCallum.
William Bernard McCann, D.C.M.
Robert McCarrell.
William McCaskill.
Donald Robert McColl.
George McConnan.
Thomas McConnon.
Irving John McCormick.
Robert McCracken.
William McCracken.
Angus MacDonald.
Alexander Macdonald.
Douglas Macdonald.
George White Macdonald.

Alfred McDonald.
Nicholas McDonald.
Robert Alexander McDonald.
William Frazer McDonald.
Ernest McDowall.
David McGilvray.
Adam McGregor.
James A. McGregor.
Robert Law McGregor.
William Easson Mackenzie.
William Robert Mackenzie.
Charles Boddington Mackie.
Bryden McKinnell, M.C.
John McKnight.
Henry MacKune.
James McLachlan.
Donald Graeme MacLaren.
Andrew McLaughlin.
William Edward McLaughlin.
Marcus McLean.
Donald Macleod.
Frederick McLeod.
Charles McMahon.
William McMaster.
Douglas McMillan.
George McMillan.
George McNab.
Robert McNae, M.C.
Thomas McNaught.
John McQuair.
Frederick McQuilliam.
Briscoe Francis MacSwiney.
Joseph Ray MacSwiney.
Archibald Weir McWilliam.
Henry McWilliams.
Myles Mack.
Arthur Maddocks.
Edward Magee.
Robert Maile.
Hamilton William Malcolm.
Thomas Manning.
James Mannion.
William Marsden, D.C.M.
William Marsh.
Edward Martin.

James Gwynne Martin.
John Edward Martin.
John James Martin.
Stanley Mason.
Hubert Hammond Massey.
Norman Mather.
Charles William Matthews.
Herbert James Matthews.
William Mawer.
Robert Maxwell.
Leonard May.
Thomas Walter May.
Enoch Mayer.
Harold Mayers.
Cecil Meadows.
John William Meehan.
Alfred Jackson Meikle.
William James Melling.
Thomas Edwin Merrick.
Clarence A. Metcalf.
Stanley Meyer.
John William Middlehurst.
Leonard Binning Mill.
Archibald Miller.
Edwin Donald Miller.
Fred Miller.
Joseph Henry Miller.
Percy How Millhouse.
Frederick Bradley Milner.
John Milroy.
Thomas Lindsay Mitchell.
Thomas Price Mitchell.
John Everard Moffat.
William Moir.
Arthur Moncrieff.
Harold Fraser Monks.
William Cameron Montague.
Frank Monteath.
Hugh Bertram Montgomery.
William Carlton Montrose.
Harold Pountney Moore.
Thomas Moore.
Thomas Moore.
Harry Moorhouse.
James Moran.

Henry Morgan.
William Morgan.
Clement Morris.
Ernest William Morris.
John Morris.
John Reginald Morris.
William George Morris
William Sydney Morris.
Richard Mottram.
George Arthur Moulton.
Allan Muir.
Robert George Muir.
Henry Charles Munro.
Alfred Edward Murch.
Arthur Murdock.
Thomas Murphy.
James Murray.
Joseph Murray.
Arthur Musker.
Ernest Musker.
Robert George Musker.
James Edwin Mylchreest.
Alfred Thomas Charles Myles.
William Nelson.
Frank Nethercott.
William Newton.
James Edward Nicholl.
Fred Nicholson.
John Samuel Nicholson.
Louis Nicholson.
Frederick Nicklin.
William Nicol.
John Charles Tawse Nisbet.
Leonard Thomas Nixon.
George Alexander Nolan.
Albert Norman.
George Norman.
John Norman.
Joseph Norris.
Percy Nugent.
William Nugent.
Albert Edward Nuttall.
John O'Brien.
Kennedy O'Brien.
Jack O'Connor.

Harold Ogden.
Charles Kelly Ogilvy.
Michael Joseph O'Hare.
William Lee Okell.
Albert Edward Orange.
Charles Orchardson.
Charles William Ormesher.
David Oswald.
Alfred Edward Ovens.
Samuel Paddock.
Thomas Packenham.
Tom Palmer.
David Parker.
Tom Parker.
William Parker.
Ernest Albert Parkinson.
Herbert Parkinson.
Thomas Parr.
George Parry.
Harold Parry.
Percy Edward Harold Parsons.
John Partridge.
David Harrower Paterson.
Edward Labarte Paterson.
James Graham Paterson.
John Paterson.
John Sutton Paterson.
Henry Edward Pattison.
George Paul.
Frederick George Peacock.
Thomas Speight Pearson.
William George Pearson.
Frederick William Peaston.
Harry Cresswell Peel.
Harold Pendergast.
William Pendleton.
Robert Pepper.
Eric Albert Peppiette.
John Phillips.
Arthur Pilkington.
John James Pilkington.
Frank Pimlott.
Arthur Wright Howard Plant.
Norman Plevin.
Tom Birtwistle Pollard.

Guy Barclay Pollexfen.
Harold Charles Ponting.
Rowland M. Poole.
Robert Lawrie Pope.
Reginald George Porter.
John Arthur Postlethwaite.
Edward Poulton.
William John Povall.
Louis Clement Pownall.
Stephen Prater.
John Sydney Preston.
James Price.
Thomas Joseph Price, M.C.
John William Pritchard.
Thomas A. Pritchard.
Charles Hubert Prosser.
William Pugh.
William Nolan Pugh.
Godfrey Lawrence Purton.
Paul Arnot Quine.
Harold Quirk.
Ernest Guy Racine.
Robert Rae.
Frank Kirby Railer.
Charles Ramus.
Sidney Ramus.
William Randell.
William Rankin.
David Rankine.
John Godwin Raschen.
William George Ravenscroft.
Bertram L. Rawlins.
Ernest Elliston Rawlinson.
Edwin James Reid.
John Reid.
John Lavens Reid.
Matthew Reilly.
John Reppke.
Joel Reynolds.
Roger Rhodes.
William Rhodes.
Donald Alexander Riddoch.
Harold Ridehalgh.
William Robert Ridehalgh.
Robert Hales Ridgway.

Henry Frederick Ries.
Norman Ogilvie Rigby.
Frederick Rimmer.
George Frederic Rimmer.
John Joseph Roach.
Archibald Younger Roberts.
Frank Roberts.
James Percy Roberts.
Percy Roberts.
Walter Roberts.
Alexander F. Robertson.
David Robertson.
George Robertson.
Edmund Robinson.
George Robinson.
Harry Robinson.
Richard Alan Robinson.
Thomas Porter Robinson.
Tom Stephenson Robinson.
George Roden.
Joseph Leonard Roe.
Frederick Albert Rogers.
William George Rogerson.
Forbes Rollo.
Harry W. Ross.
John Cassells Ross.
Thomas Herbert Rotheram.
Thomas Frederick Morvia Rowe.
Arthur Vaughan Rowlands.
Richard Rowlands.
Charles Arundel Rudd.
Stanley Herbert Rule.
Harold Salisbury.
Harry Samuel.
Arthur Sanderson.
Robert Sanderson.
Edward Sands.
Joseph Sangster.
Norman Barnewell Savage.
Alan Richard Scaife.
Clifford Schofield.
Alfred James Scott.
Arthur John Scott.
Isaac Scott.
James Harley Scott.

Victor Scott.
Thomas Scrugham.
Clive R. Sears.
William Seddon.
John Selkirk.
Peter Seymour.
Duncan Sharp.
Thomas Sharp.
Henry Sharples.
Harold Shaw.
Walter Shemwell.
Percival Henry Sheriff.
Harold Sherrington.
Louis Tibbs Shimmin.
Thomas G. Shimmin.
John William Simmons.
Arthur Neil Simpson.
William Alexander Simpson.
David McDonald Sinclair.
William Hardie Sinnatt.
William Edwin J. Skelland.
Charles Slade.
Arthur Slate.
Thomas Alexander Sloan.
Lancelot A. Noel Slocock.
Arthur William Smale.
George Smallshaw.
Robert H. Smedley.
Wallace Smedley.
Albert Smith.
Alwyn Tom Smith.
Arthur Smith.
Charles Smith.
Frank Smith.
George William Smith.
Harry William Smith.
Henry Smith.
Herbert Henry Smith.
Hugh Cameron Smith.
Joshua Smith.
Philip T. Smith.
Robert Smith.
William Southworth.
Ernest Speed.
John Gregg Speers.

Robert Speirs.
George Arthur Spencer.
Henry Gordon Spenley.
James Stanton.
William Webster Stark.
William John Steele.
Hubert Steen.
Earl Stephenson.
Harold Stephenson.
Ernest T. Stevenson.
Henry Ernest Stewart.
Edward James Still.
James Stoddart.
William Henry Stretch.
Norman Percy John Studd.
Edward William Studley.
Jerome Sullivan.
Albert Summerfield.
Robert Sutherland.
William Sutton.
Martin Swanick.
James William Swann.
Thomas Talbot.
William Henry Tamlin.
Chris Tattersall.
Brierley Taylor.
George Cowie Taylor.
James Frederick Taylor.
Robert Norman Taylor.
William Taylor.
William Taylor, M.M.
Basil Every Teague.
Christopher Tenpenny.
James Theckston.
Frederick Thomas.
Harry Edward Thomas.
Percival James Thomas.
Thomas J. Thomlinson.
Bryce Thompson.
Joseph Edward Thompson.
Victor Henry Thompson.
James Thomson.
Harry Thorne.
Harry Threlfall.
John Kennings Thurlow.

Thomas Sidney Tinsley.
Peter Tobias.
Wilfrid Toman.
Henry Travers.
Harold Trotter.
Alfred Harry Truman.
Frederick Harding Turner.
Stanley George Turner.
Thomas Morris Turner.
William Stewart Turner.
James Turton.
Arthur Twentyman.
John Tynan.
Henry Tyrer.
Henry George Tyrer.
Joseph Tyrrell.
Frederick Tyson.
Joseph Utley.
Joseph Harold Valentine.
Arthur Patrick Vance.
Eric George Vance.
George Veitch.
Frederick Vernon.
Frederick Vincent.
James Wahlers.
Cyril Wainwright.
Henry George Walker.
Horace Henry Walker.
William Walker.
William Percy Walker.
Edward Wallace.
John Smith Wallace.
Samuel Walmsley.
George William Walsh.
Kenneth L. Walter.
Augustine Ward.
Edgar Ward.
John Ward.
Frank Waterhouse.
David Watson.
Donald James Watson.
James Morris Watson.
John Hamilton Watson.
William J. Jenkin Waugh.
Thomas Henry Webster.

Joseph R. Welch.
Robert Welch.
Thomas Welsby.
John Charles Victor Westlake.
Isaiah Westwood.
Gilbert Whatley.
Norman Haviland Whatley.
James Pringle White.
Thomas White.
Joseph Whitehead.
William Levi Whitehead.
James Whitfield.
Henry Thomas Whitson.
George Whittaker.
Nicholas Whittaker.
Joseph Arnold Whittam.
. Thomas Whittle.
Harold Thomas Whyard.
John Wignall.
George Herbert Wilbraham.
Sydney Wilbraham.
Henry Wilcox.
Frederick Charles Wilkinson.
Tom Wilkinson.
Harry Willett.
Ernest Williams.
John Edward Williams.
John Owen Williams.
John Rhonwy Williams.
Matthew Williams.
Noel Griffith Williams.
Robert Williams.
William Williams.
Thwaite Williamson.
William Henry Williamson.
Arthur Wilson.
George Albert Wilson.
Joseph Wilson.
John Cowan Sydney Wilson.
Norman M. Wilson.
Ronald Bruce Wilson.
William Wilson.
William Denis Wilson.
Robert Winder.
Robert Windsor.

John Thomas Winstanley, M.M.
Robert Winterbottom.
Stanley Winterbottom.
William Henry Wiseman.
Harry Wix.
John Edward Wolstenholme.
John Wilson Wood.
Joseph Wood.
Robert Allan Wood.
William John Wood.
Louis Woodbridge.
James Woodburn.
Richard James Woodcock.
Herbert Lancelot Woodland.
Hugh Reid Woodside.
George Woodward.
Ernest Woosey.
Horace Worsley.
Joseph Worthington.
Alfred Wray.
John Wren.
George Alexander Wright.
Norman Gregory Wright.
Thomas Wright.
Francis Edward Wyatt.
Thomas Wynne.
Roderick Wynfield Wyse.
Edward Yates.
Ernest John Barlow Yates.
Everard Yates.
Edward Young.

INDEX

INDEX

W

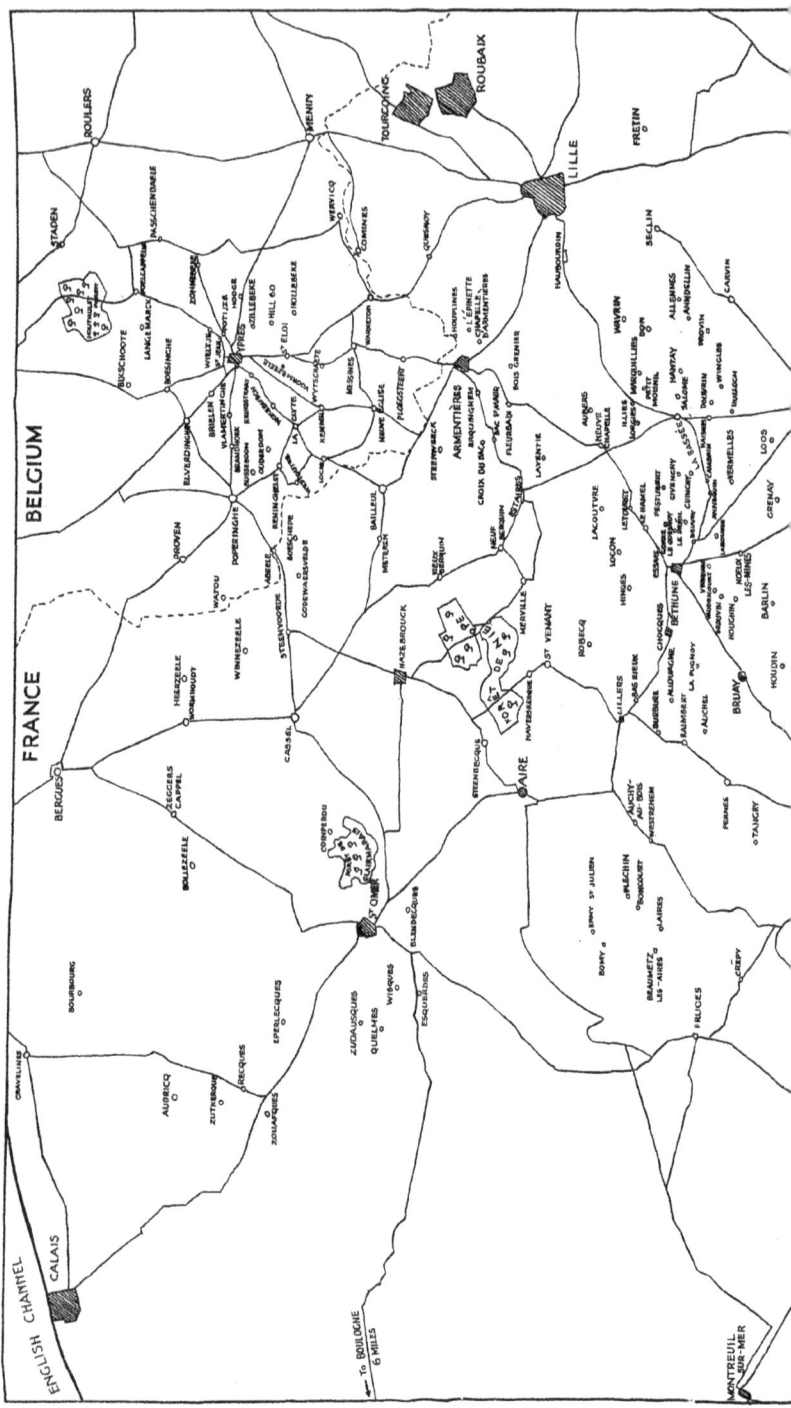

BRITISH AREA NORTH OF AMIENS — WESTERN FRONT

DOUAI
CAMBRAI
ÉPÉHY
ST. ÉMILE
VILLERS-FAUCON
LONGAVESNES
TINCOURT
VIMY
SOUCHEZ
NEUVILLE
ST. VAAST
CROISILLES
BULLECOURT
VAULX
VRAUCOURT
BAPAUME
BEAUGNICOURT
BEAULENCOURT
LE TRANSLOY
MORVAL
ARRAS
MONT ST. ELOY
AGNY
WAILLY
RIVIÈRE
ACHIET
LE GRAND
MIRAUMONT
GRANDCOURT
THIEPVAL
POZIÈRES
COURCELETTE
MARTINPUICH
FLERS
LONGUEVAL
CONTALMAISON
GINCHY
GUILLEMONT
MONTAUBAN
COMBLES
HARDECOURT
MARICOURT
PÉRONNE
AUBIGNY
SIMENCOURT
GOUY
MONCHIET
BARLY
BEAULIEU
SAULTY
RANSART
BLAIRVILLE
PASSEUX
MONCHY-
AU-BOIS
LES ESSARTS
BUCQUOY
CARNOY
NAMETZ
GREAT
BEAR
SAND PIT
AREA
MÉAULTE
ALBERT
AVELUY
BEAUMONT
HAMEL
GOMMECOURT
FONQUEVILLERS
HÉBUTERNE
AVESNES-
LE-COMTE
SOMBRIN
LA HERLIÈRE
PAS
FAMECHON
HÉNU
SUS-ST.-LÉGER
BAILLEUL-
O-AUX-CORNAILLES
ST. POL
BOURGDEMAISON
AMPLIER
BEAUQUESNES
RIBEMONT
MÉRICOURT
VILLE-SUR-ANCRE
FRÉVENT
DOULLENS
BEAUVAL
TO AMIENS
2 MILES
CANDAS
HESDIN
AUXI-LE-CHÂTEAU
BERNAVILLE
PROUVILLE
BERNÉS
PERNOIS
FLIXECOURT
VIGNACOURT
TO AMIENS
2 MILES
PONT RÉMY
LONGPRÉ
ABBEVILLE

MAIN ROADS ————
FRANCO-BELGIAN
FRONTIER ‑‑‑‑‑

MILES 5   0   5   10   15   20   25 MILES

N

www.ingramcontent.com/pod-product-compliance
Lightning Source LLC
Chambersburg PA
CBHW020806100426
42814CB00014B/352/J